A HISTORY AND ARCHAEOLOGY OF TAMESIDE

TAMESIDE 1066-1700

Michael Nevell

1991

TAMESIDE METROPOLITAN BOROUGH COUNCIL

A History and Archaeology of Tameside

Tameside 1066-1700

ISBN 1 871324 02 5

Published by
Tameside Metropolitan Borough Council

with
The Greater Manchester Archaeological Unit

Printed by
Bemrose-Shafron Printers Ltd
Chester

Preface

The Metropolitan Borough of Tameside was created in 1974 and brought together the nine towns of Ashton, Audenshaw, Denton, Droylsden, Dukinfield, Hyde, Longdendale, Mossley and Stalybridge. Since that time there has been no attempt to write a full-scale history of the area. This Borough has a rich and interesting past, and I felt that this should be documented so that we, and future generations, could increase our knowledge and understanding of our heritage.

This volume, covering the medieval and early modern period, is the first in a projected three volume History of Tameside. In its entirety the work will form an essential reference source, as well as an enjoyable read.

It is appropriate that this book should be published at this time with Tameside on the brink of a new and exciting period in its history, with major opportunities for economic regeneration and industrial development. Improved transport links will make this area more accessible to a greater number of people and these volumes will provide an important source of information for tourism initiatives in the Borough.

Councillor S. Roy Oldham
C.Eng. M.I. Mech.E
Leader of the Council

Acknowledgments

In the face of rapid change in social and economic affairs, perspectives created by our knowledge and understanding of the past can introduce balance and stability. The recent reorganization of local administrative groupings in Greater Manchester reflects and continues a process of organic change which has taken place over the centuries. The possibility of translating these theoretical historic values into practical benefits for the community arose in the course of a meeting between the leader of the Council, Councillor Roy Oldham, the Director of the Greater Manchester Archaeological Unit, Phil Mayes, the Director of Planning, Mike Eveson, through whose good offices the meeting was arranged, and Local Studies Librarian Alice Lock. Councillor Oldham pursued his belief in the value of the work and a publication programme was designed to cover the History of Tameside up to 1930 in three volumes. The responsibility for monitoring the progress of the commission for Tameside fell to Barry Delve, Assistant Director of Leisure Services (Libraries and Heritage). His support and that of the staff of the Local Studies Library at Stalybridge are gratefully acknowledged.

A number of people kindly assisted in the research and writing of this work. Dr Nick Higham and Dr Denise Kenyon read early drafts of Chapters 2, 4 and 8 and their comments and advice greatly enhanced those portions of the book. Adele Mayer read an initial draft of Chapter 9, and her suggestions were of great use. Mrs Joyce Powell kindly allowed the author extensive use of her large archive on Mottram parish, as well as the use of many of her own photographs. David Cordingley of Cordingleys Estates Agents and Surveyors, on behalf of Lord Deramore, was extremely helpful in allowing the author access to the Stamford archives in Ashton-under-Lyne. John Hodgson of the John Rylands University Library of Manchester (Deansgate) was good enough to read through Appendix 2 and correct a number of mistakes. Members of Denton Local History Society saw early drafts of Chapters 2, 3 and 4 and their comments and suggestions were most welcome. David Morris, Conservation Officer for Tameside, provided a number of useful hints as to the layout of Ashton-under-Lyne. The staff of both Preston and Chester Local Records Offices were extremely helpful during the initial research. Judith Kent, of the John Rylands University Library of Manchester, and colleagues at the Greater Manchester Archaeological Unit, Tom Burke, Norman Redhead and Greg Sanders, went to great lengths checking for spelling mistakes, bibliographical errors and factual inconsistencies. Adele Mayer and Tom Burke assisted with the graphics and Robina McNeil and Norman Redhead assisted with the photography. I must especially thank Dr Peter Arrowsmith who edited the volume with great thoroughness carrying through substantial revisions to the benefit of both content and form.

Finally my thanks to my wife Catherine and son Richard for their constant care and support.

Michael Nevell
Greater Manchester Archaeological Unit

Contents

List of Figures

List of Plates

Plates 1.1, 6.2, 6.3, 9.1 and 9.2 are reproduced by kind permission of the Local Studies Librarian, Tameside Local Studies Library, Stalybridge, Tameside. Plates 3.1, 3.2, 5.1, 10.2 and 11.1 are reproduced by kind permission of Mrs Joyce Powell. All other plates were photographed by the Greater Manchester Archaeological Unit.

Chapter 1

The Sources

'Man must transform his environment from a state in which it is less to a state in which it is more useful to himself'

(H Belloc, *An Essay on the Restoration of Property*, republished 1984, 76)

1.1 The Present Past

History and archaeology are subjective disciplines, dependent on the desires and aims of the current generation. For Ormerod (1819 & 1882) the family histories of the squirearchy and gentry of Cheshire were the central points of local history. For Earwaker (1877 & 1880) and Farrer and Brownbill (1911) the origins of the local township and parish were the chief interests. By the time Bowman embarked on her history of Ashton in the 1950s (Bowman 1960) concerns had changed once more, with the social history of the local population coming to the fore as part of the post-war upsurge in local history studies.

The purpose of this present study is to assess the role of the period 1066-1700 for the district now known as Tameside from the perspective of recent historical and archaeological studies. In order to understand our present environment we need to know how that past society developed at a local level or even on an individual basis as much as in terms of wider, national, changes. For Tameside there is a wide variety of sources for the medieval and early modern periods which can be sifted and filtered into the story of the changing landscape and people of the Borough.

1.2 Documentary Evidence

A diversity of documentary evidence has been used for the present work, and this can be divided into three main groups: legal and administrative records, wills and inventories, and contemporary map evidence.

Legal and administrative records

The main body of medieval and early modern administrative and legal documents comprises the palatinate records of Chester and the records of the duchy of Lancaster. Both include administrative and judicial material, although since Cheshire functioned as an independent administrative unit from 1071 to 1301 as an earldom and from 1301 as a palatinate the records for that county begin much earlier than those for the duchy. The charters of the earls of Chester *c* 1071-1237 have recently been published (Barraclough 1988). Records such as the Cheshire recognizance rolls are a rich mine of information both on office-holders within the palatinate and on local men from all walks of life. The puture rolls, such as those for Cheshire published by Highet (1960), provide valuable evidence for local landowners and settlements from the early fourteenth century onwards. From the Lancashire side of the Borough the Ashton custom roll and rental of 1379-1422 has been published by Butterworth (1823), Harland (1868) and Bowman (1960). Much original material relating to both counties is now held in the Public Record Office in London, in particular the details of the medieval lay subsidy for Lancashire. From time to time translations are published, among these being the Longdendale survey of 1360 (Booth *et al* 1976-8) and, most recently, Booth's calendar of Cheshire inquisitions post mortem of 1343-9 (Booth 1991).

From the sixteenth and seventeenth centuries legal evidence includes the quarter sessions records for both Lancashire and Cheshire, as well as inquisitions post mortem. There are also extensive records for tax gathering; in Lancashire these include the lay subsidy (Tait 1924) and from the early seventeenth century the parish rate for the Poor Law (Butterworth 1823). In Cheshire the situation is slightly different in that the palatinate raised its own tax, called the mise. Until recently few details of this had been published, although Clayton has now remedied that situation for the fifteenth century (Clayton 1990). Nevertheless the details for the sixteenth and seventeenth centuries remain largely unpublished, although the subsidy roll for Macclesfield hundred in 1610 is a notable exception (Driver 1953). The other main source of fiscal information for the latter half of the seventeenth century comprises the hearth tax returns, copies of which are held in Chester and Preston Local Record Offices.

Local manor court rolls have survived, in part, for only three manors in Tameside: Ashton from *c* 1600 onwards, Hattersley for 1621-57 and 1689-92, and Werneth for 1588-1658. Of the other local administrative records that have survived the most important are the parish registers for Ashton church, from 1594 onwards, and Mottram church, from 1570 onwards, and the accounts of the overseers of the poor in Ashton, from 1683 onwards.

To these can be added a large number of rich muniment collections. Much of this material is now held by the record offices, such as the Tollemache estate papers for Longdendale (Chester LRO DTW Bundles B, C, H-L). The John Rylands University Library of Manchester also holds a large collection of original documents, encompassing deeds, charters, wills and assessments, which include the Dunham Massey and Legh of Lyme muniments. However there are a number of manuscript collections still in private hands, the largest of which are the Godley deeds now held by the Society of Antiquaries (see Appendix 1) and the Stamford archives held by Cordingleys, the stewards of the Stamford estate (see Appendix 2).

Wills and inventories

The second group of original documentary material consists of wills and inventories. Most of these fall within the period 1560-1700 for which 634 survive for the parishes of Ashton and Mottram. These have been employed extensively throughout this volume. Inventories are invaluable for analysis of agricultural practices, the distribution of wealth, and industrial activities, whilst wills can be used to assess the patterns of inheritance and the size of families. This analysis is not a straightforward task, for there are many pitfalls and problems of interpretation. However, used with care probate records are an indispensable asset for the study of the sixteenth and seventeenth centuries.

Contemporary map evidence

It is perhaps surprising to note that the sources for Tameside in this period include a number of contemporary or near-contemporary maps. All have their own faults and drawbacks but they nevertheless provide valuable information about the existence and design of certain buildings and the appearance of the countryside. The earliest relevant documents are the maps of Lancashire and Cheshire by Saxton in 1577 and Speed in 1608 and 1610. These represent the landscape in only a generalized form but there is some attempt to differentiate site types into churches, chapels, towns and halls. Although other maps of Lancashire and Cheshire were produced in the seventeenth century all were reprints of these editions with minor additions.

However there are three further maps which have proved to be of enormous use to the present study. The earliest of these is the Stayley manor map of *c* 1580, published by Bowman (Preston LRO DDX 350; Bowman 1960, 113). Although the southern part of the map is now lost, it details the boundaries of the demesne and is of particular value for assessing the development of the landscape in that it includes farmsteads, field boundaries, and an elevation of Stayley Hall. However it is not drawn to any particular scale and follows the contemporary style of Saxton and Speed in giving an oblique pictorial view of the area, making assessment of distance difficult.

The second map to have survived is the Dukinfield estate map of 1692, now held in the Tameside Local Studies Library (DD 229/1). This is drawn to a specific scale, with field boundaries, roads and rivers represented in plan form as on modern maps. However this document also contains field-names and tenants' names for each parcel of land, as well as pictorial views of the main buildings within the township, including Dukinfield Hall (Plate 1.1).

Thirdly there is the Ashton estate plan drawn in 1765 (ESRCA/15). This provides invaluable evidence for the pre-industrial landscape of most of the parish of Ashton, and as such is relevant to the seventeenth-century landscape. The parish is represented in plan, and buildings other than those in the town, which are shown pictorially, are represented in the same fashion. A separate inventory listed the field-names for the parish relating them to letters on the map, but sadly this has been lost. Only the lands held by the earl of Stamford in the parish were surveyed, resulting in a number of blank areas on the map. Nevertheless, this document provides the earliest cartographic evidence for farmsteads within the parish. It also contains two insets, one of which provides the earliest depiction of Ashton church, showing it prior to 'renovation' in the nineteenth century; the other is a detailed plan of Ashton town which shows the houses, roads and boundaries of the town in plan, as opposed to the pictorial view on the actual map (Bowman 1960, 637).

1.3 Archaeological Evidence

Only three sites have been the subject of modern excavation in Tameside, the two halls of Denton and Dukinfield and the seventeenth-century glassworks at

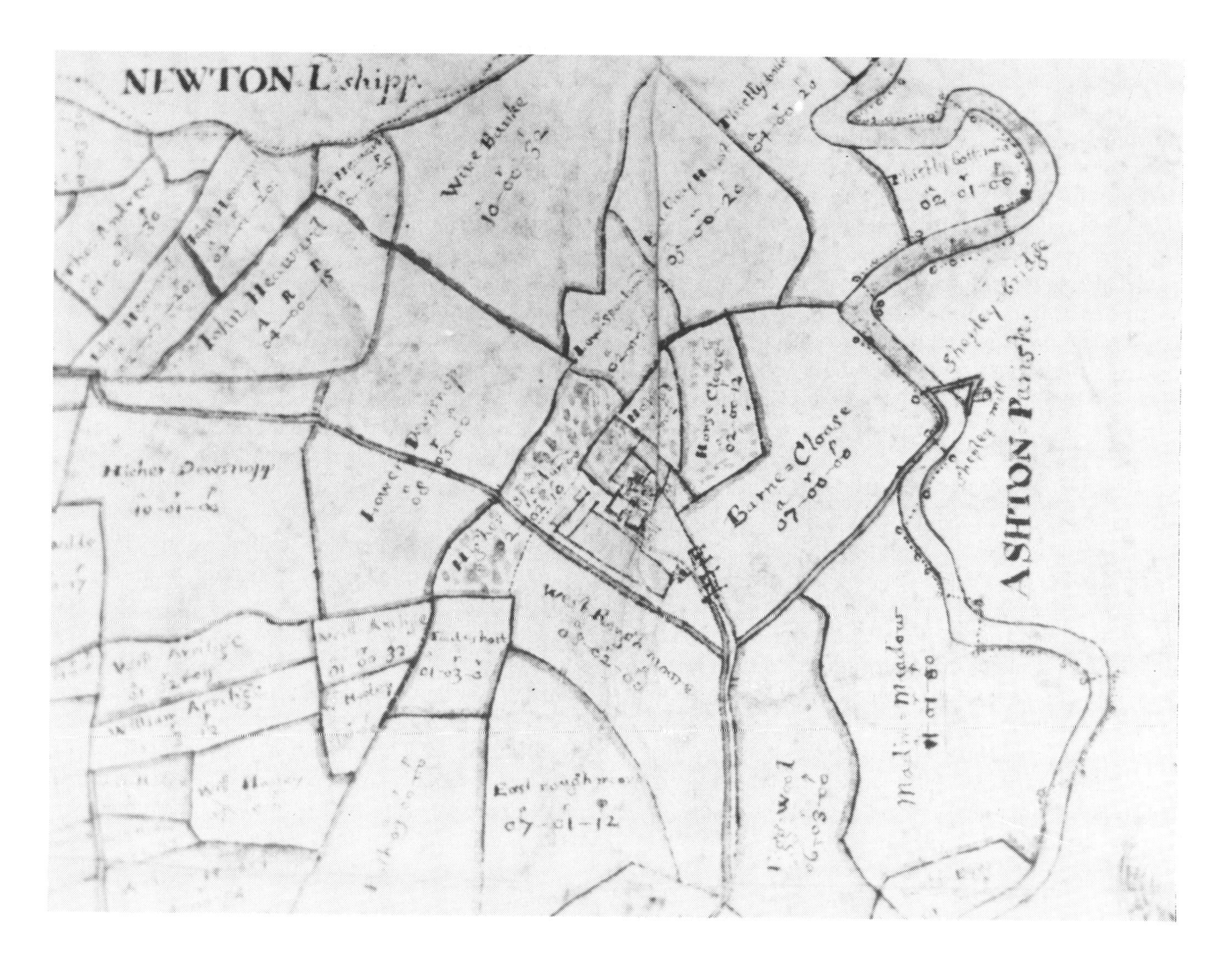

Plate 1.1 Detail of the Dukinfield estate map of 1692.
Dukinfield Hall and Chapel (centre) are shown surrounded by the demesne fields, held directly by the manorial lords, the Duckenfields. The smaller fields to the upper and lower left were leased to local tenant farmers. Early estate plans such as this provide invaluable evidence for patterns of settlement and landholding.

Haughton Green. All have been published, although for Dukinfield Hall and Haughton Green glasshouse this has only been in the form of summary excavation reports. However it was possible to re-assess the original excavation archive for Dukinfield Hall and the fruits of this research are published in Chapter 9. Since so few sites have been excavated there is a danger that too much attention could be concentrated on the mass of evidence they have produced. To avoid such an imbalance the context of these sites has been related to other buildings in the Borough in the case of Denton and Dukinfield Halls, or to other industries in the case of Haughton Green glasshouse.

Archaeological evidence does not only encompass excavated material but also includes earthworks and standing buildings. Within Tameside there are more than 30 recorded standing buildings of the period 1066-1700, and most of these are domestic structures of the sixteenth and seventeenth centuries. Nevertheless there are at least three medieval cruck-framed buildings within the Borough (Newton Hall and the lesser known Taunton Hall and Apethorn Farm), as well as two medieval churches (St Michael's, Ashton, and St Michael's, Mottram). A brief assessment of all these sites can be found in Appendix 4. The documentary evidence indicates that this number is only a small fraction of the medieval and early modern buildings built in the Borough before 1700, and it is possible that fragments of other early buildings survive, unrecognized, in the fabric of later structures. With regard to earthworks, two sites in the Borough are of particular importance. The first is Nico Ditch in Audenshaw, part of a ditch and bank system which may once have extended from Ashton Moss in the east to Moorside,

Urmston, in the west. However, although in Tameside, as elsewhere, Nico Ditch served as a boundary from at least the late twelfth century onwards, its origins probably lie in the pre-Conquest period and as such it is outside the remit of this volume. The second major earthwork is Buckton Castle, Mossley (Plate 1.2). This has often been viewed as prehistoric in origin, but there are good reasons to believe the site to be a medieval ringwork castle of the twelfth or thirteenth century. In addition several areas of 'ridge and furrow' earthworks have been identified, which may be related to medieval farming practices within the Borough; while at Mottram there are the possible remains of at least one house platform belonging to the medieval village. Such sites provide a physical expression of social and economic conditions attested within the documentary sources.

1.4 Secondary Sources

In addition to the material discussed above extensive use has been made of secondary sources. These range from national overviews such as Clarke's study of medieval England (Clarke 1984) and regional summaries such as Blackwood's assessment of the Lancashire gentry during the period 1640-60 (Blackwood 1978), to specific articles such as Cunliffe-Shaw's reconstruction of the business activities of John Shaw in the fifteenth century (Cunliffe-Shaw 1958). National assessments provide the intellectual framework for many of the arguments presented in this volume but it is the regional and local studies that have provided most of the detail.

Regional studies

Assessment of the published regional studies immediately indicates that very few encompass both of the pre-1974 counties of Lancashire and Cheshire which provided the component halves of modern Tameside. Furthermore Cheshire is by far the better served. Since the amount of original documentary material available is not especially dissimilar between the two, as a brief survey of the volumes published by the Record Society of Lancashire and Cheshire emphasizes, one must draw the conclusion that Cheshire has proved the more fashionable county. Kenyon's recent publication on the origins of Lancashire is a welcome addition to the literature on that county, but nevertheless her work (Kenyon 1991), along with that of Lowe (1972) and Blackwood (1967, 1976 & 1978) represent a belated attempt to redress the imbalance. If one turns to Cheshire one finds many volumes and articles published on that county's medieval and early modern history. Most notable amongst these are Bott's survey of corn-mill sites from 1066 to 1850, unfortunately prone to inaccuracy and omission in Tameside (Bott 1983, 1984a & 1984b), and Booth's survey of the county administration in the thirteenth and fourteenth centuries (Booth 1981), Clayton's assessment of the late medieval administration (Clayton 1990), and Morrill's analysis of the county in the period 1630-60 (Morrill 1974), which provide the starting point for any serious study of the county government of this period. To these can be added the history of the county sponsored by the Cheshire Community Council, and the twice yearly publication of *Cheshire History* which, as its title suggests, is devoted solely to publishing research on the county.

Such an imbalance has inevitably led to a bias towards evidence from the Cheshire half of the Borough. In part this can be redressed by the use of the appropriate topographical volume of the *Victoria County History* of Lancashire (Farrer & Brownbill 1911). However, a truer picture of the richness of the available sources for the Borough can be measured by the number of local articles concerning matters on both the Cheshire and Lancashire sides of the River Tame. This would suggest that the unfashionable nature of Lancashire history lies at a level above that of the local researcher or local society, and is hindering more extensive syntheses of that region's medieval past.

Local studies

When one turns to the published, and unpublished, local studies relating to Tameside a wealth of material is available. During the nineteenth century a number of pioneer local historians turned their attention to the townships of the region. These included James and Edwin Butterworth (1823, 1827 & 1842), Booker (1855), Higson (1859), Chadwick (*c* 1870), and Glover (1884). Their works vary in quality, Chadwick being perhaps the vaguest, and J Butterworth and Booker the most scholarly. Although much of what they contain is now of dubious use, these sources do provide valuable contemporary descriptions and transcripts of manuscript sources.

There are a number of early twentieth-century studies which are also of use, the chief ones being Middleton's volumes on Godley, Hyde and Denton (Middleton 1900, 1932 & 1936). However Middleton was averse to giving the sources for much of his evidence and this has greatly devalued his works. From the immediate post-war period Speake and Whitty's study of Droylsden contains an impressive collection of original manuscript material from the period prior to 1700, although it lacks any real attempt to put the development of Droylsden in its regional

Plate 1.2 Buckton Castle, Mossley.
The origins of this site are uncertain, but it is probably to be identified as a medieval ringwork castle, constructed in the twelfth century by the earl of Chester or in the thirteenth century by the lord of Longdendale.

context (Speake & Whitty 1953). The works of Bowman also contain an exciting amount of unpublished manuscript material, especially her *England in Ashton-under-Lyne* (1960), but on too many occasions her affection for Ashton overrides her critical faculties. The value of her research, particularly noteworthy for her use of the Stamford archives in Ashton-under-Lyne, is undermined by her inability on occasion to sift fact from fiction. Despite these drawbacks her work marks the first attempt to assess the landscape and social history of a large part of the Borough, although it has now been largely superseded.

Two recent works in particular illuminate the path forward for local historical studies in Tameside. These are Powell's assessment of Mottram parish in the period 1570-1680 (Powell 1976), which is especially strong on the agricultural economy, and Young's survey of the townships of Denton and Haughton prior to 1700 (Young 1982), which highlights the strength of the manorial system in that area during the sixteenth and seventeenth centuries. Sadly both remain unpublished, although Young has written a short article based on her work (Young 1985). These studies mark a recognition that the recovery of the history of medieval and early modern Tameside involves the integration of the documentary evidence with that from excavation, place-names and standing buildings. Without this previous research the present volume would have been much harder to construct.

Chapter 2

Anglo-Norman Tameside

'He [King William I] then sent his men over all England into each shire, and had it made out how many hides of land were in the shire; what the king himself had in land, and in livestock on the land; what dues he had from property each twelve months from the shire; also he let it be written down how much land his archbishops had, his diocesan bishops, his abbots and his eorls...what and how much each man who was holding land in England, in land, in livestock, and how much money it was worth.'

Extract from the Anglo-Saxon Chronicle for 1085 (Savage 1982, 213)

2.1 The Norman Conquest and Settlement

These words are the earliest surviving account relating to the Domesday Book, the inventory of Norman England compiled upon the express wish of King William I. With the creation of this work begins the medieval history of Tameside, indeed, of much of England. This monumental undertaking, completed within twelve months, provided the most comprehensive and detailed English inquisition of the eleventh century, and in much of the North-West the only substantial source until the thirteenth century. By necessity any survey of the Norman occupation of north-west England must begin with this work. However, it was written twenty years after the defeat of the Anglo-Saxon army under King Harold at Hastings. To understand the book's political and social context, and its relevance to the study of the history of Tameside, it is necessary to review, briefly, the regional developments of this formative period of Anglo-Norman society.

Although King Harold had been killed at Hastings on 14th October 1066, and William crowned king on Christmas Day, the country was far from pacified. During the period 1067-70 William was forced to fight a series of campaigns from Wessex to Northumbria in order to maintain his position (Husain 1973, 2-3). In 1069, while William was engaged in quelling a second revolt in Northumbria, the men of Chester in alliance with the Welsh rebelled and besieged Shrewsbury. Leading his army across the Pennines from York into Cheshire in the winter of 1069-70, William suppressed the revolt and established castles at Chester and Stafford to secure the region. The year 1070 is usually taken as the date at which the earldom of Chester was established, when it was granted to Gherbod the Fleming. He appears not to have taken up his new post and returned to the continent soon after (*ibid*, 3). His successor was Hugh I, the son of Richard vicomte of Avranches. The land 'between the Ribble and the Mersey' was assigned to Roger of Poitou around the same time (Farrer & Brownbill, 1906, 279) (Fig 2.1).

Post-Conquest England was a feudal society, based upon the holding of land from a superior on specified terms of service, in a chain which started from the king (Husain 1973, 14). By 1086 this hierarchical system was fully established, and most of the land was held by the king, with Norman earls, bishops, abbots, and barons as tenants-in-chief (holding lands directly from the king). One effect of the Conquest was the dispossession of nearly all of the Anglo-Saxon landholders. In Cheshire these included such major Anglo-Saxon tenants-in-chief as Earl Edwin of Mercia and his brother Morcar, earl of Northumbria (Dodd 1986, 10-11). However there were also many English tenants of only local importance who were dispossessed (Sawyer & Thacker 1987, 320-5). Many had completely disappeared by 1086 but a few, such as Gamel of Mottram, were recorded as tenants. By 1086 Englishmen accounted for only two of 180 tenants-in-chief holding estates returning an income of more than £100 per annum. About 100 of approximately 1400 lesser tenants-in-chief, and only slightly more of the 6000 or so subtenants, were English (Wood 1986, 159; Davis 1966).

In Cheshire, apart from the bishop of Chester, Earl Hugh I was the only tenant-in-chief, an arrangement unique in England. His Cheshire estates were only part of an enormous honour, which included lands in twenty other counties (Sawyer & Thacker 1987, 303-5).

Under him in Cheshire were many subtenancies, from which were to emerge the baronies of Dunham Massey, Halton, Kinderton, Malpas, Mold, Nantwich, Shipbrook and Stockport. Hugh I was the first in a succession of powerful earls, ending with the death of John le Scot in 1237, under whom the earldom maintained its own distinct character.

The lands of Roger of Poitou between the Ribble and the Mersey were themselves part of a large honour that included land in seven other counties. At the time of Domesday his original holdings in Lancashire (the land between the Ribble and the Mersey, and Amounderness to the north) had reverted to the crown, but were later restored to him with additional lands. This enlarged estate became the main constituent of the honour of Lancaster, although it was not until 1168 that we find reference to the 'county' of Lancaster (Bagley 1956, 18; Farrer & Brownbill 1906, 291). In the eleventh and early twelfth centuries the geographical term Cheshire included the land between the Ribble and the Mersey, but there is no evidence that the area was ever administered as a unit with Cheshire. The earls of Chester were in possession of this territory on only two occasions, under Ranulf II in Stephen's reign, *c* 1140-53, and under Ranulf III in the reign of Henry III, 1216-32 (Harris 1979, 2).

2.2 The Domesday Manors 1066-86

The Domesday Book includes 376 entries for the county of Cheshire in 1086 (Sawyer & Thacker 1987, 342-70) but this apparently comprehensive guide is misleading. The survey was in fact an incomplete record and the quality of information varies per hundred. For example, 33 priests are listed in 1086, but only 27 churches. In some hundreds only priests are mentioned, while in others the priests are noted always with a church. In Hamestan hundred, later to become the hundred of Macclesfield, all churches and priests were omitted, suggesting that the hundred failed to supply this information (*ibid*, 297). Such variability is especially acute in the land between the Ribble and the Mersey. Only the manors in West Derby hundred are listed in anything approaching the detail for Cheshire, whilst the information for the other hundreds here seems to be in a summary form. In Salford hundred 21 manors are grouped together in one sentence, although Radcliffe, Rochdale and Salford manors are listed separately (Morgan 1978b, R5).

The Domesday entries for Tameside can be found in three locations. The bulk are in the folios for Cheshire, but there are also references in the southern Lancashire appendix to Cheshire, and in the Derbyshire folios. The entries are as follows:

'The same earl [Hugh I] holds HAMETEBERIE [Henbury in Prestbury township] of ½ hide, COPESTOR [Capesthorne in Prestbury] of ½ hide, and HAMEDEBERIE [Henbury in Prestbury] of 1 hide that pays geld, and HOFINCHEL [unidentified] of 1 hide, and TENGESTVISIE [Tintwistle in Mottram] of 1 virgate of land, and HOLISURDE [Hollingworth in Mottram] of 1 virgate, and WARNET [Werneth in Stockport] and RUMELIE [Romiley in Stockport] of 1 virgate, and LAITONE [Leighton in Marple] of 1 virgate of land. All paid geld. Eight free men held these lands as [8] manors. In all there is land for 16 ploughs. The whole was and is waste. In Hofinghel is wood 2 leagues long and 2 wide. In Tengestvisie is wood 4 leagues long and 2 wide. In Warnet is wood 3 leagues long and 2 wide. T.R.E. [in the time of King Edward] this hundred was worth 40s, now 10s' (Sawyer & Thacker 1987, no 66).

'The same Gamel holds MOTRE [Mottram in Longdendale?]. His father held it. There [are] 1½ hides that pay geld. There is land for 4 ploughs. It is waste. There [is] wood 3 leagues long and 2 [leagues] wide and 2 hays and a hawk's eyrie' (*ibid*, no 309).

'ST MARY'S church [Manchester] and ST MICHAEL'S church [Ashton-under-Lyne?] hold 1 carucate of land in MANCHESTER exempt from all customary dues except tax' (Morgan 1978a, R5.2].

'In LONGDENDALE and THORNSETT Ligulf had 4 bovates of land taxable...All Longdendale is waste; woodland, unpastured, fit for hunting. The whole [is] 8 leagues long and 4 leagues wide' (Morgan 1978b, 1.30].

These entries would appear to indicate the presence of four manors (Tintwistle, Hollingworth, Werneth and Mottram) and one church (at Ashton) in Tameside in 1086, three of the manors being held directly by the earl of Chester and one tenanted by Gamel, held of the earl (Fig 2.2). However such an interpretation is not without difficulty. Whilst the identification of the manors of Tintwistle, Hollingworth and Werneth is secure, that of Mottram is not.

Traditionally 'Motre' has been taken to be Mottram St Andrew on the basis of an undated charter, possibly late twelfth-century, which states that 'Edward son of Gamyl, lord of Mottrum, gave to his son William land in Mottersheved in the town of Mottram', ie Mottram St Andrew (Ormerod 1882, 697). Ormerod admits that it is impossible to identify this Gamyl with the Gamel of Domesday, but presumes that he was a near descendant of the Saxon landholder. The name Gamel, however, is not uncommon, occurring for example in an Audenshaw charter of 1190-1212 (Farrer 1902, 329), nor is it confined in the Cheshire Domesday to the manor of Motre. In 1066 a Gamel held the manor of Poulton in Bebington, while in 1086 Gamel held not only Motre but also Cheadle, both of which had been held by his father in 1066 (Sawyer & Thacker 1987, 363-4). Rochdale, in Salford hundred, was held in 1066 by a Gamel who still held land in the hundred in 1086 (Morgan 1978a, R5.2). In the opinion of Sawyer and Thacker it is likely that these references to Gamel are to one man, who is also to be identified with the Gamel FitzGrifin, the holder of three manors in northern Staffordshire in 1086, and probably the son of the Grifin who held Biddulph in Staffordshire and the Cheshire manors of Weston in Runcorn and Newton by Middlewich in 1066 (Sawyer & Thacker 1987, 322).

The later occurrence of the name Gamel in Mottram St Andrew is not, therefore, conclusive evidence for the identification of that manor as Motre. Furthermore, other considerations would appear to make Mottram-in-Longdendale the more likely possibility.

The fact that Motre was assessed at 1½ hides is suggestive of a fairly large estate containing areas that were later to become separate townships. In Longdendale a number of manors in the later lordship fail to be mentioned in Domesday: Newton, Godley, Matley, Stayley and Hattersley. This phenomenon is well attested elsewhere in Domesday Cheshire (Sawyer & Thacker 1987, 333-5), but does not appear to fit the situation of Mottram St Andrew. The later manor there was not large and was flanked on the west and east respectively by the manors of Butley and Over Alderley, both of which are listed in Domesday (*ibid*, nos 101 & 208), and on the south-east by Prestbury and on the north-west by the Bollin fee of Wilmslow parish, both of which, though not mentioned by name in 1086, were probably part of the earl's manor of Macclesfield (Ormerod 1882, 646, 587); Newton, the final manor flanking Mottram St Andrew, is modest in size and appears to have been originally part of Butley (*ibid*, 669). The absence of Mottram-in-Longdendale from the Domesday survey would also be puzzling, since the presence of a parish church here rather than in one of the other Domesday manors of Longdendale argues for the primacy of this holding.

Another entry not without problems is that which refers to St Michael's church. It was Tait who first identified this with St Michael's church in Ashton-under-Lyne (Tait 1904, 6-7), a view most recently supported by Kenyon who suggests that the church, parish and manor are all probably late Anglo-Saxon in origin (Kenyon 1991, 173). In the thirteenth century Ashton manor lay within the barony of Manchester and the advowson of the parish church belonged to the lords of Manchester, implying that it was a daughter church of St Mary's in Manchester. The absence of Ashton manor from the Domesday survey does not throw doubt on this interpretation since it may be included in the 21 unnamed manors mentioned in Salford hundred in 1066 (Morgan 1978a, R5.3).

The final entry which may be connected with Tameside occurs in the Derbyshire Domesday. However the reference to Longdendale must describe the whole valley either side of the River Etherow, since it encompasses an area '8 leagues long and 4 leagues wide', and may have included not only the lordship of Longdendale but also the manor of Glossop.

Using these entries it is possible to paint a shadowy picture of Tameside in 1086. The area east of the River Tame was held by the earl of Chester, while that to the west of the river lay in the land between the Ribble and the Mersey, granted in 1070 to Roger of Poitou but in 1086 in the hands of the crown. Of the Anglo-Saxon freeholders present in 1066 perhaps only one, Gamel of Mottram, still held land in 1086, although he was now a tenant of the earl. In what was later to become Lancashire lay St Michael's church, and presumably the manor of Ashton. The Cheshire side of the Borough lay within the extensively wooded district known as Longdendale and here there were probably four manors. This side of the Borough was all 'waste', but the Domesday Book does not record whether the Lancashire side was as well. Traditionally the term 'waste' has been interpreted as the result of the devastation wrought by William on Cheshire in the winter of 1069-70. In western and central Cheshire the term is more likely to have been used in the technical sense of describing the value of the land to the lord (Sawyer & Thacker 1987, 336), but in the north and east of the county waste does seem to have been the result of that campaign. Although Longdendale was worth 40s before 1066 the manors on both sides of the river were waste in *c* 1071 and were still so in 1086.

2.3 The Norman Manors 1086-1237

In 1086 Tintwistle, Hollingworth and Werneth were still held directly by Earl Hugh I as part of a group of eight wasted manors in north-east Cheshire. This was not untypical of the situation in Cheshire at that time, where there were a number of other blocks of land, for instance in Middlewich hundred, which remained unapportioned (Sawyer & Thacker 1987, 335). This may also have been the case in Salford hundred, where 21 unnamed manors are mentioned in 1066 but are not individually accounted for in 1086. After 1086 Hollingworth and Werneth are next documented in the first half of the thirteenth century by which date they had been apportioned to local families (see Chapter 3).

West of the Tame the first unequivocal reference to Ashton is provided by a grant of land there to Orm son of Ailward by Albert Grelley, lord of Manchester,

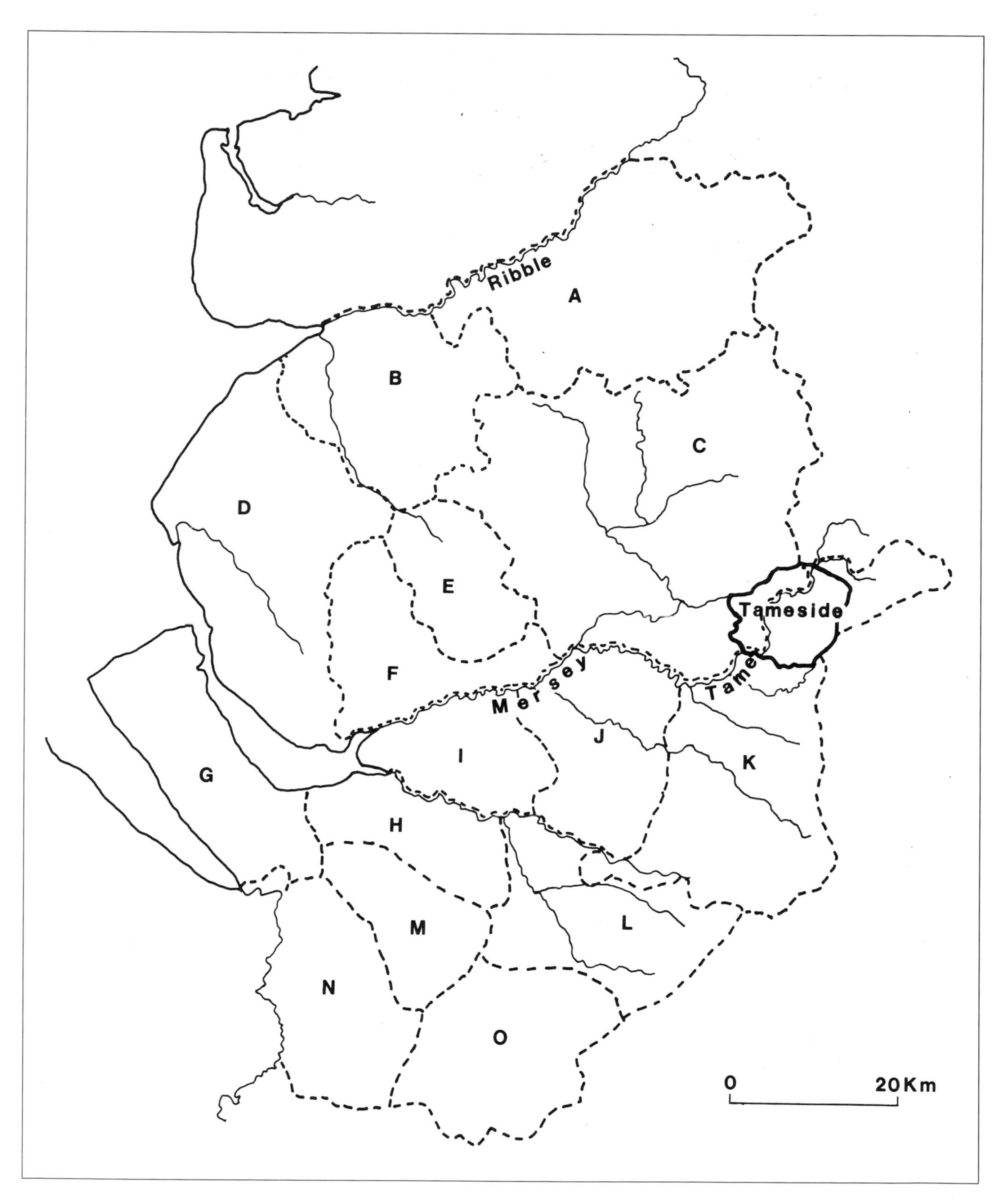

Fig 2.1 Cheshire and the land 'between the Ribble and the Mersey' in 1086, showing the hundreds and the position of Tameside. *Key:* A Blackburn; B Leyland; C Salford; D West Derby; E Newton; F Warrington; G Wirral; H Roelau (later part of Eddisbury); I Bucklow West; J Bucklow East; K Hamestan (later Macclesfield); L Northwich; M Riseton (later part of Eddisbury); N Broxton; O Nantwich.

Hundreds were subdivisions of a county. Pre-dating the Conquest, they are believed to have been originally land containing a hundred families. In Tameside the area to the west of the River Tame lay in Salford hundred, part of the land 'between the Ribble and the Mersey'; the area east of the Tame lay in Macclesfield hundred in Cheshire.

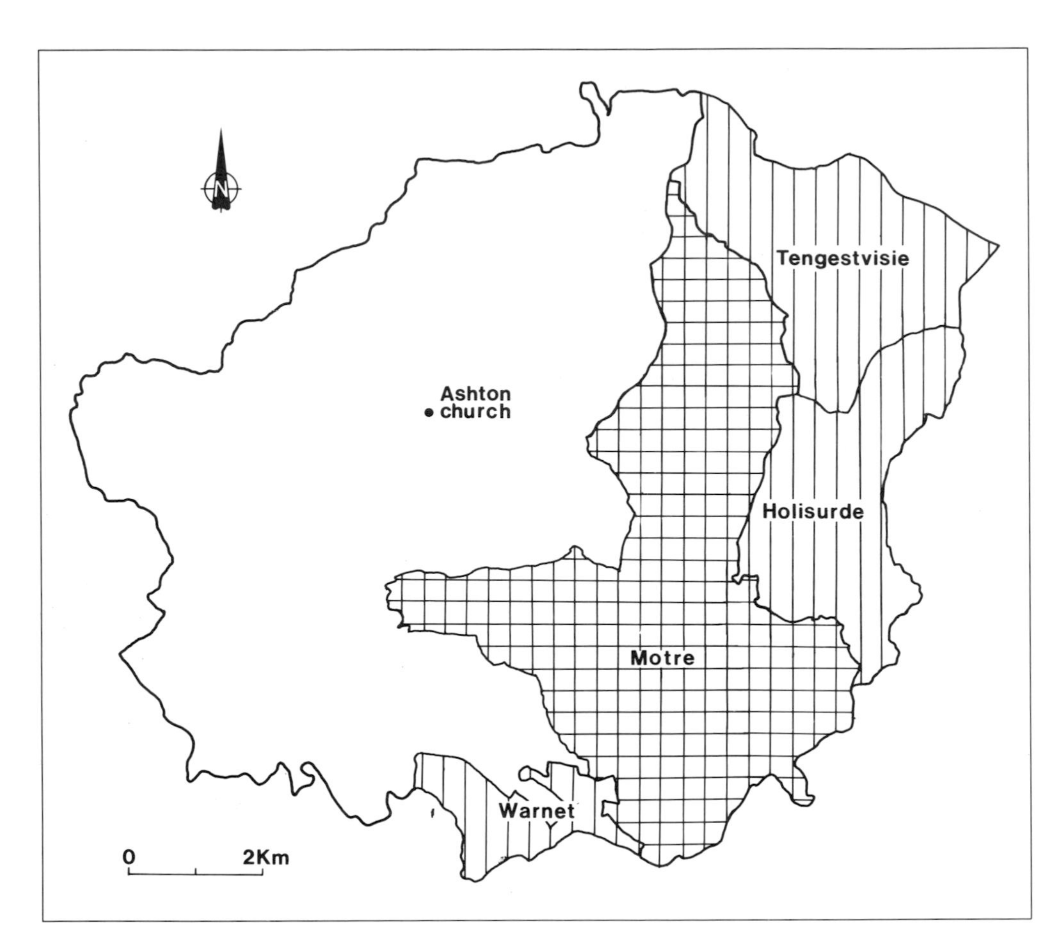

Fig 2.2 The Domesday manors of Tameside.

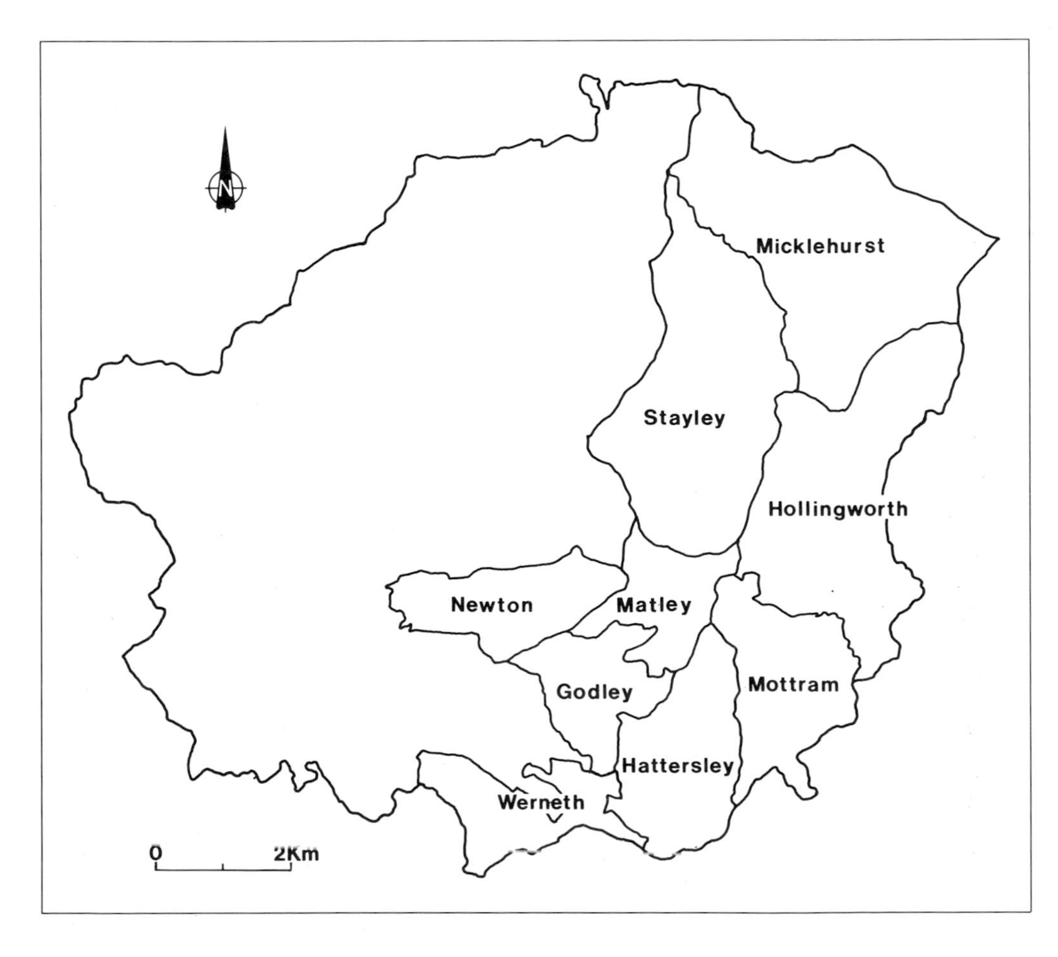

Fig 2.3 The Longdendale lordship in 1360.

probably in the mid-twelfth century (see Chapter 3). At the end of the century a moiety, that is a half, of the manor of Denton was held under the lord of Withington by Matthew de Reddish (Farrer & Brownbill 1911, 311). South-east of the Tame the Domesday manors are not mentioned again until a series of charters and deeds of the first quarter of the thirteenth century. A charter of Thomas de Burgh, lord of Longdendale, dated to 1211-25, granted land in Mottram to Adam son of Reginald. It was witnessed by Robert and Jordan 'de Staveleia', Radulfus 'de Hattresleia', Thomas 'de Holinewurthe' and Henry 'de Matteleia' (Barraclough 1957, 42). A charter of Hamo de Massey of the same period mentions Newton manor and Thomas de Godelegh (*ibid*, 43). For Godley, Hattersley, Matley, Newton and Stayley this is the first reference to their existence.

By combining the evidence from these last two charters and other documents of the period it is possible to assess the progress made by the Tameside economy up to the early thirteenth century. This evidence will be considered in greater detail in Chapter 4, but the salient points are as follows.

Firstly the fringes of the great mossland of Ashton were beginning to be exploited with wasteland being cleared along its southern edge, in Audenshaw, by the period 1190-1212 (Farrer 1902, 329). Secondly there was sufficient land under the plough, at least in Longdendale, to warrant a mill by the period 1211-25. This was possibly Woolley mill in Hollingworth and was controlled by the lord of Longdendale, along with the fishing and woodland rights of the valley (Barraclough 1957, 42; 1988, no 321). In the manors bordering the northern banks of the River Etherow assarting (clearance of woodland for farming) is mentioned in Godley in a grant of land by Thomas de Godelegh probably pre-dating 1249. The grantee was also given the right of 'passage for his swine in the wood of Godley' and licence to burn charcoal on his land (Middleton 1900, 38-9). Finally the population of Tameside in the thirteenth century may have merited not only a church at Ashton and Mottram, but also a chapel of ease at Dukinfield, for a Robert, chaplain of Mottram, and a Robert, cleric of Dukinfield, were witnesses to this same grant (*ibid*).

Such a pattern of agricultural expansion has been noted by Dodd (1986, 19-20) in Frodsham and other manors in western Cheshire for the twelfth and thirteenth centuries. The evidence for assarts and arable land indicates that the economic resources of the region were expanding, population growth was taking place, and open-field cultivation was in operation. Although this expansion was further advanced in central and western Cheshire, the Tameside manors seem to have followed these broad developments.

2.4 The Manchester Barony and the Longdendale Lordship

During the period 1086-1237 the land of Tameside fell within the remit of two major lordships. West of the Tame, with the exception of Quickmere, the land formed part of the barony of Manchester. East of the river most of the manors appear to have been part of the Longdendale lordship. The origins of the Manchester barony are obscure but its formation appears to post-date 1086 and to be connected with William Rufus's restoration of the land between the Ribble and the Mersey to Roger of Poitou (Tait 1904, 9-10). The barony included lands in three of the southern Lancashire hundreds, Salford, Leyland and West Derby, but most of it lay in Salford. This fief, or landholding, was the most extensive in that hundred and by the early twelfth century was in the possession of the Grelley family, who retained it until the early fourteenth century (Farrer & Brownbill 1906, 326). Until the end of the twelfth century Denton and Haughton may only have been townships within the manor of Manchester, but Ashton was a submanor, with its own lord, from at least the mid-twelfth century.

South-east of the River Tame the situation was rather more complicated. Ostensibly the Longdendale lordship was created in the period 1200-3 by a charter of Earl Ranulf III (1181-1232) granting the 'land of Longedenedale' to William de Neville and his wife Amabilia (Barraclough 1988, no 321). Some doubt has been cast by Barraclough on the veracity of this document but he concluded that 'on the whole, it is probably safe to accept the charter as genuine' (*ibid*, 323). If it is a forgery it can be no later than 1358 when it appears in the Black Prince's register (Dawes 1932, 296-7). This lordship consisted of two manors in demesne (that is land retained and farmed by the lord), namely Tintwistle and Mottram-in-Longdendale. By the fourteenth century Tintwistle was a market borough with its own court and the site of the lord's manor house. Mottram, on the other hand, was the ecclesiastical centre and the administrative centre of the lordship. In addition the lords of several neighbouring townships held their manors as tenants of the lord of Longdendale. In the thirteenth and fourteenth centuries these included Godley, Great and Little Hollingworth, Hattersley, Matley, Newton, Stayley, Werneth (Booth *et al* 1976-8, no 57) and Woodley, in Bredbury (Ormerod 1882, 852) (Fig 2.3). Most of these manors lay within the medieval parish of Mottram-in-Longdendale. However the territory forming the lordship would appear to be considerably older than *c* 1200.

There are several references from the mid- to late

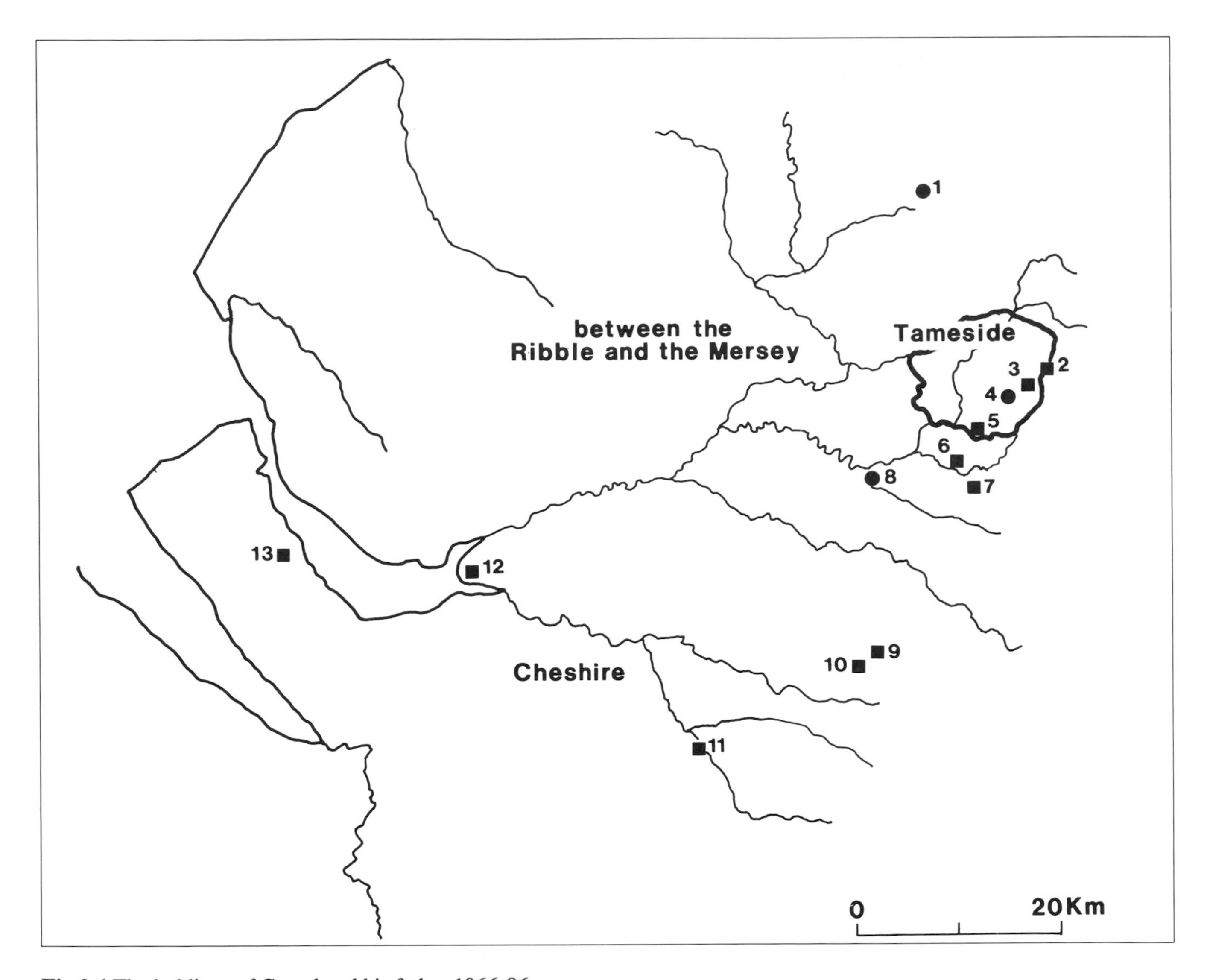

Fig 2.4 The holdings of Gamel and his father 1066-86.
Key: ■ = holding of Gamel or his father in 1066; ● = holding of Gamel in 1086.
1 Rochdale; 2 Tintwistle; 3 Hollingworth; 4 Mottram; 5 Werneth; 6 Romiley; 7 Leighton; 8 Cheadle; 9 Henbury; 10 Capesthorne; 11 Newton; 12 Weston; 13 Poulton.
The evidence of the Domesday survey suggests that prior to the Conquest this family held extensive estates in Cheshire, with Mottram as the principal manor in a group of holdings in Longdendale and north-east Cheshire.

twelfth century which might be used to support this, but which on closer inspection must all be discounted. The first is a charter of Earl Hugh II, which would appear to grant Longdendale to William and Amabilia de Neville in the period 1162-76. Apart from the names of some of the witnesses this document is virtually identical to the grant of 1200-3. However, since William did not marry Amabilia until shortly before 1202, this document cannot be an authentic charter of Hugh II (Barraclough 1988, no 170). Secondly James Butterworth cites a series of documents, otherwise unattested, which purport to show the tenure of lands in Godley, Newton, Hollingworth, Matley and Mottram in the twelfth century under a Robert de Burgh or Bros (Butterworth 1827, 152-3). However, as will be noted in greater detail in Chapter 3, these documents, which relate principally to the holdings of the Mascy family of Sale and the Wolegh family of Hollingworth, are in all probability fabrications of the fourteenth century or later. Finally one other source connects a twelfth-century Robert de Burgh with Longdendale. This is a family tree in the manuscripts of the eighteenth-century antiquarian John Watson, which claims that in the reign of Richard I (1189-99) Thomas de Burgh married Adeliza, the daughter of Thomas de Newton (Ormerod 1882, 858; Earwaker 1880, 161). However, as will be noted in Chapter 3, this too is probably a later invention.

There would appear, therefore, to be a complete lack of reliable evidence for any of the component manors of the lordship between 1086 and the early thirteenth century, and in view of this silence it seems likely that their apportionment to local lords post-dates the earl's grant to de Neville. As for the holding of the lordship by the de Burgh family, this is historical but belongs to a later date: a Thomas de Burgh married Sara the daughter of William de Neville, and when de Neville died in 1211 this Thomas succeeded to his estates (Barraclough 1957, 43).

The strongest clues that the territory of Longdendale, and possibly the lordship, were of considerable antiquity lie in the Domesday survey. In the most recent discussion of the Cheshire Domesday Sawyer and Thacker note that in a number of instances several manors are grouped together and treated as though they were a single unit (Sawyer & Thacker 1987, 318-19). In Hamestan, later Macclesfield, hundred there were only two such groupings, one of three manors, probably Somerford Booths in Astbury (*ibid*, no 300), and the group of eight manors which included Tintwistle, Hollingworth and Werneth (*ibid*, no 66). Since such 'multiple manors' were given a single evaluation in both 1066 and 1086, they are probably to be seen as pre-Conquest in origin. According to Sawyer and Thacker 'multiple manors represent territories linked under some kind of lordship, whether of one of the named tenants or some other unnamed lord' (*ibid*, 319).

It may well be the case, therefore, that the manors that came within the Longdendale lordship in the thirteenth century were part of an Anglo-Saxon lordship in 1066. However this original lordship would have been considerably larger than that recorded in the thirteenth century and later (Booth *et al* 1976-8). Of the eight manors that were listed as a group in 1086, five, Tintwistle, Hollingworth, Werneth, Romiley and Leighton, formed a compact single unit of territory, covering most of the land between the rivers Tame and Etherow, in north-east Cheshire. Two others, Henbury and Capesthorne, would have been outlying members. The location of the eighth, Hofinchel, is not known.

Unfortunately this Domesday entry refers only to eight unnamed freemen as holding these manors in 1066 and gives no indication of a pre-Conquest paramount lord. However, the probable identification of Motre as Mottram-in-Longdendale, its tenure in 1066 by the father of Gamel, and the extensive landholdings of that family documented by the Domesday survey provide a possible candidate (Fig 2.4). Gamel's own tenancy of Mottram in 1086 would then mark a concession by the earl of Chester by which he was allowed to retain the principal manor of the 1066 Longdendale holding. However, the absence of any further mention of Mottram until the early thirteenth century would suggest that it subsequently reverted to the earldom until being included in the grant to William de Neville in 1200-3.

Plate 3.1 Newton Hall.
The south elevation of the cruck-framed medieval hall dating from *c* 1380. The hall was the home of one of the oldest manorial families in Tameside, the Neutons who held the lordship of Newton from the early thirteenth to the late seventeenth century.

Chapter 3

The Manors of Tameside

'Let everybody know whether present or to come, that I Thomas de Burgh have given, granted and by this my present charter confirmed to Adam son of Reginald all the land, which Albinus held, in the territory of Mottram'

(Barraclough 1957, 42, Godley charter no 1)

3.1 The Manorial System in Tameside to *c* 1500

The medieval manor was the main administrative unit outside the large towns which had their own laws and courts (Riden 1987, 43). It could comprise a single township, parts of several townships, or a collection of individual townships. (The township was an ancient division of a parish and was only given administrative powers after the Reformation of the sixteenth century). In Tameside the single-township manor was the norm. West of the River Tame the large manor of Ashton coincided with Ashton parish and was composed of four divisions, Ashton town, Audenshaw, Hartshead and Knott Lanes. East of the river lay the Longdendale lordship, which was composed of two demesne manors, that is lands held directly by the overlord, and six other manors which were leased to lesser local lords (Fig 2.3).

The manor was 'estate' and 'state', 'for as well as matters directly relating to his tenants and the services they owed him, the lord in his manorial court could punish assault and theft, sometimes even impose the death penalty, and settle disputes between neighbours' (Walker & Tindall 1985, 20). In Tameside the special privileges of the lordship of Longdendale included the right to carry out trial by combat (Barraclough 1988, 321-2). There still exists a set of documents relating to a claim for land in Stayley in 1377/8, when the lord of Longdendale, Sir John Lovell, was prepared to let the parties concerned, Robert de Stavelegh and John de Oldham, settle the matter by combat to the death (ESRCA/4/1-3; Bowman 1960, 95-6).

As such the manor was the local expression of the feudal system, under which, in the broadest terms, society was formed into a pyramid with each level owing the stratum above services and dues, the ultimate head being the monarch.

At the lowest level of society were the peasants. In the early medieval period they are excluded from the documentation for Tameside, in part a consequence of their slight legal importance. The best evidence for the medieval peasantry in the Borough is given by the Ashton custom roll and rental of 1379-1422 (Harland 1868, 94-116). This document outlines the rents, labour services and other obligations due to the lord of Ashton from his tenants and shows a clear division between free tenants and 'tenants-at-will'. The first group included not only individuals who might be described as privileged peasants but also local landowning families, such as the Byrons of Clayton, the Staveleghs of Stayley and the Holynworths of Hollingworth, who in their own manors were lords in their own right. While free tenants had virtual security of tenure of their lands, for which they paid often only a nominal rent, the conditions of the tenants-at-will were more severe. They rented property and land for fixed terms and could be ejected for not obeying the lord's rules. It was also the tenants-at-will who provided the labour by which the lord cultivated his demesne:

> 'every tenant that plough has, shall plow two days, and he that half plough has, shall plow a day' (*ibid*, 94).

In addition to ploughing, the services of the Ashton tenants-at-will included harrowing during seeding time, carting ten loads of turves to the manor, a day's carting of corn, and four days' harvesting. Further obligations included a present to the lord of the manor at Christmas and the heriot on the death of the head of the household, specified in the rental as 'the best beast they have'.

The second social group identifiable in Tameside consists of the lesser manorial lords and their families.

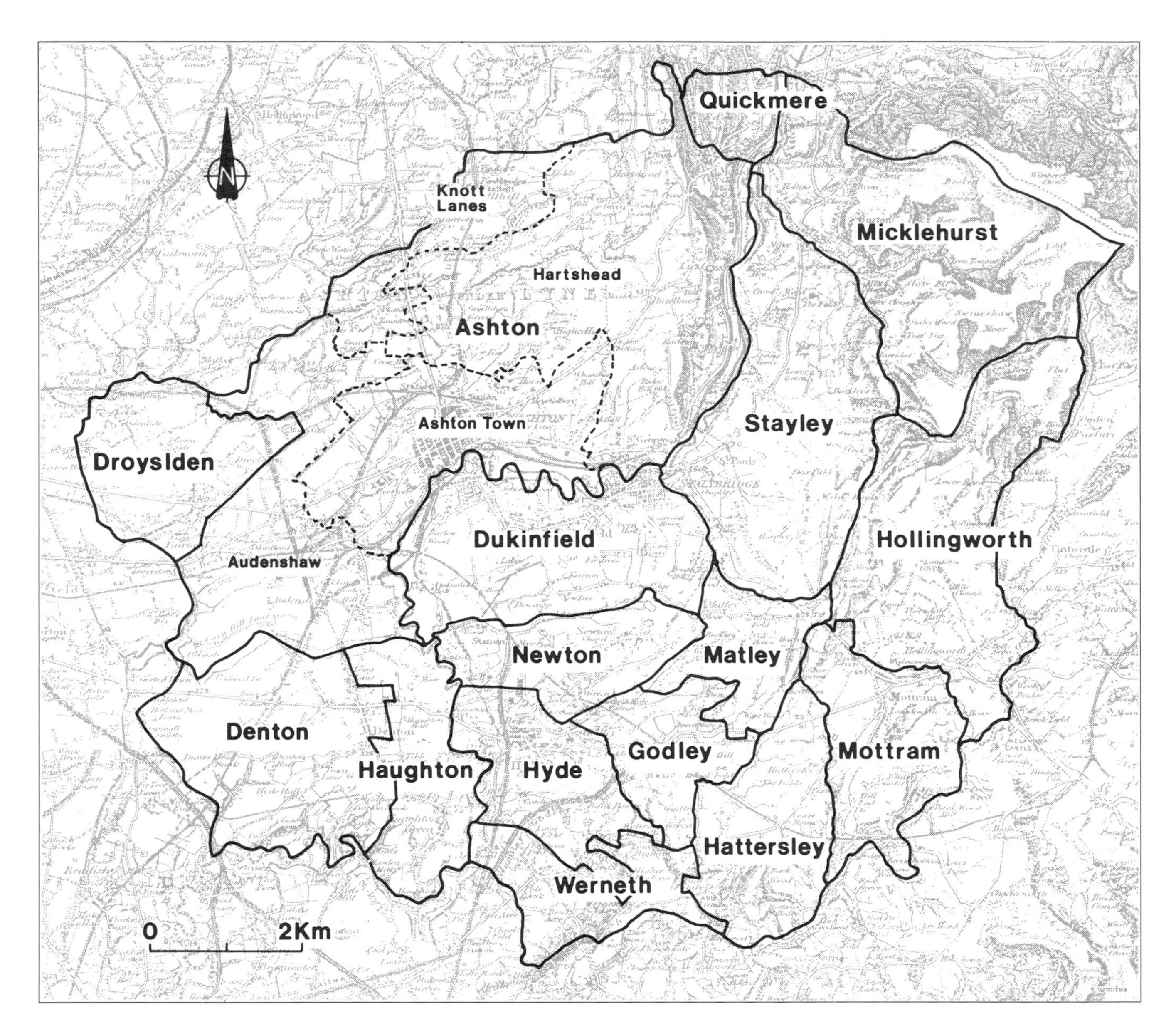

Fig 3.1 The Tameside manors and townships.
The boundaries are based on sixteenth-, seventeenth- and eighteenth-century estate plans, nineteenth-century tithe maps and the Ordnance Survey first edition 6in to 1 mile sheets, surveyed in 1844-5 and 1872. The base map used for this and other maps in this volume is the Ordnance Survey 1in to 1 mile series, surveyed *c* 1840. This lacks the precision of the 6in to 1 mile series in the location of boundaries, roads and structures but, across the Borough as a whole, provides the earliest detailed overview of the landscape.

In addition to the power which they exercised within their own manorial holdings, many of these served in a wider judicial or administrative capacity. Perhaps the most frequently attested of such duties are their appearances as witnesses to charters or as jurors on inquisitions, but in the later medieval period they are also documented in such other activities as the collection of local taxes or service on judicial commissions.

Some members of the Tameside manorial families also held posts at a national level. John de Assheton, lord of Ashton manor, represented Lancashire in Parliament in 1382, 1388 and 1390 (Farrer & Brownbill 1911, 341). The greatest prominence, however, was reached by Sir Robert de Assheton, a younger son of the same family. He held several high offices under Edward III including treasurer of the Exchequer and continued in favour at the court of Richard II, as warden of the Cinque Ports and constable of Dover (Bowman 1960, 96-7).

Above the lesser manorial lords were three greater landowners: the baron of Manchester, the baron of Dunham Massey and the lord of Longdendale (Fig 3.2). (The barons of Stockport also held lands in Tameside, but as tenants of the last two of the above named). The barony of Manchester was held as part of the honour and duchy of Lancaster, while the two other major landholders in the Borough were tenants of the earl of Chester. By the fourteenth century both the duchy and earldom were held by the crown, which on three occasions also directly held the lordship of Longdendale.

Manorial descent provides the main historical framework in Tameside for much of the period covered by this volume. Certainly for the medieval period most available documentary evidence relates to the ownership of the manors or landholdings within them. The following sections are therefore concerned with tracing the descent of each of the manors in the Borough. To place such developments in their physical context two sets of maps are also provided within this chapter. The first shows changes in manorial landholding across the Borough. The second illustrates the pre-1700 landscape in each manor or township and provides the geographical setting for many of the social and economic developments outlined later in this volume, including the development of agriculture, patterns of landholding, and the growth of industry. The existence of individual farmsteads and manorial halls in this period is based upon contemporary documentary, and in some cases physical, evidence and this is outlined in Appendices 4 and 5. In the case of Stayley, Dukinfield and Ashton use has been made of the early estate plans discussed in Chapter 1, while for Hollingworth much of the information has been derived from a description of the manor by Francis Hollingworth in 1672-84 (Chester LRO DDX 87/1a). Road alignments are based upon either these early maps or Yates' map of Lancashire of 1786 and Burdett's map of Cheshire of 1777 which, in spite of their late date, show a landscape which still preserved many of its medieval and early modern features. Evidence for medieval agriculture in the form of field-names indicating arable farming and the clearance of woodland is derived from the nineteenth-century tithe maps and apportionments.

3.2 The Descent of the Tameside Manors

Ashton

Although Ashton is not directly mentioned in the Domesday survey, its existence can be inferred from the survey's reference to a St Michael's church in the Salford hundred (see Chapter 2). It has also been suggested that Ashton was the 'Estonbury', from which Roger of Poitou granted tithes to the abbey of St Martin of Sees by a charter of 1094 (Farrer 1902, 294), but this does not appear to have been confirmed. The recorded history of Ashton manor thus effectively begins in the twelfth century. By this date the manor was rated as 2 plough-lands and formed an outlying part of the barony of Penwortham, based on the manor of that name on the River Ribble. Under the Penwortham barons it was held by the Grelley family as part of their barony of Manchester for a rent of 20s or a hawk (Farrer 1903, 34-5). By the late twelfth century Ashton was held in turn under the Grelleys by a family who adopted the local name, but the process by which this came about is far from certain.

By a grant of uncertain date Albert Grelley gave 1 plough-land in 'Eston', that is half of Ashton manor, to Orm son of Ailward on his marriage to Albert's daughter Emma (Farrer 1903, 57). The identity of this Albert Grelley is a matter of dispute. Farrer argued that he was the first known bearer of that name, and placed this grant in the early twelfth century (Farrer 1902, 404-5), but he is far more probably the second Albert Grelley, who succeeded to the lordship of Manchester at some date prior to 1154 (Tait 1904, 127-30). At some subsequent date this same Albert Grelley apparently granted out the remaining portion of Ashton, thus making the whole of the manor a single subtenancy, for a charter of Albert Grelley (probably the third bearer of that name, who had succeeded to the lordship by 1170) confirmed on

> 'Roger son of Horm and his heirs, all my lands of Haistune [Ashton], with all the appurtenances...to hold of me and my heirs, as the same Roger held of my father, and for the same service, to wit, for Haistune twenty shillings or one sparrow-hawk' (Farrer 1899, 218-19).

Roger's son Orm is named as Orm 'de Eston' in 1199-1201 (Farrer 1902, 116, 149). The apparent successor to Roger as lord of Ashton, he is also the first known member of the family to bear the local surname, subsequently 'de Assheton'.

The tenure of the manor in the twelfth century is further complicated by the evidence of a dispute of 1276. This shows that in the reign of Henry II (1154-89) a William de Kirkby had granted Ashton to Orm, from which time the Kirkbys were in effect the immediate tenants under the lordship of Manchester and it was under them that the manor was held by the Asshetons (Farrer 1902, 405). The circumstances under which William de Kirkby received Ashton are lost but it seems likely that Albert Grelley's original grant of the manor was to this William de Kirkby under whom, as intermediate lord, subsequent grants were made to Orm son of Ailward.

In addition to the difficulties surrounding the early descent of the manor, there is also the problem of its original extent, in particular concerning the Audenshaw division. There are two charters relating to Audenshaw from the period 1190-1259, which do not

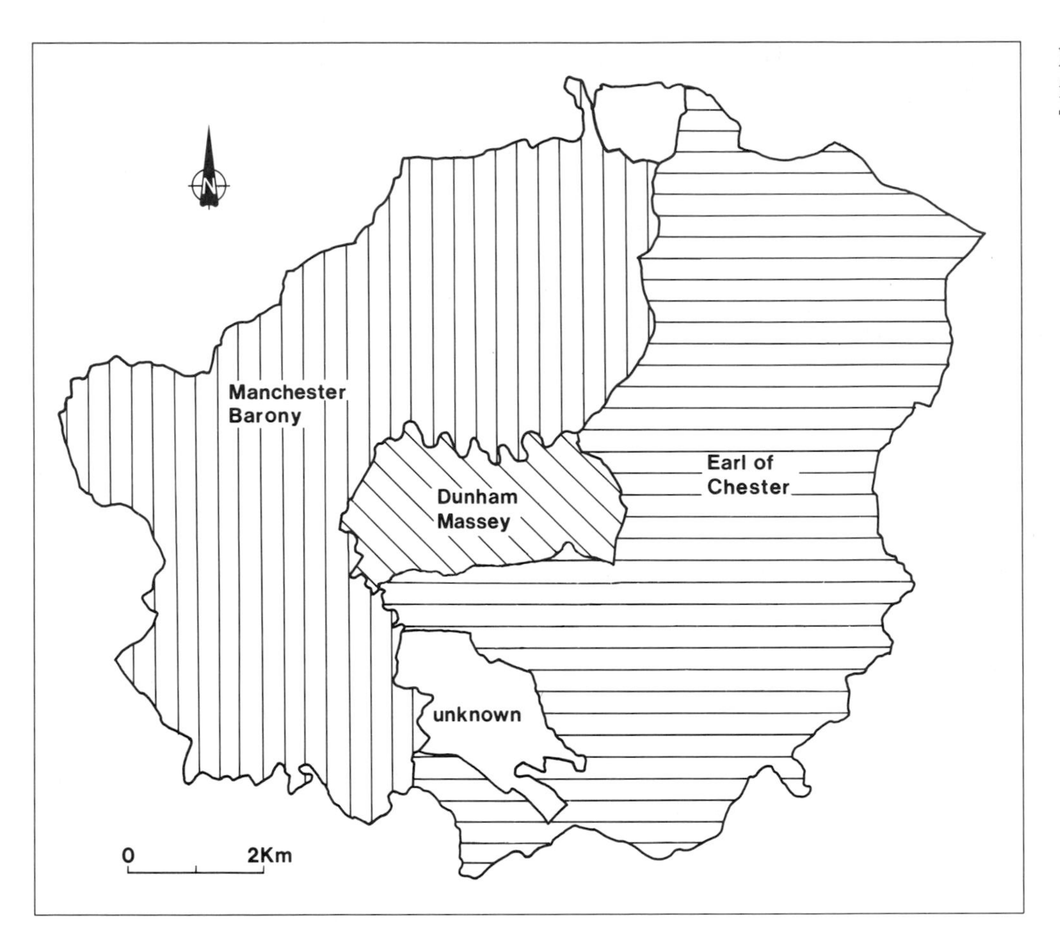

Fig 3.2 Major landholders in twelfth-century Tameside.

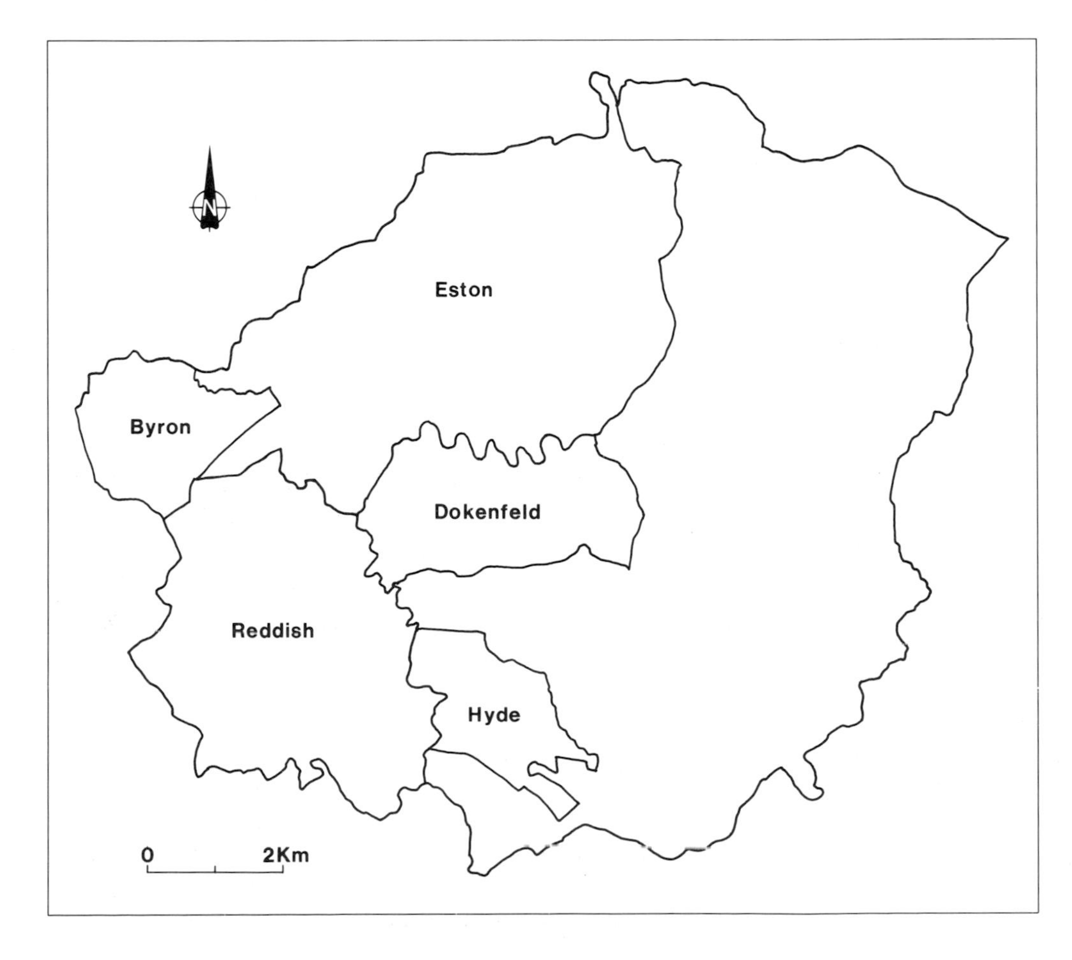

Fig 3.3 The holders of Tameside manors apportioned by *c* 1200.

mention Ashton, and are not witnessed by the lords of that manor (Farrer 1902, 328-9, 332-3). This absence is particularly striking in the case of the earliest of these charters, dating from 1190-1212, since it granted land in Audenshaw to the monks of Kersal Cell, and Cockersand Abbey is known to have received land in Ashton from Orm son of Roger in the period 1190-1202 (Bowman 1960, 128 no 11). The implication is that at this date Ashton manor did not include Audenshaw, or at least that part of it containing the Kersal Cell lands, that is to the south of Ashton Moss (Fig 3.7). Although where it lay is not clear there are two possibilities. Since the Byrons, lords of Clayton, witnessed both of the Audenshaw charters, it may have been part of their manor. The second and more likely possibility is that Audenshaw was then part of Denton manor. The original extent of that manor, as recorded *c* 1200, appears to have been 8 oxgangs. By the early fourteenth century 4 were in Denton township, and 2 in Haughton township. This leaves 2 unaccounted for, and it is possible that these were in Audenshaw (Fig 3.4). This may be supported by the charter of 1190-1212 in which the grantor of land in Audenshaw was Matthew son of Edith (Farrer 1902, 329); he may well be Matthew de Reddish who held the manor of Denton *c* 1200 (see below). However, the survey carried out in 1320 or 1322 of the estates of the lord of Manchester indicates that by this date Ashton manor had reached its full extent, that is including Audenshaw (Farrer 1907, 73).

In the thirteenth century the manor of Ashton was held by two men bearing the name Thomas de Assheton, the first being the successor to Orm 'de Eston', the second the lord in the later part of the century. The relationship between the two is not clear, but they may have been grandfather and grandson, since there is some evidence that a Robert de Assheton, son of the elder Thomas, was lord in 1246 and 1254 (Farrer & Brownbill 1911, 341). It was the right of Thomas the younger to the manor that John de Kirkby challenged in 1276 in the dispute mentioned above. Kirkby's motives are unknown, but possibly he had in mind the profitability of the manor from which his own family was in receipt of only 1d rent. The dispute was not settled until 1284 when a verdict was reached in favour of Thomas de Assheton (Farrer 1899, 162-3).

This dispute also throws some light on the development of landholdings in the manor. Kirkby's claim excluded the advowson of the church (which was held by the barons of Manchester) and 6 oxgangs. Farrer and Brownbill suggest that these were in the hands of free tenants, whom they also identify as six individuals who pressed claims against John, the son of Thomas de Assheton, in 1337; these being Richard de Stavelegh, John del Heyrod, Richard de Clayden, Robert del Hurst, William de Bardsley and John de Audenshaw (Farrer & Brownbill 1911, 341 nn 34 & 37).

When John de Assheton died in 1359, his son and heir, also named John, was a minor. This evidently presented the Kirkbys with a fresh opportunity to intervene in Ashton, for John de Kirkby successfully claimed wardship and hence gained direct control of the manor which he held until John's coming of age in 1375 (*ibid*, 341).

The lordship of the third John de Assheton, from 1402 to 1428, was of particular significance in the history of the manor. Until that time Ashton had remained very much a dependency of the manor of Manchester, to which the Asshetons were obliged to pay rent on behalf of the intermediate lords, the Kirkbys. Thus in the Manchester survey of 1320 or 1322 the first John de Assheton held Ashton manor by a rent of 'at the 4 terms 20s, and at Michaelmas one hawk or 40s', a separate rent of 2s 'at the 4 terms' being paid for the manor of Alt (Farrer 1907, 73). In 1413, however, his grandson John obtained an agreement that after the death of Thomas la Warre, lord of Manchester, these rents should cease, the subsequent payment for the manor being the nominal sum of 1d (Farrer & Brownbill 1911, 342). This concession was complemented by a second, for in 1403 la Warre had agreed that after his death the advowson of Ashton church should pass from the lordship of Manchester to John de Assheton and his heirs (*ibid*, 348). Significantly the lordship of the same John de Assheton also saw the rebuilding of the parish church.

It was under this John de Assheton and his father and predecessor that the custom roll and rental of 1379-1422 was compiled. The value of this document as evidence for the conditions of tenure of the free tenants and tenants-at-will in Ashton has been noted above. An additional point which may be made here concerns the large number of free tenants listed in this source compared with the late thirteenth and early fourteenth centuries (Farrer & Brownbill 1911, 344-5). As will be noted elsewhere, the growth of this group can be associated with changing economic conditions in the fourteenth century which were to have a profound influence on later patterns of landholding in the Borough.

The last of the Assheton lords was Thomas who succeeded to the manor in 1484. By his marriage in 1457 to Elizabeth, the daughter of Ralph Staveley (ESRCA/8), he united the manors of Stayley and Ashton (Fig 3.19). Although Thomas married four times he left no male heir and after his death in 1515 his estates were divided between George Booth, who was the son of his daughter Margaret and baron of Dunham Massey, and his other daughters, Elizabeth and Alice,

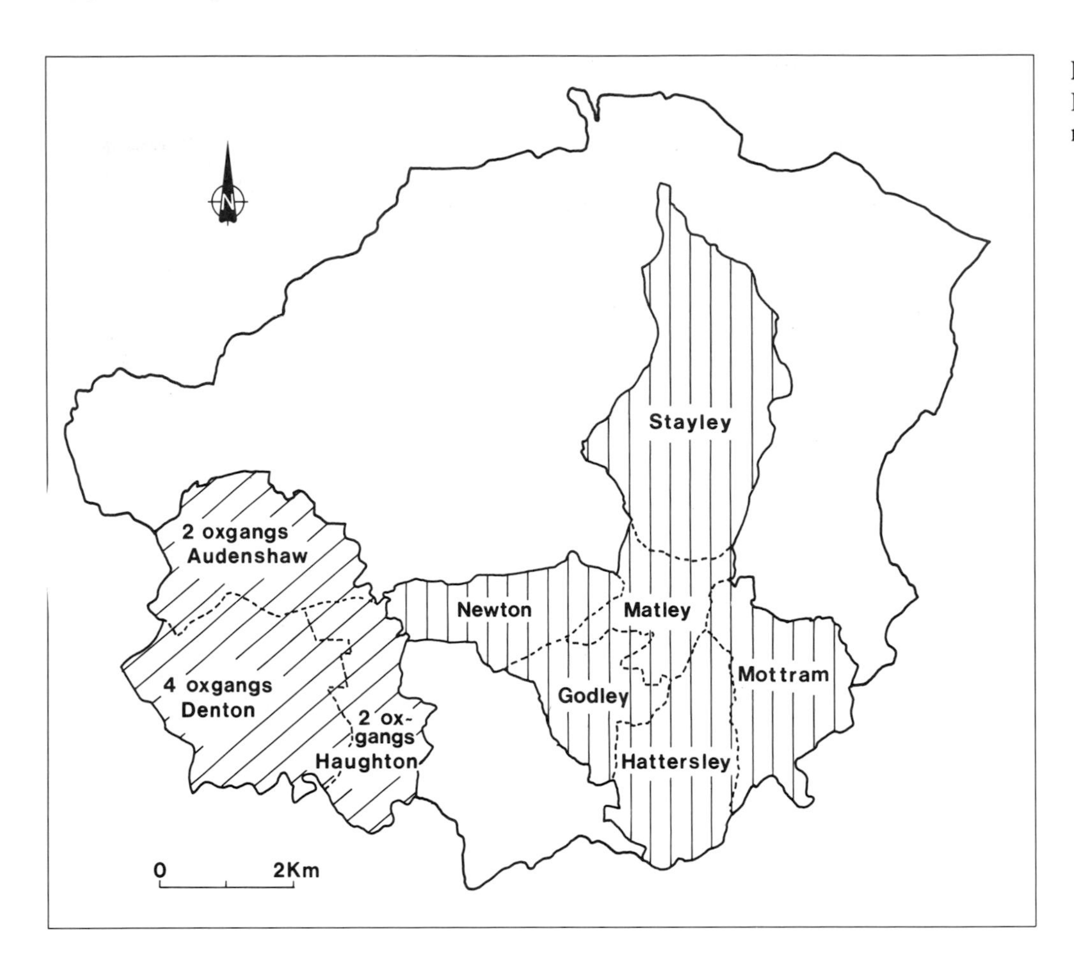

Figure 3.4 Extent of Denton and Mottram manors *c* 1200.

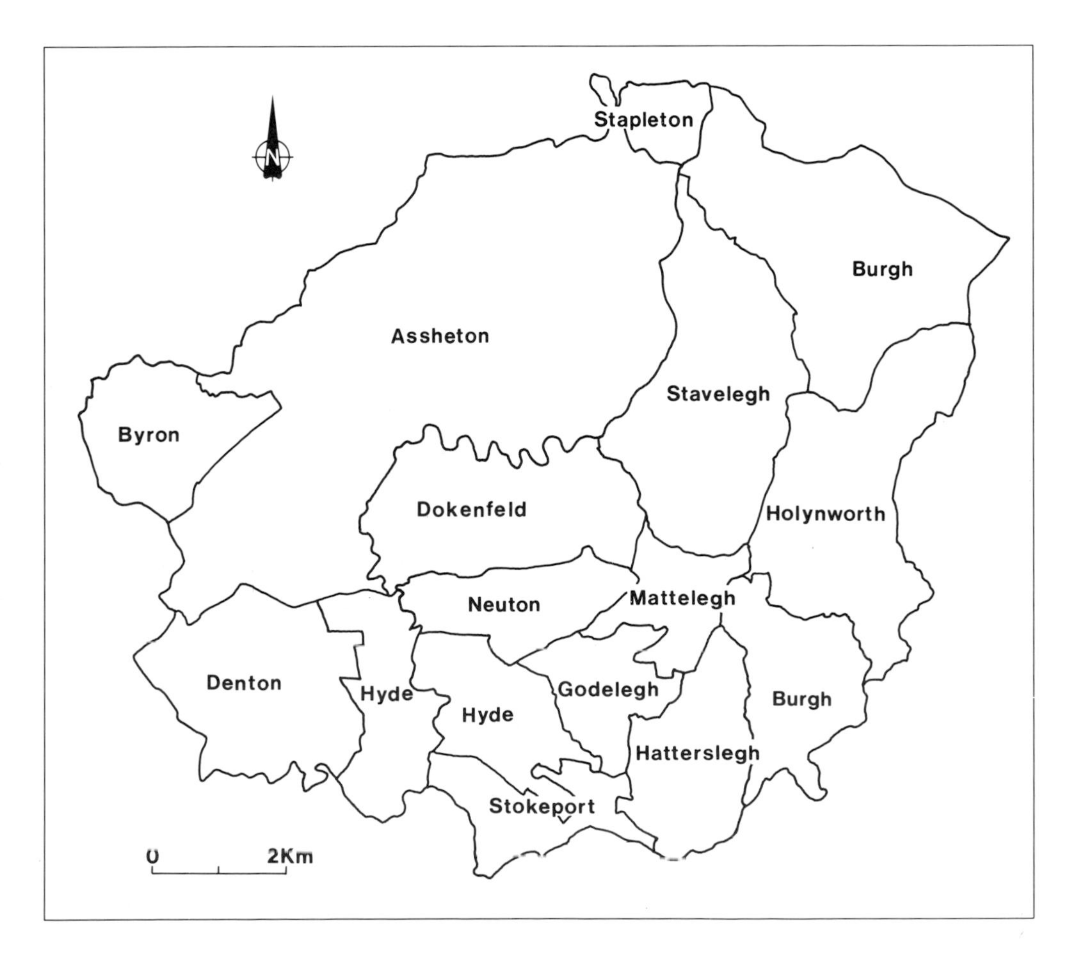

Fig 3.5 Landholdings in thirteenth-century Tameside.

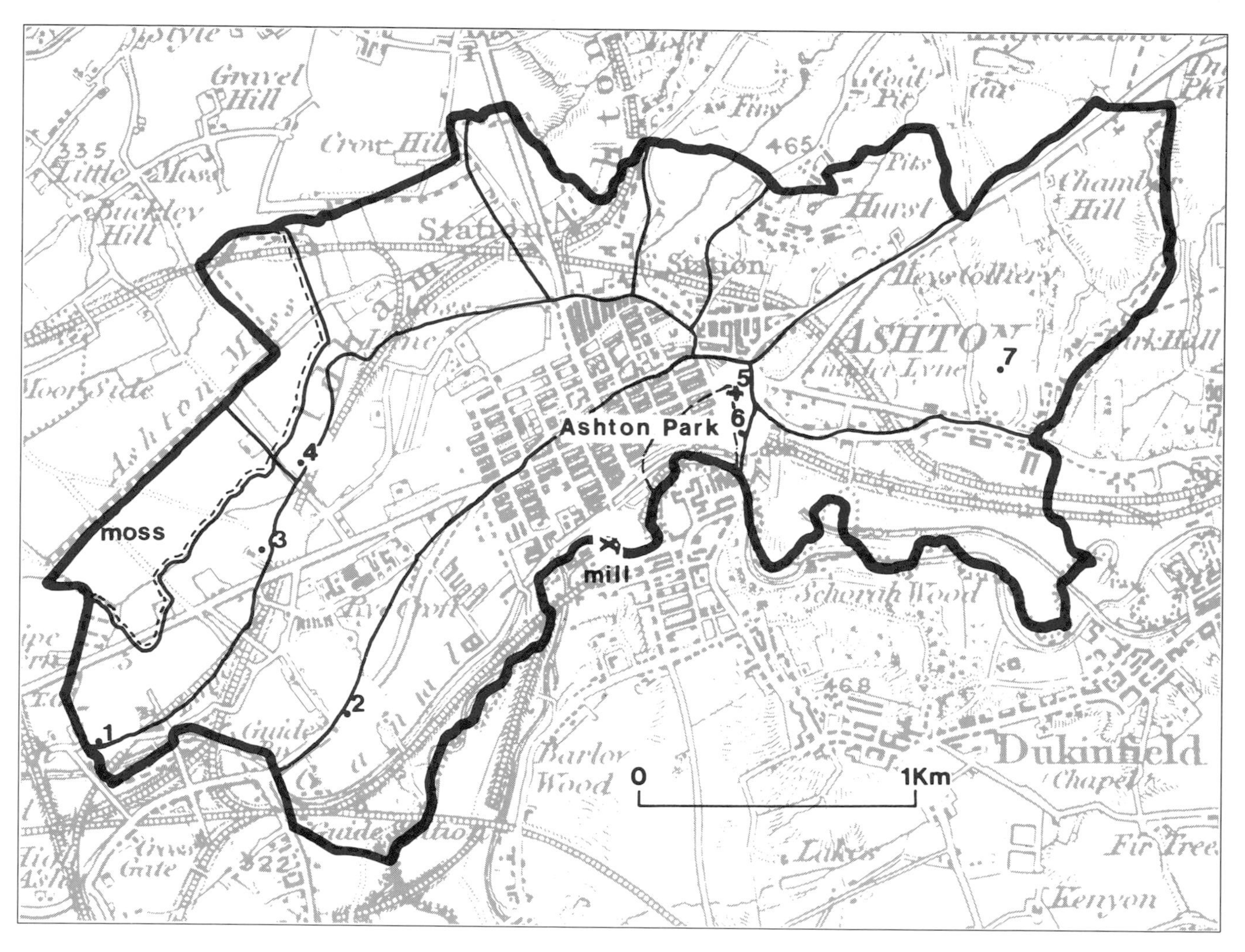

Fig 3.6 Ashton manor, Ashton town division.
Key: 1 Hayes Farm; 2 Clay Hill; 3 Knowl Farm; 4 Moss Side; 5 St Michael's Church; 6 Ashton Old Hall; 7 Parks Hall Farm.

the wife of Richard Hoghton of Hoghton in Lancashire (ESRCA/13). Elizabeth Assheton died without issue in 1553 and afterwards the manor and lands were held equally by the Booths and Hoghtons. In 1605 the Hoghtons sold their interest in these estates to the Booths, in which family they subsequently descended (Bowman 1960, 116-17).

Clayton, Droylsden township

Although a 'manor' of Droylsden is mentioned in the sixteenth century the word seems to have been used only loosely, since the township formed part of the manor of Clayton. The lands of this manor, comprising 14 oxgangs of which 4 seem to have been in Droylsden, were originally part of the demesne of the barons of Manchester but between 1194 and 1212 they were granted by Robert Grelley to Robert de Byron (Farrer 1903, 56; Farrer & Brownbill 1911, 282 n 19). By 1212 Clayton manor had passed to Robert de Byron's sons, of whom the elder, Robert, later granted his share to his brother Richard, including 'the whole vill of Droylsden', probably the earliest reference to the township (Farrer & Brownbill 1911, 282 n 22).

Clayton manor remained in the hands of the Byrons until the early seventeenth century. However, the accrual of other lands by the family from the thirteenth century onwards, both within Lancashire and without, eventually led to Clayton itself assuming less importance within their estates. Clayton Hall appears to have ceased to be their principal residence by the beginning of the sixteenth century (*ibid*, 285). In the early seventeenth century Sir John Byron sold off his Lancashire estates to settle his debts, the manor of Clayton being bought in 1621 by George and Humphrey Chetham (*ibid*).

Denton

Denton is first mentioned *c* 1200, when it was held by Matthew de Reddish as a submanor of Withington, itself part of the barony of Manchester (Farrer &

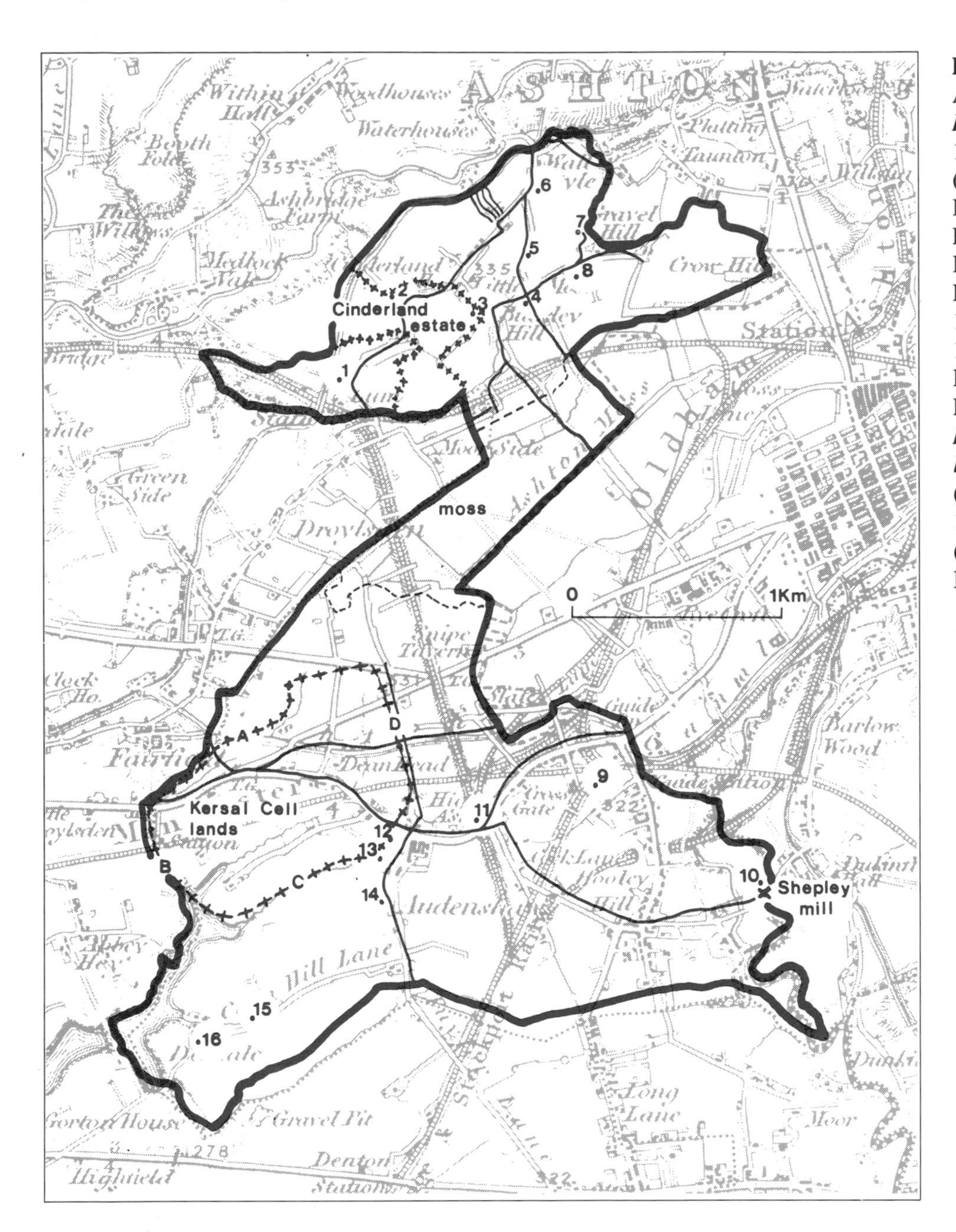

Fig 3.7 Ashton manor, Audenshaw division.
Farms and other buildings: 1 Lower Lumm; 2 Cinderland (Sunderland) Hall; 3 Buckley Hill; 4 Jaum Fields; 5 Blake Rake; 6 Well Style; 7 Gravel Hill; 8 Hope Fold; 9 Saxon Farm; 10 Shepley Hall; 11 High Ashes; 12 Red Hall; 13 Carrington Barn; 14 Hiltons Farm; 15 Audenshaw Lodge Barn; 16 Debdale Farm.
Boundary of Kersal Cell lands: A Moss Brook (probably 'Osuel's leach' in 1190-1212); B Gore Brook (Green Brook); C Kettles Brook; D Nico Ditch.

Key to manor and township maps
(Figs 3.6-8, 3.11-14, 3.16-18, 3.21-8)

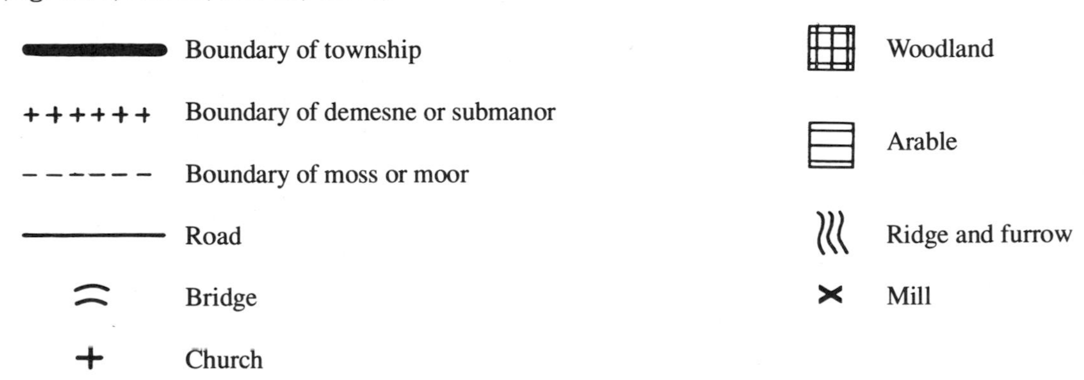

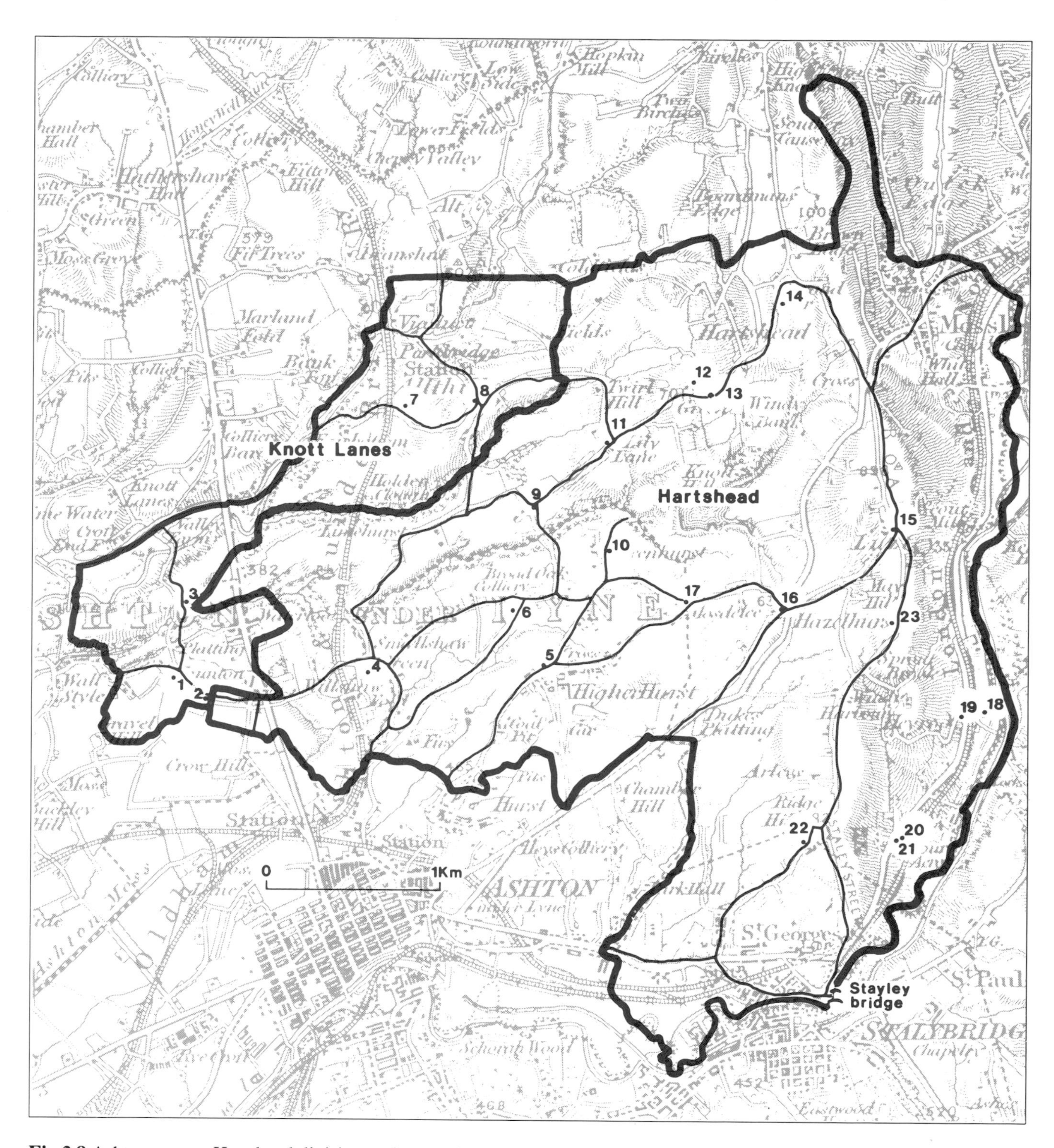

Fig 3.8 Ashton manor, Hartshead division and parts of Knott Lanes division.
Key: 1 Taunton Hall; 2 Taunton Farm; 3 Tree House Bank; 4 Smallshaw; 5 Hurst Cross; 6 Broadoak Farm; 7 Fairbottom House; 8 Althill Farmhouse; 9 Cock Bank Farm; 10 Greenhurst; 11 Lilly Lanes; 12 Hartshead Green Farm; 13 Jeremy Cottage; 14 Broad Carr Farm; 15 Luzley; 16 Hazelhurst; 17 Moss de Lee; 18 Heyrod Old Hall; 19 Heyrod Farm; 20 Woodfield Barn; 21 Woodfield Farm House (Souracre); 22 Ridge Hill; 23 Luzley End.

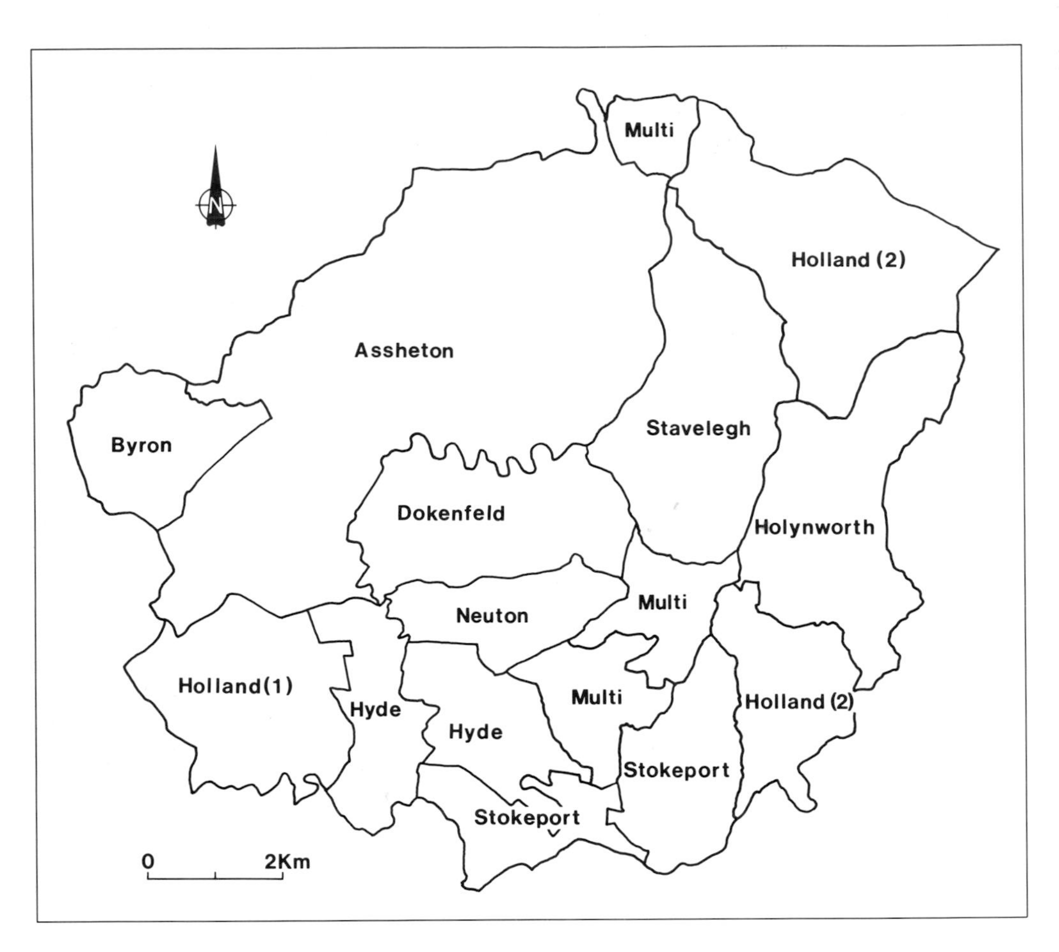

Fig 3.9 Landholdings in fourteenth-century Tameside.

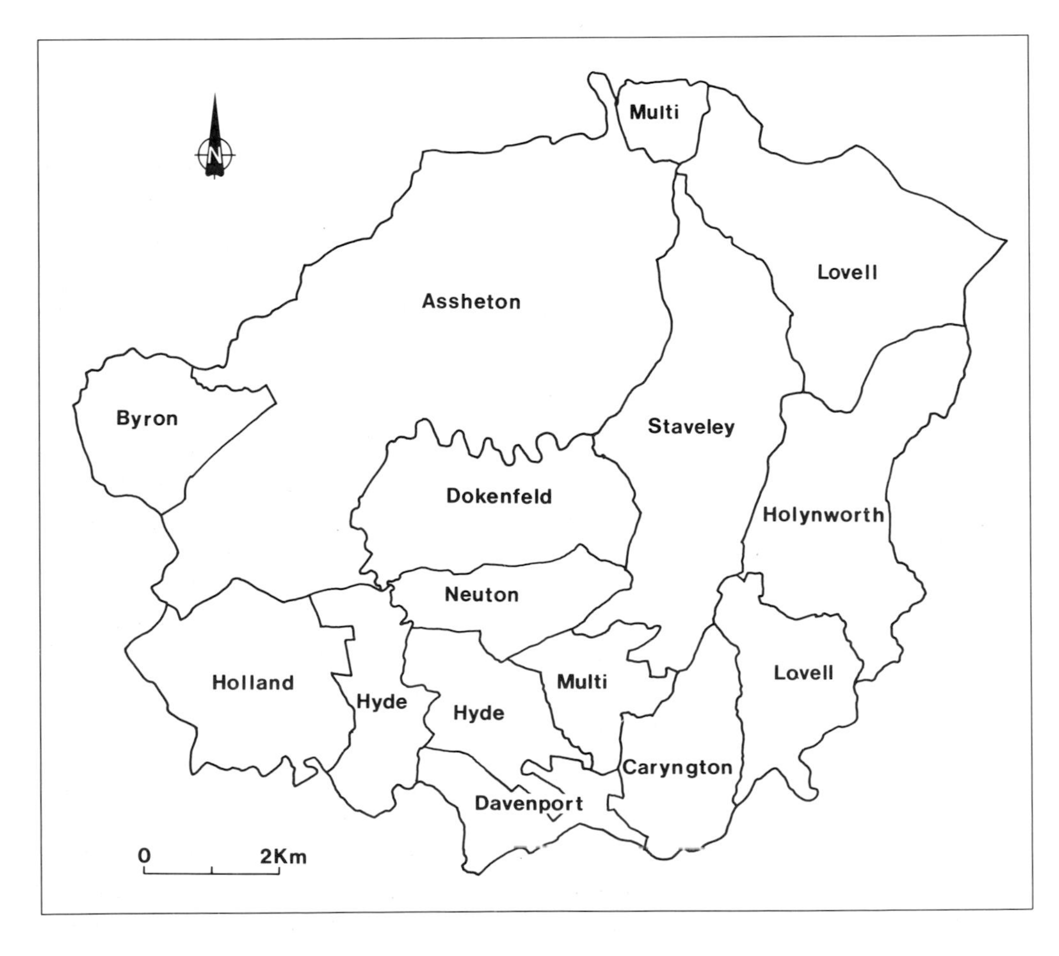

Fig 3.10 Landholdings in fifteenth-century Tameside.

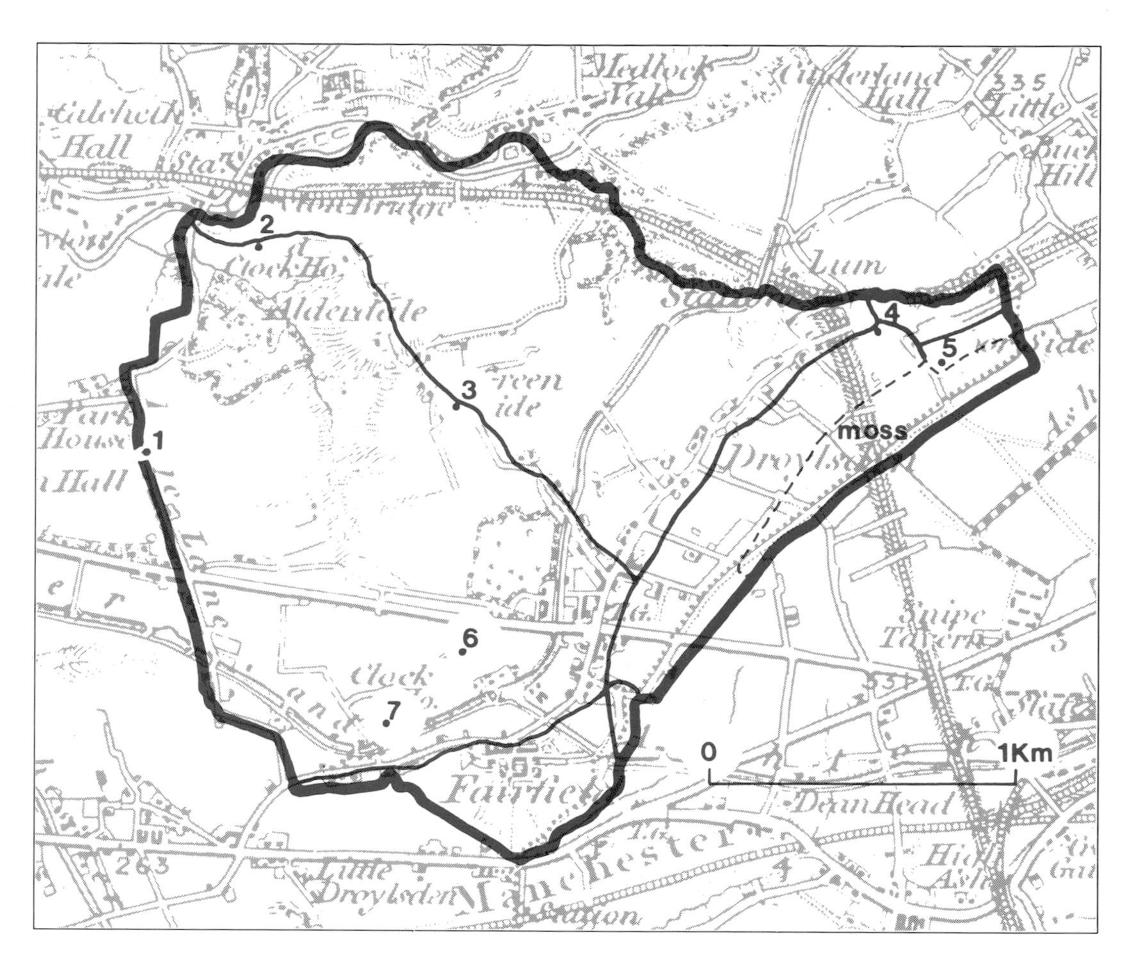

Fig 3.11 Clayton manor, Droylsden township.
Key: 1 Edge Lane; 2 Old Clock House; 3 Greenside Farm; 4 Upper Lumm; 5 Moorside Farm; 6 Birch Fold; 7 Clock House.

Brownbill 1911, 311). At this time Denton manor appears to have comprised 8 oxgangs, for later in the century Matthew granted to Richard, rector of Stockport, and his heirs, 4 oxgangs in Denton which equalled a moiety, that is a half, of the manor, at a rent of 12d (*ibid*, 311 n 5). The remaining moiety of Denton included the submanor of Haughton. Since by 1307 Haughton was composed of only 2 oxgangs (*ibid*, 322), 2 oxgangs are unaccounted for. It has been argued above that these are to be identified as Audenshaw, Matthew de Reddish probably being the Matthew son of Edith who in 1190-1212 granted land in Audenshaw to the monks of Kersal Cell.

As Young has pointed out (in Bryant & Bryant 1985, 57) the Denton family tree in the thirteenth century is somewhat complicated and it is difficult to trace the descent of the manor and its appendages. However it would appear that one Robert, rector of Mottram, held 2 oxgangs in Denton from Robert de Reddish, and that he granted this land to his daughter Cecily de Denton at 1d rent to himself and 5d to St Mary's church in Manchester (Farrer & Brownbill 1911, 311). This Robert may have been one of the clerics mentioned in two Godley charters (PSA 1850, nos 3 & 6), which would appear to date to the second quarter of the thirteenth century (see Appendix 1). He may also be the Robert de Denton whose son Richard is attested in 1246/7 (Parker 1904, 71), and perhaps the father of Geoffrey de Denton mentioned in 1241 (Farrer 1899, 80).

His daughter Cecily was twice married, to a Norris of Heaton Norris and to Robert de Shoresworth. This Robert and Cecily granted all their Denton lands to their son William de Shoresworth *c* 1280 (Farrer & Brownbill 1911, 311). There seem to have been three other sons who held land in the manor. Roger 'son of Cecily de Denton', attested *c* 1274 (Preston LRO DDHu 12/2 & 3), Geoffrey, attested in 1280 (Farrer & Brownbill 1911, 311 n 7), and Alexander. In 1299 Cecily, now widowed, modified the gift of 1280 by granting half of her father's land to this last son. In 1325/6 Alexander granted his lands to Adam de Ryecroft, vicar of Huyton, who at once regranted them to Thurstan de Holland, the son of William Holland and Margaret, granddaughter of William de Shoresworth (*ibid*, 311). This Thurstan appears to have

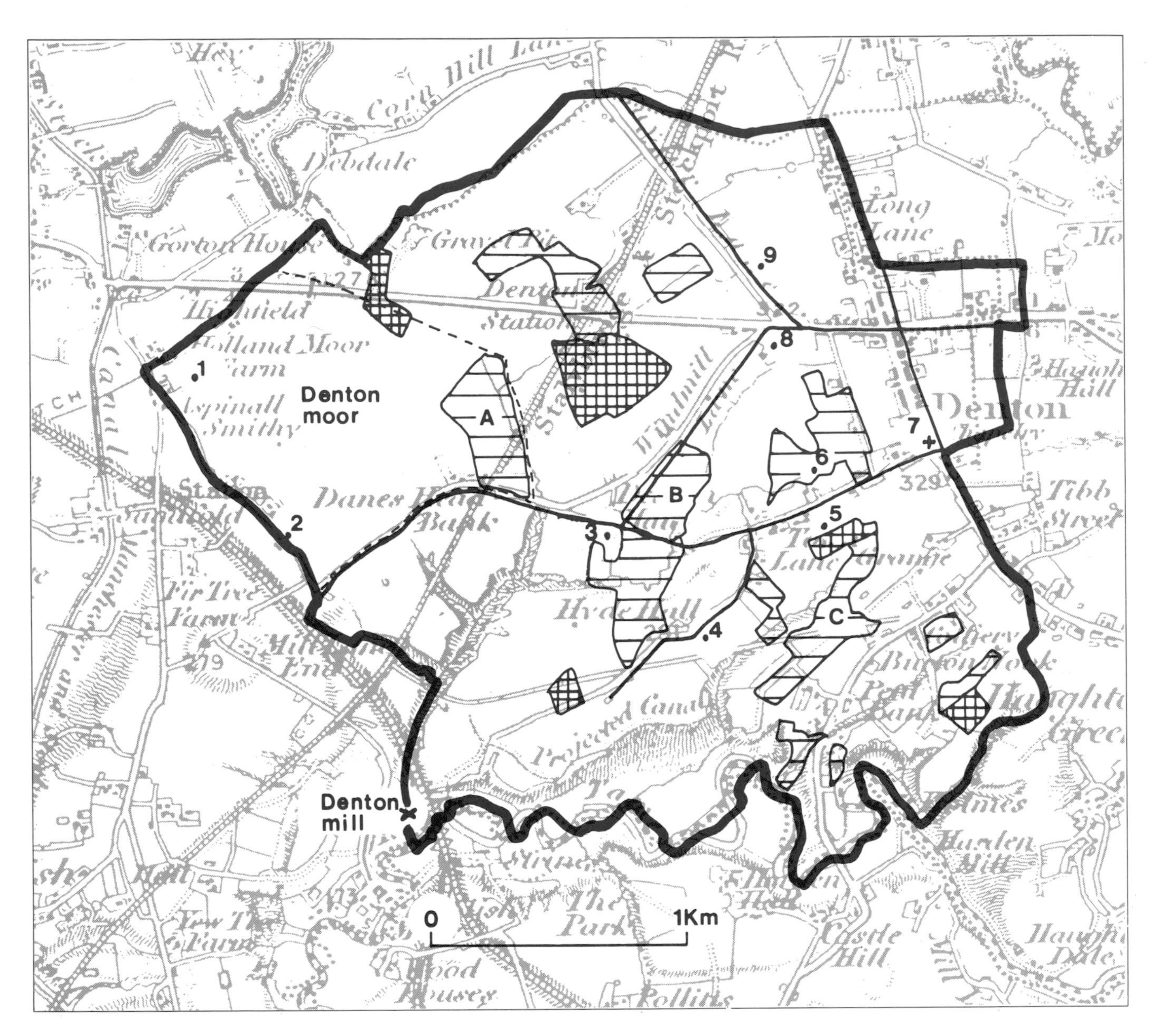

Fig 3.12 Denton manor.
Farms and other buildings: 1 Holland Moor Farm; 2 Thornley Lane Farm; 3 Denton Hall; 4 Hyde Hall; 5 Town Lane Farm; 6 Lees House; 7 St James' (Lawrence's) Church; 8 Bridge House Fold; 9 Taylor Lane Farm.
Field-names: A Twenty Acre and Little Twenty Acre; B Tom Acre, Further Hall Field and Nearer Hall Field; C Longshut, Cockshut, Nearer Cockshut, Further Cockshut and Hair Platt.

acquired a further 2 oxgangs of the manor from the heirs of the Moston family (*ibid*, 312).

The manor remained in the Holland family until the late seventeenth century. In 1683, when Edward Holland died unmarried, the manor and other lands passed to his sister Elizabeth, the wife of Sir John Egerton of Wrinehill (*ibid*, 314).

Dukinfield

Like many of the manors south-east of the River Tame Dukinfield is not mentioned in 1086. It may possibly have been part of Mottram manor at this date, although the fact that it was not later included in the Longdendale lordship may tell against this. However by the reign of Henry II (1154-89) 'Dokenfeld' was held by the barony of Dunham Massey and, together with 'Bromale' (Bramhall), was granted by Hamo de Massey, the second baron, to Matthew de Bromale (Earwaker 1880, 9). This manor was subsequently held under the lords of Bramhall by a family who bore the local name, the earliest recorded appearing to be Sir Robert 'de Dokenfelt' who is attested *c* 1260-70 (Earwaker 1877, 69; 1880, 40; Ormerod 1882, 812). He may also be the Robert, cleric of Dukinfield, attested in the second quarter of the thirteenth century

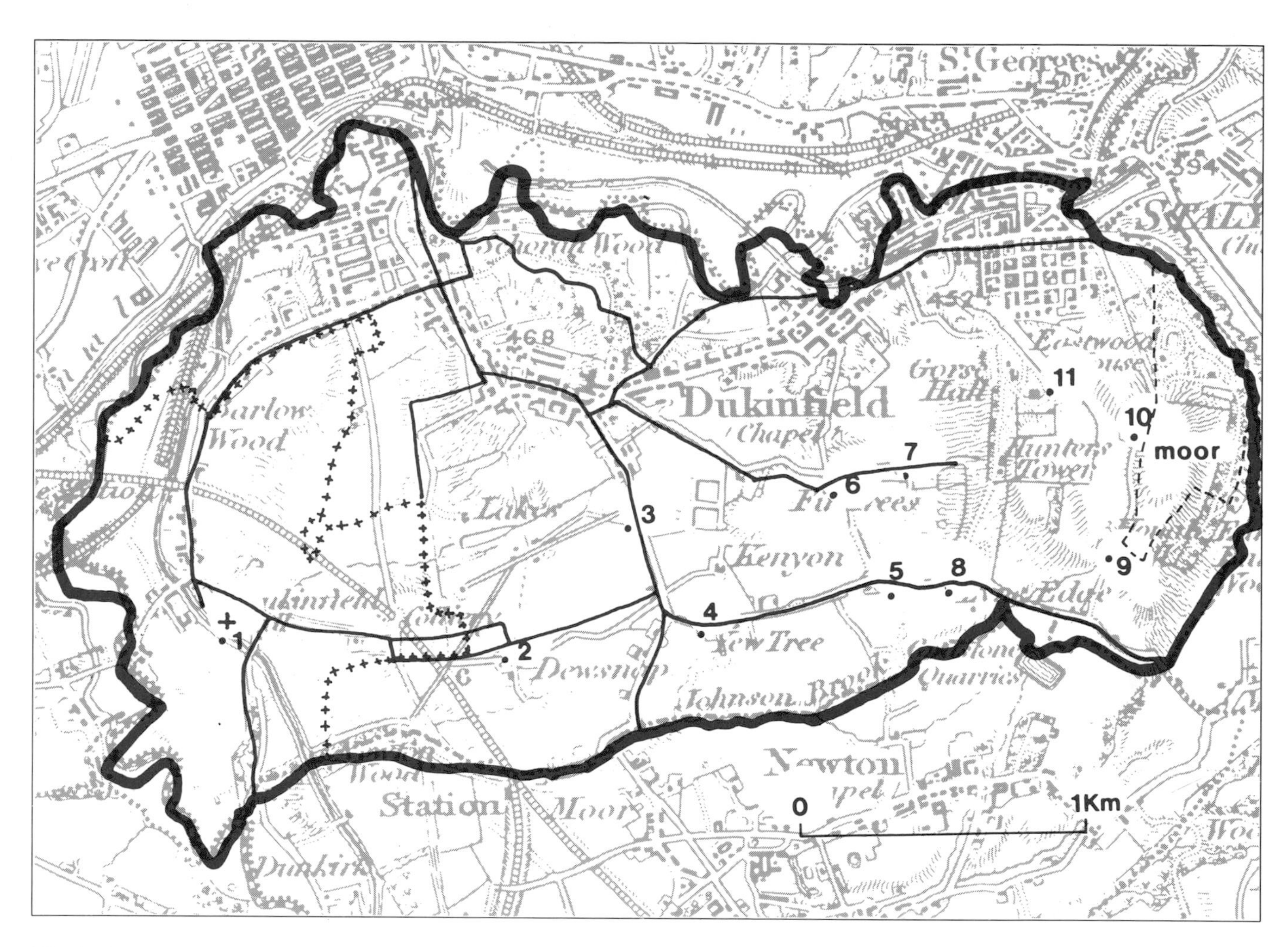

Fig 3.13 Dukinfield manor.
Key: 1 Dukinfield Hall and Chapel; 2 Dewsnip Farm; 3 Unnamed farm; 4 Yewtree Farm; 5 Bazier Farm; 6 Firtree Farm; 7 Knights House Farm; 8 Linehedge Farm; 9 Broadbentfold; 10 Hough Hill; 11 Gorse Old Hall.

(PSA 1850, no 3; Barraclough 1957, 44). In the early fourteenth century the manor appears to have been held by William de Stokeport, chaplain, perhaps as intermediate lord, for in 1327 he granted Dukinfield and Brinnington to Robert de Dokenfeld, both of which manors subsequently descended in the Dokenfeld or, later, Duckenfield family (Ormerod 1882, 812).

In the fifteenth century there are a number of references to the family serving in local government. Robert de Dokenfeld was a collector of the subsidy in Macclesfield hundred in 1403 (CRR 1875, 159), in 1416 (Ormerod 1882, 813) and in 1435 (Earwaker 1877, 241). His son John was probably one of the four governors of Stockport church listed in 1464 (*ibid*, 362) and was one of the mise collectors in 1465 (Clayton 1990, 199). His successor Robert served on a commission responsible for the arrest of outlaws in 1481 (Ormerod 1882, 813).

Two seventeenth-century members of the family are also of note. Robert Duckenfield died in 1630 and his will and inventory indicate for the first time the existence of coal pits in this part of Tameside. Through his second marriage to Frances Croston he acquired lands in Mobberley parish (Chester LRO D/73/1 & 2). His son Colonel Robert Duckenfield acquired property and land in the neighbouring Hyde township (Chester LRO DDX 16/2), but is best known for his role in the Parliamentarian campaigns in the North-West during the Civil War (see Chapter 6).

Godley

The early history of Godley, prior to the thirteenth century, is not recorded. The place is not mentioned in the Domesday survey, and although there are references purporting to show the tenure of lands here in the twelfth century, these must be discounted. According to Butterworth, 'it is recorded in ancient deeds now in existence at Dunham Massey, in Cheshire, that Richard Massey, of Sale, and Robert Massey, of Assheton, and others, as tenants, held lands in the manors

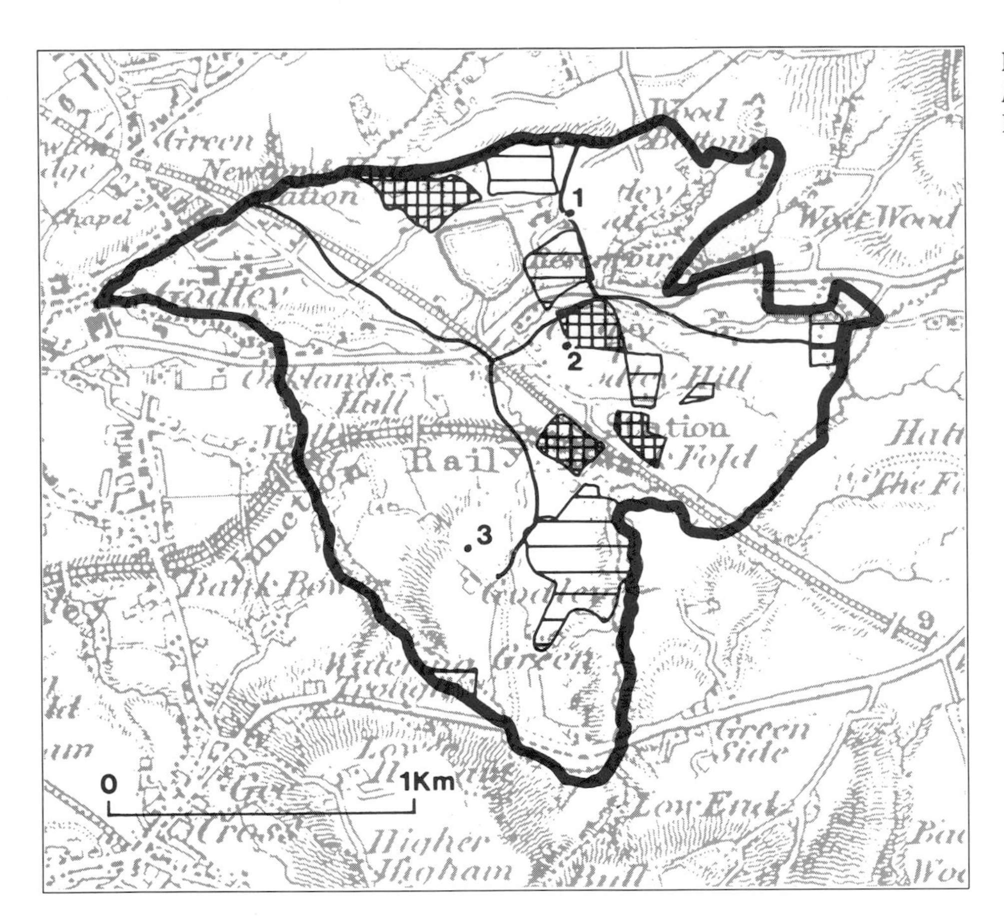

Fig 3.14 Godley manor.
Key: 1 Tetlowfold; 2 Godley Hall; 3 Oliverfield Farm.

of Godley and Newton, under de Burgh, or Bros, as lord paramount, in the year 1189, with the old field in the town of Hollinworth, and the meadows of Wooley...It is also added in the same deed...that the said Richard Massey, of Sale, enclosed the meers of Matteleigh and Godeleigh, (Matley and Godley)' (Butterworth 1827, 152-3). The Mascy family of Sale at least are known to have held such lands, but no other evidence appears to place their tenure earlier than the mid-fourteenth century (see below).

The absence of any authentic reference to Godley prior to the early thirteenth century is in sharp contrast to the wealth of material after that date. Apart from the records for Ashton, those available for Godley form the largest group of medieval documents known from Tameside; 51 of these documents are held by the Society of Antiquaries in London, while a second group was presented to the Manchester Free Library in 1874 (see Appendix 1). Together they provide information that helps to dispel the degree of discrepancy between Ormerod's descent (1882, 860-3) for the manor and that of Earwaker (1880, 156-61), and make it possible to construct a family tree for the extensive Godelegh family of the thirteenth and early fourteenth centuries (Fig 3.15).

Charter number 1 dates from 1211-25 and is a grant by Thomas de Burgh, lord of Longdendale, to Adam son of Reginald of land in Mottram part of which was previously held by Albinus and part by de Burgh himself (Barraclough 1957, 42). This is probably the original grant of the manor of Godley to the family which assumed the local name (*ibid*, 44). Adam, son of Reginald, had two brothers, William and Thomas, and all three held land in Godley. The lordship itself seems to have passed from Adam to his son Robert, descending in turn to Robert's son Henry. In 1308/9 he agreed that the lordship should pass after his death to Robert, a member of the second branch of the family, who held land in Godley through his father Henry and grandfather Thomas, the brother of Adam (Fig 3.15). In 1318, however, Robert sold his lands in Godley to William de Baggilegh (Middleton 1900, 39; Earwaker 1880, 156), to whom Henry de Godelegh also sold his own lands in the following year, 1319 (charter no 13).

However, the family continued to hold some part of the manor, probably through a third branch that included Robert, son of Hugh (*c* 1211-25) (charters nos 2 & 4) and Ralph son of Matthew (charters nos 7 & 8). This branch seems to have retained some of the family estates into the second half of the fourteenth century, for in 1360 John son of John de Godelegh paid 1d a year to the lordship for one messuage and 24 acres of land in Godley (Booth *et al* 1976-8, no 98).

William de Baggilegh was the son of Sir William de Baggilegh, knight of Baguley near Northenden and lord of Godley until his death sometime after 1332

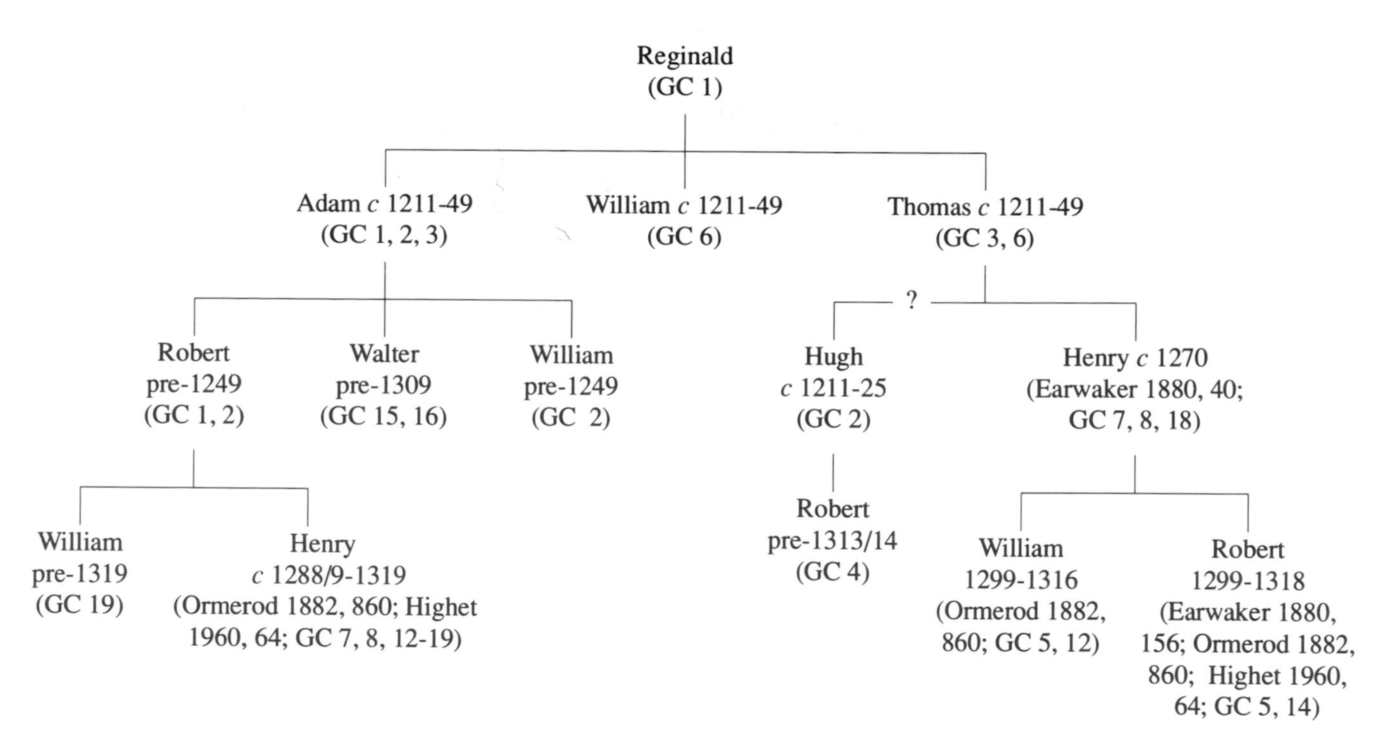

Fig 3.15 The descent of the Godelegh family in the thirteenth and early fourteenth centuries. GC = Godley charter(s), on which see Appendix 1. Dates given are the known floruit of each individual. The position of the following within this descent is uncertain: Richard de Godelegh, pre-1325 (GC 20); Hugh de Godelegh, *c* 1211-25 (GC 2), father of Robert de Godelegh (GC 4); Matthew de Godelegh (GC 7, 8), father of Ralph de Godelegh (GC 7, 8) and a second son, name unknown (GC 7); John son of John de Godelegh, 1360 (Booth *et al* 1976-8, no 98).

(Earwaker 1877, 340). Isabella, one of his two sisters, married John de Hyde of Hyde *c* 1270 (Earwaker 1880, 40). Either through this marriage or by purchase, a moiety of Godley passed to the Hyde family (Ormerod 1882, 861), probably in or before 1335 when Robert de Hyde is recorded as holding lands there (Taylor F 1975, no 3410). By a process which is equally obscure the other moiety of the manor was divided into two. The Longdendale survey of 1360 records John de Hyde as holding half the manor, with two quarters divided between Howel ap Oweyn, William the son of William de Tranemol, and Katherine the heir and daughter of Geoffrey de Honford (Booth *et al* 1976-8, no 98). John de Hyde and the other joint lords of Godley are also named in the survey as holding land in 'le Hage' in Mottram (probably the Haigh or Hague) (*ibid*), and reappear in 1362, by which date William de Tranemol and Katherine de Honford were married, as joint lords of Newton (Earwaker 1880, 161). Presumably both of these holdings had, like Godley, been previously part of the Baggilegh estate.

In 1364 John de Hyde sold his share of Godley and Newton, along with a quarter of the manor of Matley, to Richard de Mascy of Sale (Ormerod 1882, 861). An agreement of 1377 shows the same Richard de Mascy still holding a moiety of Godley but the other half as now divided between William Boydell (the heir to Howel ap Oweyn), Robert de Mascy of Alturton and 'William de...', possibly William de Tranemol (*ibid*, 861-3). The same agreement refers to the 'Oldefylde' in Hollingworth and 'the meadow of Wolegh' for which de Mascy paid a rent of 4s 8d. These are the lands, it should be noted, which according to the charter cited by Butterworth were supposedly held by Richard de Mascy as early as 1189 but which, on the evidence given above, did not in fact come into the family until 1364.

The division of Godley manor into a moiety and two quarters remained during its subsequent history. By the fifteenth century the Boydell quarter passed to the 'de Redych' (Reddish) family, the other quarter to the Mascies of Kelsall (*ibid*, 863). The Mascies of Sale, however, retained their moiety until 1665/6 when Richard and William Massey leased their lands in Godley, Sale, Matley and Newton manors to William Jackson, mayor of Nottingham, and others (Chester LRO DDX 464/3).

Hattersley

The earliest documentation for Hattersley occurs in the early thirteenth century when the manor was held under the Longdendale lordship by the Stokeports as part of the Stockport barony, a tenure which is first attested for Robert de Stokeport who died in 1239 or 1249 (Ormerod 1882, 792, 864). The Stokeports in

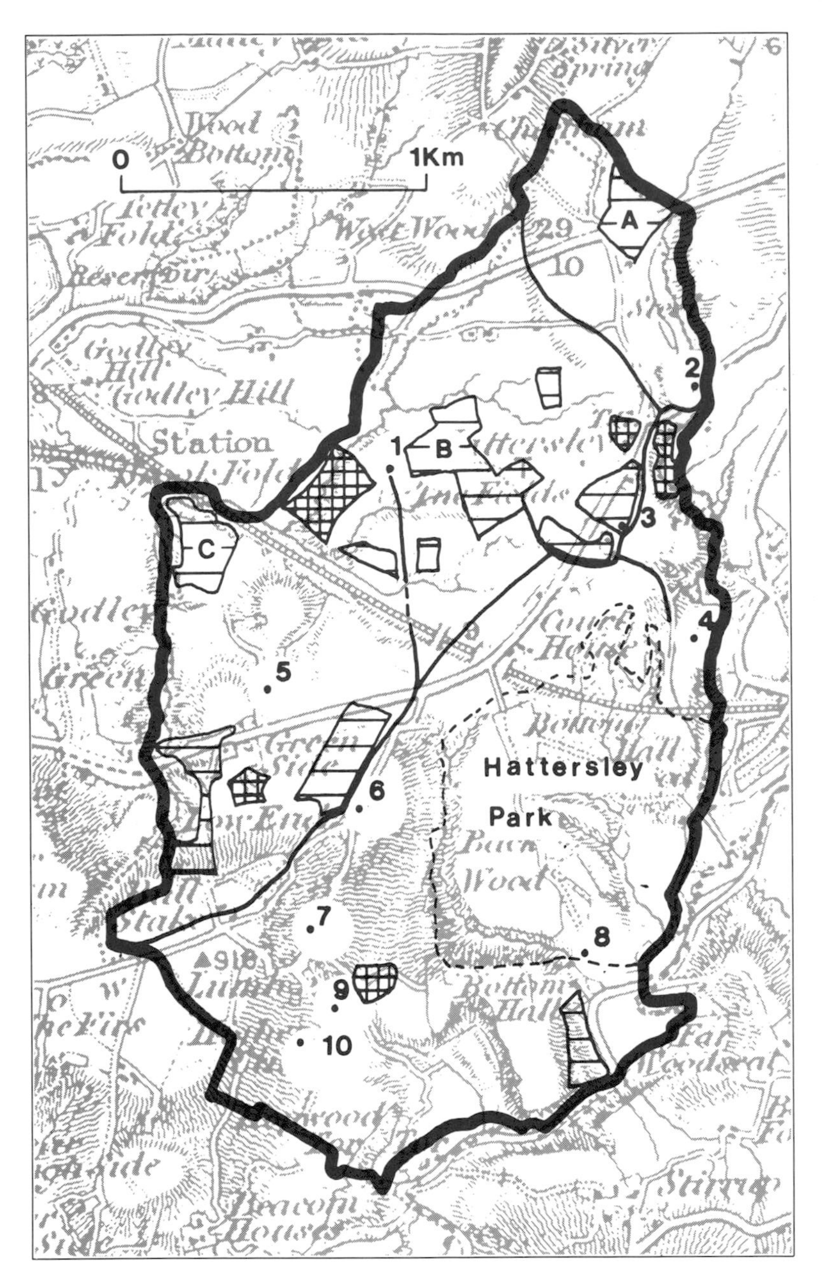

Fig 3.16 Hattersley manor.
Farms: 1 Fields; 2 Millhill; 3 Pinfold; 4 Clough; 5 Butterworths (later Greenside); 6 Lane End; 7 Rhodesfold; 8 Bothams Hall; 9 Lower Cliff; 10 Higher Cliff.
Field-names: A Great Field; B Great Field, Near Bent, Far Bent, Lower Bent; C Great Field, Acre.

turn appear to have granted Hattersley to a family bearing the local name, the first known member of which is Radulfus 'de Hattresleia' who was a witness to Godley charter number 1 in the period 1211-25 (Barraclough 1957, 42). In or prior to 1292, however, Thomas, son of Richard de Hatterslegh, granted all his land in Hattersley back to his lord, Roger de Stokeport, and Lucy his wife (Ormerod 1882, 864). Although this same Thomas may be attested as a tenant in Hattersley in the early fourteenth century (Highet 1960, 64), the local family are not otherwise heard of again. Roger de Stokeport was the brother of Richard lord of Stockport who had granted him the manor of Woodford and other lands, including evidently Hattersley and Werneth (Ormerod 1882, 688, 864). It has been claimed that Roger died childless, but a William son of Roger de Stokeport is attested as holding lands in Werneth in 1342-3 (Highet 1960, 67), and is probably the William de Stokeport who in 1333 granted a moiety of Hattersley, a sixth of Stayley and lands in Mottram to Adam de Bredbury and his wife Cecily (Ormerod 1882, 864).

The grant of 1333 may partly explain the situation in 1360 when the Longdendale survey records that one half of the manor was held by Richard de Eton, lord of Stockport, and the other by Sir William de Caryngton (Booth *et al* 1976-8, no 98). This division may still have held good in 1370 when the inquisition of Isabel, daughter and sole heir of Richard de Eton recorded that she held 'a place in Hattreslegh' under the Longdendale lordship (Ormerod 1882, 864). However, between that date and 1422, when George Caryngton granted Hattersley and other property to Nicholas Bird, chaplain (*ibid*), the whole of the manor

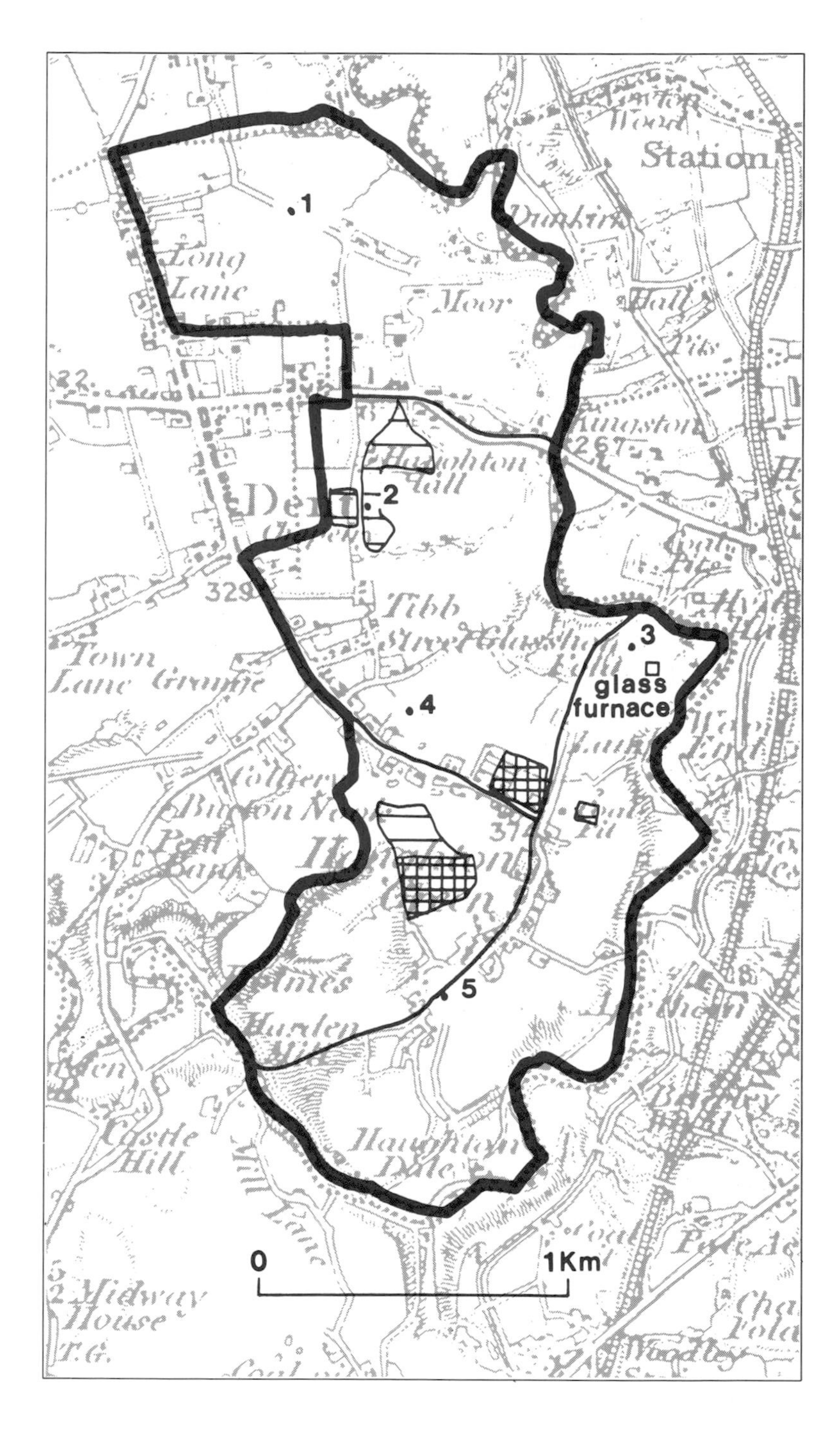

Fig 3.17 Haughton manor.
Key: 1 Thorp Fold; 2 Haughton Hall; 3 Glass House Fold; 4 Lowe's Farm; 5 Haughton Green.

appears to have passed to the Caryngton family. The circumstances of this transfer are lost, although it may be significant that in the early 1370s John Warren, successor to the Stockport lordship, disposed of the manor of Werneth (see below). The acquisition of Hattersley manor by the Caryngton family at this time may have been facilitated by the fact that until 1374 Sir William de Caryngton was also the steward of the lordship of Longdendale (see below). The manor remained in this family until 1577 when John Carrington died, leaving his daughter Jane as his only heir. She married George Booth and so brought the manor within the extensive holdings which the Booths already possessed in Tameside (Earwaker 1880, 153-4).

Haughton

The origins of Haughton manor are obscure but it seems likely that it was originally a division of the manor of Denton, possibly forming with Audenshaw a moiety of that manor (see above). By the early thirteenth century Haughton manor was in the possession of the Hyde family of the manor of Hyde, across the Tame, Robert the son of Matthew de Hyde being lord of Haughton *c* 1225 (Ormerod 1882, 809-10). Its subsequent descent followed that of Hyde manor (see below).

Plate 3.2 Hollingworth Hall.
Built in the seventeenth century, the hall was the home of the senior branch of the Hollingworth family; a junior branch of the same family resided at Hollingworth Old Hall, now known as Mottram Old Hall. Both branches were descended from John de Holynworth, living in the early fourteenth century, although the division of the manor into two separate estates would appear to date back to the thirteenth century. Hollingworth Hall was demolished in 1944.

Hollingworth

The manor of Hollingworth is the 'Holisurde' of the Domesday survey, held in 1066 by an unnamed freeman and in 1086 by the earl of Chester (Sawyer & Thacker 1987, no 66). Its subsequent history, prior to the early thirteenth century, is not recorded. Although a document cited by Butterworth referred to the 'Old Field' in Hollingworth in 1189, this has been shown to be fictitious (see above, pp 27-9). Similar doubts must also be cast on Butterworth's assertion that 'from other documents it is further understood that Robert de Burgh granted certain lands, about 1139...to Radalph de Woleigh, or Wolegh', these lands being Woolley in Hollingworth and 'a continued range of land' in Mottram, including Broadbottom, the Haigh and Hillend (Butterworth 1827, 152-3). The Wolegh family, who clearly took their name from the place, are elsewhere attested from the thirteenth century (Ormerod 1882, 872). Their tenure of land in at least Broadbottom and the Haigh is documented in other sources, but that evidence again relates to no earlier than the mid-fourteenth century (*ibid*, 864; Booth *et al* 1976-8, no 98).

The earls probably retained direct control of Hollingworth until 1200-3 when Earl Ranulf III granted the 'land of Longedenedale' to William de Neville. By 1211-25, however, Hollingworth seems to have been granted by the lord of Longdendale to a family which bore the local name, for a Thomas 'de Holinewurthe' occurs as a witness to Godley charter number 1 (Barraclough 1957, 42).

It would appear that by the mid- to late thirteenth century this local family was divided into two branches, each holding half of the manor. The first of these branches came to an end when William, son of Robert de Holynworth, died leaving a daughter, Petronell, as his sole heir; this was in or before 1289, for in that year Petronell and her husband Roger Booth granted all their land in Hollingworth to Roger de Hyde and his wife, Margery (Ormerod 1882, 869).

The second branch of the family continued to hold land in the manor, the earliest known member being John de Holynworth, first attested *c* 1309 (Middleton 1900, 38; PSA 1850, no 15). He is probably to be identified as the John de Holynworth who in 1325/6, according to Earwaker, was granted 'the manor' of

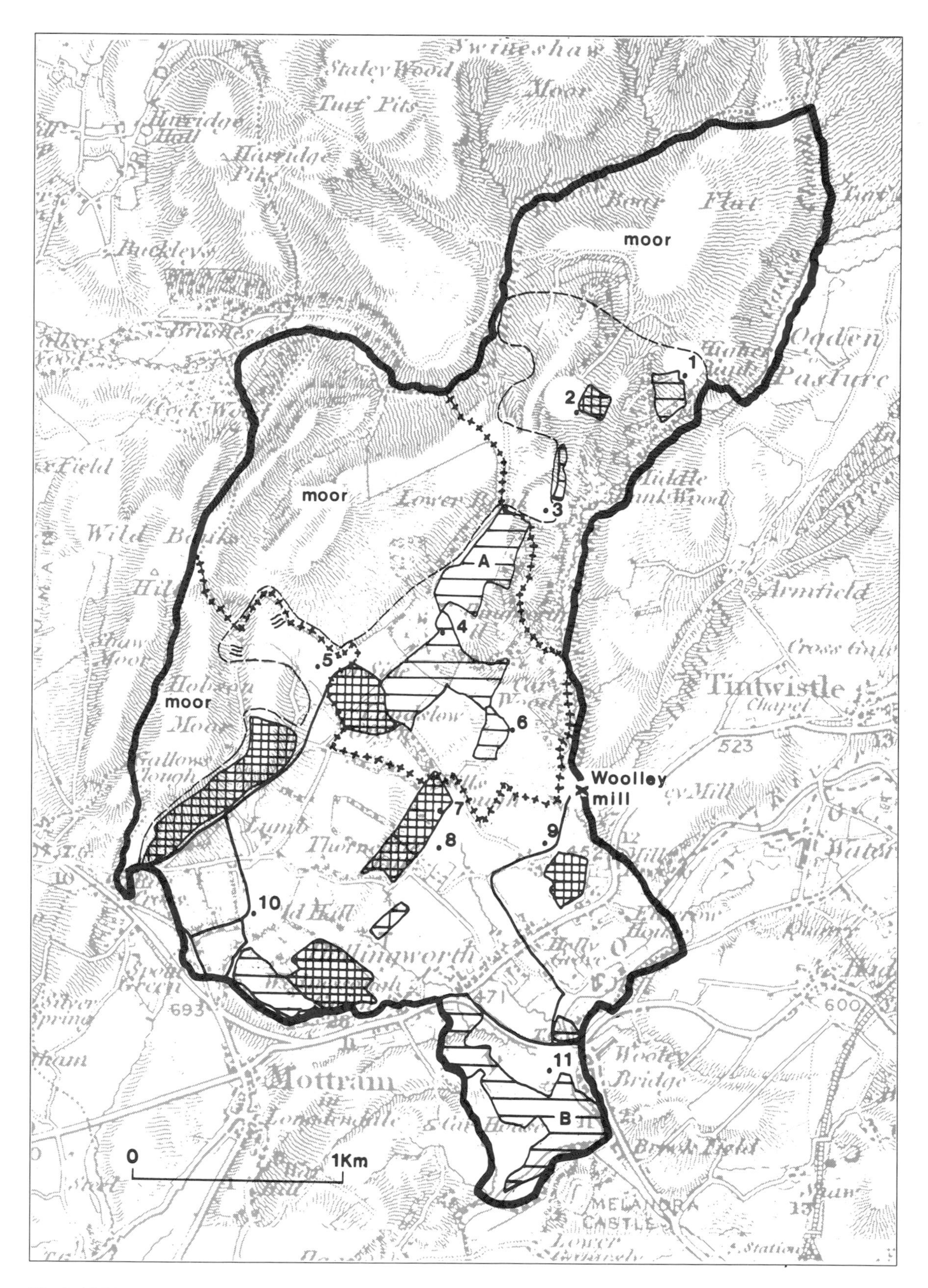

Fig 3.18 Hollingworth manor.
Farms and other buildings: 1 Higher Bank; 2 Middle Bank; 3 Lower Bank; 4 Hollingworth Hall; 5 Moorside Farm; 6 Widowscroft Farm; 7 Thorncliffe Farm; 8 Thorncliff Hall; 9 Meadowbank Cottages; 10 Hollingworth Old Hall (Mottram Old Hall); 11 Woolley Farm.
Field-names: A Further Riggs Fold, Middle Riggs Fold, Nearer Riggs Fold; B Riddings, Wet Acres, Great Meadow, Megg Field, Wet Acres, Long Loons.

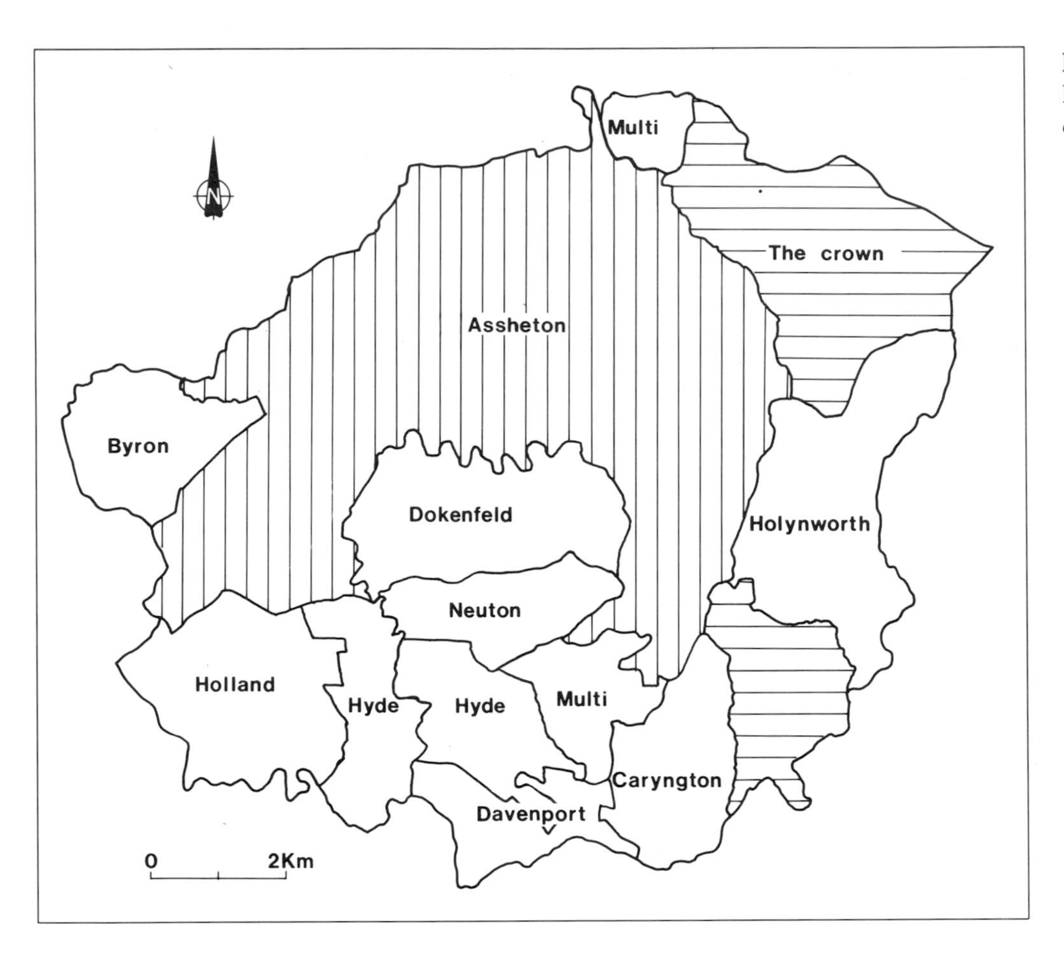

Fig 3.19 Major and lesser landholders in Tameside *c* 1500.

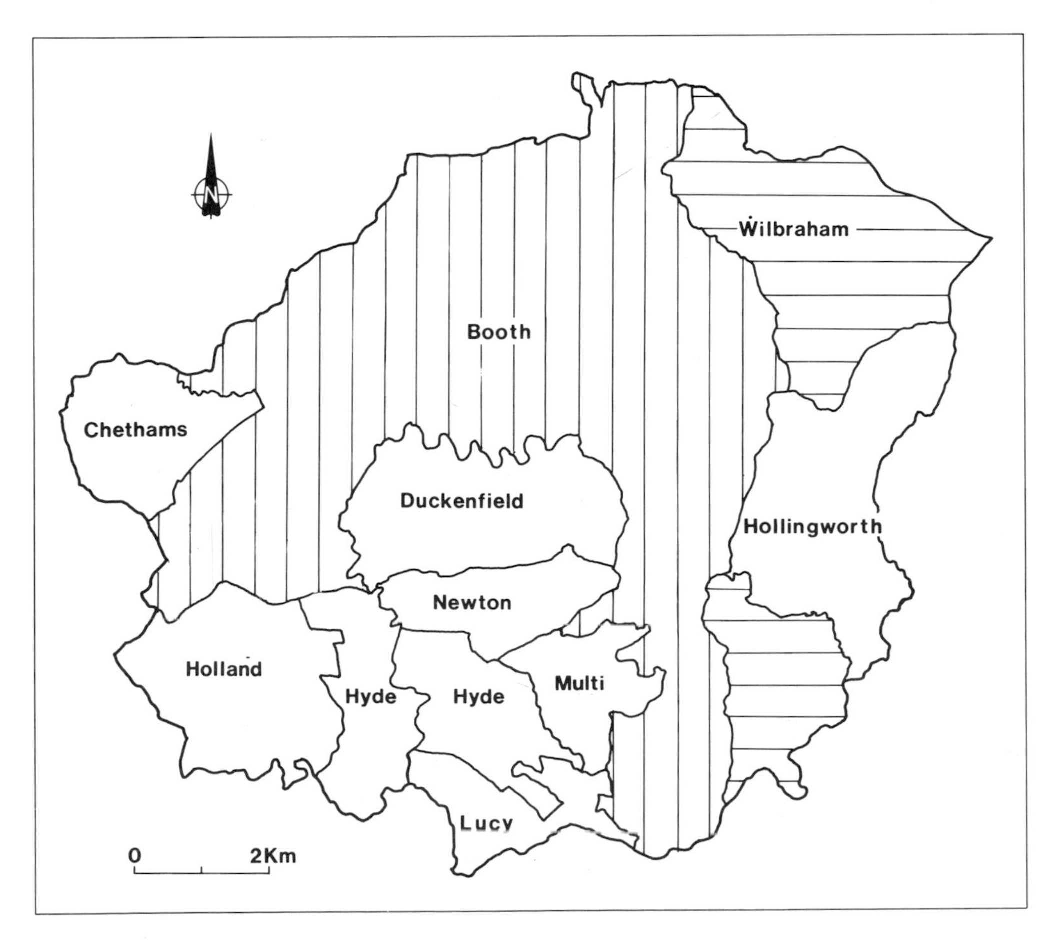

Fig 3.20 Major and lesser landholders in seventeenth-century Tameside.

Hollingworth by Henry Payn, chaplain, his successors being named as his son John de Holynworth and his daughter-in-law Ameria (Earwaker 1880, 142). This grant, which probably confirmed an existing tenure, would appear to have been of only part of the township, for according to a descent of the Hollingworth family, drawn up by Francis Hollingworth in the period 1672-84,

> 'William de le Solor the sonne of William de le Solor grants to Robert sonne of John Hollingworth his mannor of Hollingworth Anno 10 Edwardi filii Edwardi [1317]' (Chester LRO DDX 87/1b).

Both grants have an equal claim to authenticity. Of the grantors, the puture rolls record a William 'de le Soler' as holding land in Hollingworth in the early fourteenth century, along with Robert and Dikon 'de le Soler' (Highet 1960, 64). Henry Payn may be identified with the 'lord Henry chaplain' attested in Hollingworth in the puture roll of 1342-3 (*ibid*, 66). That same source also mentions a John and Robert de Holynworth who are explicitly identified as brothers (*ibid*). Furthermore, a Great and a Little 'Holynworth' are included in the Longdendale survey of 1360, the first being held by a John de Holynworth (Booth *et al* 1976-8, no 121), the second by a Robert de Holynworth (*ibid*, no 104).

The division of Hollingworth between two branches of the Holynworth family, each descending from the John de Holynworth of the early fourteenth century, has been traced by Ormerod (1882, 869-71) and Earwaker (1880, 142-6), but only from the early fifteenth century. However, the grant recorded by Francis Hollingworth, cited above, dates that division to a century earlier. Although the evidence remains incomplete, it may be suggested that William de le Solor and Henry Payn each held a moiety of the manor. Payn was overlord to John de Holynworth the elder, while de le Solor held the lands given in 1289 to Roger de Hyde and his wife. John de Holynworth's share of the manor, the Great Holynworth of the 1360 survey, descended through his, presumably eldest, son John. However, in 1317 William de le Solor granted Little Holynworth to a second son, Robert, thereby installing a junior line of the Holynworth family in lands held by an earlier branch prior to 1289.

The division of Hollingworth between John de Holynworth and his son Robert continued through their descendants, each of the two branches retaining its respective share until well after 1700. The junior branch, descended from Robert, lived at the Old or Nether Hall, the senior at Hollingworth Hall (Ormerod 1882, 869-71) (Plate 3.2)

Hyde

Like many of the manors south-east of the River Tame Hyde is not mentioned in 1086. It may have been part of Mottram manor, although, as with Dukinfield, the fact that it was not part of the Longdendale lordship may tell against this. However, unlike Dukinfield, it does not appear to have been amongst the parcel of land granted to the de Masseys of Dunham, as part of that barony. According to Ormerod (1882, 807) by the reign of King John (1199-1216) the Baggileghs held Hyde manor, half of this being held under them by a family who took the local name and whose earliest known member was Matthew de Hyde. In this regard it is interesting to note that a William 'de Bagileia' was a witness to a deed of the period 1211-25 concerning land in Newton (Barraclough 1957, 43).

During the course of the thirteenth century the Hyde family also acquired the manor of Norbury in Cheshire (Ormerod 1882, 807) and lands in Denton, including the manor of Haughton (Farrer & Brownbill 1911, 315-16; see above). The marriage of John de Hyde to Isabella, daughter of Sir William de Baggilegh, and the Hydes' subsequent acquisition, either through this marriage or purchase, of a share of the Baggilegh estates have been noted above (see pp 28-9). Whatever the precise means of acquisition were, the Hydes became lords of the moiety of Hyde manor which they had previously held from the Baggileghs, as well as obtaining the Baggileghs' lands in Godley and Newton probably in or before 1335. By purchase in 1340 the Hydes further extended their estates by obtaining the manor of Matley (see below). The lands acquired by the family in the second quarter of the fourteenth century did not, however, remain long in their hands. By 1360, one quarter of Matley was held by Henry de Holynworth (Booth *et al* 1976-8, no 98). In 1364 John de Hyde sold his share of Godley, Newton and a quarter of Matley to Richard de Mascy of Sale, while by 1389 the Hydes had lost the remaining share of Matley, amounting to half of the manor (Ormerod 1882, 869).

The Hydes retained their moiety of Hyde, and the manors of Norbury and Haughton into the seventeenth century (*ibid*, 809), at which date the family also rented farmland in Brinnington and Romiley (Chester LRO DDX 16/1-5). Between 1614 and 1621 Hamnett Hyde added to the family's estates by acquiring the manor of Newton (Stewart-Brown 1935, 106). After his death in 1643 these extensive estates passed to his grandson Edward, who took an active part on the side of Parliament in the Civil War (see Chapter 6).

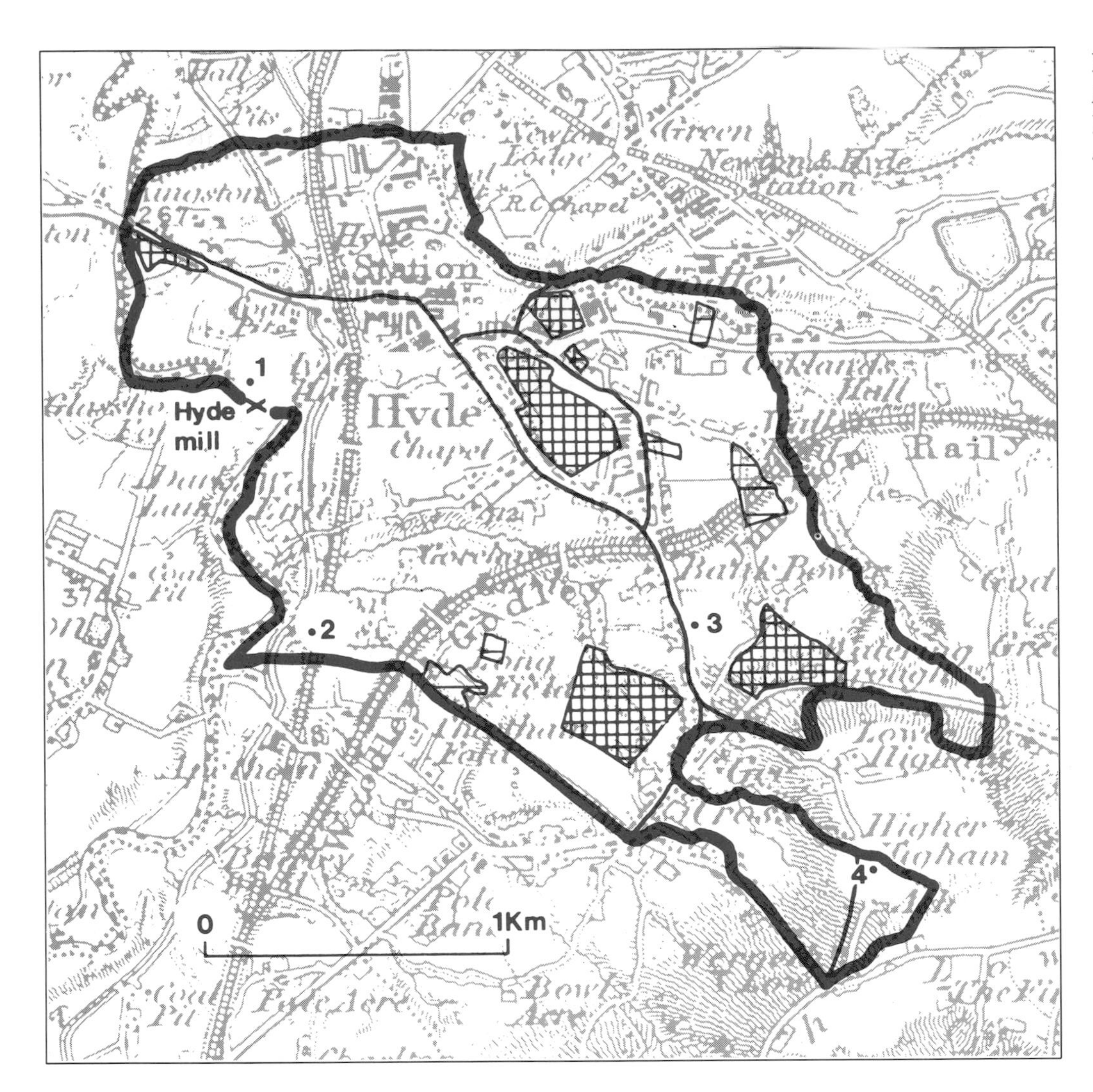

Fig 3.21 Hyde manor. *Key:* 1 Hyde Hall; 2 Foxholes; 3 Smithyfold; 4 Higher Higham Farm.

Matley

There is a spurious reference to lands in Matley in 1189 (see pp 27-9) but the earliest reliable evidence dates from the early thirteenth century, by which date it appears to have been held under the Longdendale lordship by a family bearing the local name (Ormerod 1882, 868), a Henry 'de Matteleia' appearing in 1211-25 among the witnesses to Godley charter number 1 (Barraclough 1957, 42). From the thirteenth century the same family also seems to have held a sixth part of the manor of Godley (PSA 1850, no 4).

The Matteleghs held both Matley and a sixth share of Godley until 1341 when William de Mattelegh sold them to Philip Chetwynd who in the same year regranted Matley to William, son of John de Hyde (PSA 1850, no 21; Ormerod 1882, 868). However the family remained in the manor until at least 1360 when a William de Mattelegh was recorded in the Longdendale survey as renting land valued at 2s 4d (Booth *et al* 1976-8, no 104). It is clear from the survey that the manor was split between two major landholders, John de Hyde holding a moiety and one quarter (as two separate holdings) and Henry de Holynworth the remaining quarter (*ibid*, no 98). In 1364 the estate was further divided by the sale of John de Hyde's quarter of the manor to Richard de Mascy of Sale whose family held this land until the seventeenth century (Ormerod 1882, 868). The survey of 1360 suggests that the Hydes' claim to the remaining moiety was of doubtful legitimacy (Booth *et al* 1976-8, no 98). By 1389 this share was forfeited to the lord of Longdendale, for in that year John Lovell, then holding the lordship, granted this moiety to Robert de Stavelegh (Ormerod 1882, 869). It must be added that the forfeiture of this moiety may have raised a question mark over the legitimacy of other Hyde holdings in Longdendale. It may not be coincidental that in or after 1364 the Mascies of Sale appear to have fabricated documentary evidence to the effect that the lands in Matley and elsewhere which in reality they had obtained from John de Hyde had been held by them from as early as the twelfth century (see above).

The grant of Matley to the Staveleghs was confirmed in 1410 (Earwaker 1880, 155). In 1457 the lordship passed to the Asshetons as a result of the

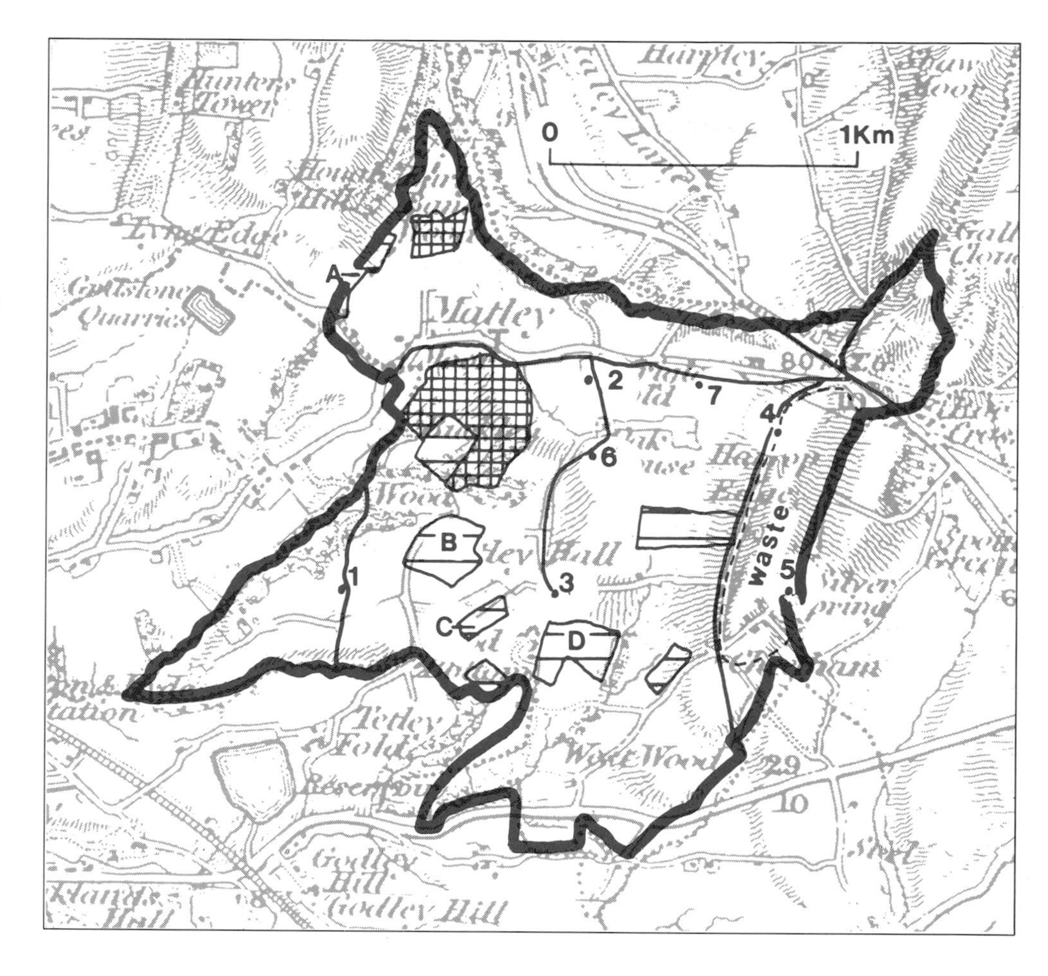

Fig 3.22 Matley manor.
Farms and other buildings: 1 Lower Matley Hall; 2 Wrigleyfold; 3 Higher Matley Hall; 4 Harrop Edge; 5 Paddock Farm; 6 Taylor Fold; 7 Bardsley Gate.
Field-names: A Longfield; B Little Townfield; C Ryecroft; D Middle Longlands, Highmost Longlands, Nearer Broadfield, Further Broadfield.

marriage of Thomas Assheton to Elizabeth Staveley. After the death of Thomas in 1515 this estate descended with Stayley and Ashton to the Booths of Dunham Massey, who retained possession throughout the seventeenth century (Figs 3.19 & 3.20).

Mottram

The history of Mottram manor is inextricably linked with that of the Longdendale lordship. As argued in Chapter 2, prior to the Conquest Mottram may have been the principal manor of an extensive lordship, held in 1066 by the father of Gamel. Although by 1086 Gamel had been allowed to retain Mottram, this was as a tenant of the earl of Chester who assumed the paramount lordship. According to Butterworth 'the manor of Mottram-long-den-dale, with its appendages, belonged to Robert de Burgh, or Bros, and was granted to him by king Stephen, in the year 1138 or 1139' (Butterworth 1827, 152). We have already seen that other references provided by Butterworth regarding the tenure of lands in twelfth-century Longdendale by a Robert de Burgh are spurious, and this final piece of evidence is no exception. In 1138-9 north eastern Cheshire was under the direct rule of Earl Ranulf I of Chester, so that any grant of land should have been made by him, not the king. Most likely, after 1086 the manor reverted to the earldom and was not granted out until 1200-3 when Earl Ranulf III gave the 'land of Longedenedale' to William de Neville. On de Neville's death in 1211 his son-in-law Thomas de Burgh succeeded to the Longdendale lordship.

The original Mottram manor probably consisted not only of Mottram itself but also Godley, Hattersley, Matley, Newton and Stayley (Fig 3.4). By 1225, however, these other divisions of the manor appear to have been granted out to local lords, the most graphic instance of this being provided by Godley charter number 1 in which Thomas de Burgh gave to Adam son of Reginald land in 'Mottram', probably Godley itself (Barraclough 1957, 42; see above). Mottram proper was retained by the lords of Longdendale for themselves, as their administrative and religious centre, and one of two demesne manors, the other being Tintwistle. However the de Burghs were not resident lords of the manor, their main estates being in central Cheshire. They must have appointed stewards to administer the lordship, but it is not until the fourteenth century that these are first mentioned.

The exact date of Thomas de Burgh's death is unknown but 'Thomas, the son of Thomas de Burgh, lord of Longdendale' made a grant of land to the Mattelegh sometime in the middle years of the thirteenth

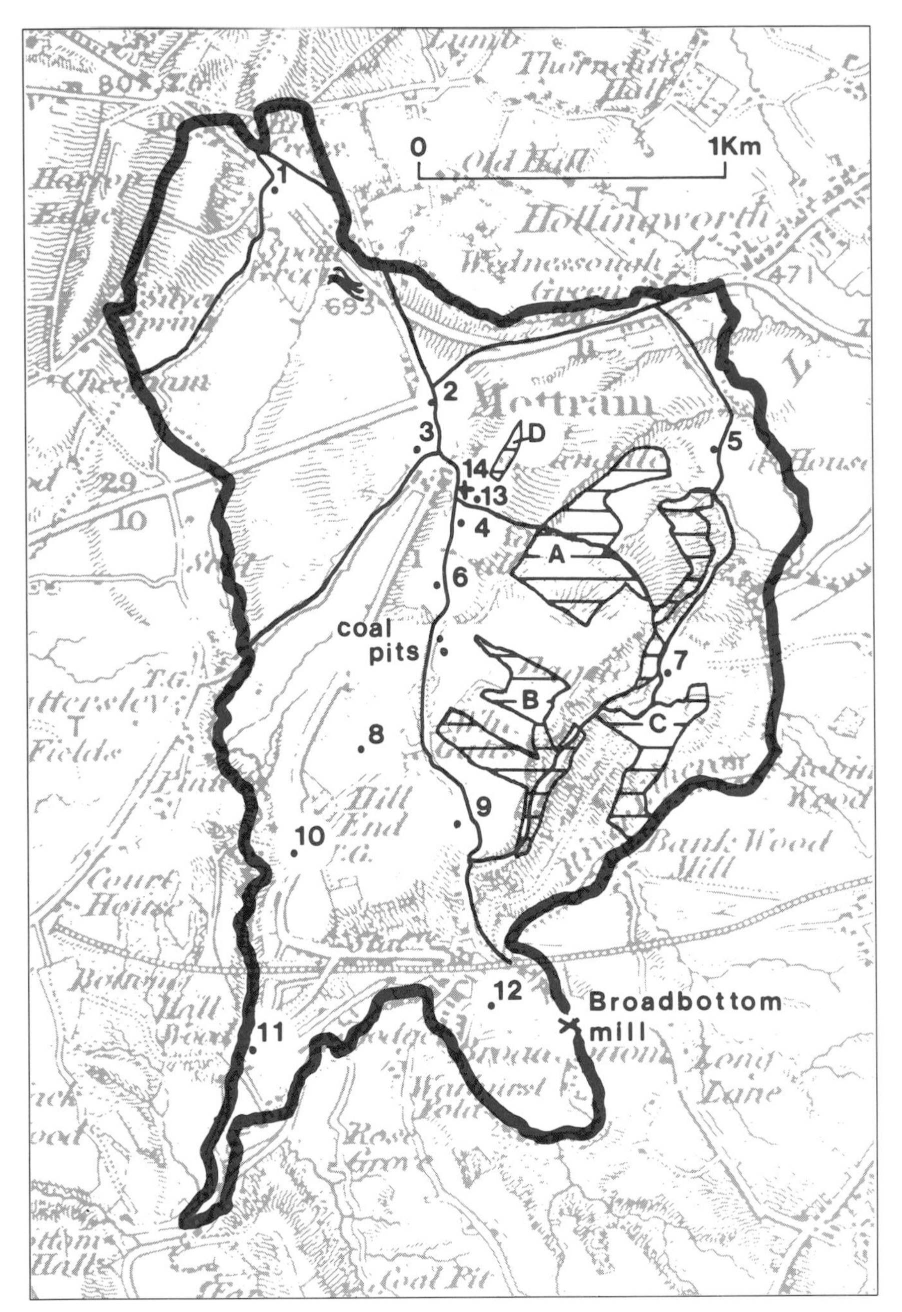

Fig 3.23 Mottram manor.
Farms and other buildings: 1 Lower Roe Cross; 2 Old Post Office; 3 Packhorse Inn; 4 Warhill Farm; 5 Carr House Farm; 6 Parsonage Farm; 7 The Haigh (Hague); 8 Hillend; 9 Brown Road; 10 Hurstclough; 11 Hodgefold; 12 Broadbottom Hall; 13 Mottram Grammar School; 14 St Michael's Church.
Field-names: A Ridground, Lower Ryding and Longcroft; B Great South Field; C Hanging Acre; D Town Field.

century (Earwaker 1880, 155). This may be the same Thomas de Burgh who in 1260 received 20s for goods taken for the use of Lord Edward, the future Edward I, who had been granted the Cheshire estates of the former earls (Studd 1985, 12 no 32).

In 1318 a Thomas de Burgh granted Longdendale to Thomas, earl of Lancaster (Ormerod 1882, 851), who in turn gave it to his supporter, Robert de Holland, this last grant being confirmed by the king in 1320 (*ibid*). However, after the earl of Lancaster's rebellion against the king and his defeat and execution at Boroughbridge in 1322, Holland forfeited all his lands to the crown (Booth *et al* 1976-8, no 57), which in the 1320s made three presentations to Mottram church (Ormerod, 1882, 851). Presumably a steward was appointed to administer the Longdendale lordship, but there is no record of this. Holland received his lands back in 1327 and held Longdendale as a tenant of Lancaster's barony of Halton, to which he paid 3s 4d a year in rent (Dawes 1932, 411-12). He died in 1328, having passed on Longdendale to his son, Robert.

However in 1357 this grant was challenged by the administrators of the Black Prince, who then held the earldom of Chester, on the basis that Holland had not received the earl's permission; accordingly the lordship was forfeited to the earldom (Booth *et al* 1976-8, no 57). The legitimacy of this forfeiture has been questioned on the grounds that such permission was normally only required when lands were held by 'knight service or serjeantry'(*ibid*). However, under the terms of the grant of 1200-3 to William de Neville,

Plate 3.3 Mottram parish church and village from Harrop Edge.
Probably the 'Motre' of the Domesday survey of 1086, Mottram was later one of the two principal manors of the lords of Longdendale. The church and medieval settlement lay on a prominent ridge with extensive views along the Longdendale valley.

the lordship was indeed held by 'half a knight's fee' (Barraclough 1988, 321). It might of course be suggested that this charter, which appears in the Black Prince's register of 1358 (Dawes 1932, 296-7), was a forgery, designed for this very purpose, but this requires the burden of proof. Whatever the reason for the forfeiture, the Longdendale lordship remained in crown possession until 1374. During this period the territory was administered by a crown appointed steward. In 1361 Sir William de Caryngton was granted a ten-year lease of the whole of the lordship, at an annual rent of £40 (Booth *et al* 1976-8, no 121 n 97). In 1366 Sir William's lease was cancelled for slowness of payment, but was returned to him in April 1368 at the same rent (*ibid*). On 28th November 1374 the lordship was returned to Robert de Holland's heir, his granddaughter Matilda (*ibid*, no 57). She had married Sir John Lovell of Titchmarsh, and since his main estates lay in central Cheshire he too appointed a steward, this office being held in 1377 by Henry le Mareschal (ESRCA/4/1-3). The lordship remained in the hands of the Lovells until the death of a later John Lovell in 1465. His son, also John, was then only seven years of age and in consequence the lordship was leased by the crown to Sir William Stanley (Ormerod 1882, 852). John Lovell came into his inheritance in 1477 but he was a supporter of Richard III and, having been charged with treason in November 1485, appears to have died after the battle of Stoke in 1487. His estates were confiscated by the crown, a survey of these in 1488 recording that he had held 'the manor and demesne of Longdendale, with all its members, the vill of Tyngetwisell, and the advowson of Mottrum, held from the king as earl of Chester; value per annum £41' (*ibid*, 853).

The lordship appears to have remained in the crown's possession only until 1489 when it was granted to Sir William Stanley, lessee from 1465 to 1477 (Clayton 1990, 118-19). By this time he was Henry VII's chamberlain of the royal household and

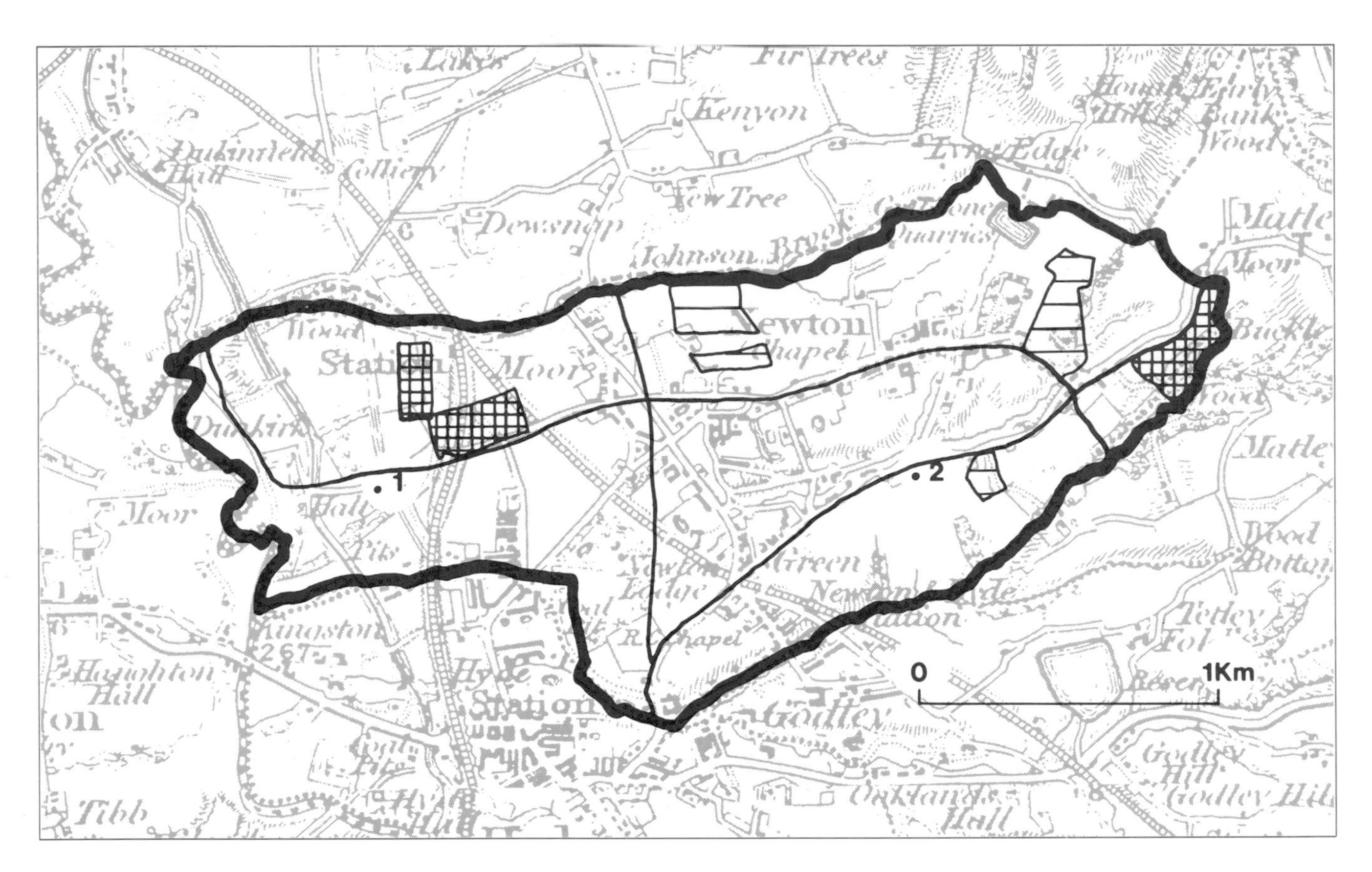

Fig 3.24 Newton manor.
Key: 1 Newton Hall; 2 Goodiers Farm.

controlled much of North Wales and the northern Marches, as sheriff of Flint and chamberlain of Chester (Ives 1976, 34). In 1495, however, Stanley was executed, having been charged with treason as a supporter of Perkin Warbeck. The Longdendale lordship came for a third time into crown possession, in which it remained until 1554. During this time the lordship was administered once more by crown appointed stewards, to whom it was leased like any other royal estate of the period. It is not clear who was the steward of Longdendale immediately after 1495. It may have been William Smith, groom of the wardrobe, who gradually accumulated a significant number of Stanley's properties, but no records survive to confirm or deny this. However by the early 1520s Ralph Egerton was steward, and it was from him that William Brereton took over in 1525 (*ibid*, 15). Brereton's enormous wealth and power led to his downfall and execution (see Chapter 5), so that in 1536 Edmund Peetham was appointed steward. In 1546 the last crown appointed steward, Ralph Standish was granted Longdendale for 21 years. However in 1554 the lordship was granted by Mary I to Richard Wilbraham of Woodhey, Cheshire (Chester LRO DTW Bundle L). Longdendale remained in the Wilbraham family until the late seventeenth century. In 1691 a grant of perpetuity was made to Sir Thomas Wilbraham (*ibid*), on whose death the lordship passed to his son-in-law Lyonel Tollemache (Earwaker 1880, 117).

Newton

Newton is not mentioned in the Domesday survey of 1086, but the township may then have formed part of Mottram manor (see above). The date at which Newton was established as a separate manor is a matter of some difficulty. Two sources suggest that this may have been as early as the twelfth century, but both need to be treated with caution. The first is the 'ancient deeds' at Dunham Massey which, according to Butterworth, recorded that in 1189 'Richard Massey, of Sale, and Robert Massey, of Assheton, and others' held lands in the manors of Godley and Newton under the lord de Burgh or Bros (Butterworth 1827, 152-3). As noted earlier, there are good reasons to believe this claim to be a fabrication of the fourteenth century (see above, pp 27-9).

The second dubious piece of evidence is a pedigree in the manuscripts of the eighteenth-century antiquarian John Watson, now in the Bodleian Library, Oxford. According to this, Thomas de Burgh married

Adeliza, the daughter of Thomas de Newton, in the reign of Richard I (1189-99); the manor subsequently passed to their daughter Agnes de Burgh, who married Richard de Stokeport; their eldest son, Robert, styled himself Robert de Newton and was the ancestor of the later lords of that name (Ormerod, 1882, 858). Both Earwaker (1880, 161) and Helsby (in Ormerod 1882, 858) cast doubt on this evidence and, although Barraclough has come to the defence of at least the marriage of Thomas de Burgh and Adeliza (1957, 43), such scepticism appears to be warranted.

Barraclough himself provides the evidence which appears to give a truer picture, citing a grant (attested in the Shakerley deeds) of Newton by Thomas de Burgh to Robert, son of Richard parson of Stockport. This same grant would appear to be mentioned in a charter of Hamo de Massey of the period 1211-25; in this de Massey confirms Robert, cleric of Stockport, as lord of Newton, as granted by Thomas de Godelegh and confirmed by Thomas de Burgh (Barraclough 1957, 43). There can be little doubt that the Robert son of Richard parson of Stockport of these grants is the same as Robert de Newton son of Richard de Stockport in Watson's pedigree. However, while that pedigree has Robert succeeding to the manor through family descent, the grants show a rather different situation, in which Robert received Newton from Thomas de Godelegh who in turn held it under Thomas de Burgh. Of these two possibilities, the second is undoubtedly correct; for although the evidence of the Shakerley deeds consists only of a later abstract of de Burgh's grant to Robert, the de Massey charter survives in the original.

In reality Newton, along with the rest of Mottram manor, probably reverted after 1086 to the earls of Chester who retained it until 1200-3, when along with the other components of the lordship of Longdendale it was granted to William de Neville. In 1211 the Longdendale lordship passed to Thomas de Burgh as de Neville's son-in-law and heir. Newton, however, did not remain long in the direct control of the lord of Longdendale, for the 1211-25 charter indicates that either de Neville or de Burgh had granted it to Hamo de Massey, baron of Dunham. De Massey himself did not directly hold Newton for long; between 1211 and 1225 the manor was given to Thomas de Godelegh who in turn granted it to Robert, cleric of Stockport.

The immediate descent of the manor after 1211-25 is lost but Robert the cleric may have been ancestor to the Robert 'de Neuton' attested in 1276 and 1306 and through whom the lordship appears to have subsequently descended (Ormerod 1882, 858-9). The manor remained in this same family until 1692 when John Newton died a bachelor and the estate passed to his five sisters (*ibid*, 859).

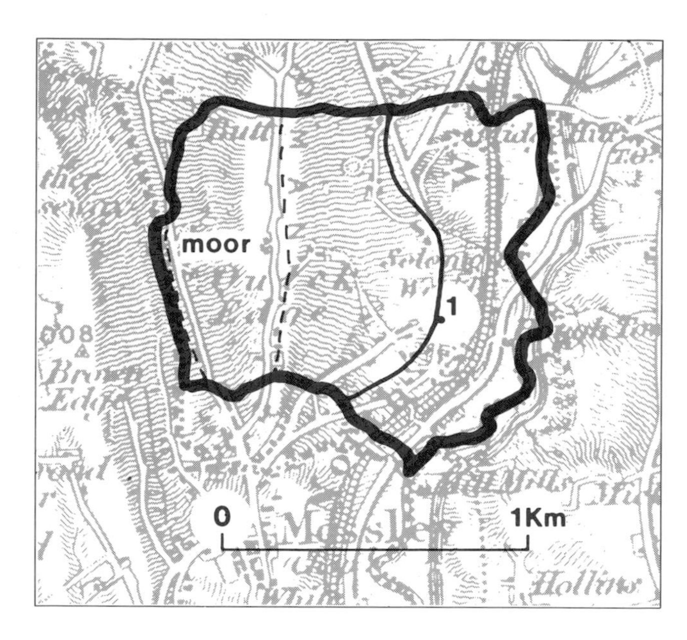

Fig 3.25 Quickmere 'manor'.
Key: 1 Mossley Manor House.

The circumstances under which the manor passed to Robert the cleric would seem to have a direct bearing on the later history of the manor. In 1360 the Longdendale survey lists Robert 'de Neuton' as holding the manor as tenant of the Longdendale lordship (Booth *et al* 1976-8, no 98). However in his inquisition post mortem taken in 1362 he is described as holding Newton from the same four landholders who held the manor of Godley (see above), so that it would seem that the intermediate lordship of Newton, which had been held in 1211-25 by Thomas de Godelegh, had descended with the lordship of Godley.

The 'manor' of Quickmere in Saddleworth (Mossley district)

Following the Conquest the manor of 'Thoac', the early name for the area known as Saddleworth, was held by Roger of Poitou as part of his extensive landholdings in southern Lancashire and the West Riding of Yorkshire (Page 1912, 148). By 1150 it had descended to the Stapletons (Smith 1987, 13), from whom it passed to the Scargills, recorded as lords here in the early fifteenth century (Bowman 1960, 124). By the early sixteenth century the manor had changed hands once more, passing to the Tunstall family. In 1590 Francis Tunstall sold all his lands and manorial rights in Saddleworth to Sir John Ramsden of Longley Hall near Huddersfield (Petford 1987, 84). In turn the Ramsden family sold the estate in 1654 to William Farrer of Eswood near Mytholmroyd for £2950 (Smith 1987, 13).

Quickmere was one of four divisions of Saddleworth township, and in the sixteenth and seventeenth

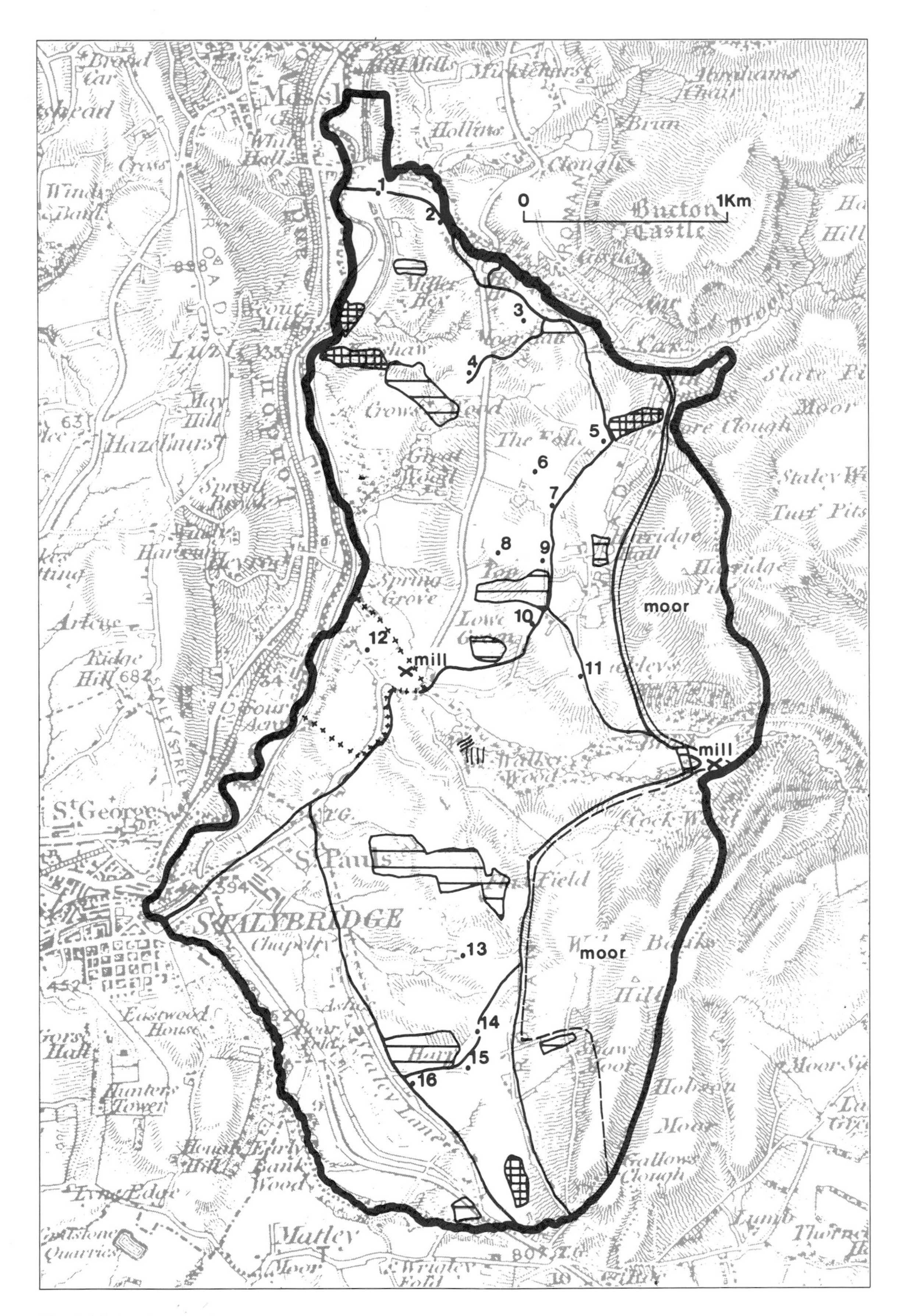

Fig 3.26 Stayley manor.
Key: 1 Inglenook Cottages; 2 Spring Bank Farm; 3 Moorgate Farm; 4 Oakfield; 5 Unnamed farm; 6 Little Bank; 7 Unnamed farm; 8 Wood Farm; 9 Hilltop Farm; 10 Sungreen; 11 Buckley Hill; 12 Stayley Hall; 13 Sidebottom Fold; 14 Cockers Farm; 15 Herpley Farm; 16 Heaps Farm.

Plate 3.4 Stayley Hall.
Documentary evidence suggests that a manorial hall has stood on this site since at least the fourteenth century. The existing structure is a sixteenth-century timber-framed building which was clad in stone sometime after 1580.

centuries at least would appear to have been a separate manor. The evidence for this is a series of documents concerning the enclosure in 1624-5 of Quick Moor and Quick Edge (Petford 1987, 84-91), in which the Leghs and Booths were each described as half lords of 'Quick more'. These documents also state that neither the Ramsdens nor the Tunstalls, as lords of Saddleworth, ever held rights to any part of Quick Moor or other lands there (*ibid*, 86). The origin of this situation is unclear. The same source claims that the Booths' rights to the moor had descended to them through the lordship of Stayley. However, there is no mention of Quick Moor in either the will of Ralph Staveley, lord of Stayley, in 1456 (ESRCA/7/1-3) or in 1517 in the inquisition post mortem of Sir Thomas Assheton (ESRCA/13), who inherited the estates of Ralph Staveley and who in turn was succeeded by the Booths. The precise nature of Quickmere's status prior to 1625 is thus difficult to ascertain; it may have been an independent manor, or a submanor of Saddleworth. Whatever the case, the enclosure agreement reached in 1624-5 gave Ramsden not only a half share of Quick Moor and a third share of Quick Edge but also the title 'chief lord of Quickmere' (Petford 1987, 86), which by this agreement became firmly established as a division of Saddleworth manor.

Stayley

Stayley is not mentioned in the Domesday survey of 1086 but may then have been part of Mottram manor (see above). Following the grant of the 'land of Longedenedale' by Earl Ranulf III to William de Neville in 1200-3, Stayley was granted to a family who bore the local name and whose earliest known members, Robert 'de Staveleia', his brother, also called Robert, and Jordan 'de Staveleia', appear as witnesses to Godley charter number 1 in 1211-25 (Barraclough 1957, 42). This family, however, were not the direct tenants of the lord of Longdendale. A

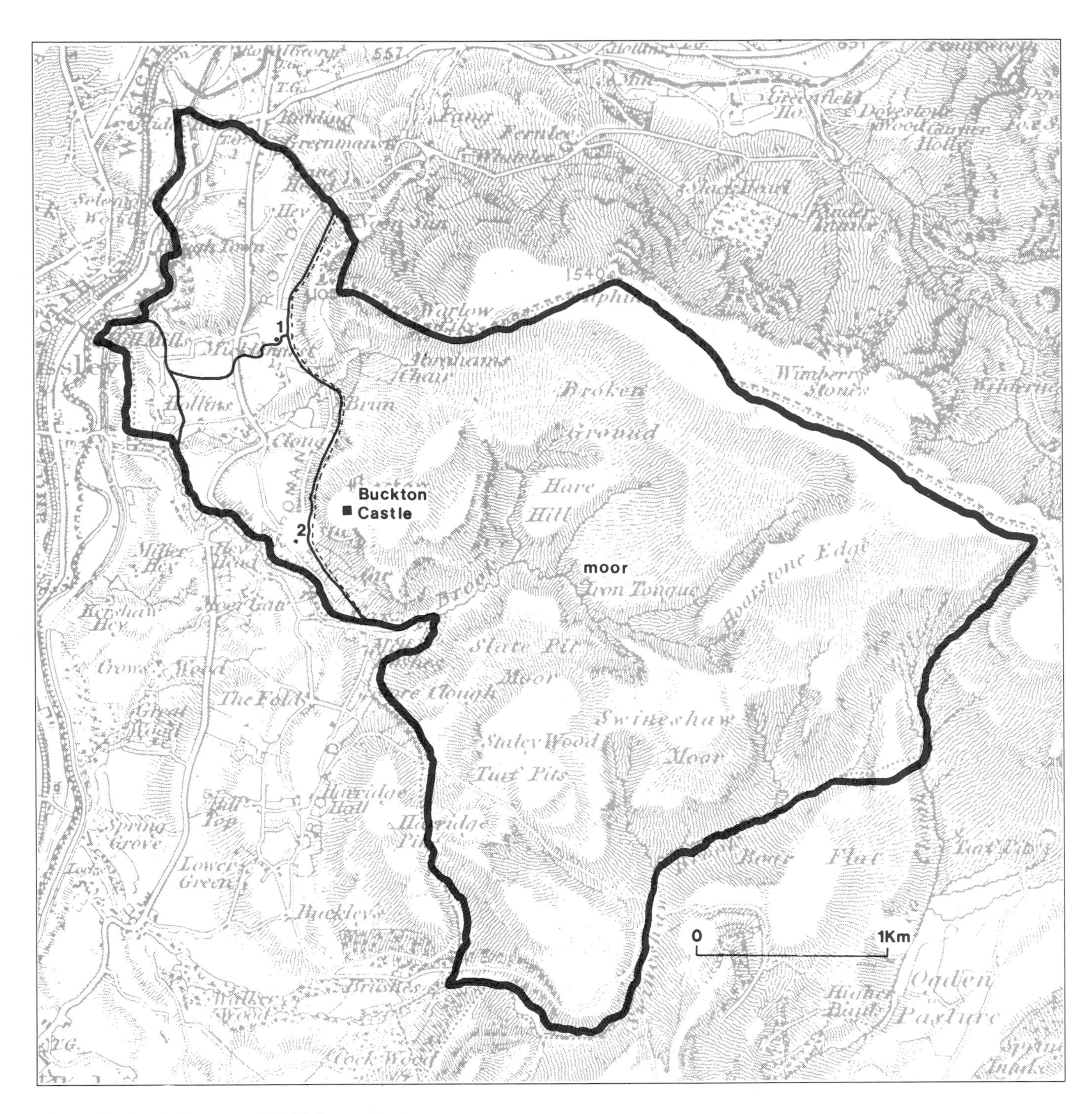

Fig 3.27 Tintwistle manor, Micklehurst district.
Key: 1 Howard's Farm; 2 Castle Farm.

document of 1272-3 shows that the manor of Stayley was then held by Thomas de Macclesfeld and that Robert de Stavelegh, who married Thomas' daughter Dionysia in that year, was a tenant (Earwaker 1877, 165; Ormerod 1882, 864). Similarly in 1357 the inquisition post mortem of Jordan de Macclesfeld shows that he held Stayley under Robert de Holland, lord of Longdendale (Ormerod 1882, 865). The extent of the Staveleghs' own holdings in Stayley is unclear. In 1333 a sixth part of Stayley was granted by William de Stokeport, chaplain, to Adam de Bredbury, but it is uncertain whether this division was originally carried out by the Staveleghs or the Macclesfelds, in which last case the Staveleghs may have held only part of the manor (*ibid*).

In 1456 Ralph Staveley, the last of the male line, bequeathed his estates to his daughter Elizabeth, with the wish that she married Thomas Assheton (ESRCA/7/1-3). As a result of this marriage in 1457 the estate passed to the Assheton family (ESRCA/8), and subsequently followed the same descent as Ashton manor, passing ultimately to the Booths of Dunham Massey.

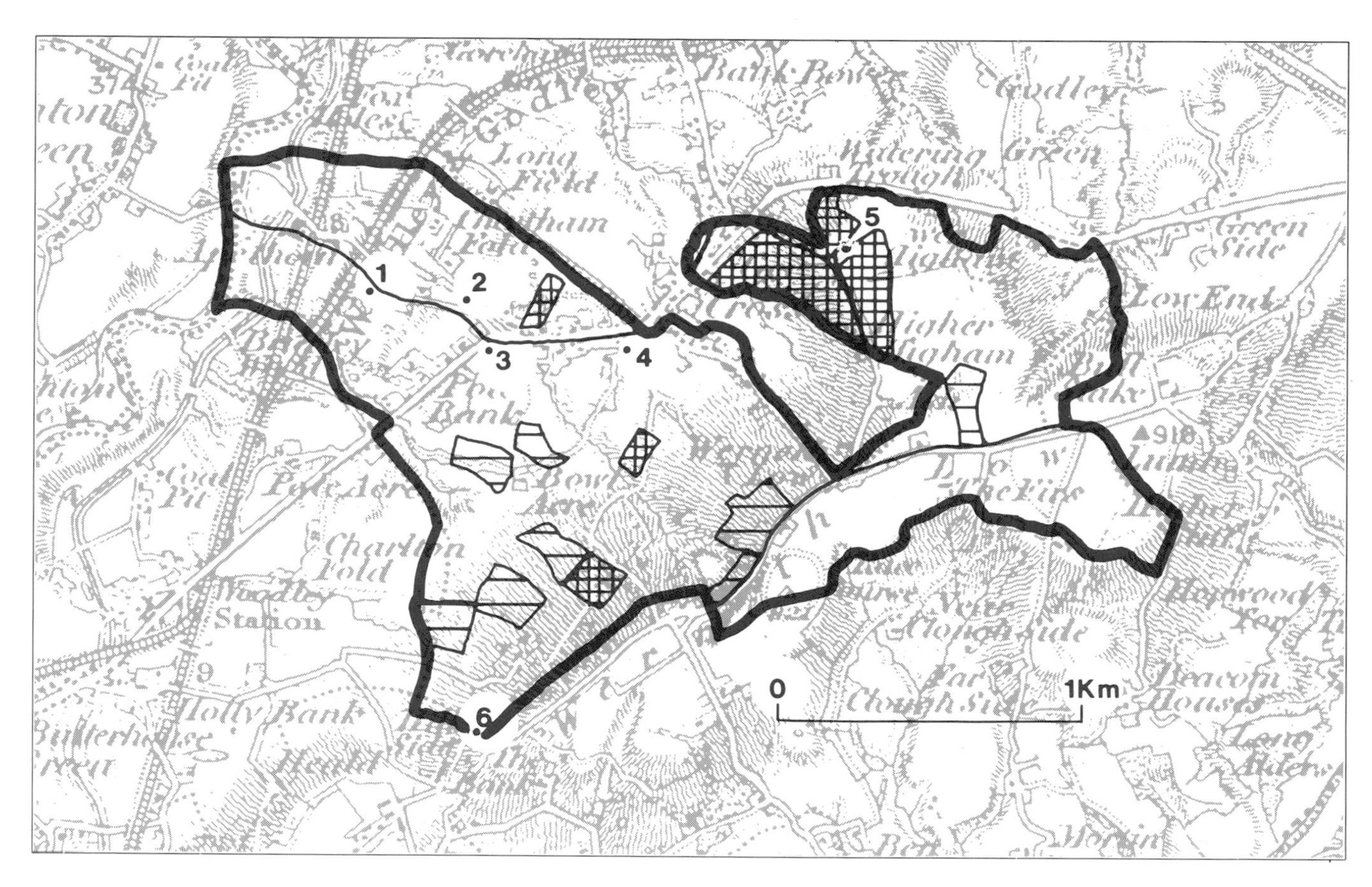

Fig 3.28 Werneth manor.
Key: 1 Apethorn Farm; 2 Gerrards Wood Farm; 3 Gerrards Fold; 4 Geecross Fold; 5 Lower Higham Farm; 6 Hillside.

Tintwistle (Micklehurst district)

The Micklehurst district was originally in the township and manor of Tintwistle, which is listed in the Domesday survey as containing 1 virgate of land, described as waste in 1086, and woodland 4 leagues long and 2 leagues wide (Sawyer & Thacker 1987, no 66). In 1066 it was held by an unnamed freeman, possibly as a tenant of a larger lordship held by the father of Gamel of Mottram. In 1086, however, it was held directly by the earldom of Chester, a situation which probably continued until 1200-3 when it formed part of the grant of the 'land of Longedenedale' to William de Neville (see Chapter 2). Tintwistle, like Mottram, was retained as a demesne manor by the lords of Longdendale and the two manors accordingly follow the same descent (Earwaker 1880, 170; see above). The manor of Tintwistle itself was extremely large and, like Ashton, was composed of four districts, Micklehurst, Arnfield, Tintwistle and Woodhead, the earliest record of these being the Longdendale survey of 1360 (Booth *et al*, 1976-8). This also records that two of the four districts, Arnfield and Micklehurst, were in fact subdivided, the first into 'Great' and 'Little' Arnfield, the second into 'Mukelhurst' and 'Lytelhurst' (*ibid*, no 126). By the time of the Longdendale survey of 1600 Lytelhurst had disappeared, but there were still four divisions in the manor, 'Arnefield', 'Aovur [Over] Tinihtwisell', 'Longdendale' and 'Miclhurste' (Chester LRO DTW/2477/B/9).

Werneth

Werneth appears as 'Warnet' in the Domesday survey, where it is described as waste, containing woodland 3 leagues long and 2 leagues wide, and assessed at less than 1 virgate (Sawyer & Thacker 1987, no 66). It was held in 1066 by a freeman as a manor, and like Tintwistle may have formed part of a larger Anglo-Saxon lordship. In 1086 Werneth was held directly by the earl of Chester but was subsequently held by the lords of Longdendale, probably as part of the 'land of Longedenedale' granted in 1200-3 to William de Neville (see above).

By the middle years of the thirteenth century Werneth, like Hattersley, was held under the Longdendale lordship by the Stokeports, a tenure which is first attested for Robert de Stokeport who died in either 1239 or 1249 (Ormerod 1882, 792). Similarly in 1360 Werneth was listed in the Longdendale survey as being held of the lordship of Longdendale by Richard de Eton, lord of Stockport (Booth *et al* 1976-8, no 131).

However, there is some evidence to suggest an early grant of the manor to the de Masseys. In particular the inquisition post mortem of Isabel, daughter and heiress of Richard de Eton, in 1370 records that while her lands in Hattersley were held of the Longdendale lordship those in Werneth were held of the barony of Dunham Massey (Ormerod 1882, 794). At a later date the Arderne family of Romiley are also attested as holding land in Werneth as tenants of the Dunham barony (*ibid*, 848). The involvement of the barony is puzzling, but it may be the case that, as at Newton, the original grant of Werneth by the lord of Longdendale was to the baron of Dunham and that it was he who granted the manor to the Stokeports.

In Werneth a locally named family may in turn have been tenants of the Stokeports in the thirteenth century, for a William de Werneth granted his claim to part of the waste in the manor to Richard de Byron in a deed of the latter half of that century (Farrer & Brownbill 1911, 283 n 24). By the fourteenth century, however, the manor appears to have been held directly by the Stokeports, for in 1342-3 a William son of Roger de Stokeport held land here (see above, p 30), perhaps the same William de Stokeport attested in Werneth in 1355-7 (Highet 1960, 68, 71).

Following the death of Isabel de Eton in 1369 Werneth seems to have passed with the rest of the Eton-Stokeport estates to Sir John Warren. However in 1372 an agreement was made by John de Davenport of Henbury and Thomas his son, with Sir John Warren, whereby the former obtained lands in Bredbury, Romiley, Werneth and Etchells, at the yearly rent of 1d (Earwaker 1877, 458). The 1372 agreement was superseded by another between the same parties in 1382 (*ibid*). Although the manor is not explicitly mentioned in either of these documents the Davenport control of Werneth would appear to date from this period.

This transfer of the manor may have a bearing upon a curious reference to Werneth in a survey of the tenants of John Lovell, lord of Longdendale in the 1370s:

> 'Hatterleigh and Wernith, which are held from the same [John Lovell], val. 40s are held from the same John, in capite, by the same service' (Ormerod 1882, 852).

The dual assessment of Werneth and Hattersley presumably dates back to their original tenure by the Stokeports. However, unlike other entries in this survey no tenant is mentioned by name, possibly due to the changed circumstance of the two manors.

Werneth descended as part of the extensive Davenport estates until the death of William Davenport in 1640 when Isabel, his daughter and heir, inherited these lands. Since she was only four at the time of her father's death, she was made a ward of Sir Fulk Lucy, whom she later married, *c* 1656 (Earwaker 1880, 109, 417). Between 1662 and 1699 the Werneth estate was sold by the Lucy family to the Bretlands of Thorncliff, in Hollingworth (*ibid*; Ormerod 1882, 872).

3.3 Patterns of Landholding 1066-1700

By the thirteenth century all the Tameside manors were established with the possible exception of Quickmere and, apart from Mottram, Tintwistle and perhaps Werneth, were held by local families (Fig 3.5). West of the River Tame, all the early apportioned manors were held under the barony of Manchester: Ashton appears to have been granted out by the mid-twelfth century; Clayton, including Droylsden, and Denton by *c* 1200; Haughton, a submanor of Denton, by 1225. East of the Tame, Dukinfield, which was part of the barony of Dunham Massey, was granted out by 1189, and Hyde, the overlordship of which is uncertain, perhaps not much later (Fig 3.3). The situation in the Longdendale lordship is rather different in that all of its component manors appear to have been retained by the earl of Chester until 1200-3 when the lordship was granted to William de Neville. However, with the exception of Mottram and Tintwistle which were retained as demesne, these too had been allocated by 1225.

The evidence from the later medieval and early modern periods indicates that much of this early distribution of ownership was maintained throughout the period covered by this study. Of the eleven local families recorded as holding manors in the thirteenth century, seven were still lords in 1500, (Assheton, Byron, Duckenfeld, Holland, Holynworth, Hyde, Neuton), and five were still the chief manorial landholders in the seventeenth century (Figs 3.19 & 3.20).

There were two periods during which ownership of manors changed. The first of these was the first half of the fourteenth century, a period characterized by the fragmentation of some manors and the introduction of new, external, landholders (Fig 3.9). These decades witnessed the break-up of Godley and Matley manors, the immediate though short-term beneficiaries being the Hyde family of Hyde. In Godley this process began with the sale of most of the Godelegh family estates to William de Baggilegh in 1318-19. By 1360 the manor was split between John de Hyde, and three others. Matley manor was sold by William de Mattelegh in 1340. By 1360 there were two major landholders here, John de Hyde and Henry de Holynworth. Further fragmentation can be seen in Hollingworth and Tintwistle.

New manorial lords took over three of the ancient manors. Denton passed to the Holland family in

1325/6 and in addition the local manorial families in Hattersley and probably in Werneth were replaced by direct ownership from the Stokeports by the second quarter of the fourteenth century. In the 1370s these two manors were split between the Davenports and the Caryngtons, both absentee landlords. The fourteenth century witnessed a change in environmental and social constraints leading to a move away from demesne and arable farming towards pastoral farming and the growth of the tenant (see Chapter 4). It is possible that some of the changes in manorial ownership during this period were the result of these wider influences.

These new arrangements resulted once more in a stable landholding pattern until the second period of change in the late sixteenth and early seventeenth centuries, coinciding nationally with the break-down of the medieval manor as the main local administrative unit. By 1515 the Booths of Dunham Massey had part-inherited the manors of Ashton and Stayley from the Asshetons, as well as land in Matley. In 1577 John Carrington left the manor of Hattersley to the Booths, providing them with a large arc of land from Audenshaw in the west to the River Etherow in the east. In 1621 the Byron family sold Clayton manor, including Droylsden, to George and Humphrey Chetham, while *c* 1656 Werneth passed by marriage to Sir Fulk Lucy. However by the seventeenth century the social and economic importance of manorial ownership was limited by a wider development, noted later in this volume – the growth of the freehold farmer.

Chapter 4

The Medieval Economy

'Know that by our special favour we have granted to our beloved and faithful knight John de Assheton that he and his heirs in perpetuity may have in the township of Ashton-under-Lyne in the county of Lancaster two fairs per annum...and...a market every Monday'

(Charter of Henry V, February 13th 1414, John Rylands Library EGR1/5/1/1)

4.1 Agriculture

During the medieval period significant differences in topography, soil type, and climate led to a wide variety of agricultural practices within the North-West. Zones of mixed farming with a bias towards either pastoral or arable agriculture predominated in a number of areas, for instance in western Cheshire for arable agriculture, and on the western Pennine flanks for pastoral activity. In general soil conditions for the cultivation of cereal crops were not good east of the Central Cheshire Ridge. In south-east Lancashire and north-east Cheshire much of the land was poor, consisting of peat, marsh, and thin soils in the lowlands, and millstone-grit outcrops in the uplands such as Rossendale and the western Pennine fringe. North of the River Mersey the climate is not particularly suitable for the growth of crops, with the modern July temperature averaging less than 15 degrees centigrade, and rainfall around 75cm per annum on the lowlands, increasing to over 190cm on the western Pennines (Crowe 1962, 28-33).

However in the eleventh, twelfth and thirteenth centuries the average yearly temperature for the British Isles appears to have been *c* 0.7 to 1.0 degrees centigrade warmer than today (Lamb 1982, 170). Crowe estimates that within the Mersey Basin a temperature rise or decrease of 0.5 degrees would increase or lower the height at which cereal might be cultivated by *c* 70m (Crowe 1962, 44). In the North-West the current marginal limit for cereal cultivation lies at *c* 200-250m OD (*ibid*), but in the early medieval period, therefore, this could have been as high as *c* 390m OD. Conversely a deterioration in the climate after 1300 meant that by the late sixteenth and early seventeenth centuries summer temperatures in England averaged between 0.6 to 0.8 degrees centigrade below those of the twentieth century (Lamb 1982, 203), in which case the upper limit for cereal cultivation could have been as low as *c* 100m OD. Such rises and falls in temperature have important implications for the evidence for medieval agriculture in the North-West as a whole, and in particular within Tameside where east of the River Tame most of the land lies above 100m OD (Fig 4.1).

Such evidence falls into three groups. The smallest is actual physical evidence for medieval agriculture, classically in the form of ridge and furrow earthworks, but there also exist in Tameside a number of field patterns that probably pre-date the seventeenth century. Secondly there is the evidence provided by field-names, which are mostly recorded by the nineteenth-century tithe schedules or awards but also occur occasionally in medieval deeds. Thirdly there is documentary material, the earliest of which is provided by the Domesday survey.

Tameside and the Domesday record

It must be stated at the outset that the description of the Domesday manors in Tameside is brief and patchy. West of the River Tame the manors of Salford hundred were dealt with en bloc, so that no specific agricultural information survives. East of the river only four manors are mentioned, Tintwistle, Hollingworth, Mottram and Werneth, although the whole valley of Longdendale receives a reference in the Derbyshire Domesday (see Chapter 2). The survey does, however, allow us to compare the situation in 1066 with that in 1086.

Firstly, in 1066 woodland was mentioned in three of the four manors; in Tintwistle where there was woodland '4 leagues long and 2 wide', in Werneth where there was woodland '3 leagues long and 2 wide'

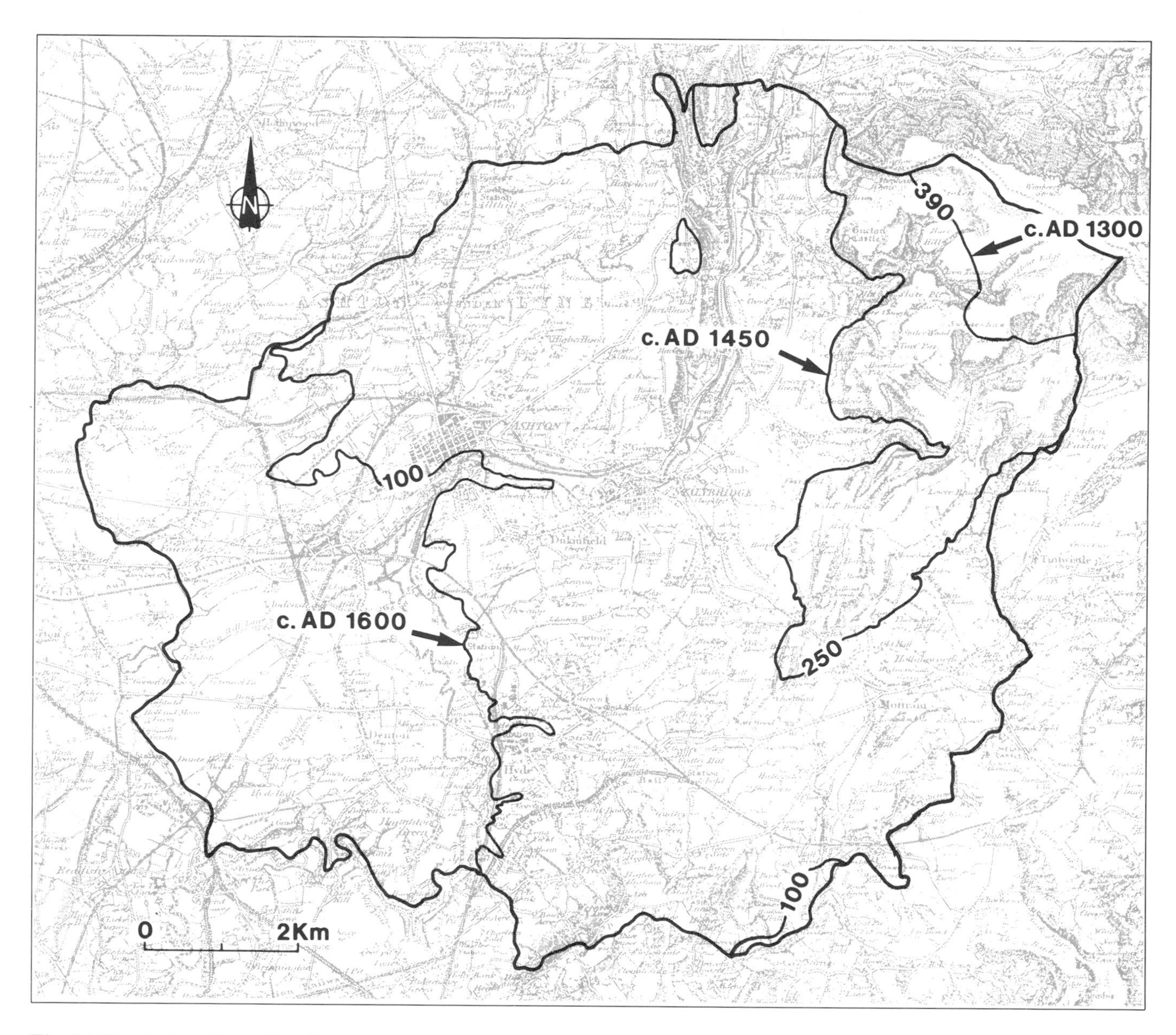

Fig 4.1 The limits of cereal agriculture *c* 1300 to *c* 1600.
The lowering of the height at which cereals might be cultivated was a result of a deteriorating climate and led to an increasing dependency upon the raising of livestock.

(Sawyer & Thacker 1987, no 66), and in Mottram where there was woodland also '3 leagues long and 2 leagues wide' (*ibid*, no 309). Finally in the whole of the Longdendale valley, which probably included land either side of the River Etherow, there was woodland '8 leagues long and 4 leagues wide' (Morgan 1978b, 1.30). Within the four Domesday manors there was land of less than 1 virgate in Werneth, of 1 virgate each in Hollingworth and Tintwistle, and of 1½ hides in Mottram: in total enough probably for ten ploughs, although only the four in Mottram were specified. Indeed the relative agricultural wealth of Mottram manor in 1066, compared to its fellows, can be seen by the presence of two hays (hedged fields cleared from the woodland). In part this can be explained by the size of that manor, which probably included the townships of Godley, Hattersley, Matley, Newton and Stayley, and by the lowland valley location of much of this territory, lying as it does between the rivers Tame and Etherow. The relative agricultural wealth of these townships still stood out in the sixteenth and seventeenth centuries but was based largely on a pastoral economy (Powell 1976). However in 1086 the whole of this area was wasted, although it is likely that the woodland was not touched by the devastation of the winter of 1069-70.

The agricultural potential of Tameside in 1086 is best demonstrated by a comparison of the relative values of Salford and Macclesfield hundreds with the rest of Cheshire and southern Lancashire. While it would be dangerous to assume a direct relationship between values and resources, generally the greater the resources of a holding, as expressed in plough-lands, plough-teams and recorded population, the higher its value. The distribution of plough-teams in 1086 indicates that the richest areas were the Wirral peninsula and Dudestan (later Broxton) hundred, each with more than 20% of the total recorded ploughs. Salford hundred had only 25 plough-teams, between 5% and 9% of the total, whilst Macclesfield had less than 5%, with only fourteen plough-teams recorded (Fig 4.2). Nevertheless almost everywhere there was a deficiency of plough-teams in comparison with estimated agricultural potential in the form of plough-lands, which for the whole of Cheshire and southern Lancashire totalled 1040, almost double the number of recorded teams. Plough-team densities were considerably greater in western Cheshire, in the Wirral and Dee valley. The average there of 1-1.2 per square mile is almost double the nearest figures, those for the Weaver basin and the area around Halton, and far in excess of the extremely low densities of 0.1 in the eastern hundreds of Salford and Macclesfield (Sawyer & Thacker 1987, 338). In part, at least, this may be a reflection of the distribution of better quality agricultural land, since Macclesfield was dominated by the foothills of the western Pennines, and Salford by the Rossendale uplands and the great expanses of lowland bogs at Chat Moss, Red Moss and Ashton Moss. However this difference is also apparent from an assessment of the decline in the monetary values of the hundreds between 1066 and 1086 (Table 4.1). After Leyland hundred, Macclesfield suffered the greatest fall in value during this period, with an 82% drop, followed by Salford hundred, with a 78% drop. Indeed all the lands between the Ribble and the Mersey, bar Blackburn hundred, suffered drops in excess of 62%, whilst those lands in western Cheshire suffered the least, and in Bucklow West and Northwich hundreds the values in 1086, compared to 1066, actually rose.

Most of the land held by the earl of Chester in Macclesfield hundred was rated as waste, and the possibility exists that this was a concession to the earl by the crown, rather than a true reflection of the economic potential of these manors. The absence of any church holdings from the hundred may have further served to lower its value. The scant details provided for most of the lands between the Ribble and the Mersey may also involve an underestimate of their value. Nevertheless, in absolute terms in 1086 Salford hundred, at £8 4s 0d, and Macclesfield hundred, at £5 9s 0d, were amongst the poorest hundreds, whilst in terms of value per square mile they were the lowest.

However Husain records that nationally the values of manors and hundreds in Domesday Cheshire were amongst the lowest in England. Only twelve manors in the county were valued at £3 or over, of which five were situated in the Dee valley. Most holdings were worth less than £1, 'whereas in Northamptonshire, for example, fewer than thirty were assessed at so low a figure' (Husain 1973, 33). Thus in 1086 not only was Tameside in the poorest agricultural region of Domesday Cheshire and southern Lancashire, but its wasted manors lay in one of the most underdeveloped areas of Norman England.

Hundred	1066 Value	1086 Value	Change	%Change
Leyland	£19-18-02	£3-00-00	–16-18-02	–85%
Macclesfield	£30-01-00	£5-09-00	–24-12-00	–82%
Salford	£37-04-00	£8-04-00	–29-00-00	–78%
West Derby	£30-16-00	£8-12-00	–22-04-00	–72%
Warrington	£14-18-00	£4-10-00	–10-08-00	–70%
Newton	£10-10-00	£4-00-00	–6-10-00	–62%
Bucklow East	£7-18-00	£3-16-00	–4-02-00	–52%
Eddisbury	£53-14-08	£29-10-02	–24-04-06	–45%
Broxton	£91-04-01	£51-18-03	–39-05-10	–43%
Wirral	£70-10-00	£41-06-07	–29-03-05	–41%
Blackburn	£32-02-00	£20-11-00	–11-11-00	–36%
Nantwich†	£27-12-08	£17-12-00	–10-00-08	–36%
Chester	£54-11-00	£52-12-08	–1-18-04	–4%
Northwich†	£10-09-00	£10-13-00	+0-04-00	+2%
Bucklow West	£7-07-00	£11-12-00	+4-05-00	+58%

†Not including revenue from salt works

Table 4.1 The value of the Domesday hundreds in Cheshire and southern Lancashire, 1066 to 1086.

Land clearance and agriculture c 1100-1500

The evidence for agricultural development in Tameside from the twelfth to fifteenth centuries is far from complete, but such as there is tallies with the climatic changes noted above. In the late twelfth and thirteenth centuries there are clear indications of a rise in arable agriculture, coincident with the period of high summer temperatures which would have allowed cereal production to have extended into the uplands to a height of *c* 390m (see above). However, as the climate deteriorated in the fourteenth and fifteenth centuries, this period of expansion would appear to

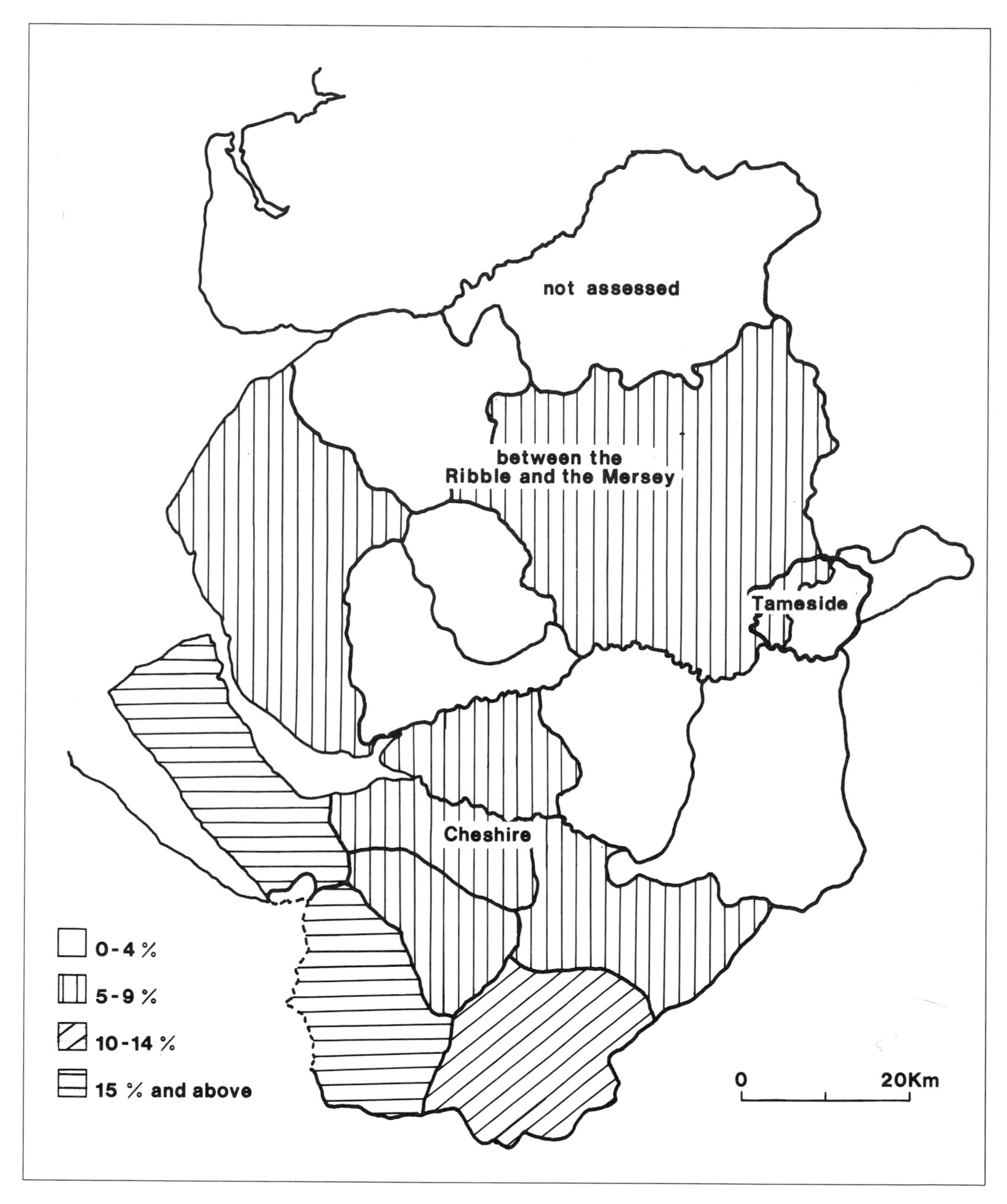

Fig 4.2 Plough-teams in the Cheshire and south Lancashire hundreds in 1086.
The number of plough-teams, each probably consisting of eight oxen, serves as a useful indication of the amount of land under cultivation in each hundred. In 1086 Tameside lay within one of the least productive areas of the North-West, itself one of the most underdeveloped areas of Norman England.

have been followed by a retreat from those areas of production above 200-250m OD, and an increasing dependency on a mixed economy or one dominated by livestock.

East of the River Tame the earliest references to arable farming and land clearance date to the thirteenth century and can be found in the Godley charters. The first of these, of the period 1211-49, granted to Thomas Faber certain lands and rights in Godley, including his right to 'free the land of wood by cutting it' (PSA 1850, no 3; Middleton 1900, 38-9). The second, dated to 1211-25, is Godley charter number 1, the grant by Thomas de Burgh to Adam son of Reginald of lands 'in Mottram', probably Godley manor (see Chapter 3). This grant included both the land which Albinus had previously held and 'two acres of my own cultivation...with all common liberties in wood, in field, in pasture' (Barraclough 1957, 42). In a third deed, of the period *c* 1288-1319, Henry de Godelegh granted to 'William his brother the whole of a plot of land in Matley called 'assarta'', a name indicating agricultural land created by woodland clearance (PSA 1850, no 19; Middleton 1900, 39).

West of the River Tame the earliest references to agriculture belong to the late twelfth and early thirteenth centuries. In Audenshaw woodland was being cleared during the period 1190-1212, for the land which was granted by Matthew son of Edith to the monks of Kersal Cell lay 'between the assart of William the son of Gamel and Kettlescroft'(Farrer 1902, 328) (Fig 3.7). Matthew also granted to the monks all his common rights 'in woodland, in field, in meadow, in pasture' (*ibid*), indicating the presence of cultivation in Audenshaw at this early date. The place-name element 'riding', meaning 'cleared land', is found in a deed of 1274 relating to Denton (Bowman 1960, 91), and by 1346 in Ashton the demesne land included 40 acres of arable land, valued at 12d per acre, 12 acres of meadow at 2s per acre, and 20 acres of woodland at 12d per acre (Farrer & Brownbill 1911, 341 n 38).

Agricultural expansion in the twelfth, thirteenth and early fourteenth centuries can be seen in much of northern England (Miller 1975, 7-8), but it is worth noting that evidence quoted by Dodd (1986, 19-20) suggests a concentration of woodland clearance in eastern Cheshire, a pattern observable east of the Tame. During the thirteenth century the medieval population of England was at its peak, with possibly 5 or 6 million people working the land by the end of the century (Clarke 1984, 20). In contrast, it seems likely that by the end of the fourteenth century the population stood at only *c* 3 million (*ibid*). This drastic and rapid decline was due to economic pressures at the turn of the thirteenth century exacerbated by climatic deterioration leading to agricultural failures in the early fourteenth century (Lamb 1982, 186-7), the effects of which can be seen in western Cheshire (Hewitt 1967, 12-13). These events culminated with the Black Death of *c* 1348-9 and its recurrences in 1360-2, 1369 and 1375. As a consequence of these factors, the medieval agrarian economy of England underwent a number of profound changes. Marginal lands which had been brought into cultivation during the population increase of the thirteenth century were abandoned in the fourteenth (Platt 1978, 97-9, 129-31). There followed a move from demesne farming, that is the farming of the lord's lands through the labour of his tenants, to tenant farming, where the lord rented out large sections of his estates. In Tameside this last change is most evident in Ashton manor where there is a substantial rise in the number of free tenancies recorded in the custom roll and rental of 1379-1422 from those attested in the late thirteenth and early fourteenth centuries (see Chapter 3).

Direct evidence for the Black Death in the Borough is difficult to find, although an indication of its effects may be provided by the two burgages left vacant in Tintwistle in 1360 and by the number of multiple owners, eleven burgages being held by three individuals out of a total of 26 (Booth *et al* 1976-8, no 126). However evidence for environmental deterioration may be provided by the presence of ridge and furrow on land above 200m OD now given over to pasture. Ridge and furrow earthworks represent the classic form of medieval arable agriculture in which open, or unenclosed, fields were farmed in common by the tenants of the manor in the form of intermingled strips. Both Youd and Sylvester have argued that the common fields of Lancashire and Cheshire were divided into furlongs or groups of ridges; that these major divisions were further divided into holdings often called 'butts' or 'doles'; and finally that 'butts' and 'doles' were in turn ploughed into ridges known as 'acres', 'flatts', 'lands' or 'selions' (Sylvester 1956; Youd 1961). Other terms associated with such strip-farming are 'shut', 'road' and 'loon'. In Tameside ridge and furrow earthworks can be found not only above the 200m OD contour on marginal land in Hollingworth and Mottram but also in more sheltered locations at Stayley, at *c* 160m OD, and at Little Moss, at *c* 100m OD (Plate 4.1; Appendix 4). Furthermore, the documentary evidence is consistent with a move away from grain production in the later medieval period. In both Hollingworth and Mottram manors there is evidence for medieval open-field agriculture in the form of field-names (see below), but by the late sixteenth and seventeenth centuries a series of wills, inventories and estate surveys show that farms in both manors were dependent on livestock for their income.

Plate 4.1 Ridge and furrow near Mottram Old Mill.
Such earthworks are difficult to date but may be relics of medieval open-field farming.

The evidence for arable agriculture

West of the River Tame early evidence for open-field agriculture is provided by a thirteenth-century document in which Roger, son of Cicely de Denton, was granted the 'Mabiliflat' and the 'Harperflat' (Young 1985, 18-19); the precise location of these lands is uncertain but other field-names suggestive of open-field farming, such as 'Tom Acre' (Town Acre), 'Cockshut', 'Longshut' and 'Twenty Acre', are recorded on the tithe award to the east of Denton Hall (Preston LRO DRM1/37; Fig 3.12).

In Ashton manor the best evidence for open-field agriculture comes from that part of the estate now in Oldham. The 'Lees Field' lay on the northern edge of the manor (centred upon SD 952 043) and was composed of a series of open-field strips. These were still held by twelve tenants in 1841, when a map was made of the common field before its enclosure (Higson 1917, 48). The strips varied in size from 1 acre to less than ½ acre, and many still retained individual names in the nineteenth century, such as 'Brierlands', 'Rails Half Acre' and the 'Platt Dole', although the earliest named was 'Meadow Spot' in 1663 (*ibid*). These strips are only referred to for the first time in 1592 (*ibid*, 40), but their origin lay in the medieval period, when the 'Lees Field' was under crop. By 1841 the field was used for grazing cattle. When this change-over occurred is not clear, but the Ashton court leet records of 1692 describe at least part of the field as meadow (Bowman 1960, 24). Since the field lay at *c* 210m OD it is likely that it was affected by the deteriorating climate of the fourteenth and fifteenth centuries.

Elsewhere within the manor of Ashton conclusive evidence for open-field agriculture is harder to find. Both the 1346 survey of the manor (see above, p 52) and the custom roll and rental of 1379-1422 suggest that the economy of the manor was based on mixed farming. The last document in particular shows the exploitation of mossland, pasture land and arable land to have been of equal importance. That there were substantial tracts of arable land under cultivation near Ashton village is indicated by the duties of the tenant-at-will. In 1422 these included providing ploughs and labour for the cultivation of the lord's demesne, as well as harrowing and harvesting this same land. Reference to fields later in the document might imply open-field agriculture but the context is too vague to be sure (Harland 1868, 94-116).

East of the River Tame the evidence is even more fragmentary, although the distribution of 'heys' and arable-type field-names implies a wooded landscape, where isolated fields were held and tilled in common. The earliest date for arable agriculture in this area of the Borough, as noted above, relates to thirteenth-century Godley. However, the most detailed material is found in the Longdendale survey of 1360 which records a corn-mill at Tintwistle (Booth *et al* 1976-8, no 98), and the yearly cost of farming out the 'arable land' of the valley as £12 (*ibid*, no 116). Furthermore in certain manors the survey lists specific services related to reaping and harvesting, and thus indicating manorial cultivation. Robert de Neuton held Newton manor and William de Caryngton and Richard de Eton held Hattersley manor by services that included the provision of one man for three days at harvest time and one plough for three days at Lent (*ibid*, no 98). Though this evidence indicates only that crops were grown in the lordship, not that open-field agriculture was practised, there are further references in the same document which would suggest the existence of fragmented or scattered holdings. Richard de Diewysnape, for instance, held ½ bovate of land and John de Radeclyf ½ rood of land, both in Mottram (*ibid*, nos 98 & 121).

For further evidence it is necessary to assess the field-names recorded on the mid-nineteenth-century tithe awards for this area. These indicate the presence of scattered open fields in most of the townships east of the River Tame, except Dukinfield, but with specific concentrations in Matley, Hattersley, Mottram and Hollingworth. In Matley township it is apparent from the tithe award (Chester LRO EDT 268/1 & 2) that field-names such as 'Longfield', 'Longlands', 'Broadfield', 'Ryecroft', and 'Townfield', are concentrated around Higher Matley Hall (Fig 3.22). However in Hattersley field-names such as 'Great Field' and 'Acre' are scattered over the northern part of the township (Chester LRO EDT 192/1 & 2), and not in one specific area (Fig 3.16).

Further testimony for arable agriculture in medieval Longdendale comes from a series of seventeenth-century wills and inventories relating to Mottram and Hollingworth manors. The will of William Robotham in 1614 and the inventory of Reginald Rowbothom in 1672 list field-names associated with the Haigh farm, south-east of Mottram village (Chester LRO WS). Several suggest open-field agriculture: 'Great South Field', 'Ridground', 'Lower Rydinge', 'Longcrofte', 'Henginge Acar' and 'Symons Roade' (Fig 3.23). Their origin must pre-date the seventeenth century since it is clear from William Robotham's inventory in 1614 that his holding was based primarily on livestock and not arable agriculture. It is also possible that the origin of this particular farm is related to lands in the 'Hagh' or 'Haghe' mentioned from the mid-fourteenth century onwards (Ormerod 1882, 864; Booth *et al* 1976-8).

Immediately north of Mottram, in Hollingworth manor, a survey of the demesne of Hollingworth Hall from 1672-84 lists a number of suggestive field-names, including 'Great Riggs Field', 'Middel Riggs Field' and 'Further Riggs Field' (Chester LRO DDX 87/1a). To these can be added the 'Oldefeld in Holynworth', a field-name which can often indicate the original nucleus of a settlement and which is also mentioned from the mid-fourteenth century (Booth *et al* 1976-8, no 116). It is clear from the tithe award (Chester LRO EDT 204/1 & 2) that these fields clustered around the hall itself, although there is a second group of field-names suggestive of open-field farming below the hall, on the banks of the River Etherow, including 'Wet Acres', 'Long Loons' and 'Great Meadow' (Fig 3.18). John Hollingworth's will of 1662 (Chester LRO WS) indicates that his wealth lay in livestock, which amounted to over £153, compared to only £30 in 'corne and hay'. It would thus seem likely that the field-names around the hall originated before the seventeenth century in open-field practice, like those by the Haigh.

Mills and milling

A useful indicator of the importance of grain production during the medieval period was the presence or absence of a corn-mill. However references to mills in the documentary evidence usually emphasize their legal or financial aspects (Hewitt 1967, 23). The custom of mill soke required tenants of a manor or residents of a borough to grind all the grain which they grew or consumed at the mill of their lord, thereby providing him with an additional source of income. This system encouraged the construction of a mill in every manor or borough which had a stream with sufficient force to turn a wheel.

Within Tameside evidence survives of the duties relating to the two medieval mills in Longdendale and Ashton. In 1360 the Longdendale survey records that several of the local lords, including those of Hollingworth and Hattersley, were required to provide

Plate 4.2 The mill dam at Woolley mill.
The manorial mill of the lords of Longdendale, Woolley mill is first documented in the 1530s but is probably the mill listed in the Longdendale survey of 1360. There was still a working mill here in the nineteenth century. The dating of the earthern dam is uncertain, but the 1360 survey shows that certain tenants of the lord of Longdendale were required to provide labour for the construction of earthworks at the mill.

labour for the construction of earthworks at the mill of Tintwistle (Booth *et al* 1976-8, no 98). In Ashton the custom roll and rental of 1379-1422 stipulates that tenants were bound to use only the manorial mill and to pay one sixteenth of their corn for this service (Harland 1868, 95, 109). The relative value of these two mills can be gauged by the proportion of manorial income they accounted for. In Longdendale *c* 1360 the mill brought in £4 out of a total income of between £35 and £40, or 10% to 11% (Booth *et al* 1976-8, no 68). In Ashton in 1422 the mill was leased for 16s 4d out of a total of £36 15s 6¾d, or 2% (Harland 1868, 101, 116).

The Domesday survey provides the earliest record of the number of corn-mills in medieval England, but in dealing with the material for Cheshire and southern Lancashire one must be aware of the limitations of the evidence. North of the Mersey no mills were recorded, although that does not mean that there were none to list, whilst in Cheshire only eighteen were noted (Bott 1983, 62). Even allowing for these difficulties, Bott's analysis of the national distribution of mills listed by the Domesday survey (*ibid*, 63) indicates that Cheshire was far behind the main arable farming areas in 1086, that is Dorset, Hertfordshire, Norfolk, Northamptonshire, Oxfordshire and Wiltshire, each with more than one mill for every 4 square miles of land. In Cheshire this figure was only one mill for every 57 square miles. In thirteen counties the revenue from corn-mills was more than £10 per 100 square miles of land, but in Cheshire it was less than 10s (*ibid*), while the annual revenue from mills alone in the counties of Kent, at £231, and Wiltshire, at £216, was almost equivalent to the revenue of £246 from every kind of land and property in Cheshire (*ibid*, 62). Some of these differences could be partly accounted for by the uneven nature of the Domesday evidence for Cheshire, but Bott's more detailed examination of the distribution of mills in adjacent counties indicates that recorded mills were as scarce in north-western Derbyshire, northern Staffordshire and the far north of Shropshire as in southern and eastern Cheshire (*ibid*, 65).

In view of this evidence it is no surprise to find that only one mill was recorded in Macclesfield hundred in 1086, and that at Macclesfield itself (Sawyer & Thacker 1987, no 60). Although not necessarily a complete record of the mills in the hundred, the implication of low arable activity along the western foothills of the Pennines is supported by the low number of plough-teams in this hundred (see above). It might thus be reasonable to assume that the growth in the number of corn-mills in Tameside indicates either an increase in arable production or a growth in population, or possibly both.

The earliest mill references in the Borough can be found in the charter of Matthew son of Edith, which relates to a grant of land in Audenshaw to Kersal Cell in the period 1190-1212 and in which the right to the 'mills' was retained by the lord of the manor (Farrer 1902, 329). If the reference is to be taken as genuine, and not part of a standard legal formula, then we have to look for the location of these mills. There would appear to be two probable sites. It has been argued in Chapter 3 that Audenshaw, along with Haughton, is likely to have belonged to Denton manor at this date, and that the grantor of this charter was Matthew de Reddish, then lord of Denton manor. Within the original thirteenth-century extent of Denton manor there lay only one mill, that known as Denton Old Mill (Fig 3.12). Although this is not referred to until a series of deeds beginning in 1409 (Taylor 1951, nos 606, 607, 609, 613) this would be the most likely location for one of these early thirteenth-century mills. The other possible mill location is on the west bank of the Tame in Haughton manor. In 1270 William de Baggilegh granted to his daughter Isabella and her husband John de Hyde, 'a weir for their mills in Haughton' (Earwaker 1880, 40), and Haughton mill is mentioned again in deeds of 1307 and 1446 (Farrer & Brownbill 1911, 322-3 n 3; Cunliffe-Shaw 1958, 17). By the early seventeenth century the mill in Haughton may have been replaced by a mill on the eastern side of the river, in Hyde manor (Chester LRO WS Robert Hyde 1639) (Fig 3.21).

The earliest reference to a mill in Longdendale can be found in Godley charter number 1, of 1211-25. In this the grantee of land 'in Mottram', Adam son of Reginald, was required to grind his corn in the mill of the grantor, Thomas de Burgh, lord of Longdendale (Barraclough 1957, 42). In 1360 the manorial mill of the Longdendale lordship, 'at Tintwistle', was probably located on a tributary of the River Etherow between Hollingworth and Tintwistle manors, on the site of the later Woolley mill (Fig 3.18; Plate 4.2). This was certainly the site of the manorial mill in the sixteenth century. In the 1530s William Brereton, steward of Longdendale, leased the manorial mill to the Wolegh family (Ives 1976, 247), while the lease of the stewardship to Ralph Standish in 1546 and the grant of the lordship to Richard Wilbraham in 1554 both specified the right to Woolley mill as belonging to the Longdendale lordship (Chester LRO DTW Bundle L). However 'le Oldemulneton' occurs as a place-name in Mottram manor in 1313 (Dodgson 1970, 315), suggesting a mill earlier than Woolley mill and evidently abandoned by 1360 since it does not occur in the Longdendale survey. One possible location for this mill is the site of the later Mottram Old Mill, on Hurstclough Brook (SJ 9889 9596) recorded as an old woollen mill on the tithe award (Chester LRO EDT 281/1 & 2). An alternative and perhaps more likely location is the site of the later Broadbottom mill on the River Etherow (Fig 3.23), although this itself is not mentioned until 1608 (Chester LRO WS Anthony Wilde 1608).

While four corn-mills may be recorded for the thirteenth century, possibly only one new corn-mill is attested in the fourteenth and fifteenth centuries, namely Ashton Old Mill on the River Tame (Fig 3.6). Although only first recorded, in the custom roll and rental, in 1399 (Bowman 1960, 72), the existence of a settlement at Ashton in the twelfth and thirteenth centuries might lead one to suspect a very early date for this site. By 1422 there is reference in the rental to 'both the corn-mills' (Harland 1868, 101, 109). This may indicate that the Asshetons had added a second mill site by this date, but its location is not known and the reference may be to a second millstone rather than a second building. In 1422 the rental also records a 'Walk Miln', but this was a fulling mill, used in the finishing process of woollen cloth (*ibid*, 96; Bowman 1960, 414-15). The last mill to be referred to in medieval Tameside was located in Stayley manor and was mentioned in 1430 (Dodgson 1970, 318). Whether this was a corn-mill is unclear since the actual reference merely describes it as 'Staveleymulne'. However in the next reference, in 1533, there were two mills in the manor, possibly both on Mill Brook, one a water-mill, the other for fulling (Ormerod 1882, 867) (Fig 3.26). The function of the 1430 mill is not known, but in view of the location of Stayley manor, between 130 and 400m OD, it may have been severely affected by the deterioration in the climate, so that a

Plate 4.3 Apethorn Farm, Werneth.
Although later encased in stone and brick and converted to use as a cottage and shippon, this building was originally a cruck-framed longhouse built in the fifteenth century. A longhouse combined the living quarters of a farmer and his family and the stallage of livestock and storage of produce under one roof, and was probably the dwelling of many of the tenant farmers of medieval Tameside.

fulling mill, exploiting the fifteenth-century trend towards pastoralism, might be more likely at this date.

In general, the pattern of corn-mill references in Tameside is broadly similar to that observed in Cheshire by Bott, and mirrors the rise and fall in both the population of medieval England and the expansion and subsequent contraction of arable agriculture. According to Bott's survey, in Cheshire twelve mills are documented for the first time between 1087 and 1186, to add to the eighteen recorded in 1086 (Bott 1984a, 34). The period 1187-1286 saw an increase in this number with references to 30 new mills. The peak was reached in the period 1286-1336 with 99 mills appearing for the first time (*ibid*, 35-6). Thereafter the rate of growth slackened considerably and in the period 1336-1485 there were only 24 new corn-mills recorded in the county as a whole (*ibid*, 36). It is not clear how many of these sites continued in use throughout the medieval period, but nationally some corn-mills were abandoned by the beginning of the fourteenth century (Platt 1978, 97), and it would be logical to assume that the declining population from this period onwards would have needed fewer corn-mills. In Tameside the single reference to 'le Oldemulneton' in Mottram, in 1313, may hint at this decline in established sites.

The evidence for pastoral agriculture

In many parts of northern England stock-farming was the main form of agricultural activity during the medieval period. Cattle tended to graze the lowlands and lower slopes of the Pennines, and sheep the uplands (Miller 1975, 11-12). Many of the upland areas were only used as summer pasture lands (*ibid*, 13). Macclesfield hundred appears to have been a great supplier of cattle, possibly as early as the late eleventh century (Morgan 1978a, 1.25), but certainly by the fourteenth century. In particular the accounts of Macclesfield manor from 1347-62, whilst perhaps not representative of the whole hundred, do indicate that this area had a long history of stock raising (Hewitt 1967, 31-2). The importance of livestock in this area is emphasized by the Cheshire puture rolls for the fourteenth century which indicate that cattle rustling was rife in the hundred (Highet 1960, 48-9). Furthermore it is clear that cattle were brought into Macclesfield from all over the county in order to improve the stock. In the thirteenth and fourteenth centuries Cheshire cattle were regularly driven to London (Hewitt 1967, 33-4).

The evidence for cattle rearing in Tameside is tentative but a document of 1354 records the theft from John de Holynworth, of Hollingworth, of three oxen and eighteen cows (Dawes 1932, 144). Elsewhere in the Borough it would appear that cattle may have been grazed in common, as in other parts of Lancashire (Youd 1961, 23-5). The earliest reference to this may occur in Godley charter number 1, of 1211-25, in which Thomas de Burgh granted to Adam de Godelegh 'all common liberties in wood, in field, in pasture' (see above). Common pasture rights in Godley are also mentioned in a deed of the period *c* 1288-1319 (PSA 1850, no 19; Middleton 1900, 39). In the Longdendale survey of 1360 livestock are mentioned in two instances; firstly as plough animals and secondly in connection with fines for animals straying through the valley (Booth *et al* 1976-8, nos 98 & 131). A number of meadows are also referred to in the survey.

West of the Tame the Ashton custom roll and rental of 1379-1422 provides evidence for the keeping of pigs within the manor, but makes no mention of cattle (Harland 1868, 111-12). Meadows, however, are mentioned in the Ashton survey of 1346 (see above), while a series of documents relating to the boundaries of Ashton Moss *c* 1425 provides a useful insight into animal husbandry in Ashton and Droylsden. As a result of a dispute over the moss's boundary between John de Assheton's and John de Byron's land, an inquisition of the inhabitants of Droylsden was taken. From this it is clear that livestock, including sheep and cattle, were grazed on the moss, with one tenant, Thumlyn Gibson, having as many as fourteen or fifteen cows there (Speake & Whitty 1953, 65).

Woodland and waste enclosure

Where no open fields existed, agriculture was based on enclosed fields, defined by hedges, walls or banks. These fields often appeared at the limits of open fields on land previously woodland or waste and were most common in areas of low population and dispersed settlement (Taylor C 1975, 94). It is possible to follow the general trend of clearance by examining the distribution of field-names associated with such fields. In Tameside there is extensive field-name evidence recording the presence of 'intakes' or 'hays', field-names associated with waste and woodland clearance.

West of the River Tame 'intake' field-names are found in the Ashton custom roll and rental, in association with 'Palden Wood', probably on the northern edge of the manor near Strine Dale, Oldham. The Ashton rental also records a 'moor hey' and 'hayscroft' at Ryecroft Farm on the southern edge of Ashton Moss (Harland 1868, 94-116), whilst in Denton a number of 'hay' field-names, north-east of the hall, were documented by 1383 (Young 1985, 19).

However it is east of the River Tame that these field-names predominate. Whilst they are rare in the riverside lowland manors of Dukinfield, Newton and Hyde, they are especially noticeable in upland areas such as Stayley and Hollingworth. In these latter two manors 'intake' and 'hay' field-names are concentrated between 200m and 300m OD, on the slopes of the valley, immediately below the moorlands of Buckton and Hollingworth (Figs 3.26 & 3.18). Likewise the distribution of such field-names in Werneth manor show as a cluster around the fringes of Werneth Low at around *c* 210m OD (Fig 3.28). In lower lying manors, that is between 150m and 200m OD, stretches of enclosed woodland may also be identified by such evidence. In particular, in Matley there were two groups of 'hay' field-names in the northern part of the manor that suggest such activity (Fig 3.22). Though much of this activity is difficult to date without supporting documentary evidence, only available for thirteenth-century Godley where the clearing of woodland is specifically mentioned in two deeds of the periods 1211-25 and *c* 1288-1319 (see above), it does fit the known pattern of medieval exploitation of upland fringe areas.

Parkland

A final form of enclosure requires mention since this effectively took the lands concerned out of the agricultural system. This is the enclosure of waste or woodland to provide parkland for the hunting of game, in particular deer. In 1335 John de Assheton was given a grant of royal free warren, that is exclusive rights to hunt game, in his demesne lands in Ashton (ESRCA/3). Two years later he was granted a licence to impale or enclose Lyme Park in the north of Ashton manor (Farrer & Brownbill 1911, 341 n 38). There was also a smaller park immediately west of the manorial hall and village of Ashton (Fig 3.6). This 'Little Park' is first mentioned in 1379, when along with 'the Hall-yards', it was named as an area of the demesne from which pigs were excluded (Harland 1868, 112).

In Longdendale the hunting of deer by the lord is mentioned in connection with the 'hagehag'; this was the obligation of certain tenants to provide labour for the preparation of a deer-hay, possibly at the Haigh (Booth *et al* 1976-8, no 98). In Hattersley manor a park at Botham's Hall was still remembered in the early seventeenth century (Ormerod 1882, 546). Perhaps by this date the park had already been cleared for agricultural use, as indicated by the number of 'hay' field-names here on the nineteenth-century tithe award (Chester LRO EDT 192/1 & 2; Fig 3.16).

4.2 Mossland Exploitation

During the medieval period Ashton Moss lay mostly within the manor, parish and township of Ashton. This valuable resource was exploited from at least the late medieval period, with piecemeal enclosure around the fringes of the moss from the beginning of the fifteenth century. The Ashton custom roll and rental records that in 1422 the leasing of turbary rights (the right to dig peat, which was used for fuel) brought in £5 for the lord of the manor – a figure which represents nearly a seventh of the yearly income of £36 15s 6¾d from his estate (Harland 1868, 102). An instance of the value of the moss is the amount paid by Sir John Byron in 1422 to rent a portion of the moss, 16s – a payment almost equivalent to the cost of renting the manorial corn-mill at 16s 4d (*ibid*).

About the year 1400 and again in 1425 Sir John de Assheton and his son, also John, had disputes with the Byrons regarding the 'meres' or boundaries between their respective sectors of the mosslands. In 1400 an inquest was appointed to meet upon the moss to decide upon the boundaries. In the event, angry words were exchanged between the two families, the meeting proved inconclusive, and it was not until 1425 that the matter was settled (Bowman 1960, 43-6). Since this dispute affected the Droylsden side of the moss as much as the Ashton side, sworn statements were taken from both sets of inhabitants. Those relating to Droylsden have survived and indicate some of the uses to which the mossland was put at this time. Its primary use was as a source of fuel, but it was also valuable summer pasture land. As noted above, livestock were grazed on the moss, with one tenant having fourteen or fifteen cows there.

The agreement reached in 1425 also survives and provides the earliest description of the boundaries of Ashton Moss. Although it only deals with the northern part of the morass, from Droylsden to Little Moss, it serves as a useful mark from which to assess the process of enclosure. It is apparent that even at this date parts of the moss had already been drained, for the Ashton custom roll and rental records a number of intakes along the southern edge of the morass (Harland 1868, 94-116). Even so in the late medieval period the extent of the moss appears to have been nearly double that recorded in the early twentieth century (Ordnance Survey Drift Geology map, sheet 85, revised edition 1913), with the roads of Moorside Street and Back Lane defining its northern boundary, and Slate Lane and Lees Lane defining its southern edge (Fig 7.1).

4.3 Trade and Trading Activities

In the North-West the rise and decline of medieval trade can be followed in the number of market charters granted down to 1500. Before 1200 only three markets and fairs are known in the North-West, but in the thirteenth century some 27 new markets and fairs were established. The number of new foundations declined in the period 1300-50 with only ten new markets and fairs recorded, and between 1350 and 1400 none. A slight recovery in commercial fortunes may be represented by the appearance of four new fairs and markets in the fifteenth century (Morris 1983, 29). Most of these charters related to local trading centres, such as the borough towns of Altrincham or Wigan, but markets were not the exclusive right of boroughs and many of the settlements in the North-West had a market or fair but lacked formal borough status. In Tameside Ashton-under-Lyne had a market and two fairs by 1414 but was not a borough, whilst at Tintwistle borough status and the presence of a market can be inferred but not proved.

Trading activities in twelfth- and thirteenth-century Tameside are virtually impossible to recover because there is neither the archaeological nor documentary evidence to provide such information. The earliest such material dates from the fourteenth century, and includes some evidence for long-distance trade. In 1352-3 new stones for the mill at Cogshall, Cheshire, were brought from Tintwistle (Hewitt 1967, 24), whilst it is possible that Longdendale may have taken part in the cattle drives to London and in the stock rearing activities of the Macclesfield area (*ibid*, 33-4). During the fourteenth century it is likely that Tintwistle, rather than Mottram, acted as the local market centre for Longdendale, and whilst no market charter has survived the reference to 26 burgages here in 1360 and the presence of the lord's manor house in 1370 suggest that the settlement may have been of borough status (Booth *et al* 1976-8, no 126). Its impor-

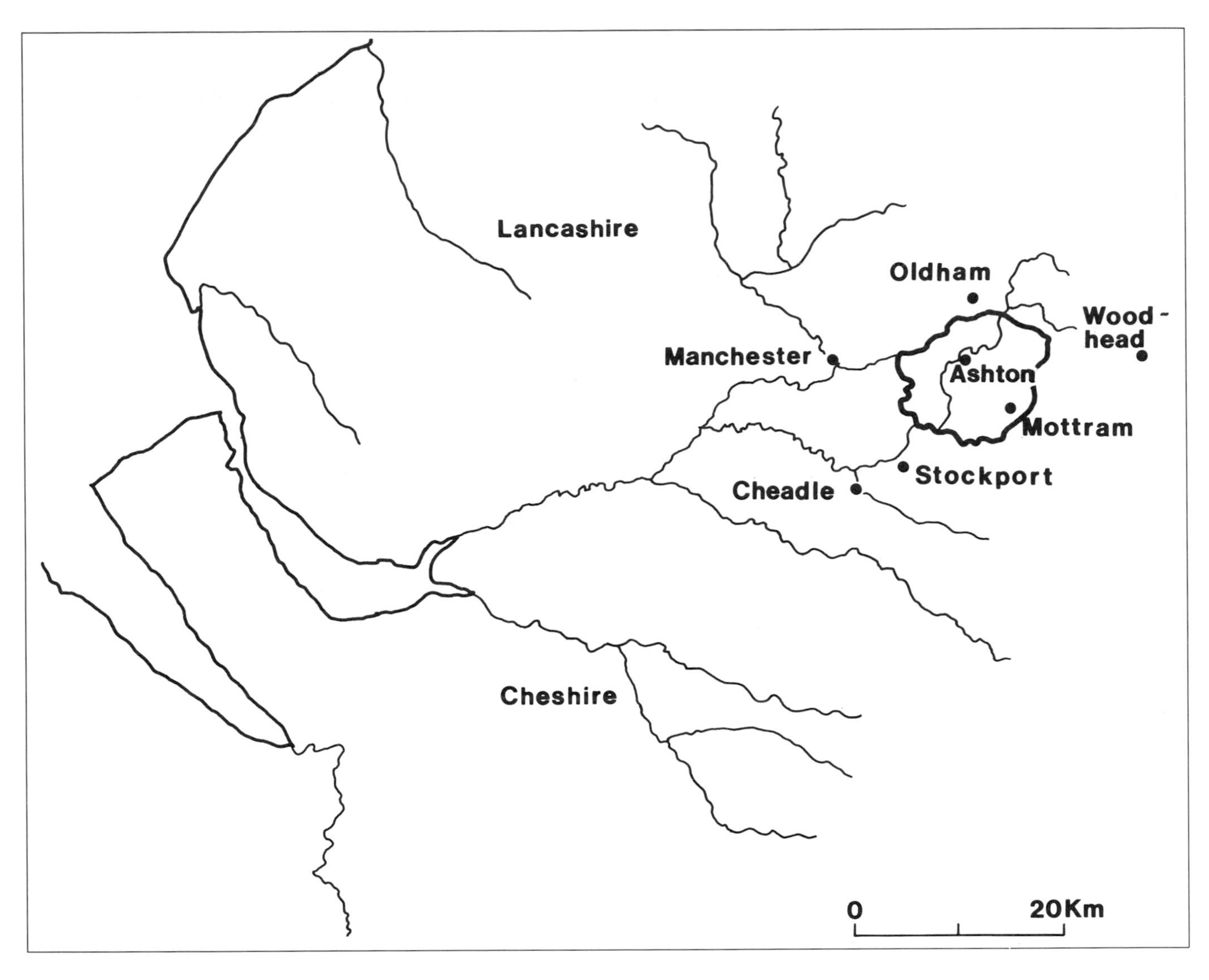

Fig 4.3 The location of Sir Edmund Shaw's bequests in 1487/8.
The location of these donations may serve as a pointer to the local business interests of the Shaw family of Dukinfield, fifteenth-century traders in wool and finished cloth.

tance may also have been boosted by the reliance of the Longdendale economy on livestock rearing, in which case the existence of livestock fairs at Tintwistle would have become especially important in the local economy. If this was the case, the decline in Tintwistle's fortunes in the fifteenth century may have been the result of the wider phenomenon of climatic and population decline. Morris has noted that many of the boroughs that were established in the North-West up to the mid-fourteenth century lay in marginal agricultural areas, like Tintwistle, and probably represented a speculative investment by the local lord, in this case the lord of Longdendale (Morris 1983, 30). In the changed conditions of the fourteenth and fifteenth centuries Tintwistle was unlikely to survive as a major local centre. Its fate was probably sealed by the presence of Glossop on the opposite side of the River Etherow, which by the sixteenth century was the major centre in the valley for local trade, especially in the form of livestock fairs (Scott *et al* 1973, 17-19).

Most of our evidence for medieval trade in Tameside comes from the fifteenth century. Although a settlement had long existed at Ashton prior to that date, the earliest reference to a market here was made in a grant of 1414, confirmed in 1608 (John Rylands Library EGR1/5/1/1 & 2). Butterworth claimed to have seen a manuscript ascribing the granting of a market to 1284, but the lack of any mention of an earlier market in the 1414 grant makes this highly unlikely, and this document must be treated as spurious (Butterworth 1842, 78). The grant gave permission for the holding of two fairs annually in the town of Ashton-under-Lyne, on 1st-3rd July and 10th-12th November, and a market every Monday. The profits from the fairs and markets went to the lord of the manor, and in 1422 totalled 2 marks (26s 8d) (Harland 1868, 102).

During the fifteenth century a number of landowners in Tameside began to acquire land and trading interests beyond southern Lancashire and northern Cheshire. In 1402 Robert Staveley acquired land and interests in Leicester, interests which the family still held in 1457 when Ralph Staveley's will was drawn up in that town (ESRCA/6 & 7). Perhaps the best evidence for the changing economic circumstances of the landholders of the Borough can be found in the records of John Shaw of Dukinfield, a mercer. As we have already seen the economic changes of the later fourteenth century produced an increase in tenant farmers. This in turn gave rise to an ancillary merchant class, who were able to deal readily with the produce of farms and sheep walks. These merchants not only bought the wool clip, but also traded in finished cloth and lent money to the producers.

John Shaw's father held the submanor of the Shagh in Saddleworth in 1379 (Cunliffe-Shaw 1958, 15), but he himself appears to have lived in Dukinfield, where he had business dealings with the Tame valley townships and the markets at Manchester, Stockport and Warrington. Cunliffe-Shaw argues that he was probably the cloth exporter entered in the Hull customs roll of 1391/2 (*ibid*, 16), but fuller details of John Shaw's trade are supplied by the palatine of Lancashire plea rolls. These indicate that the mercer died before 1444, when his widow Margaret and his son Edmund, as executors, claimed debts against Ralph de Assheton of Ashton-under-Lyne and Sir Nicholas de Longford of Withington, the amounts being 50s 7d, and £8 8s 3d respectively. That these figures represented cloth sales can be seen from the details of the claim against Ralph de Assheton who in September 1441 had purchased from John Shaw, at Warrington, 8 yards of woollen cloth, 11 yards of russet coloured woollen cloth, 6 yards of 'checker', and 6½ yards of green coloured woollen cloth of 'kersay' for 42s ½d (*ibid*, 17). In two further pleas the same executors claimed debts of 60s 0d and £8 1s 4d against John Hyde, gentleman, of 'East Halghton', Denton.

Cunliffe-Shaw argued that John Shaw's local business interests were indicated by the bequests made in the will of his son Sir Edmund in 1487/8 (Fig 4.3). These highlighted the pack-horse routes across the southern Pennines via Longdendale and Saddleworth. Sir Edmund granted a gown of Welsh frieze and 12d to 200 poor men in the towns of Saddleworth, Oldham, Ashton, Mottram, Stockport, Manchester and Cheadle. Furthermore he bequeathed 40 marks to each of the churches of Ashton, Stockport and Mottram, in the last case this money being for building a steeple. He also founded a grammar school at Stockport parish church, where his father and mother were buried, and a chantry chapel at Woodhead, at the top of the Longdendale pack-horse route.

Plate 5.1 Hillend, Mottram.
This yeoman farmhouse was built in 1604 by the Redditch family, probably by Raphe Redditch following his marriage in the previous year. The house is one of the earliest of a number of new dwellings constructed in Tameside in the seventeenth century by prosperous tenant farmers.

Chapter 5

Tudor and Stuart Society

'A trew and perfect Inventory of all the goods and chattells moveable and immoveable of the late Alexander Newton of Newton Gentleman deceased, prised and valued the 29th of March 1617 by John Tetlow: Robt Winterbottome, Henry Hurst: Richard Chadwicke: Wm Benisonn and John Turner: 1617

Imprimis at his ffarme house at Roadesse. 4.horses xii Li...

Itm at his house at Newton Hall in plate xiiii silver sponnes weighing xxiiii onzes & a quaterre & halfe an onze: ffourre white bowles weighing:44:onzes one bowle parcell gilt.9.onzes one white salt ii onzes & halfe a quaterre & one little white tunne 5 onzes & a halfe xxii Li...'

(Chester LRO WS Newton 1616/17)

5.1 Landholding Classes and Social Status

Although in the sixteenth and seventeenth centuries the beginnings of industry are discernible in Tameside, the economy of the Borough remained primarily agricultural and the landowning classes continued to dominate local society. However, within that group were great variations in sources of income, wealth and status, which had their origins in the later medieval period. By 1500 there were two major landholders in the Borough: the Asshetons, with lands in Ashton, Stayley and Matley, and the lord of Longdendale, at this date the crown, directly holding the demesne manors of Mottram and Tintwistle (Fig 3.19). A small group of ancient local families still held a number of the medieval manors, including Clayton, Dukinfield, Denton, Hollingworth, Hyde and Newton, although Godley and Matley were divided between two or more manorial lords. Finally, below these manorial landholders were various tenants. In the early sixteenth century they still formed a relatively shadowy group. However, by the late sixteenth and seventeenth centuries there is a body of evidence to enable an assessment of their social and economic importance within the Borough.

The value of land in the politics of the day can be seen in the career of William Brereton, steward of Longdendale from 1525 until his execution in 1536 (Ives 1976, 1-2). He was the sixth son of Sir Randolph Brereton of Malpas, Cheshire, the chamberlain of the county palatine. Born around 1490, he entered royal service, along with his three brothers, and by 1521 he was a groom of the king's chamber, and from 1524 groom of the privy chamber. As holder of this last post he had close contact with the king and in consequence was able to gather a mass of royal offices, which by 1530-1 made him the greatest royal servant in Cheshire and North Wales. He also controlled a number of lucrative royal farms, such as Longdendale from 1525, grants of land in Chorlton from 1527, and the estate of the dissolved abbey of Lesnes in Kent from 1534 (*ibid*, 12-15). His position in Cheshire has been described as the result of deliberate calculation, by which he used his authority to benefit his family and to influence Cheshire politics as the head of a ruling faction. When he held court at Holt Castle in the summer of 1534, he was attended by most of the gentry in Cheshire and the border and was able to hang his chief enemy, John Eyton (*ibid*, 2). In Ives' opinion Brereton's downfall in 1536 was not only because he was implicated in the adultery of Anne Boleyn but also because he had accumulated so much independent power in Cheshire and the Marches (*ibid*). His influence was akin to the old earls of Chester and in the Tudor state his power-base proved to be too much of a threat.

Regionally, in Cheshire and Lancashire, the sixteenth century witnessed the growth of a number of local landed magnates, amongst the most prominent being the Booths of Dunham Massey. This family held the ancient barony of Dunham, their power-base being in the Altrincham area. However in 1515 the family inherited a third share of the Assheton estates in Tameside, through George Booth's mother Margaret

Assheton (ESRCA/13), the other co-heirs being Elizabeth Assheton and Sir Richard Hoghton. With the death of Elizabeth Assheton in 1553, the Booths and Hoghtons each held a half of the Assheton estates. In 1577 the Booths further increased their estates in the Borough by the acquisition of Hattersley manor, through the marriage of Jane Carrington to Sir George Booth (see Chapter 3). In 1581 with the death of Alexander Hoghton, the last male descendant of Alice Assheton, the Booths should have become sole inheritors of the Assheton estates. Instead, the Hoghton share passed unlawfully to Alexander's half-brother and it was not until 1605 and by payment of £5000 that the Booths acquired this inheritance (Farrer & Brownbill 1911, 342; Bowman 1960, 115-17).

Outside the holdings of the Booths and the demesne manors of the lord of Longdendale, some manors were still held and, to a greater or lesser degree, farmed by their ancient manorial families in the late sixteenth and seventeenth centuries (Fig 3.20). These included the Duckenfields of Dukinfield, who owned virtually all that township but farmed directly only 112 acres (Tameside Local Studies Library DD229/1). In 1571 the inquisition post mortem of Robert Hyde recorded that he held a moiety of the manor of Hyde and over 600 acres of land within it (Ormerod 1882, 809). In the 1670s Francis Hollingworth farmed 688 acres of Hollingworth township, although 400 acres of this was moorland (Chester LRO DDX87/+1a). Also in Hollingworth, in 1620 Raynold Bretland of the Thorncliff Hall estate, then a submanor within the township, held 150 acres (Ormerod 1882, 872). In Newton township the virtual lack of tenant farmers suggests that the manorial lords farmed most of the land directly.

Farmland within the Borough not held directly by these major landowners or lesser manorial lords was rented to diverse groups of tenants. Some of these were free tenants, either freeholders, with virtual security of tenure and paying only a nominal fixed chief rent, or tenants for life, where a man's heirs might be required to reapply for the tenancy. Others were tenants-at-will, or customary tenants, holding property for an agreed fixed term and liable to services as well as a monetary rent. Most of the small farmers of Ashton fell into this last category (Bowman 1960, 33-4). By the seventeenth century some free tenants had reached a sufficient level of prosperity for the social distinctions between themselves and the manorial lords to be blurred under the common term of 'gentleman'. The growth of a prosperous class of tenant farmers in the Borough can also be traced in the number of 'yeoman' farmhouses constructed during the seventeenth century (Plates 5.1, 5.2 & 9.2; see also Chapter 9).

Two contemporary surveys from opposite parts of the Borough reflect the diversity of farmers and farms that existed in late sixteenth- and early seventeenth-century Tameside. The Mottram and Tintwistle survey of 1600 (Chester LRO DTW/2477/B/9) and the parish survey of Ashton in 1618 (Butterworth 1823, 155-66) both give details of tenants, size of holding, and rent payable per annum. These show that most land was rented out both in Ashton, under the Booths, and in the demesne manors of the Longdendale lordship, then held by the Wilbrahams. They also illustrate differences in landholdings between the mixed farming zone west of the River Tame and the predominantly pastoral zone east of the river.

In Ashton the average rented holding was around 13 acres. There were, however, a number of larger tenancies held by freeholders, which in the case of Cinderland Hall, at least, amounted to a submanor (Farrer & Brownbill 1911, 345) (Fig 3.7). Among those freeholders styled as 'gentlemen' were John Sandiford of Audenshaw with over 100 acres, Robert Assheton of Shepley with at least 88 acres, the Chadwicks of Taunton Hall with 78 acres, and William Bell of Cinderland Hall with 60 acres. However a few, such as Robert Holland of Denton or Miles Marland of Hurst, called themselves yeomen.

East of the Tame, in Mottram and Micklehurst, the average size of rented landholding was 33 acres, more than twice that in Ashton. The evidence of the 1600 survey is complemented by the wills and inventories for Mottram parish. In the period 1570-1680 these record the presence of 44 'yeoman' farmers, with holdings of 20 to 80 acres, and 81 'husbandmen', who appear to have rented land of less than 20 acres (Powell 1976, 20-1). It is not possible to compare these figures directly with the Lancashire side of Tameside, where only 35% of the wills and inventories extant from 1560-1680 give occupations in their titles, as opposed to 80% from the Cheshire side, but sixteen individuals are named as husbandmen and 29 as yeomen (Earwaker 1879, 1881 & 1887a).

5.2 Poverty and Affluence

Tudor and Stuart society was bedevilled by rapidly rising inflation. Although we can only crudely follow these price rises, there is evidence of a general rise in the order of five times between the decades 1501-10 and 1641-50, when the long upward movement finally ended. However the rise in the price of food in the same period was nearly seven times (Coward 1980, 14). Although monetary factors, such as the debasement of the coinage in the Tudor period, may have contributed to this rise (Platt 1978, 208-9), the major force was population pressure which outstripped the resources of English agriculture. The stresses that this imposed on society surfaced in Tameside in two main areas: the attitude of society towards the poor, and the relative value of wills and inventories for the period.

Local and national government found considerable difficulty in coping with the problems of poverty and vagrancy throughout the sixteenth and early seventeenth centuries, despite the increasing legal penalties. Poverty was initially more extensive in the towns than in the countryside, and as early as 1539 the mayor of Chester had laid down regulations in order to distinguish between the deserving and undeserving poor (Beck 1969, 69). This distinction was carried into succeeding Poor Laws. In 1572 an Act established a compulsory Poor Rate in every parish, whilst in 1598 two statutes were enacted which became the basis of the national poor relief system in England until 1834. The first was concerned with the able-bodied poor who were to be returned to the parish of their birth, the second with the aged or sick poor who were either to be given pensions, food or clothing, or to be put into workhouses. The responsibility for organizing poor relief was placed on the parishes, who were to appoint overseers to administer poor relief and to collect the compulsory rate (Coward 1980, 56).

Although the establishment and operation of the compulsory Poor Rate was extremely patchy in seventeenth-century England, Ashton parish provides some evidence for its working in the Borough. The overseers of Ashton were the churchwardens and their elected assistants and the earliest evidence for their activities is the assessment of Ashton in 1618, which was 'to remain a precedent for the whole parish' (Butterworth 1823, 155-66). The Poor Rate was levied, either annually or more frequently as needs arose, on every landholder in the district, and in that year brought in £2 9s 1d. Although there are few records for the early part of the seventeenth century, a number of documents from the middle of the century indicate the scope of the overseers' activities. In 1651 the overseers were ordered to erect a small cottage to house a 'poor young woman', who had the 'french pox', and who otherwise would not have received shelter (Bowman 1960, 324). A letter of complaint from 1657 grumbled at the way the assessment was raised by the overseers, emphasizing the increasing frequency of the levying of the Poor Rate (*ibid*, 510).

Regular poor relief accounts survive from 1682, usually as part of the churchwardens' accounts (Bowman 1950, 60-82). These record various expenses, including, in 1689-90, 3s for carrying coal to 'Old Grace Saxon', and in 1691-2 expenses for going to Manchester to buy cloth for the poor (Bowman 1960, 510). However the cost of poor relief continued to rise throughout the century, so that in 1699 the overseers had to borrow money on six occasions from the land tax (*ibid*).

As a complement to these official ministrations to the poor, there were also instances of individual philanthropy. In 1619 Elizabeth Booth left in her will the sum of £2 10s per annum to be distributed by the overseers of the poor in Ashton, whilst in 1676 John Sandiforth gave in his will £5 to establish 'a stock for the Towneshipe of Assheton to be paid into the Overseers hands of the sayd Towneshipe for the reliefe of the poor when mony is out of purse' (*ibid*, 509). Nevertheless analysis of the published wills and inventories for the parish in the period 1560-1680 would suggest that such donations were the exception.

Indeed, the parish community was often as vigorous, if not more so, in restricting the numbers of paupers within their jurisdiction and therefore keeping down the escalating cost of poor relief. As early as 1609 the court leet was endeavouring to limit the number of vagrants in the parish, by forbidding the keeping of undertenants (*ibid,* 513). This problem recurred throughout the century, in entries for 1630, 1634-5, 1651 and 1679 (*ibid*). The run of bad harvests in the 1620s and 1630s caused special problems. In 1632 the court leet was forced to emphasize its policy, by restating that no inhabitant of the parish should lodge any vagrants (*ibid*), whereas in the previous year the constables of the parish had stated that, although they had been directed to apprehend any vagrants, none were known (*ibid*, 512). Naturally such processes also worked in reverse; in 1664 Abraham Radcliffe, 'a sturdy vagrant beggar' was forced by the city of Derby to return to his birthplace at Littlemoss in Ashton parish (*ibid*, 514).

Whilst the poor can be discerned in Ashton parish, elsewhere in Tameside they are relatively obscure and information concerning them is difficult to recover. This is not the case for the numbers and wealth of those higher up the social scale. These are revealed by probate inventories or, where no inventory is available, often by wills. However wills are not very satisfactory indicators of total wealth, since they do not always give details of real property. The will of Robert Duckenfield in 1621 mentions his room above the hall, his best horse, and other bequests to his children, but gives no total of his wealth nor any indication of the family's extensive landholding in the township, although a number of pieces of land are mentioned (Chester LRO WS). This might be of less consequence when most of the property was personal, but even here full details are not given. Whilst probate inventories are a more satisfactory indicator of wealth, they too have shortcomings. Some inventories were not totalled, others incorrectly. There is no consistent method of noting the debts, some being included in or

Plate 5.2 Broadbottom Hall, Mottram. Built in 1680, this was the home of the Wilde family, tenant farmers who also leased Broadbottom mill from the lordship of Longdendale.

at the end of an inventory, others in or at the end of a will. If the will pre-dates the inventory by any length of time, some of the debts mentioned will have been paid, making the lists of debts in the two documents at variance with each other. Finally since the inventories were appraised by three or four neighbours, they vary considerably in their detail. The most common habit of the appraisers was to use group headings and not to give details, with the result that much information, such as the composition of livestock holdings and the details of household furnishings, is lacking (Powell 1976, 3). Nevertheless their intensely local nature makes them an invaluable source for this period.

Within Tameside 634 wills and inventories are known covering the period 1560-1680; 309 from west of the River Tame, and 325 from east of the river. For the Lancashire side of the Borough lists of wills are provided by Earwaker (1879, 1881, 1887a), and selective examples have been published by Earwaker (1884) and Bowman (1960). The Cheshire side of the Borough is somewhat better served as a result of Powell's survey of the 227 Mottram parish wills and inventories from the period 1570-1680.

The value of these Mottram wills and inventories varied from 17s 6d to £710 0s 8d, but the median value of personal property was £50. However Ashmore's assessment of the inventories of the Lancashire gentry from 1550-1700 indicated that some of the landowners in the county were extremely wealthy. Sir John Radcliffe of Ordsall's inventory amounted to £1468 on his death in 1590, whilst Sir Cuthbert Clifton of Lytham had goods valued at £3100 in 1634 (Ashmore 1958, 97-8). Of the 35 wills and inventories which Ashmore examined most appear to have been valued at well over £500, making even the largest wills from Mottram look ordinary. When compared with the towns of Manchester, where the average was £101 in the sixteenth century, and Leicester, where it was £28 between 1557 and 1612 (Willan 1980, 84), the Mottram average of £50 does not appear too measly.

However the relatively high level of the Mottram figure, compared to Manchester, may be largely due to the later period covered by the Mottram study, 1570-1680, during which prices rose by four times (Coward 1980, 14).

A closer analysis of the Mottram totals reveals that 18% of all wills and inventories were below £15, 31% between £15 and £50, 23% between £51 and £100, and 28% above £100 (Powell 1976, 25). However wills and inventories worth less than £15 peaked at 37% of all extant documents from 1601-10, and did not approach this figure again until 1671-80 when they accounted for 21% (*ibid*). Furthermore there are hints that the figures for the Lancashire part of Tameside may have been broadly similar to those in Mottram parish. In the period 1660-80 wills and inventories west of the Tame valued below £40 accounted for 48% of the total (Earwaker 1887a), whilst in Mottram parish wills and inventories below £50 accounted for 51% of the total.

When we look at the distribution of the wealth in these inventories it is noticeable that the ancient manorial families accounted for many of the inventories above £100. These included Alexander Newton of Newton at £710 0s 8d in 1617 (Chester LRO WS), Robert Hyde of Hyde Hall, at £272 11s 1d in 1639 (Chester LRO WS), John Hollingworth of Hollingworth Hall at £378 2s 0d in 1662 (Chester LRO WS), and Alexander Hollingworth of Hollingworth Old Hall at £225 18s 6d in 1695 (Chester LRO WS). However there were also yeoman farmers amongst this category, including John Booth of Hall Bank Farm whose inventory in 1646 came to £192 6s 0d (Chester LRO WS), Reinold Goddard of the Waterside at £135 12s 0d, and even carpenters such as John Handford of Newton whose inventory totalled £220 (Powell 1976, 30). West of the River Tame the inventory of Ralph Hall, yeoman, of Moss de Lee, Hartshead, totalled £505 3s 5d in 1663, whilst that of John Cocke of Cocke Bank in Hartshead, a pack-horse trader, amounted to £307 in 1590 (Bowman 1960, 556-61).

Clearly, it was possible to achieve a similar level of wealth as the ancient families by means other than farming, and the most profitable way appears to have been by money lending. It is interesting to note that many inventories indicate that large amounts of money were owing to the deceased. In 1623 Thomas Heape, a yeoman of Stayley, was owed £401 4s 7d out of a total inventory worth £469 6s 3d (Powell 1976, 24); Ralph Hall was owed over £360 out of his total inventory of £505 (Bowman 1960, 558-62); whilst in 1614 Alexander Lees was owed £116 out of a total inventory of £126 2s 0d (Powell 1976, 24).

At the other end of the scale those wills and inventories worth less than £15 in Mottram parish illustrate how little the poor might have. In 1610 Thomas Colyer of Hollingworth had a cow and ten sheep in his inventory of £8 11s 8d, whilst in 1616 Ellin Garsyde of Mottram was a poor widow whose only assets were a cock and goods valued at £5 10s 6d (*ibid*). The inventory of Gregory Knott of Tintwistle totalled 17s 6d at his death in 1671, containing merely cooking utensils, a chaff bed, sheets and blankets and 'one littel tabelle and other odde things' (*ibid*, 30). Between these two extremes lay the mass of inventories, which belonged to husbandmen and yeoman farmers, and which appear to have been largely debt free (*ibid*, 25).

The surviving number of wills from Mottram parish, at 227, represents only 9% of the total of 2497 burials during the period 1570-1680, and further work might well reveal more detail as regards affluence and poverty in the parish. Ashmore pointed out that the wages recorded in the Shuttleworth accounts during the building of Gawthorpe Hall between 1600 and 1605 varied from 2d a day for an unskilled worker to 6d for the more skilled (Ashmore 1958, 60). To this could be added 4d or 6d for food provided, to achieve an idea of contemporary purchasing power for the average labourer. Even though wages were slightly higher in the latter half of the sixteenth century, any inventory over £25, on these figures, would represent the equivalent of two years' work for a member of the wage-earning classes. Thus one might suspect that many of the lost wills and inventories from Mottram belonged to this poorest group of society.

Chapter 6

Civil War Tameside 1642-60

'8-4-45 Duckenfield [Hall]. I received your letter and shall be very forward to further the design upon Chester, it concerning so much the good of this county. But my regt hath lain so long at the siege of Beeston without pay that many of them are grown sick and dis[contented?], so that I cannot persuade them to march presently, unless your gentlemen of the county would be pleased to take order for some pay for them. And that they may find good quarters or good store of provisions where they march, the store whereof of the country is much exhausted, otherwise extreme impoverished. 'your kinsman to command'.'

A letter from Colonel Robert Duckenfield to Sir George Booth (Dore 1984, no 175)

6.1 The Allegiance of the Tameside Gentry

Much of the drama and turbulence of the period 1642-60 involved national figures and national institutions, but these found their counterparts in local politics and society. At first sight Civil War Tameside might appear to be a barren area for such local conflicts, but although the Borough failed to host a major battle, or even a minor skirmish, it did furnish energetic figures who provided the regional expression of the national issues of the time.

Unfortunately there is very little material from this period concerning the majority of the population in the North-West, namely the peasantry, and little more can be found for the urban, yeoman and merchant classes. The evidence that does survive can be classified firstly as personal documents (letters, diaries, estate accounts), secondly as official documents (quarter sessions records, composition records, sequestration orders, financial accounts), and thirdly as contemporary accounts and pamphlets. As such most of the evidence is confined to that problematic group, 'the gentry'.

The gentry

The definition of the term 'gentry' in the seventeenth century has exercised historians considerably, and there are conflicting views as to what made a man a 'gentleman'. As Morrill has highlighted, these reflect the contradictions within contemporary sources in which the same individual might be given differing status titles (Morrill 1979, 69). Cliffe defined the gentry of Yorkshire in the armigerous sense, while Lloyd defined the gentry of south-west Wales as all those who claimed to be so (Blackwood 1967, 77-8). In his study of the Lancashire gentry Blackwood (1978, 4-5) charted a middle course by accepting all those who were consistently styled gentlemen in official records, a view which has been followed by Morrill (1979, 73). When Blackwood's criteria are applied to Tameside, a list of twelve gentry is established (Fig 6.1). On the Lancashire side of the River Tame these gentlemen were identified from the Lancashire freeholders' list of 1600, the muster rolls of 1632, the knighthood composition lists of 1631-2, the lay subsidy rolls of 1641, the protestation rolls of 1642 (Blackwood 1978, 5-6), and the Ashton parish survey of 1618 (Butterworth 1823, 155-66). On the Cheshire side the main primary source is the subsidy roll of 1610 (Driver 1953, 63-4).

In addition to these twelve local gentlemen, there were three absentee landlords who held significant land in Tameside. The foremost of these was Sir George Booth the elder of Dunham Massey, who owned lands in Ashton, Stayley, Matley and Hattersley townships. Secondly there was Sir Richard Wilbraham of Woodhey, who was lord of Longdendale and directly held the manors of Mottram and Tintwistle, and finally there was Isabel Davenport, who was only four years old in 1640. Her lands in Werneth were held in trust by Sir Fulk Lucy of Henbury, whom she eventually married in 1656.

The opposing sides

Who were the Royalist and Parliamentarian gentry of Lancashire and Cheshire? According to Blackwood

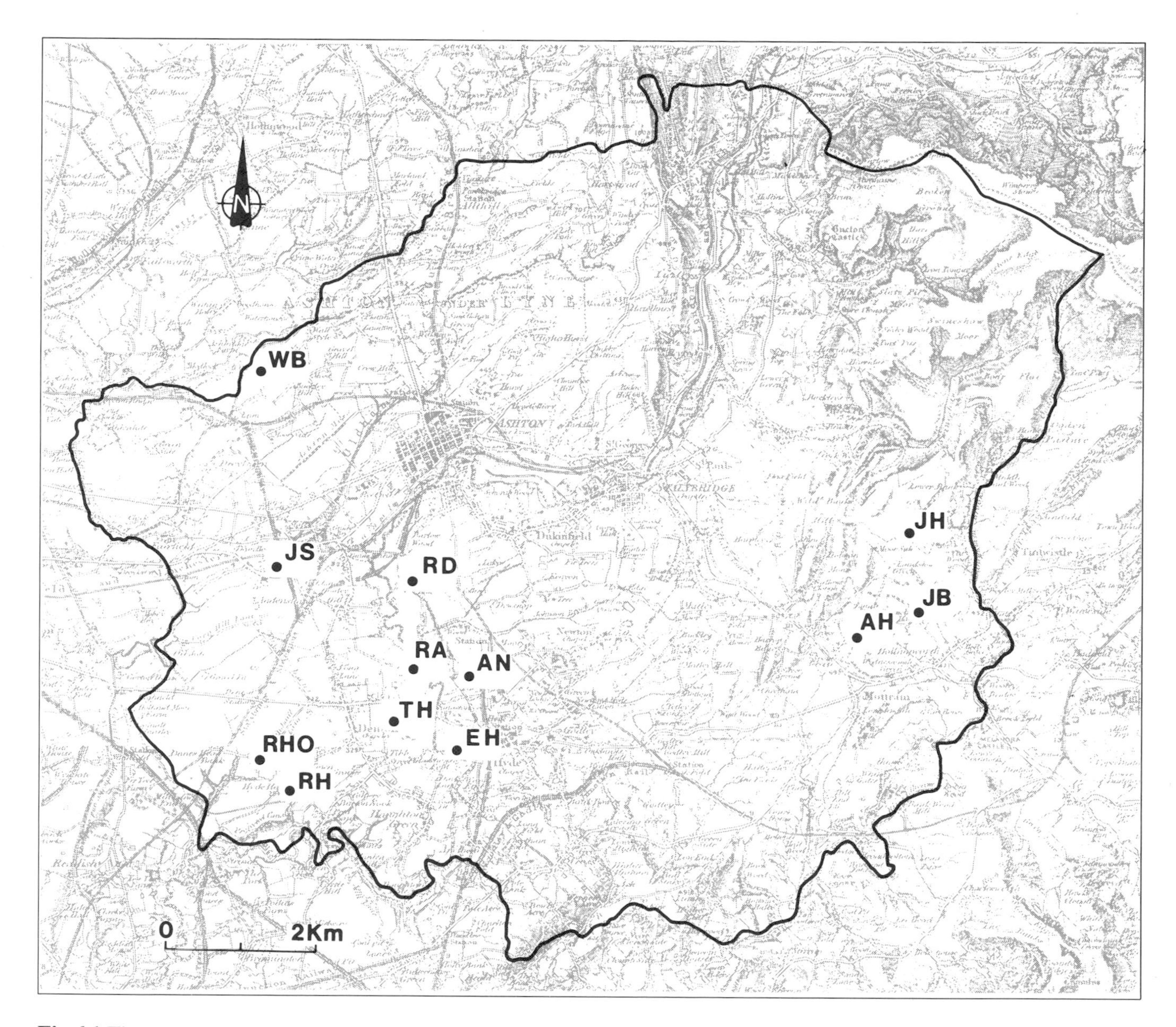

Fig 6.1 The gentry of Civil War Tameside.
Key: RA Robert Assheton of Shepley Hall, Audenshaw; JB John Bretland of Thorncliff Hall, Hollingworth; WB William Bell of Cinderland Hall, Audenshaw; RD Robert Duckenfield of Dukinfield; AH Alexander Hollingworth of Hollingworth Old Hall; EH Edward Hyde of Hyde and Norbury; JH John Hollingworth of Hollingworth Hall; RH Robert Hyde of Hyde Hall, Denton; RHO Richard Holland of Denton; TH Thomas Houghton of Houghton Hall, Denton; AN Alexander Newton of Newton; JS John Sandiford of High Ashes, Audenshaw.

they were those who, at some time between 1642 and 1648, served either the king or Parliament in a military or civil capacity (Blackwood 1978, 37). In this last respect they can be found on the committees and in the offices through which the counties functioned in the 1640s. These posts can be divided into two groups, the first of which constituted the normal organs of county government prior to 1642; these included the deputy lieutenancy, the chief office holder of the county, who was responsible for law and order, and the commissioners of the peace, responsible for administering law and order in each hundred. The second group of posts were new organs of government created by Parliament and the king. These included the military governorships of Chester and Manchester, the first a Royalist centre, the second Parliamentarian; the county committees, which were the chief ruling Parliamentarian body in each county; the sequestration committees responsible for fining, and confiscating the property of, Royalist supporters in each hundred; and the accounts sub-commissioners whose duty it was to raise the monthly Parliamentary financial contribution from each hundred.

However the issue is not as clear cut as Blackwood's definition suggests, and between the two poles of firm Parliamentarians and firm Royalists there were many shades of support. In Cheshire, of over 400 gentry families 360 can be associated with the two 'opposing' sides (Morrill 1974, 14-16). However, Morrill and Dore (1967, 61) have argued that many of the gentry of the county only became involved in the war reluctantly, with many attempting to remain neutral throughout the conflict in an effort to maintain their normal way of life. In Lancashire it may be suspected that many of the 482 families whose allegiance is unknown also attempted to remain neutral, while the figures of 177 Royalist and 91 Parliamentarian families (Blackwood 1978, 46-7) may have included many whose support was only given reluctantly. Furthermore, contemporary sources indicate that many families in the region offered help to both sides, depending on their changing fortunes (Morrill & Dore 1967, 47).

In Tameside we are fortunate in having information relating to all bar one of the gentry, although the quality of this material varies from individual to individual. Ten of the fifteen Tameside gentry gave some support to the Parliamentarian cause during the years 1642-8, one appears to have been a Royalist, while three probably stayed neutral. On the Parliamentarian side nine individuals took an active part in the military or civil proceedings of the Civil War.

Three were commissioned as colonels: Richard Holland, Sir George Booth the elder and Robert Duckenfield. Richard Holland, along with other gentry of south-east Lancashire, came to the aid of Manchester when it was besieged by Royalist forces in 1642 (Ormerod 1844, 45). He was governor of Manchester from 1642-6 (*ibid*, 222-31), involved in the storming of Preston in February 1643 (*ibid*, 74), supposedly responsible for the near loss of Wigan in April 1643 (*ibid*, 226-7), and took part in the battle of Nantwich in January 1644 (Atkinson 1909, 108). However he was accused of lukewarmness and even cowardice by Colonel Rosworm, a foreign engineer serving with the Parliamentarian forces in Lancashire, and was in London early in 1645, probably to answer these charges (Dore 1984, no 20 n 5). By May 1645, however, he was back in Lancashire (*ibid*, no 593), and was probably present at the siege of Lathom House, the principal Royalist stronghold in the county (Blackwood 1978, 68 n 47; Dore 1984, nos 621 & 640). In January 1646 Holland may have assisted William Brereton, the Parliamentarian commander in Cheshire, in the final stages of the siege of Chester (Dore 1990, nos 1101 & 1222). He was also one of the three most active members of the sequestration committee for Lancashire during the period 1643-8, signing at least sixteen documents (Morrill 1974, 83; Ormerod 1844, 90).

Sir George Booth was a major local landholder with extensive estates in northern and eastern Cheshire and south-west Lancashire. In the summer of 1642 he appears to have headed a large body of Cheshire gentry who attempted to remain neutral by threatening the armed intervention of the county against the forces of both king and Parliament (Morrill 1974, 57). However in September 1642 Booth declared for Parliament by not attending the king's summons when he visited Cheshire in that month (*ibid*, 60). He was active in the Parliamentarian civil administration of the county during the period 1643-9, as governor of Nantwich in 1643 (Dore 1966, 33), a deputy lieutenant during 1640-6, an accounts sub-commissioner during 1643-8, and effective head of the moderate Parliamentarian group in Cheshire against Brereton during 1646-9 (Morrill 1974, 83, 182).

Robert Duckenfield began his career at the siege of Manchester in 1642 (Ormerod 1844, 45), but most of his military activities took place in Cheshire, where he was one of Brereton's closest and most trusted commanders (see below).

A further six of the Parliamentarian gentry acted as captains in the period 1642-8. Robert Assheton of Shepley Hall served as a captain in the First Civil War and was high constable of Salford hundred in 1650 (Bowman 1960, 61, 261).

John Bretland of Thorncliff in Hollingworth was an agent of Sir George Booth, leader of the moderate Parliamentarians in Cheshire (Morrill 1974, 216-20). As such he was involved in negotiations with Thomas Leigh at Adlington Hall in 1642, in an attempt to keep the county neutral, and with Robert Tatton at Wythenshawe Hall in 1643, in an attempt to persuade the latter to change to the Parliamentarian side. In 1644 he was appointed sub-commissioner of accounts in Cheshire and seems to have received his military commission from Booth in January 1646 (Morrill & Dore 1967, 68-9; Morrill 1974, 217). Bretland's career highlights the divisions within the Cheshire Parliamentarians during the 1640s. As early as 1645 radicals such as Colonel Duckenfield were complaining about his actions (Dore 1984, no 415). This culminated in 1647 in the sequestration of his estate, worth £556 16s 8d, by the Macclesfield committee on the grounds that he was a Royalist (Morrill 1974, 112). The issue led to a split between the Macclesfield committee and the county committee, so that Bretland was able to fight this decision in London over the next seven years, until he finally cleared his name in 1654 (Morrill & Dore 1967, 67-74).

Edward Hyde of Hyde and Norbury raised troops for Parliament in late 1642 (Earwaker 1877, 429-30; Morrill 1974, 79-80), but contrary to Dore's assertion there is no evidence that he was the Hyde who came to

Plate 6.1 Hyde Hall, Denton.
The hall, built in the sixteenth and seventeenth centuries, was the seat of a junior branch of the Hyde family of Hyde and Norbury. In the 1640s the hall was the home of Robert Hyde, a Parliamentarian who came to the aid of Manchester in 1642 and who was later a member of the Lancashire sequestration committee.

the assistance of besieged Manchester in September 1642 (Dore 1984, no 422 n 1). He raised a further troop of horse in 1642/3, taking them to Nantwich in February 1643 (Hall 1889, 36), and took part in the battle of Middlewich in the following month (Atkinson 1909, 27). By 1645, however, he had resigned his commission (Morrill 1974, 80). Hyde was very active for Parliament in the civil administration of Cheshire, being a deputy lieutenant in the period 1643-6, when he was a lukewarm supporter of William Brereton (Dore 1984, no 159 n 3, no 422 n 1). He supplied money to Brereton in November 1645 and was asked by him to collect Brereton's soldiers' backpay due from Macclesfield hundred, where he may have been on the sequestration committee (Dore 1990, nos 780 & 893; 1984, no 456). He was also a member of the commission of the peace during the period 1646-50 (Morrill 1974, 83, 186).

Alexander Newton of Newton served in Colonel Duckenfield's regiment of foot as a captain during the First Civil War, and probably signed the death warrant of two mutineers at Dodleston in April 1645 (Dore 1984, no 197, no 186 n 1). In 1648 he took part in the Second Civil War campaigns against Lord Hamilton, again probably under the command of Colonel Duckenfield (Ormerod 1844, 312; Dore 1966, 71-2).

John Sandiford of High Ashes, Audenshaw, was described as a captain in 1646 (Bowman 1960, 220), and had probably served under Colonel Richard Holland in Lancashire. However in 1645 he opposed Sir George Booth's method of raising troops from among his tenantry in Ashton-under-Lyne for service at the siege of Chester (Dore 1990, no 846). This so enraged Booth that he complained to Brereton, who in turn wrote to Parliament, recommending exemplary punishment (*ibid*, no 934), but no record survives to show that this was implemented. Sandiford's will of

1676 indicates that he continued to live in High Ashes during the Interregnum and after the Restoration (Preston LRO WS).

Robert Hyde of Hyde Hall, Denton, took part in the defence of Manchester during the siege of 1642 (Ormerod 1844, 45, 52) and in 1643 served on the county commission of ecclesiastical enquiry, set up to review the local conduct of the Church of England (*ibid*, 91). He was also active as a member of the Lancashire sequestration committee during the period 1643-6, and can be found witnessing a number of committee letters to William Brereton, Lords Fairfax and Leven, and to Colonel Robert Duckenfield in 1645 (Blackwood 1978, 65; Dore 1984, nos 585, 594, 640 & 641).

Sir Richard Wilbraham of Woodhey, lord of Longdendale and one of the leading landowners in Cheshire with over 30,000 acres, was active on the civil side of the Parliamentarian war effort (Morrill 1974, 14). Although, with Sir George Booth, he had tried to keep Cheshire neutral in the summer of 1642 (*ibid*, 57), he subsequently declared for Parliament (*ibid*, 65 n) and was arrested by the king on his visit to the county in September of that year (Hall 1889, 25-6). He remained in custody, first in Chester and later in Shrewsbury, and died in April 1643 (*ibid*, 48). He was succeeded by his son Sir Thomas Wilbraham, who was active in the civil administration of Cheshire as a commissioner during the period 1643-6 (Morrill 1974, 224).

Turning to those three individuals who appear to have remained neutral, William Bell of Cinderland Hall, Audenshaw, was one of four itinerant preachers for Lancashire sponsored by the king, and later minister of Huyton church, near Childwall, Liverpool (Bowman 1960, 63; Ormerod 1844, 338). In December 1644 he was named as one of the committee of ordination, set up by Parliament to approve ministers (Ormerod 1844, 208). He was the son-in-law of Robert Hyde of Denton, having married his daughter Anne (Bowman 1960, 220), and the brother-in-law of William Meeke, the Puritan minister of Salford (*ibid*, 260). Despite his later ejection from Childwall in 1662 for nonconformity, and his strong Puritan ties, he appears not to have played an active role on the Parliamentarian side in the 1640s.

Alexander and John Hollingworth of Hollingworth were part of the same family, but John's branch was the senior and resided at Hollingworth Hall (Plate 3.2), whilst Alexander resided at the Old Hall (now known as Mottram Old Hall). Although John's family was probably Catholic – his wife Prudence and her servant Dorothy Goodwin were named as recusants in 1640/1 (Bennett & Dewhurst 1940, 104) – there is no evidence that either family were Royalist, or indeed Parliamentarian.

The only attested Royalist amongst the Tameside gentry was Thomas Houghton of Houghton Hall, Denton. In 1649 he was fined £2 10s for taking up arms against Parliament in the First Civil War (Stanning 1891, 300-1). Nothing more is heard of him, and there are no further records of his activities on the Royalist side in Lancashire.

The wealth and status of the Tameside gentry

Blackwood has amply demonstrated the problems of assessing the economic standing of the gentry in the 1640s. He has argued that 'private archives are quantitatively limited and the papers of the Compounding [sequestration] Committee qualitatively poor' (Blackwood 1976, 55). Nevertheless if we wish to assess the status of the Tameside gentry during the Civil War we need to know at least a little of their economic background. Blackwood suggests the examination of the subsidy rolls immediately prior to 1642 to be probably the best way forward, despite their deficiencies (*ibid*, 55-6).

The Lancashire subsidy roll for 1641 and the Cheshire subsidy roll for 1610 (admittedly out of date by 1642, but the only detailed document readily available for Macclesfield hundred) indicate that two of the three absentee landlords in Tameside, Sir George Booth and Sir Richard Wilbraham, were by far the richest, with incomes in excess of £1000 per annum. Indeed Sir Richard's son and heir, Thomas, had the third largest income in Cheshire in 1648, at £2500 per annum (Morrill 1974, 206). Below these, with incomes between £500 and £750 per annum, were the three most powerful local families in the Borough, the Duckenfields, Hollands and Hydes. Of the remaining families three (Hollingworth of Hollingworth Hall, Newton, and Hyde of Denton) had incomes between £250 and £499, four between £100 and £249 (Houghton, Assheton, Bell and Sandiford), and two below £100 (Hollingworth of Hollingworth Old Hall and Bretland of Thorncliff). Compared to Blackwood's figures for the whole of Lancashire, where 37% of all gentry incomes are unknown (Blackwood 1976, 57), we are fortunate in only having one such case in Tameside, namely Isabel Davenport. More significantly, the percentage distribution of wealth in Tameside is closer to the Yorkshire and Cheshire levels, than to that of Lancashire (*ibid*, 58), suggesting that the Tameside gentry in the mid-seventeenth century were wealthier than their counterparts in many areas of Lancashire. Even so these figures would suggest that there was a considerable gulf between the county elite, such as Sir George Booth and Sir Richard Wilbraham, and the local gentry of the Borough. This difference is best seen in terms of the political power wielded by these two groups before 1642.

Sir Richard Wilbraham was an active JP in the 1620s and 1630s, attending most sessions at Chester and Nantwich between 1625 and 1638. His marriage connections included the rest of the county elite: the Davenports, Delves, Dones, Grosvenors, Savages and Venables (Morrill 1974, 9-14). These he used to good effect in October 1640, when a group of the leading gentry met to draw up a petition asking the king not to call upon the county militia for the war against Scotland. Sir Richard drafted the text and circulated it amongst the gentry of south and west Cheshire, before sending it to Sir George Booth to be canvassed in north and east Cheshire (*ibid*, 30). Sir George Booth was almost as influential as Sir Richard in the two decades before the war. He was one of only three JPs who served on average more than twice a year in the 1620s and 1630s (*ibid*, 9), the others being Sir William Brereton and Henry Mainwaring.

Of the remaining Tameside gentry the Bretland, Duckenfield, Holland, Hollingworth and Hyde families had all gained some political experience in the decades before 1642, but only on the fringes of power. In some cases the generation who took part in the Civil War had no previous political experience. John Bretland's grandfather was a witness to inquisitions post mortem at Stockport and Macclesfield in 1601 and 1602 (Driver 1953, 61), but otherwise the family does not seem to have been involved in the county administration. The Duckenfields, an ancient family whose service to the crown is well attested in the fifteenth century (see Chapter 3), could only muster Robert Duckenfield's appearance as a juror at the inquisition of Sir William Brereton in 1610 in the years before 1642 (Driver 1953, 61). Admittedly Colonel Robert was only eleven years old when his father died in 1630, but the family seem to have been content before that date in their capacity as local lords of the manor. Richard Holland's great-grandfather had been a JP in the mid-sixteenth century (Watson 1966, 57), and his grandfather had been a collector of the lay subsidy in 1600 (Tait 1924, 70), and a JP, responsible for collecting the poor relief, in 1601 (Quintrell 1981, 71). However his father Edward appears to have taken no part in the county administration, and before his appointment as governor of Manchester in 1642 neither had Richard. The activities of the Hollingworths were confined to the early 1620s when John Hollingworth's father and uncle witnessed inquisitions post mortem (Stewart-Brown 1934, 8, 141-2, 193; 1935, 97, 104). The last of the Hydes to be involved in the county administration was Robert Hyde, as a JP and a commissioner for the collection of the 1610 mise in Macclesfield hundred (Driver 1953, 63).

6.2 The Military Career of Robert Duckenfield

Robert Duckenfield's date of birth is unknown but he was baptized on 28th September 1619 (Bulkeley 1889, 116-17). His father succeeded to the family estates in 1621 (Stewart-Brown 1934, 193-4), but died in 1630 leaving Robert, at only eleven years of age, heir to the family manor house and lands (Chester LRO WS). In his will Robert Duckenfield senior left the care of Robert, and the estate, in the hands of his wife, Frances. Robert was involved in the Civil War from the very beginning, assisting the Parliamentarians in their successful defence of Manchester in September 1642 (Ormerod 1844, 45, 52). This early enthusiasm for the Parliamentarian side may be explained partly by his family background during the 1620s and 1630s and partly by the attitude of his relations to the events of 1642.

The Duckenfields were one of a number of medieval families who still held considerable estates in Tameside in the early seventeenth century. The others included the Hydes of Hyde, the Hydes of Denton (a junior branch of that family), the Hollands of Denton, the Newtons of Newton, and the Asshetons of Shepley. All these families had strong marital connections, particularly between the Duckenfields, Hydes and Hollands, stretching back to the fifteenth century (Ormerod 1882, 817). These connections were continued into the early seventeenth century. Richard Holland's will of 1619 (Earwaker 1884, 213-14) indicates that one of his daughters, Jane, was married to Robert Duckenfield's grandfather (Ormerod 1882, 818), that a further daughter, Margaret, was married to William Brereton, father of the Parliamentarian commander (Dore 1990, 33), and that his cousins included Samuel Hyde of Norbury and Robert Hyde of Denton. In the 1621 will of Robert Duckenfield, grandfather of Colonel Robert, Hamnett Hyde of Hyde is mentioned as an executor, whilst in Robert senior's will of 1630 both William Brereton of Handforth, and Robert Assheton of Shepley received grants of land in north-east Cheshire (Chester LRO WS).

Perhaps more significant than these marital ties were the religious leanings of Robert's relations and neighbours in the 1630s. In his will of 1630 Robert's father wanted his wife to have his children educated 'with the advice of Sir William Brereton Baronet [a kinsman and Puritan], Mr Alexander Horrux, Preacher at Deane Church in Lancashire, Robert Assheton of Shepley [a Puritan], and Godfrey Heron of Stockport', or any two of them as she thought best (Chester LRO WS). Further Puritan links can be found in the Hyde and Holland families, who were noted Puritans in both Lancashire and Cheshire during the 1630s (Morrill 1974, 52); the three patrons of the church at Denton were Hamnett Hyde of Hyde and Norbury, William Hyde of Denton and Richard Holland of Denton, all cousins of Robert Duckenfield (Arrowsmith 1985, 7). Furthermore it was Richard Holland who was responsible for the appointment of the nonconformist minister John Angier to the living of Denton church in 1632, with the agreement of the other two patrons (Booker 1855, 70-1). It is thus probable that the young Robert Duckenfield grew up in the Puritan atmosphere of his relations and neighbours.

Thus, when his kinsmen Richard Holland and Robert Hyde of Denton raised troops in aid of the besieged Parliamentarian forces at Manchester in 1642, it is not surprising that Robert followed their lead and did likewise (Ormerod 1844, 45). Towards the end of 1642 he was appointed the Propositions Money collector 'for the whole of Macclesfield Hundred', and had received £625 by the end of 1642 (Hall 1889, 241 no 3; Morrill 1974, 101). When his cousin Edward Hyde, who was living at Hyde Hall during the period 1640-3, started to raise a troop of soldiers for Brereton's forces in late 1642 (Earwaker 1877, 429-30), Robert followed suit, appearing with Edward at Brereton's Nantwich headquarters in February 1643 with a troop of soldiers for his kinsman's use (Hall 1889, 36-7, 243 no 6). This marked the real beginning of Robert's career, and he was to see near continual military service until 1651.

Having brought his troops to Nantwich, where he was described as captain (Ormerod 1844, 36), he was later involved in the battle of Middlewich in March 1643 (Dore 1984, no 91 n 1). His movements during the rest of the year are unclear but according to Dore it was during 1643 that he was made a colonel by Brereton (*ibid*). He was also appointed one of the sequestration commissioners for Cheshire (Morrill 1974, 86). Early in 1644 Robert Duckenfield was involved in relieving besieged Nantwich, an action which culminated in the battle of Nantwich on 25th January 1644 (Hall 1889, 117; Dore 1966, 35-8). His first command was the siege of Wythenshawe Hall in February 1644 (Earwaker 1880, 314); Duckenfield finally took the house on the 25th of the month, after bringing two pieces of ordnance from Manchester (Ormerod 1882, 608 n 'a').

With the advance of Prince Rupert into Cheshire in May 1644 Colonel Duckenfield, with Colonel Mainwaring, was ordered to defend Stockport (Hall 1889, 252 no 20). Contrary to some reports, such as that of William Davenport of Bramhall, that these commanders and their troops fled the advancing prince (Earwaker 1877, 430), Duckenfield and Mainwaring appear to have put up stiff resistance. As Rupert's infantry approached the town on 25th May Duckenfield positioned his men behind hedgerows in ambush. However, they were flushed out by Colonel Washington's dragoons and, after a charge from Rupert, the Parliamentarians were forced back into Stockport, and the town lost. According to the contemporary Royalist pamphlet *Mercurius Aulicus*, all the Parliamentarian cannon, much ammunition and 800 prisoners were captured (Hall 1889, 130 n 2). In October Colonel Duckenfield was at Stockport with other members of the Macclesfield sequestration committee, where he heard William Davenport's defence against the charge of support for the Royalist cause (Hughes 1980, 114).

Although Duckenfield's movements during the rest of the year are unclear the Brereton letter books provide detailed information regarding his service during 1645-6. They indicate that during the winter of 1644/5 he took part in the siege of Beeston Castle and saw action in the Wirral (Dore 1984, no 175). However by April 1645 Duckenfield and his regiment were back in Tameside, from where he was ordered to join Brereton's main army at once, for the siege of Chester (*ibid*, no 174).

The particular difficulties Colonel Duckenfield suffered in raising his regiment during May are well illustrated by the letter books. On 5th May Colonel Duckenfield was still at Dukinfield Hall, from where he wrote a letter complaining of the actions of John Bretland and the presence of a Parliamentarian Yorkshire regiment at Stockport whose actions were discouraging his troops from moving (*ibid*, no 415). This latter difficulty did not stop the colonel from joining his colleagues by the 9th at Nantwich (*ibid*, no 456). The next day he was at Tarporley with most of the rest of the committee of Cheshire (*ibid*, no 469). However the problem of the Yorkshire regiment had not been resolved and on the 12th, when Duckenfield was at Hoole Hall, some of his troops threatened to mutiny over the issue (*ibid*, nos 499-501). From 14th to 16th May he was based at Tarvin (*ibid*, nos 519, 521 & 545), but it is clear that not all his troops had joined him in west Cheshire, for on 26th May Duckenfield was in Mottram trying, unsuccessfully, to encourage a company of foot to march with him (*ibid*, no 638) (Fig 6.2).

For the rest of the year Colonel Duckenfield was closely involved in the siege of Chester, and during most of December he was acting governor of the suburbs, as the senior Parliamentarian officer in the absence of Brereton who was in southern Cheshire. At Chester he was probably based in Brereton's headquarters at the mayor's house in the eastern suburbs (Dore 1990, no 1143 n 2), and was present at the surrender of the city on 1st February 1646 (*ibid*, no 1260).

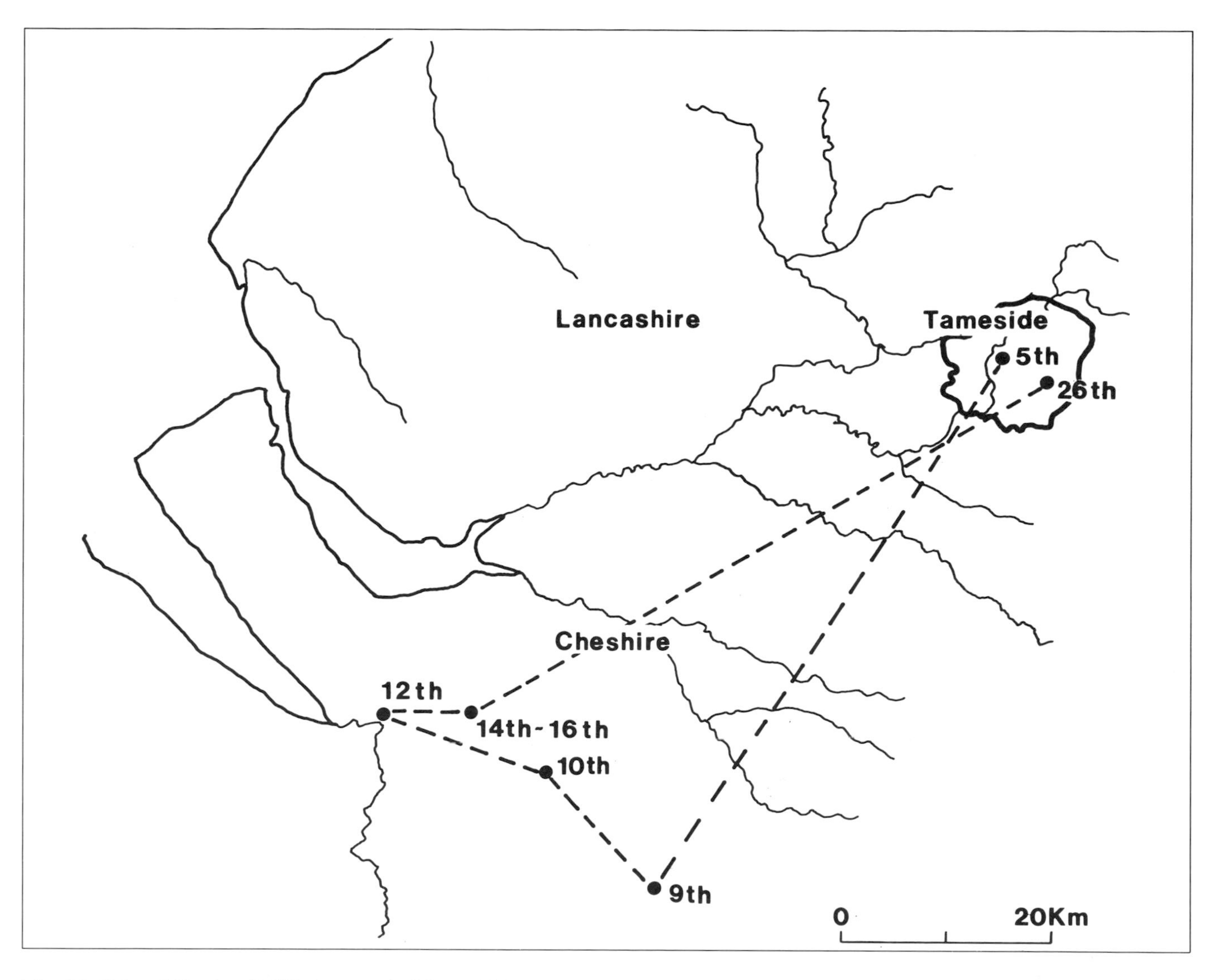

Fig 6.2 Colonel Duckenfield's journey in May 1645.
Duckenfield left Dukinfield Hall to join the Parliamentarian siege of Chester. However the refusal of a company of his troops to leave their homes in Mottram forced him to return to Tameside in an attempt to quell this mutiny.

His movements during much of 1646-7 are unclear, but a letter held by Tameside Local Studies Library throws some light on these otherwise obscure years. This letter was addressed to Mr Jolly of Droylsden, at the end of the seventeenth century or early in the eighteenth century, in reply to a request for information concerning 'Justice Dukenfield's grandfather' (see Appendix 3). Jolly's great-grandfather had written a set of memoirs in which Colonel Duckenfield was mentioned. These indicated that in September 1647 Duckenfield was raising troops on Fairfax's orders for the campaign in Ireland. Furthermore by 3rd February 1648 Duckenfield had 'ye Comand of ye Garrisons of Shrewsbur[y], Lancaster, Liverpool, & Ludlow'. Finally, by 13th February Duckenfield had been charged with the raising of a regiment of foot for the defence of Chester.

The feverish activity recalled in this letter was in response to the outbreak of the Second Civil War. In December 1647 Fairfax wrote to Colonel Duckenfield about the disbandment of his troops (Earwaker 1880, 13). However, as a consequence of the Scots' rebellion in support of the king, Duckenfield was made military governor of Chester and overall commander of Parliamentarian forces in the North-West in February 1648 (Hall 1889, 215). On 24th May 1648 the proceedings of the House of Commons record that Duckenfield held a meeting with the gentlemen of Cheshire and promised to raise a further three regiments of foot and one of horse (Earwaker 1880, 13). With the heightened danger during the Scots' march south in July, Duckenfield was granted a commission of martial law in Chester to try those implicated in a plot to betray the city to Lord Hamilton (Hall 1889, 214-15). It is not clear whether Colonel Duckenfield

Plate 6.2 Dukinfield Hall.
The hall was the ancestral home of the Duckenfield family. Excavation in 1982 showed that there was a hall on this site in the medieval period which was rebuilt in the mid- to late sixteenth century. Further alterations, including the addition of a new wing, were made in the seventeenth century and may have been the work of Robert Duckenfield in the 1620s or his son, Colonel Robert Duckenfield, in the 1650s or later. In the late nineteenth-century the hall was divided into separate cottages. It was demolished in 1950.

fought in the battle of Preston on 17th August, in which Cromwell shattered Hamilton's forces, but it would seem more likely that he remained at Chester.

In 1649 he was made high sheriff of Cheshire and in 1650 governor of Chester for a second time (Earwaker 1880, 13). It is possible that he was reappointed to this last position in response to the landing of Charles II in Scotland in June 1650, and the beginning of the Third Civil War. On 20th August 1650 he was again raising troops for Parliament, this time four regiments of 700 foot (Ormerod 1882, 816). Duckenfield is not mentioned again until September 1651, when as governor of Chester he was directed by Parliament to summon the court martial for the trial of the earl of Derby, who had been defeated at Wigan on 25th August 1651 (Earwaker 1880, 13). Lord Derby was executed on 16th October. Colonel Duckenfield's final military action in this campaign seems to have been the capture of the Isle of Man, where he and Colonel Birch landed on 25th October. The countess of Derby and her children were betrayed to Duckenfield by a Captain Christian and the island captured without any fighting (Ffarington 1856, 156 no 27; Ormerod 1882, 816).

6.3 Change or Continuity?

The popular attitudes and concerns of the period

The impact of the Civil War on the ordinary mass of people is difficult to gauge, but there are a number of documents from the period 1642-60 that throw a little light on the attitude not only of the gentry, but also of those groups below them in society. In the 1650s most of this material comes from the quarter sessions records and the occasional private memoir or letter. However in the 1640s the common place book of William Davenport of Bramhall, kept between 1613 and 1650 (Morrill 1975, 118), and the archive compiled by William Brereton during 1645-6 (Dore 1984; 1990) allow a glimpse of the collective feelings of particular groups of tenantry recruited by Edward Hyde and Robert Duckenfield.

Davenport's common place book records a petition from a group of 24 of his tenants in Bramhall on 17th September 1642, in which they urged their lord to take up arms. Their petition concluded with the words

> 'For howsoever wee would not for the world harbour a disloyall thought against his Maiestie yett wee dare not lifte upp our handes against that honorable assembly off Parlament, whom we are conffydently assured doe labour both for the happiness of his Maietie and all his kingdome' (Earwaker 1877, 430).

Davenport was keen to remain neutral and attempted to defuse the situation by delaying a reply. However the following day the petitioners and other tenants took matters into their own hands by enlisting in the regiment of Edward Hyde of Hyde and Norbury (*ibid*). For tenants to follow their manorial lord into battle might suggest traditional feudal loyalty, but to petition their lord in support of Parliament, and then to join Hyde's regiment suggests that this is an authentic record of 'popular' tenant feeling.

Towards the end of the First Civil War there is evidence for a very different aspect of the independence of the local tenantry, that is an unwillingness to serve. In November 1645 Sir George Booth the elder attempted to raise troops in order to aid William Brereton in the siege of Chester. He recruited a number of companies in Wilmslow and Bowdon, where some of his own tenants refused to serve (Dore 1990, no 846). However his greatest problems arose when he attempted to recruit 200 tenants from the parish of Ashton-under-Lyne. Booth invoked covenants in their leases in order to force them to join the siege of Chester (*ibid*). John Sandiford of High Ashes in Audenshaw objected to Booth's action, claiming it to be without precedent, with the result that only 50 tenants responded to Booth's summons (*ibid*; see also above, p 71).

During 1645-6 the Brereton letter books contain a number of references to complaints made by the troops under Duckenfield's command. These grievances fell into two categories: firstly discontent over backpay, secondly disquiet at the quartering of other soldiers in the neighbourhood of Mottram parish. Arrears of pay for the troops was a national problem, and one that persisted throughout the three Civil Wars. In April 1646 a petition to Parliament estimated that the arrears to troops stood at £80,000 (Morrill 1974, 126). In April 1645 Duckenfield complained twice to Brereton about the lack of pay, arguing that his regiment had been so long at the siege of Beeston Castle without pay that they were now reluctant to march (Dore 1984, nos 175 & 206). Finally in May 1645 Duckenfield was forced to return to Mottram in an attempt to encourage his troops to move but the soldiers complained that Captain Booth's regiment had been paid whilst they had not (*ibid*, no 638). By the middle of 1647 Duckenfield calculated that the accounts due to himself and his officers and men amounted to £5443 paid and £4056 in arrears (Morrill 1974, 127).

However there was an issue even stronger than the lack of pay: the fate of their homes and families. This caused Duckenfield's troops to desert en masse twice, in March 1644 and in May 1645 (*ibid*, 154). In the first instance Duckenfield complained that his soldiers had gone back to the land and refused to return for fear of their homes being plundered (*ibid*). On the second occasion his troops actually presented a petition to Brereton stating that supplies were being taken from their homes by Parliamentarian troops of the Yorkshire regiments (Dore 1984, no 501).

The evidence for popular attitudes during the 1650s comes from different sources, consisting mainly of judicial and manorial records, and private letters. In particular the quarter sessions records indicate that life for most people continued much as before. They contain much material which is 'varied but rarely political' (Mackey 1983, 11), with disputes over wills, common land and apprentices more notable than any political comments on the times. In 1652 Lawrence Bennett petitioned the justices in Manchester for a licence for an alehouse in Ashton-under-Lyne. The petition included the signatures of Robert Duckenfield and Robert Assheton (Bowman 1960, 309-10). However there is no record of the suppression of alehouses in the town, as Major General Worsley attempted to do throughout Cheshire (Mackey 1983, 26).

A notable exception to these ordinary concerns is a series of letters and petitions to the Cheshire justices in the period 1649-51. These are concerned with the effects of the Civil Wars, in particular the provision of pensions for many of Colonel Duckenfield's troops (Bennett & Dewhurst 1940, 135-6), a matter in which Duckenfield himself intervened, with a letter to the Cheshire committee for the militia (*ibid*, 117). However, as the diary of Thomas Mainwaring of Cheshire indicates, even the life of an active justice during the 1650s could be routine. Mainwaring was one of those who continued to co-operate with successive governments, attending the assize courts, quarter sessions and the monthly assessment meetings (Mackey 1983, 21) yet he did not find this incompatible with sharing a common life with Royalists. His diaries show that he often dined with both Royalists and Parliamentarians at the same table (Morrill 1974, 261). Perhaps the most surprising aspect of these diaries is the lack of political news or views. He still travelled around meeting family and friends, and they returned the compliment, but there is a noticeable lack of information from other parts of the country. What seems to have mattered to Mainwaring were family and county affairs.

Further material suggesting a return to more settled times and relationships during the 1650s can be found in the manorial records of Ashton-under-Lyne and Hattersley. Both manors were owned by Sir George Booth the elder at the beginning of the period. Despite the passing of these lands to his son, the younger Sir George, who was gradually alienated by the Republic, the local manorial administration continued to function as it had done throughout the 1640s. A complete record of the suite rolls from Hattersley survives for the period 1634-57, although the court book only covers the period 1621-46 (Manchester LRO M95 Chapman Papers Box 13). These indicate that there was continuity of tenant families, with no major change in the tenant-lord relationship. The court leet records from Ashton-under-Lyne also survive from the 1650s. The parish concerns included the proper running of alehouses (Bowman 1960, 308), the weekly market (*ibid*, 293), the boundaries between Ashton and Dukinfield (*ibid*, 605) and provision for the poor (*ibid*, 510). However there was also much relating to the usual concerns of tenants; the mending of fences, pasture rights, rights to woodland and the moss (*ibid*, 55). Occasionally wider political matters did intrude, but only obliquely. Thus when the court met in April 1649, immediately after the abolition of the monarchy, it was held 'for the Custodians of the Liberties of England'. That held in October 1651 was 'for the keepers of the liberties of England by authority of parliament', whilst in 1655 the court was held 'for his highness Oliver Lord Protector of the Commonwealth' (*ibid*, 592-3).

However the court records from Werneth manor do indicate a disruption in the tenant-lord relationship that in part is attributable to the disorders of the period. The manorial court book survives for the period 1588-1658, but there is a break between 1640/1 and 1657 (Chester LRO DAR/I/16). When the records resume, they are once more concerned with ownership of the rights to crops, the repair of farm buildings and their use. When Sir Fulk Lucy took control of the manor in October 1657, he discovered that the tenants had banded together and kept their own court book during the preceding sixteen years. Thus the first record of the court meeting for 1658 was an angry note stating

> 'Item We ffind that there is Another Court Booke Kepte ffrom us whiuch wee ought to have hande with this Court Booke' (*ibid*).

In the resumed records for 1657/8 it is clear that some tenants had sold their farms during the period 1641-57 without the lord's permission. For instance one tenant, Robert Higham, of Higham Farm, had been busy enlarging his estates by buying land from Reginald Thorniley and Thomas Hyde.

The opinions of those groups below the gentry appear to have been recorded only when they touched the lives of the gentry or impinged on the manorial or judicial system. The information that does survive would suggest that such groups, like many of the gentry, were only concerned with wider political issues when they were directly affected, either by the fighting or by the decisions of the national government. It was the local manor and township which were of prime importance throughout the period.

Politics and power 1642-1700

We have already seen that most of the Tameside gentry were on the fringes of county power prior to 1642. How far did the period 1642-9 lead to a change in the long-term political and social fortunes of these families? During the 1640s there was little overall change in the composition of civilian administrators in either Cheshire (Morrill 1974, 30, 83) or Lancashire (Blackwood 1978, 77-88). An obvious feature of this period was the continuity of pre-war gentry families in many of the key civilian appointments. Pre-war deputy lieutenants, like Sir George Booth, sat on the wartime Cheshire county committee. Indeed Sir George's dominance in the county, as head of the moderate Parliamentarian party, steadily increased in the period 1642-9, being both an accounts sub-commissioner from 1643-8 and a deputy lieutenant (Morrill 1974, 182). The Wilbraham family were also active in the Parliamentarian civil administration. Although Sir Richard the elder had died in the custody of the king in 1643 (Hall 1889, 48) his son and heir Sir Thomas remained a JP and a supporter of Parliament for much of the 1640s (Morrill 1974, 224).

However three families, whose service records in the decades prior to 1642 were virtually non-existent, became actively involved in the period 1642-9. The roles of Richard Holland and Edward Hyde in local administration have been noted above. Robert Duckenfield found time between his military duties to be involved in the civilian administration as a deputy lieutenant, a local sequestrator and a JP (Bennett & Dewhurst 1940, 135-6). Thus Blackwood's observation that in Lancashire the need for more men in government during and after the war led to a shift in power towards those families who previously had little part in county affairs (Blackwood 1978, 87) is almost certainly applicable to Cheshire as well.

The cost of quartering Parliamentarian troops, and the upkeep of the Parliamentarian war effort in Cheshire, affected a number of families in Tameside, most of whom were not active in either the military or civil war effort. In particular there survives a series of accounts from Hollingworth township compiled in August 1645 (Earwaker 1880, 150-2). These give costs for quartering men and horses and supplying arms and victuals, and indicate the kind of burden feared by Duckenfield's troops when they mutinied in May 1645. The greatest sum owed was to the Hollingworth family, who had remained neutral throughout the conflict despite their Catholic leanings. Alexander Hollingworth of the Old Hall was owed £82 6s 8d, whilst John Hollingworth of the manorial hall was owed £70 16s. Neither gentleman was particularly wealthy. John's total estate was worth only £378 when he died in 1662 (Chester LRO WS), his income being little more than £300 per year, whilst Alexander's income was less than £100 per year. The sums involved represented a considerable portion of their wealth, and may in part account for the decline in the estates of these two families over the next generation. When Alexander's son John died in 1686 the Old Hall estate was worth only £133 18s 6d (Chester LRO WS). Other gentlemen in the Hollingworth accounts who incurred costs included John Booth of Hall Bank Farm who was owed £20 5s, although at his death in January 1646 his estate was worth £192 6s (Chester LRO WS). Finally John Bretland of Thorncliff, who later fell foul of the radicals within the Cheshire Parliamentarians (see above, p 70), was also owed £20 5s. Since at least three of these individuals remained either neutral or were sequestered, there must be a suspicion that those who were not regarded as being wholly loyal were made to suffer the most.

During the 1650s there was a noticeable decline in the number of gentry families serving as members of both the Lancashire and Cheshire county committees, particularly those greater gentry in office prior to 1649. Although the greater gentry formed a majority of committee members before this date, after they were a minority (Blackwood 1978, 82; Morrill 1974, 257). Furthermore this situation was repeated in other offices within Lancashire. During the Interregnum two of the twelve Lancashire sheriffs were recently created gentlemen and two were only merchants (Blackwood 1978, 85). According to Blackwood the greatest social change in Lancashire after the Civil War occurred in the county militia. Between 1628 and 1642 all 29 Lancashire militia officers belonged to the greater gentry, but when the Lancashire militia was reorganized in 1650 of 27 officers only two belonged to this class while ten were not even 'plain gentlemen' (*ibid*, 85-6). In Cheshire the membership of the county committee and the commission for peace seems to have been confined to a narrow group of ten to twelve individuals during the Interregnum who included few of the greater gentry. Of the ten most active justices between 1646-59 only one, Sir George Booth senior (who died in 1652), was of the county elite (Morrill 1974, 258). Morrill concluded that this non-participation was the result either of repulsion at the king's execution or resentment at the continuing power of the army (*ibid*, 257).

This disillusionment can be seen clearly in the impact of the Interregnum on those Tameside families who were part of the county government before 1649. Sir Thomas Wilbraham was excluded from the administration in Cheshire for openly opposing the execution of the king (*ibid*, 224). Whilst Sir George Booth senior continued to serve the Cheshire county administration until his death in 1652, his heir, Sir George Booth the younger, refused to co-operate with the Republican government because of the abandonment of Parliamentary rule (*ibid*, 318). Furthermore, when Booth the younger attempted a royalist rebellion in Cheshire in 1659 many of the gentry who did not support the uprising remained neutral. Only radicals like Robert Duckenfield and Richard Holland came to the defence of the Republic, most of the landowners of Cheshire, and probably Lancashire, having been alienated (*ibid*, 311-12). Robert Duckenfield himself, although elected to Parliament in 1653 and placed on the Council of State in the same year, was sufficiently disillusioned with Cromwell to refuse his instructions to raise a troop of horse during the Royalist uprising by Penruddock in March 1655:

> 'I desire to imitate Caleb and Josua in the wildernes, as neare as may be, and not to seeke a confederacy with those, who limitt God to their passions, and against whom God hath an evident controversy etc. I believe firmely that the roote and tree of piety is alive in your lordship, though the leafs theirof, through abundance of temptations and flatteries, seeme to mee to be withered much of late' (*ibid*).

The only individual involved in the county governments of the 1640s who remained so throughout the 1650s was Edward Hyde. He was one of the ten most active justices during the period 1649-59 signing 144 documents (Morrill 1974, 258). Hyde was also one of

Plate 6.3 Denton Chapel.
This nineteenth-century photograph shows the chapel prior to its alteration in 1872. The timber-framed building was erected in 1531-2 as a chapel of ease. In 1632 Richard Holland persuaded the patrons of the chapel to accept the nonconformist preacher John Angier as chaplain. Angier remained in this post after the Restoration until his death in 1677.

Cromwell's candidates for the Parliamentary election of 1656 (*ibid*, 288). However by 1659 he was sufficiently disillusioned with the Republic to support Peter Brooke, head of the party of alienated Cheshire landowners, in the election of 1659 (*ibid*, 295).

In Lancashire Blackwood has argued that over half of those families who had supported Parliament or the Republic had lost their gentility by the end of the century and that, although this was in part due to the extinction of the male line, the largest group of affected gentry were those who held office after 1648 but were denied it after the Restoration (Blackwood 1978, 101). In Tameside it is difficult to observe this pattern. Edward Hyde, who had served the Republic throughout much of the 1650s, was made a commissioner of the peace after the Restoration (Morrill 1974, 310). Colonel Duckenfield was tried after the Restoration for his part in the trial of the earl of Derby in 1651 and is said to have been 'afterwards imprisoned in the county' on the charge of conspiring to overthrow the monarchy (Ormerod 1882, 816). Duckenfield died in September 1689 and was buried at Denton church (Bulkeley 1889, 117). In spite of the active part which he had played in the Civil War and the Republic, his son received a baronetcy in 1665 (Ormerod 1882, 816). Indeed by the end of the century the Duckenfield family had increased its wealth, with the acquisition of lands in Mobberley (Chester LRO D/73). Furthermore although Colonel Duckenfield had retired from county politics his son was high sheriff of Cheshire in 1675 (Earwaker 1880, 15).

Many of the other gentry families recorded in Tameside before 1642 were also recorded as such after the Restoration. The hearth tax returns for Salford in 1666 record Robert Assheton, William Bell, Robert Hyde and John Sandiford as being of gentry status (Tait 1924, 106, 114). The Asshetons, Sandifords and Hydes were all still in possession of their estates and social position at the end of the century (Booker 1855, 33, 137), although only Robert Hyde's son seems to have been active in the county administration during the latter half of the seventeenth century. As for Sir

George Booth the younger, the reward for his rebellion in 1659 was his elevation to the peerage as the first Lord Delamere in 1661 and the return of the family's estates (Bowman 1960, 119).

Some families did disappear. The male line of the Hollands of Denton and the Newtons of Newton was extinct by the end of the seventeenth century (Farrer & Brownbill 1911, 314; Ormerod 1882, 859). However of the three gentry families whose estates were either sequestered or had troops billeted on them in the 1640s only one, that of Thomas Houghton of Houghton, seems to have disappeared by 1666. Both branches of the Hollingworth family continued to reside in the township well into the eighteenth century, albeit as minor local gentry who took no part in county government (Ormerod 1882, 870-1). The Bretland family, whose troubles in the late 1640s and early 1650s were extensive, prospered greatly in the latter half of the seventeenth century, acquiring the manors of Werneth and Romiley from the Lucy family between 1662 and 1699 (*ibid*, 872; Earwaker 1880, 109).

Despite the fact that Tameside appears to have been a strongly Parliamentarian and nonconformist area, the long-term effect of this support on the gentry of the Borough would appear to have been minimal. We cannot conclude, as Blackwood has done for Lancashire as a whole, that those who held power in the 1640s and 1650s were excluded from it after the Restoration, nor that the economic fortunes of the Parliamentarian gentry were seriously impeded by the return of the king.

Chapter 7

Agriculture and Industry *c* 1500-1700

'Anne Bower de Goden brooke drowned in a pitt upon ye Litlemore'

(Mottram parish registers, 7th February 1617, Chester LRO MF41/1)

7.1 Agriculture

Evidence for agricultural practice in Tameside during the sixteenth and seventeenth centuries can be found in a variety of sources, but two are of special significance, the first being wills and inventories. For the period 1560-1680 a total of 325 wills and inventories survive from the Cheshire side of the Borough, and 309 from the Lancashire side. The use of these sources is not without problems, not least of which is the question of how many such documents were made and have survived (see also Chapter 5). Nevertheless, they provide valuable information about the distribution of wealth, agriculture, industrial activities and domestic arrangements from the poorest labourer to the wealthiest landlord. The second major source comprises the manor court rolls, which provide useful information on manorial customs, land tenure, rents and agricultural practice. The Ashton court roll, which begins *c* 1600, has been partially published (Bowman 1960). However two further court rolls survive which are less well known. For Hattersley the court book survives from the period 1621-46 and the suite rolls from 1634-57 and 1689-92 (Manchester LRO M95 Chapman Papers Box 13). For Werneth the court book survives from the period 1588-1658 (Chester LRO DAR/I/16).

In assessing the agricultural economy of Tameside in this period two factors need to be taken into account, the regional background and influence of climate. As Kenyon has recently noted (1991, 16), the consistently low level of rural productivity in the North-West is reflected in the wealth and population statistics available for the medieval and early modern period. In 1334 Lancashire's tax assessment was the lowest after that of Northumberland (*ibid*). The lay subsidy of 1524/5 indicates a similar position and matters do not seem to have improved significantly during the rest of the sixteenth century (Sheail 1972, 117-20) nor by the end of the seventeenth century (Tait 1924, xxxiii-v).

The importance of climatic influence on agricultural potential has already been stressed for the medieval period and applies equally to the sixteenth and seventeenth centuries. Although the nadir of climatic deterioration was reached in the 1590s (Lamb 1982, 203), when England was affected by a succession of appalling harvests (Coward 1980, 15), the climate did not improve significantly until after 1700. In Tameside the marginal limit for cereal cultivation remained around 100m OD, although land above this level still supported pasture (Fig 4.1). The agricultural fate of land above this marginal limit should be an indication of the stresses within the economy of Tameside during this period.

Mixed farming

Two of the four farming regions identified by Thirsk in Lancashire and Cheshire dominated early modern Tameside. These were the Lancashire mixed farming region, which extended from Preston in the north to Manchester and Ashton-under-Lyne in the south (Thirsk 1967, 86), and the Cheshire pastoral region which included Mottram parish in the north-east (*ibid*, 83). West of the River Tame the Lancashire mixed farming region included the townships of Denton, Haughton and Droylsden, as well as the Audenshaw and Ashton town divisions of Ashton parish. The remaining divisions of Knott Lanes and Hartshead appear to have been marginal areas for mixed farming, lying above 100m OD. East of the River Tame the mixed farming area included most of the lowland townships of Dukinfield, Newton and Hyde. The evidence suggests that the two most important elements of the agricultural economy in this area were grain production and stock rearing. However there is also evidence for dairy, sheep and pig farming.

Plate 7.1 Audenshaw Lodge Barn.
This brick barn was built in the late seventeenth-century. Audenshaw is situated in the low-lying western part of the Borough which in the seventeenth century supported a mixed farming economy.

Cereal production, despite the deteriorating climate, continued in the western part of the Borough during the sixteenth and seventeenth centuries. In many of the inventories of the period grain crops are classified under the general heading of 'corne'. It seems likely that, at least west of the River Tame, this was often oats, although there is also evidence for the growing of barley, malt, rye and wheat crops. In March 1574, for example, William Bagenlay of Haughton had 10s worth of meal and malt, whilst in 1598 Ralph Hyde, a labourer, had 40s worth of oats and barley, a figure which may reflect the high prices of the 1590s resulting from the disastrous harvests of the period (Young 1985, 22). Tithe documents for Denton and Haughton from 1693 provide a unique insight into the farming practices of this area, since they give the names of tenants together with the amounts of oats or barley and the sum agreed for the tithe. These indicate that at the end of the seventeenth century around one third of barley was grown in proportion to oats in Denton, whilst in Haughton barley was one seventh of the total crop (*ibid*, 22; Preston LRO DDEg 4d/13).

In Audenshaw and Ashton there is evidence that enough surplus grain was produced to sell at markets outside that at Ashton. In 1647 three men from Ashton parish were fined 'ffor measuringe Malt before the Market bell did Ring' in Manchester (Earwaker 1887b, 14-15). One of the offenders, William Walker, committed the same offence in the following February, while in 1650 Miles Mayall and Anthony Audenshawe were fined at Manchester 'for sellinge wheat before the Market Bell was rung' (*ibid*, 20-1). The use of fertilizers, in the form of marl, is attested from the fifteenth century in Ashton manor (Bowman 1960, 404), but in the seventeenth century thcrc is also evidence for manuring, the Ashton court book recording judgements on this matter in 1629 and 1655 (*ibid*,

403). However, within the lowland region of Tameside there is little other indication of agricultural improvement, beyond enclosure (see below).

The second major element of the mixed farming regime of this area was stock rearing. The relative importance of these two elements within western Tameside is difficult to assess, but there is at least one documented instance of the growing importance of cattle rearing in the seventeenth century. Through a series of wills and inventories Young has traced the development of the farming interests of the Baguley family of Haughton during the late sixteenth and seventeenth centuries (Young 1982, 29; 1985, 24-5). In 1594 William Baguley had cattle worth £3 6s 8d, and corn valued at £1 14s. He was also a licensed trader and leased a further corn crop. The will of Robert Baguley in 1619 indicates that the value of the cattle had risen to £13, with £7 10s worth of 'corne'. In 1634 Alexander Baguley had corn growing in the ground worth £4 but by far the most important element of the farm were his cattle, now worth £34. Even when allowance is made for inflation this was a substantial increase over their value in 1619. The family also hired and sold cattle, practices more noticeable in Mottram parish.

Figures for the average herd size in western Tameside are not readily available, but the average for the Lancashire mixed farming region was ten (Thirsk 1967, 87). These herds usually consisted of cows, calves and young bullocks. The will of Richard Barlow of Haughton, for example, from 1546 records that he had three twinters (two year old cattle), two stirks (one year old cattle), two cows and two calves (Young 1985, 22). Along the River Tame during the late sixteenth and early seventeenth centuries herd sizes among the valley townships could be as large as those in the pastoral regions of Tameside. In 1617 the inventory of Alexander Newton of Newton Hall records 22 kine, eleven stirks, ten calves, eight oxen and two bulls (Chester LRO WS). In Ashton in 1590 John Cocke of Cocke Bank had eight kine in calf, seven stirks, three calves, three heifers in calf, two barren kine, and one fat heifer (Bowman 1960, 557).

Such differences in herd sizes in part reflect the variations in wealth and the size of landholdings within the Borough. The Ashton parish survey of 1618 (Butterworth 1823, 155-66), and the Denton and Haughton surveys of 1645 (Booker 1855, 7-8, 133-4) indicate that in the lowland townships there was a great difference between the mass of small farmers and the few large freehold farmers. We have noted in Chapter 5 that the average holding of the customary tenants of Ashton parish in 1618 was just 13 acres, whereas most of the freeholders, such as William Bell, John Sandiford or Robert Assheton, had large estates of 60 acres or more. A similar pattern of landholding can be identified elsewhere in the Lancashire lowlands (Thirsk 1967, 87). Furthermore a number of the farmers of lowland Tameside were engaged in a wide range of activities. In 1617 Alexander Newton, besides his 53 cattle, had 12 acres 'of corne in the ground', oats, barley, and wheat crops, 33 sheep, and turkeys, hens, geese, bees and coal-mining interests (Chester LRO WS). John Cocke of Cocke Bank despite having 24 cattle, £12 worth of corn, and £8 worth of hay in 1590, made most of his money as a pack-horse trader (Bowman 1960, 556-8). Abraham Cooke of Denton, yeoman, not only had oats, barley and hay worth £8 13s 4d when he died in 1679, but he was also in possession of a smithy and 2cwt of iron (Young 1985, 25). In 1630 Robert Booth of Haughton owned horses worth £4, beef £8, hay 50s, pigs 40s, hens 4s and five spinning wheels valued at 5s 6d (*ibid*, 24). The Baguleys of Haughton, in addition to growing grain and raising stock, were also involved in woollen production (see below).

Pastoral farming

East of the valley-side manors of Hyde, Newton and Dukinfield the countryside was dominated by pastoral farming, although as with most of lowland Tameside there was considerable diversity in subsidiary incomes. The agricultural economy of the northern Cheshire plain was dominated by pasture land and cattle, although farmers also supplemented their income with crops such as barley, oats, wheat, vetches, peas and beans (Thirsk 1967, 83). Eastern Tameside lay on the extreme north-eastern edge of this area and, along with the upland areas west of the River Tame around Quick Edge and Hartshead Pike, formed a physical link with the pastoral region of eastern Lancashire.

Mottram parish during the period 1570-1680 has been studied in detail by Powell, and the following discussion owes much to her survey. The likely effect of the deteriorating climate on the upland areas of the Borough has been noted above. Significantly between 1590 and 1620 the references to ploughs and harrows, as a proportion of the extant inventories in Mottram parish, dropped from 57% in the decade ending in 1590, to 10% in the decade ending in 1610, and 13% in the decade ending in 1620 (Powell 1976, 17). Conversely the inventories indicate a swing towards livestock rearing with references to oxen and pigs peaking in the decade 1611-20 (*ibid*, Tables 9 & 16).

Although in upland Tameside, as in the lowlands, there was considerable variation in the size of landholdings, the average farm size in the uplands was somewhat greater, that in Mottram and Tintwistle in 1600 being 33 acres (see Chapter 5). In part the larger landholdings of this area must have been dictated by the type of agriculture possible, namely pastoral farming which of necessity needed more land.

Powell's study reveals that the ownership of cattle was widespread throughout the period, with 71% of all inventories examined including cattle and oxen (Powell 1976, 9). The townships with the most references to cattle were Tintwistle with 44 inventories, Mottram and Stayley, both with 26, and Hollingworth with fifteen. These were the highest townships within Tameside, being wholly above 100m OD. As in the mixed farming region in the west of the Borough, herd sizes varied considerably. At one extreme was Robert Harrison of Matley, who in 1593 had one cow valued at £2 6s 8d out of an inventory totalling just £4 13s 4d (Chester LRO WS). At the other extreme was John Hollingworth of Hollingworth, esquire, who in 1661 had 27 beasts, including two oxen, worth £76 10s out of a total inventory of £380 2s (Chester LRO WS).

The average herd size over the period was nine, although 22% of all inventories with cattle had three animals or less (Powell 1976, 9). However, towards the end of the period there was a decline in average herd size towards five or six, the emphasis in these smaller herds probably being on dairy products for home consumption. Bullocks, as well as being kept for fattening, were probably also used as draught animals. Oxen certainly were, especially on the heavier soils of Tintwistle, Stayley and Hollingworth from where most references can be found (*ibid*, 10).

Sheep were also common in this pastoral region with nearly half, or 113, of the inventories examined containing references to them. Tintwistle, with its large acreage of pasture, was the primary sheep-farming area, with over 40%, or 47, of all sheep-keeping inventories (*ibid*, 10). However, Hollingworth, Mottram and Stayley townships were also areas of sheep farming. In 1638 the local farmers of Hollingworth negotiated passage through the manor demesne lands in return for a 'promise to give yearly to the same John [Hollingworth] one day shearinge' (Chester LRO DDX 87/2). The largest flocks are found in the late sixteenth and early seventeenth centuries. In 1577 Thomas Heaward of Hollins had at least 240 animals, in 1606 John Cottrell of Tintwistle had 389, whilst Nicholas Sykes of Crowden had 356 valued at £80 4s in 1608. After *c* 1610 the only flock approaching this size was that of John Hollingworth who in 1661 had 310 sheep (Powell 1976, 10-11). The small size of the majority of flocks probably meant that most families kept sheep for home use of meat and wool (Hodson 1978, 76).

Although pigs were kept throughout the parish and were mentioned in 40% of all inventories, only ten inventories included more than two, suggesting that they were kept only for domestic use. In the more populous lower lying townships of Godley and Matley more people raised pigs than in the sheep-rearing townships of Stayley, Hollingworth and Tintwistle (Powell 1976, 12).

The other element of the pastoral economy of upland Tameside was the cultivation of fodder crops and some grain for domestic consumption. In the high townships of Mottram parish, where there was almost no suitable arable land, adequate provision of fodder must have been a perennial problem (*ibid*, 15). A total of 56%, or 128, of all inventories included hay, straw and pasturage. An indication of the amounts involved may be gained from an inventory of 1623 when hay was sold at 1d a stone or 13s 4d a ton. In 1673 John Butterworth of Hattersley had £1 worth of hay, whilst in 1678 Edmund Massie of Godley, yeoman, left to his son 'my little Gray horse, a stacke of hay now at backe of the Barne and summers grase for his horses' (*ibid*).

References to 'corne', either stored or growing in the ground, are found throughout the parish, in 48 inventories, but as with western lowland Tameside it is not clear what grains were included under this description. However, oats stored and growing in the ground occur in only 23 inventories, and wheat in as few as three (*ibid*, 15-16). The infrequency of these references serves as a useful indicator of the relatively low level of cereal cultivation within this region and supports the view of Powell that 'corne as it appears in Longdendale inventories...must refer to wheat grown for animal feed' (*ibid*, 16).

Mention of other crops is also infrequent. Barley occurs in eleven inventories and was used for brewing and for animal feed. In Godley there are single references to buckwheat and beans, also used as animal foodstuffs (*ibid*). The other main crops were hemp and flax. 'Flaxlands' appears as a field-name on the tithe map and apportionment of Mottram, in the wet low-lying land near the River Etherow, and further 'flax fields' appear in Stayley (*ibid*). In 1627 the Hattersley court book listed amongst the duties to the lord of the manor 'days of swingling' (Manchester LRO M95 Chapman Papers Box 13). A further product of these wetlands was alder wood or 'owlers', used for basket making. George Hopwood of Hattersley had owlers worth 4s in 1635 (Powell 1976, 16), whilst the Hattersley court book for 1627 recorded that Robert Worth the elder sold to John Mosse 'soe much owler wood as comes to XXd' (Manchester LRO M95 Chapman Papers Box 13).

Enclosure

Enclosure of waste land or woodland continued throughout the medieval period and into the sixteenth and seventeenth centuries. There were three cases in Tameside where moorland was enclosed by the local gentry which led directly to a loss of common rights. The best documented instance was the enclosure in 1624-5 of Quick Moor in Saddleworth township. This enclosure included Quick Edge, lying in the part of the Quickmere division now in Tameside (Fig 3.25).

The enclosure of the moor was probably initiated by Sir John Ramsden of Longley Hall, Almondbury, near Huddersfield. The family had steadily increased its landholding in Saddleworth throughout the sixteenth century, and in 1606 William Ramsden, John's father, acquired a half of the old enclosed lands of Quick, with their common rights on Quick Edge, from William Stubbs of Congleton (Petford 1987, 84). Quick Moor was a large common moorland stretching from Badger Edge, across High Moor and Wharmtown down to Quick Edge and comprising around 1500 acres. However there were two other claimants to Quick Moor, Sir George Booth and Mr Thomas Legh. In order to determine the nature and extent of each lord's rights an extensive investigation was undertaken. Since fragments of the documentation produced by this enquiry have survived Petford was able to piece together the procedure (*ibid*, 85-8). Once the principal division had been agreed upon, the exact extent of each claimant's rights was assessed by a series of detailed questions posed to each of the inhabitants of Quick. A final agreement was reached at Oldham on 22nd July 1624 and stipulated that Quick Edge was to be treated separately from Quick Moor and be divided equally between Ramsden, Booth and Legh. Quick Moor was divided in two; Ramsden received one half and the other was divided into three equal parts, two of which were given to Sir George Booth and the third to Thomas Legh. Compensation for those who could prove their common rights was agreed in March 1625, and in that year a map was drawn of the newly enclosed land. A copy of this survives from *c* 1755 (Barnes *et al* 1983, 9-15).

At the end of the sixteenth century Denton Moor was also enclosed by the local gentry (Fig 3.12). In 1322 the survey of Manchester manor indicated that the moor covered 200 customary acres and was divided between six main holders. At that stage each had been allowed to enclose 25 acres. A lengthy suit concerning the Withington fee and the enclosure of Denton Moor survives from 1595-7 and indicates that the moor then consisted of 292 customary acres (Preston LRO Slater Heelis Box D Bundle 57; Young 1982, 11). The enquiry appears to have taken a similar form to that for Quick Moor, with questions and depositions from witnesses. This showed that prior to final enclosure in the 1580s a number of encroachments had taken place upon the moor, and that there were groups of housing, some of ancient origin, surrounded by areas of enclosed land. However many of these intakes were enclosed by the licence of the lords from before the time of the witnesses' memory (*ibid,* 12). There were at least eighteen tenants, the majority of whom held land of less than 1 acre. One of the largest of these areas was 3 acres which had been deliberately set aside by consent of the 'lords of the moor' to be employed 'for the maintenance of the chapel', that is Denton chapel. In addition to these 'it was agreed by the lord and freeholders of Denton and Halghton that every acre in an intake to be enclosed should pay 20d for the upholding of the chapel lately built' (*ibid*).

The suit of 1595-7 indicates that in *c* 1584 those with the greatest interest in the moor agreed to enclose 292 acres of it, an area representing approximately one sixth of Denton township. Richard Holland had 79 acres, Robert Hyde of Hyde 88 acres, Adam Hulton 46 acres, Robert Hyde of Denton 38 acres, Ralph Haughton of Haughton Hall 22 acres, Alexander Barlow 7 acres, Robert Assheton of Shepley 5 acres, and Alexander Reddish 1 acre. Not all of the inhabitants of Denton agreed with this move and a number approached the lord of Manchester, Nicholas Longford, complaining that the new enclosures would take away their traditional rights of pasturing (*ibid*, 15). However nothing seems to have come of this approach, despite the fact that Booker records a document entitled 'ffor the p'secutinge of the suite conserninge Denton more' from April 1597, taxing the grantees of the suit £1 7s 4¾d per acre on the lands enclosed, in order to defray the cost of the suit (Booker 1855, 5). Such local opposition is rarely recorded, although that does not mean that it did not exist.

The common right to pasturage on Werneth Moor is seemingly first referred to in the thirteenth century when a William de Werneth granted his claim to part of the waste in the manor of Werneth to Richard de Byron (Farrer & Brownbill 1911, 283 n 24). However by the mid-seventeenth century much of Werneth Moor appears to have been enclosed. The evidence for this can be found in the Werneth court book for the period 1588-1658 (Chester LRO DAR/I/16). Entries for 1657 and 1658 mention the repair of boundaries and hedges on the moor, suggesting that this part of the moor had already been enclosed in the early seventeenth century. Furthermore this appears to have led to a loss of common grazing rights, as it had done on Denton Moor. The court book includes a list of rents from *c* 1658 for 'Werneth Moore Ground', worth £7 2s 9½d. It would appear that the moor had been divided into twelve 'tenements', in total valued at £61 5s and leased to fourteen individuals, the rents varying from 1s 3d paid by both Robert Cleaton and Thomas Berre to 19s 6d paid by William Bennesson.

Mills

The above evidence suggests that there is little indication of new areas of arable cultivation being developed in Tameside in the sixteenth and seventeenth centuries. Rather, land above 100m OD was being turned over to cattle and sheep farming. In consequence the growth in the number of references to mills in Tameside during this period may have been prompted by a rising population, and where we lack detailed documentary evidence some of these new sites could have been fulling establishments.

In Tameside four of possibly five corn-mills working in the late medieval period continued in use throughout the sixteenth and seventeenth centuries. Of these only the Longdendale manorial mill at Woolley (Fig 3.18) was located outside the Tame valley. By 1530 at the latest the Woolley family held the lease for the mill from the lord of Longdendale (Ives 1976, 247). The family are mentioned throughout the sixteenth and seventeenth centuries, in wills (Chester LRO WS) and more frequently in the Mottram parish registers. A 'Robert Woley de Milne' occurs in the baptism records on several occasions between 1603 and 1620 and a 'John Woley de Milne' similarly between 1630 and 1647 (Chester LRO MF41/1). The Brereton records indicate that in the 1530s the income of the mill was derived chiefly from corn-milling, and that the soke, or catchment area, for the mill was the whole of the Longdendale lordship, not merely the demesne manors of Mottram and Tintwistle (Ives 1976, 247). This would make the mill one of the two most important in sixteenth-century Tameside in terms of income and workload.

The other chief mill site was the Old Mill at Ashton, on the River Tame (Fig 3.6). The importance of this mill, which served virtually the whole of the parish of Ashton, is highlighted by the number of times that complaints concerning it occurred in the Ashton court book during the seventeenth century. The Booths appear to have guarded their mill soke assiduously throughout this period. Bowman records three occasions in the seventeenth century, 1630, 1648 and 1692, when the manor court fined certain parishioners for taking corn to be ground outside the parish when they 'ought of right shall grind theire Corne and graine at the lordes milnes' (Bowman 1960, 40). Furthermore in 1648 the manor court recorded that the miller, John Fidler, had taken a greater share of corn than was his right (*ibid*).

Denton Old Mill (Fig 3.12) was an ancient structure possibly dating from the thirteenth century (see Chapter 4) and occurs infrequently in documents of the period, for instance in 1656 (Preston LRO QSP 132/39). It was not referred to as a corn-mill but presumably this was still its function since Denton was mixed farming country.

Haughton mill is not attested after the fifteenth century (see Chapter 4). By the seventeenth century, however, a mill had been established on the opposite bank of the river in Hyde (Fig 3.21). This mill is first mentioned in the inventory of Robert Hyde of Hyde Hall, Hyde, in 1639 (Chester LRO WS). This listed the contents of the mill, which included three measures at 3s 4d and 'one wyre dryeinge sive' at 6s. That this mill was for grinding grain was confirmed by the contents of the 'milne chamber' which included

'3 hoopes of oate malt 2 hoopes of milne malt }	13s 4d
halfe hoope of wheate	3s 0d
halfe hoope of shillinges	2s 8d
2 hoopes of hard corne	8s 0d'

A mill in Stayley is first recorded in 1430, but may have been for fulling (see Chapter 4). A second mill had been added by 1533, when Elizabeth Assheton, widow of Sir Thomas Assheton, gave to Ralph Chetham and Henry Marland land in Stayley, Newton and Matley including a moiety of one fulling mill and one water-mill (Ormerod 1882, 867). That both mills were in Stayley is confirmed by the inquisition post mortem of Sir George Booth in 1580 (Bowman 1960, 117). Although it is not entirely certain, both may have been located on Mill Brook (Fig 3.26). A Katherine Meller of 'Staylie water milne' left a will in 1610 (Chester LRO WS), whilst an Alice 'widow of John Meller de Milne in Staly' was buried in August 1656 (Chester LRO MF41/1).

Although Bott noted only one new mill site in Tameside during the sixteenth and seventeenth centuries, at Broadbottom (Bott 1984b, 35), there are in fact references for six new mills. The second mill at Stayley is the only one first attested in the sixteenth century, but five mills, including that in Hyde, occur for the first time in the seventeenth century. The earliest of these references are to Broadbottom mill (Fig 3.23). It has already been suggested in Chapter 4 that 'le Oldemulneton' (Dodgson 1970, 315) may have been sited on the River Etherow at this point. However by 1360 this mill had been abandoned and evidence of a mill at Broadbottom does not reoccur until 1608. In that year the inventory of Anthony Wilde, ostensibly a yeoman farmer, makes it clear that he was also the miller at Broadbottom. The inventory included 'boards & sawed boards husbandry geare and one paire of milne stones xiiiLi xis viiid' (Chester LRO WS), indicating that this water-powered mill was a corn-mill. In 1623 his son, Richard Wilde, was described as the miller of Broadbottom mill (Chester

LRO WS), while a John Wylde of Broadbottom mill was buried at Mottram in June 1636 (Chester LRO MF41/1).

At the end of the seventeenth century three further mills are mentioned for the first time. A widow Hardy of Hattersley mill was buried in April 1681, whilst a Priscilla Garsyde of Hattersley mill was buried at Mottram in March 1684 and a Robert Garsyde in February 1685 (*ibid*). The exact location and function of this mill is not clear but it may have been situated on Hurstclough Brook at Millhill (Fig 3.16). Secondly a further water-mill on the River Tame is recorded on the Dukinfield estate map of 1692 (Tameside Local Studies Library DD 229/1) (Fig 3.13). This indicates that the structure, described as Shepley Mill, was located on the left bank of the river and was fed by a mill leat run from above a weir across the river. The function and antiquity of this mill are unknown.

Finally a description of the demesne of Hollingworth manor in the 1670s refers to two water-mills in the township, one for corn and the other a fulling mill (Chester LRO DDX 87/1a). The presence of a fulling mill here in the latter half of the seventeenth century is also suggested by the inventory of John Hollingworth esquire who in 1661 had 'ironware belonging to the house and Mill' worth £2 and 'certen Walkers Earth' worth 10s (Chester LRO WS). The exact location of the fulling mill is not known, but the corn-mill was the medieval manorial mill for Longdendale, later known as Woolley mill (see above). It would seem likely that the fulling mill was on the same tributary as the corn-mill, although it is possible that this site lay on the north bank of the Etherow.

7.2 Mossland Exploitation

The exploitation of the valuable economic resource of Ashton Moss in the medieval period has been discussed in Chapter 4. Between 1425 and 1617 Ashton Moss was divided into rooms or allotments for rent by the tenants of the manor. However the common rights to graze were not infringed and officers, such as the bailiff, with moss reeves and moor lookers, were responsible for managing the whole area. In the early eighteenth century there were three of each of the latter two officials whilst special 'pinners' or 'pounders' were responsible for stray cattle on the moss (Bowman 1960, 46). The court leet records for this period provide extensive evidence for the use and abuse of the moss and its attendant rights (*ibid*, 46-8), and it is clear from these records that certain parts of the moss went under special names. There is reference to 'Shadow Moss' in 1613, and 'Linden Moss' in 1622. A 'Donome Moss' mentioned in 1617 may be associated with the place described in the 1422 rental as 'Doneam Moss', from which every tenant had to convey, yearly, ten cartloads of turves to the manor house.

In 1692 the court leet records noted 157 moss-rooms needing attention, whilst in April 1722 some 225 holders of moss-rooms were presented at Ashton court for neglecting to clean out their ditches on the moss (*ibid*, 47-8). As late as 1807 the moss reeves were still reporting those who failed to abide by the ancient rules.

Piecemeal enclosure of the moss continued into the early seventeenth century, by which date most of Little Moss had been reclaimed. A conveyance of 1614 by the Booths, relating to the Cinderland Hall estate on the north-west fringe of the moss, listed a number of field-names suggestive of enclosure, 'Blackcroft', 'Midlest Rushie', 'Halfacre' and 'Further Rushie' (John Rylands Library EGR1/5/2/1). In 1615 further fields on the same estate were sold, including 'Nearer Rushie Hey' and 'Further Rushie Hey' (*ibid*, EGR1/5/2/3). A conveyance in 1623 between Robert Graver of Droylsden, yeoman, and Robert Leech of the Lume (Lumb farm) mentioned two closes in Droylsden along the edge of the moss, 'Narre Moore Intack' and 'Further Moore Intack' (*ibid*, EGR1/5/2/4). Finally, in 1692 a messuage in Littlemoss was leased to William Edmundson, which included closes called 'Two Rushy Heys', 'Black Croft' and 'Moor Field' (*ibid*, EGR1/5/2/15).

By the end of the seventeenth century much of the northern fringes of Ashton Moss, specifically the shallow deposits that made up Little Moss to the north, and the deposits within Droylsden township had been reclaimed as pasture land. Even so the moss continued to be a valuable source of common grazing and fuel throughout the eighteenth century. The estate plan of Ashton parish of 1765 (ESRCA/15) provides valuable evidence for the extent of Ashton Moss in the mid-eighteenth century and the number of farms around its fringes. Most of the land south of the later line of the Ashton and Manchester railway was still uncultivated at this time, the exception being around Moss Side Farm which was already established. North of this line it can be seen that the Littlemoss area was dominated by small dispersed farmsteads. In 1765 these included Jaum Farm and Jaum Fields Farm, Hope Fold Farm, Swinecote Hall, Gravel Hill Farm and Well Style Farm (Fig 7.1). The farmstead known as Top o'th'-Lane appears to be a post-1765 foundation. There is reason to suppose that this was also the extent of the moss *c* 1700. As such it was the last extensive area of common grazing left in Tameside.

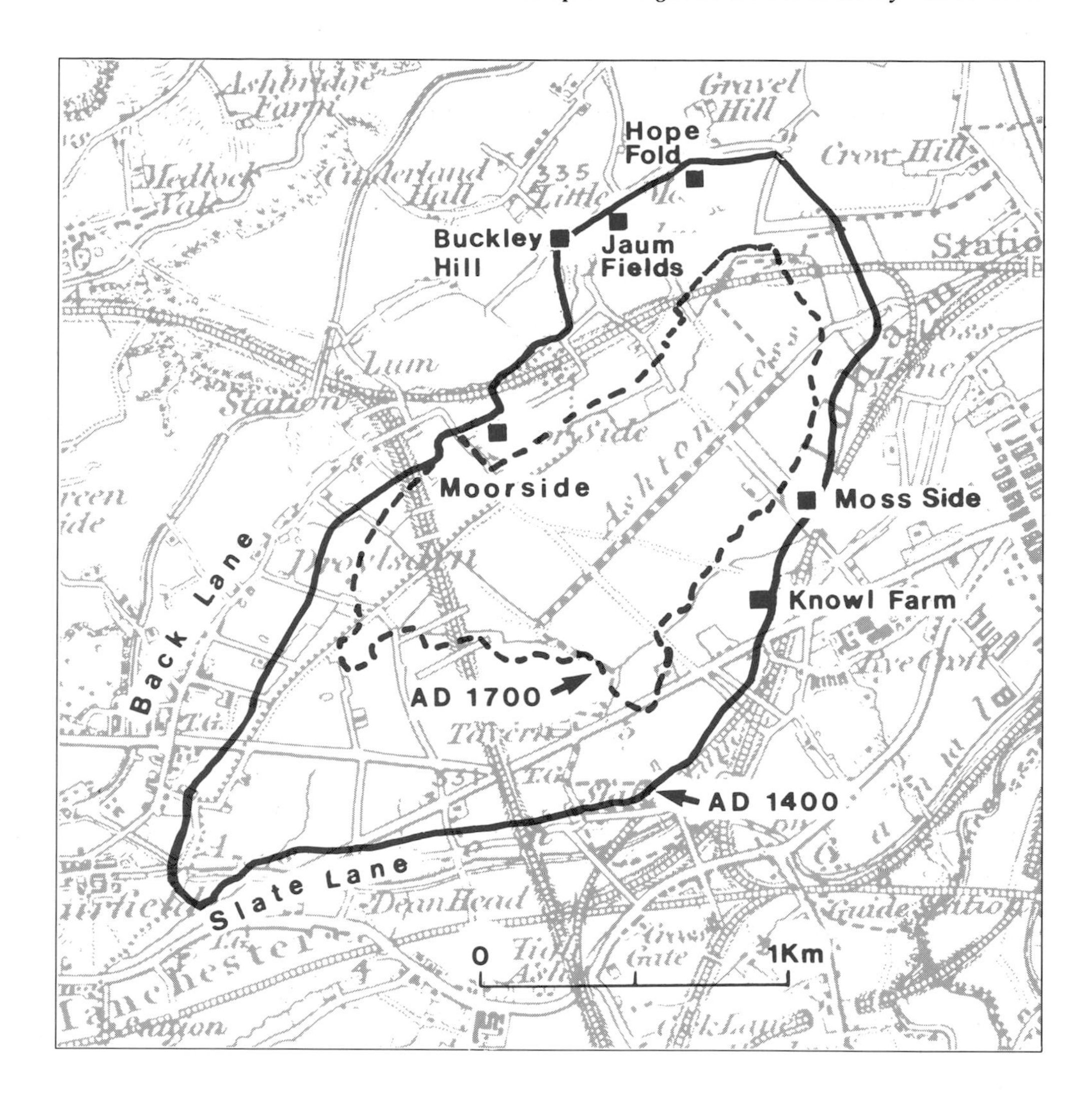

Fig 7.1 Extent of Ashton Moss *c* 1400-1765.

7.3 Growth of the Textile Trade

The production of woollens in Tameside can be traced back to the early fifteenth century when a fulling mill is attested at Ashton, and possibly also in Stayley. Trade in woollens is also first documented in this period, when John Shaw was plying the pack-horse routes across the southern Pennines (see Chapter 4). However, the textile trade may not have significantly expanded until the latter half of the sixteenth century, when Richard Thornton, Richard Assheton and John Cocke, all inhabitants of Ashton, were dealing in woollen and flax products. In 1553 Thornton travelled to London to sell friezes, finding buyers also at Loughborough and Stourbridge (Lowe 1972, 60), while Assheton was trading in Liverpool in 1593 (*ibid*, 17). The best documented Tameside textile trader of the late sixteenth century, however, was John Cocke of Cocke Bank. His will of November 1590 indicates that he was a dealer in flax and linen cloth. His possessions amounted to £307, but debts owed to him amounted to a further £33. Two women together owed him 22s 8d for four stones of flax. His inventory mentions

> 'yarne to be forty pieces of sackinge £48; yarn to be six pieces of bolstering £5 2s; in cloth woven and at weaving £48; wares sent into the country £33' (Preston LRO WS; Bowman 1960, 556-8).

As Lowe has pointed out, the interpretation of this entry depends upon the phrase 'at weaving' (Lowe 1972, 52-3). Bowman takes this to be evidence of a putting-out system, whereby Cocke provided raw materials to weavers in his employment but working in their own homes (Bowman 1960, 419). On the other hand Cocke himself owned two looms so that, as Lowe suggests, the cloth may have been woven in his own house (Lowe 1972, 53). Nor does the list of debts owed to him by local people mention all the commodities involved. However, Lowe concludes that Cocke probably sold raw materials on credit and bought linen cloth from other weavers, and that he may have had some of his yarn woven by men to whom he paid wages (*ibid*). It would also seem that Cocke's business was expanding, for much of his time was spent travelling with his nine pack-horses to market centres in the Midlands and eastern England (*ibid*).

Plate 7.2 Ashton Moss.
Much of the Littlemoss area on the northern side of the moss was reclaimed for agriculture by the early seventeenth century, but the central core remained a growing raised moss, used as pasture in summer but unpassable in winter.

Evidence for the industry in the seventeenth century is to be found in particular in the wills and inventories of both the Lancashire and Cheshire sides of the Borough. These and other documentary sources suggest differences in the pattern of development in each of these two areas, although common to both was the use of textile production as a secondary income. Almost all households probably still relied on farming as their primary means of support.

In Denton and Haughton much of the evidence for textile manufacture is associated with the production of linen. In the seventeenth century a seventh of the wills and inventories from these townships include reference to one or more looms, and spinning wheels are mentioned in a similar proportion (Young 1985, 23). In some cases these may have served only the personal needs of the household, but in other instances yarn or cloth was evidently being produced for the market.

Among this last group of producers was Robert Booth of Haughton who in 1630 owned five spinning wheels valued at 5s 6d. His inventory indicates that he was involved in the production of linen thread, for he possessed a turnell and a hetchel, implements used for dressing flax (Young 1985, 24). Booth's five wheels may indicate not only a commercial operation but also the hiring of labour from outside his household. This last practice is also implied in the inventory of William Bridgehouse in 1647 which specifies that his looms were 'for the use of the house' (*ibid*).

Another family who may have employed outside labour are the Baguleys of Haughton. The inventories of this family in the late sixteenth and seventeenth centuries show an increase from £12 5s 8d in 1594, to £53 3s 10d in 1619 to £173 0s 2d in 1634 (Young 1985, 24-5). Their farming interests and increasing involvement in stock rearing have been noted above (see p 84), but part of their wealth may be attributable to the production of cloth. The inventory of William Baguley from 1594, indicates that he had looms. In

1619 Robert Baguley had looms worth 6s 8d and spinning wheels worth 1s 4d. In 1634 Alexander Baguley had spinning wheels for which he had 1s 4d worth of swine's grease, tow and yarn worth 15s.

Individual textile workers, who may have been in the employment of another or working independently, are attested throughout the seventeenth century in Denton. Otho Robertson, Thomas Robertson and Charles Low, linen weavers of Denton, appeared at the Manchester quarter sessions in 1620-1 (Axon 1901, 157, 159). Alice Mosse in 1664 and Anne Marlor in 1673 were described as spinsters. Jonathan Hollinshed of Denton was described as a weaver in his inventory of August 1685, when he had one loom worth 8s, while in 1686 John Brombell had a spinning wheel and three pounds of hemp yarn worth 1s 6d at his house in Denton (Young 1985, 24). The reference to individuals as 'weavers' or 'spinsters' may indicate that textile production, rather than farming, was their primary source of income, but this is not certain.

A similar pattern can be identified for the textile industry in seventeenth-century Ashton. The inventory of John Slater of Hartshead in 1610 shows that he owned three spinning wheels and had debts owed to him of 8s 8d for hemp (Bowman 1960, 416). Others involved in the industry can be identified by their occupational titles. Jane Assheton, spinster, for example, is named in 1627, and James Lees, flax-dresser in 1687 (*ibid*, 416-17). Thomas Andrew was named as a woollen 'webster', or weaver, in 1627 and John Shaw of Ashton town as a wool-spinner in 1672 (*ibid*, 416).

By the 1690s individuals involved in the textile trade at Manchester were wealthy enough to buy property in Ashton parish. In 1692 a farm in Littlemoss belonging to William Edmundson, a Manchester dyer, was leased to James Mosse of Manchester, a woollen draper, and Samuel Brookes for £20 a year (John Rylands Library EGR1/5/2/15). A deed of March 1700 makes it clear that William Edmundson had purchased this property, but that his son was now leasing the farm to new tenants (*ibid*, EGR1/5/2/16).

East of the River Tame the development of the industry can be more readily traced as a result of Powell's study of the Mottram wills and inventories. Her study indicates that a total of 67, or 29%, of all the inventories during the period 1570-1680 contained 'some item of textile equipment, varying from the single pair of cards in a carpenter's inventory of 1647, to the two woollen looms, tenters and wheels of a clothworker, priced, with some joinery tools, at £6 13s 4d' (Powell 1976, 27). However, the distribution of these references suggests that it was not until after 1660 that the industry began to expand, with 24 of the 35 instances of spinning wheels coming from the period 1660-80 (*ibid*). Of the fifteen references Powell found to looms, six were in the inventories of stated textile workers, a seventh being named as a husbandman (*ibid*).

Powell's analysis of the references to raw materials, wool, flax and hemp, showed them to be roughly equal in number at the end of the sixteenth century. By 1630 flax and hemp were mentioned half as many times again as wool, but by 1680 they had fallen to around 25% of the total references to raw materials (*ibid*, 28). Several types of cloth were also mentioned in the inventories. Nicholas Sykes of Crowden had ten yards of 'Russet' and two yards of 'white Kersey' in 1608. Fustian, which combined wool with the new material cotton, was listed in only three inventories, in 1617, 1638 and 1671 (*ibid*).

In contrast to the evidence for the townships west of the Tame, the Mottram wills and inventories appear to provide little if any indication of the use of hired labour in the textile industry, and no suggestion of a putting-out system. Rather commercial textile manufacture would seem to have been undertaken by independent weavers, possibly representing, as Powell suggests (*ibid*, 27-28), only a relatively small percentage of local landholders.

7.4 Other Industries

Coal mining

Despite the rich outcrops of coal seams in the Ashton, Denton, Dukinfield, Newton and Hyde areas, the centres of the Industrial Revolution coal-mining industry in Tameside, there appears to be little if any indication of medieval exploitation of these deposits. Elsewhere in Lancashire and Cheshire the evidence points to the growing importance of coal mining from the sixteenth century onwards (Crofton 1889), an expansion which coincides nationally with a decreasing supply of timber. This same pattern of growth can be identified in Tameside where the documentation suggests that the industry was well established by the early 1600s.

Coal-mining rights were commonly reserved by the manorial lord, who might in turn lease them to others. As early as the grant of the stewardship of Longdendale to Ralph Standish in 1546, the crown, then holding the lordship of Longdendale, retained the rights to mines and quarries, a prerogative which was confirmed in the grant of the lordship to Richard Wilbraham in 1554 (Chester LRO DTW Bundle L). Similarly in a lease of 1624 by Sir Richard Wilbraham to Robert Ashworth of Mottram, and a series of later leases of 1683-4 by Sir Thomas Wilbraham, the lordship specifically reserved the right to search and dig for stone, slate and coal (Chester LRO DTW

Bundle J). The extent to which the mineral deposits of Longdendale were being exploited in the mid-sixteenth century is uncertain, but the stipulations of 1546 and 1554 at least show that their potential was recognized.

By the early seventeenth century, however, there is evidence that coal was being mined in Mottram manor. The Mottram parish register records the burial in 1617 of Anne Bower, drowned in the 'pitt upon ye Litlemore' in Mottram (Chester LRO MF41/1). Other entries are for the burial of John Bothome of Broadbottom mill on 1st December 1614, 'slayne in ye colepitt', and Ralph Bower in February 1634, also 'sleane in a Colepitt' (Powell 1976, 21), but the location of these pits is unfortunately not specified. In 1624 the terms of the lease of Robert Ashworth of Mottram included the carriage of ten loads of coal (Chester LRO DTW Bundle J/1a), while 'coals got from Mottram' occur in two inventories of 1671 (Powell 1976, 21).

In the first half of the seventeenth century mining is also attested east of the River Tame in Hattersley, Newton and Dukinfield. In 1627 the Hattersley court book included the carting of coal among the duties of the tenants of that manor (Manchester LRO M95 Chapman Papers Box 13). In 1647 a Henry Holte wrote to William Rowcroft, the steward of the manors of Ashton, Stayley and Hattersley, requesting the lease of 'the Cole pit in Hattersley'. Holte's letter refers to the early exploitation of this site. In the previous year the 'Boarer Robt Coller' had 'sank a shaft and recevered [recovered] the workes being Lost before' (Bowman 1960, 467). Mining in Newton is attested in Alexander Newton's inventory of 1617 which listed 'Coales at the Colepitt' worth £3 (Chester LRO WS). In Dukinfield coal pits are mentioned in 1630 in the will of Robert Duckenfield (Chester LRO WS), while in November 1681 the Ashton parish register records the burial of 'John Fletcher killed in Duckenfeild coale pitt the 4th day as he was hookeinge the baskett by the fall of the greate stone' (Brierley 1928, 445).

West of the River Tame in Ashton manor the exercising of mining rights by the manorial lord is shown in 1650 by a verdict of the court leet that no tenants 'who have Cole mynes in their tenements shall disturb anie whosoever that comes to bye Coles at the lord's pitts' (Bowman 1960, 465). Coal mining in Ashton is attested from at least the early sixteenth century. Pits are documented in particular at Fairbottom and Alt in the north of the township, while in 1627 the court leet gave Samuel Andrew, 'Collier' the right of way to the Dig Bank, immediately south of the old parish churchyard (*ibid*, 466-7).

The extraction of coal in seventeenth-century Tameside was probably limited to shallow workings sunk into outcropping seams. Little physical evidence for such workings survives within the Borough although reference to a pit on 'Litlemore' in 1617 (see above) may be suggestive. Littlemoor is an area of heathland at *c* 200m OD, immediately south of Mottram village (SJ 993 947), and the Mottram tithe and the Ordnance Survey first edition 6in to 1 mile maps both record the presence of four oval ponds here in the nineteenth century. Two of these still survive today and may represent the remains of bell pits, associated with early coal mining (see Appendix 4).

Some of the coal dug in Tameside was no doubt used as fuel on the hearths of local homes. In 1638 John Hinchcliffe, a Mottram husbandman, had peats and coals worth £3; in 1671 William Hyde of Mottram, yeoman, had a coal sack; whilst in 1679/80 Richard Holson of Hollingworth had a coal rake listed amongst his kitchenware (Chester LRO WS). Some coal, however, was used in local domestically-based industry. John Harrop, the Mottram smith in 1636, had coals and turves worth 13s 4d (Powell 1976, 21), while Robert Newton of Newton, yeoman, had coals worth 5s, two firegrates and also a furnace in 1662/3 (Chester LRO WS). One industrial site using coal is of special significance, namely the coal-fired glassworks at Haughton Green.

Glassmaking at Haughton Green

The presence of at least one glass furnace might seem somewhat incongruous in seventeenth-century Haughton, but by this period there was a ready market among the local landholders, not least in connection with the many halls and yeoman buildings then being refurbished. Initially glass furnaces had used wood as fuel, but in 1615 this was prohibited by royal proclamation. In that same year Sir Robert Mansell, vice-admiral of England, acquired the sole rights of manufacture, and operated the industry through a system of leasing (Hurst Vose 1989, 115).

It is possible that the glassmaking industry was already established at Haughton by that date, for in January 1598 the burial of 'Ales' the daughter of William Kenion, glassmaker, was recorded in the register of Stockport parish (Young 1982, 31). However, a series of later references to glassmakers in the Stockport registers, from 1615 to 1644, may be safely associated with the operation of the Haughton Green glassworks under Sir Robert Mansell, although it is not until 1636 that the location of the glassworks is specified in this source by name (Earwaker 1877, 406 n 'w'). Three notable glassmaking families or individuals are associated with the Haughton works: Francis Bristow, recorded here in 1618-19, the Du Houx family who were leasing the glassworks from

Mansell in 1621, and the Pilmeys, who provided the last reference to the glassworks with the burial at Ashton parish church on 17th December 1653 of George, son of Mr John Pilmey (Young 1982, 31-2; Hurst Vose 1989, 116). The demise of the glasshouse was possibly connected with the death of Sir Robert Mansell in 1653 (Young 1982, 32).

Excavations were carried out at the Haughton Green glassworks in 1969-73 by Pilkington Glass Museum under the direction of Ruth Hurst Vose (1989, 115-16), the first such investigation in England of an early coal-fired glass furnace. According to Hurst Vose the major historical significance of the Haughton Green furnace was its unique incorporation of a deep wind-tunnel running beneath the sieges (the platforms on which the crucibles, or glassmaking pots, rested). In addition to window glass the site produced high quality vessel glass, requiring considerable specialist knowledge on the part of the glassmaker (*ibid*).

Chapter 8

Settlement and Population

'May 24th, 1649...Ashton, with the neighbouring parts, lying at present under the sore stroak of God in the pestilence'

(Ormerod 1844, 278)

8.1 The Development of Rural Settlement

Place-name evidence

Any analysis of the development of the rural communities of medieval and early modern Tameside must begin not with the Domesday entries but with a review of the place-name evidence. We have already noted in Chapter 2 that the Domesday survey probably records four manors within the Borough (Mottram, Werneth, Hollingworth and Tintwistle) and St Michael's church in Ashton. It also makes it clear that large areas of the Borough were wooded and that waste and under-used land were widespread in 1086. However the absence of dependent settlements in the Domesday survey does not automatically mean that they did not exist (Aston 1985, 87). This is most clearly seen when the Anglo-Saxon place-name elements for Tameside are studied.

There are three main elements present in the Borough which probably indicate late Anglo-Saxon settlement activity (Fig 8.1). These are the 'tun', 'leah' and 'worth' elements. 'Leah' and 'worth' are woodland related place-names, although 'leah' names were often used in a semi-habitative sense, referring to settlements established in woodland clearings or a wooded landscape (Gelling 1984, 195-207). The most characteristic place-name element used in this period was 'tun', the Old English generic employed to denote a farmstead or settlement, and thus pre-Conquest settlement. Kenyon suggests that in the North-West it was used to describe settlements which lay in open, relatively unwooded, countryside and along river valleys (Kenyon 1991, 106). In Tameside most of the 'tun' elements lay along the River Tame in the lowland part of the Borough, for instance at Denton, Haughton, Newton and Ashton, whilst Taunton lay on a southern tributary of the River Medlock (Ekwall 1922, 29-30; Dodgson 1970, 316). East of the River Tame British and Anglo-Saxon place-name elements in Werneth and Mottram respectively suggest that these were also areas of pre-Conquest settlement (Dodgson 1970, 302-3, 313-14).

The distribution of 'leah' and 'worth' place-name elements may suggest settlement expansion in the late Anglo-Saxon and early Norman periods, specifically along the upper reaches of the Tame valley and around the Mottram area. West of the River Tame only one 'leah' element has so far been identified, at Shepley which lies on the west bank of the river midway between Denton and Ashton. However around the upper reaches of the Tame, in Stayley manor and the Hartshead division of Ashton, there is a collection of 'leah' names recorded by Ekwall and Dodgson. In Hartshead most of these names can be found on the eastern flanks of Hartshead Pike, which rises from *c* 120m OD to over 270m OD at Luzley and Mossley (Ekwall 1922, 29). However early clearance on the western slopes of Hartshead may be suggested by the place-names Moss de Lee and Lilly Lanes (Fig 3.8). East of the Tame there is a band of 'leah' elements running north to south through Stayley, Matley, Godley and Hattersley manors (Dodgson 1970, 306-7, 312, 317-18). Similar clearance place-name elements can be found at Hoviley in Hyde manor (*ibid*, 279), on the western slopes of Werneth Low, and in Hollingworth at Thorncliff, anciently 'Thorntelegh', and Woolley (*ibid*, 309-10).

Further early activity in Hollingworth manor, on the Pennine slopes below Hollingworth moor, is indicated by the place-name element 'worth'. In the past this has been taken as evidence of secondary settlements of the late Anglo-Saxon period, but Kenyon has suggested that it may also indicate the smallest internal subdivisions of estates of this period (Kenyon 1991, 107). The manor of Hollingworth would seem

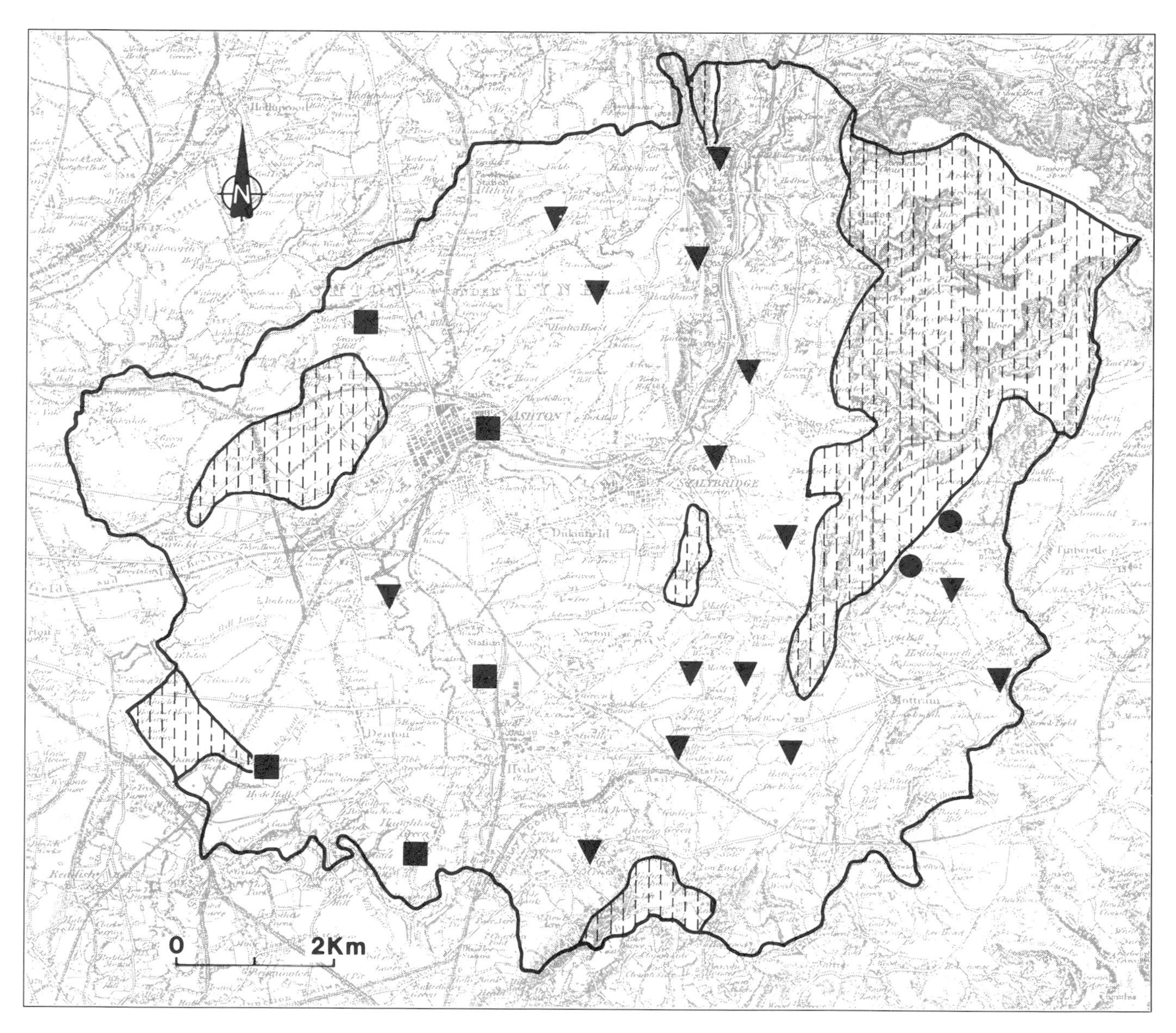

Fig 8.1 Place-name evidence for late Anglo-Saxon and early Norman settlement in Tameside.
Key: ■ = 'tun'; ▼ = 'leah'; ● = 'worth'; ¦¦¦ = moor.
The 'tun' elements may be associated with a first phase of late Anglo-Saxon settlement along the river valleys, the 'leah' and 'worth' elements with a second phase of settlement in woodland areas.

to have formed part of a group of place-names with this element, running in an arc around the hills to the east and north of Manchester and denoting the presence of ample upland grazing areas (*ibid*).

Although the precise dates of these place-names are open to debate (*ibid*, 138), the evidence suggests a two-phase colonization of the landscape. The first phase took place in the late Anglo-Saxon period and was characterized by 'tun' place-names in valley situations. The second phase occurred during the late Anglo-Saxon and early Norman periods and was characterized by 'leah' and 'worth' place-name elements clustering amongst the foothills of the western Pennine flank (*ibid*). By the time of the Domesday survey in 1086 many of these settlements may already have existed but, being of submanorial status, went unrecorded.

Medieval settlement

The development of settlement during the period 1066-1500 can be traced not only in the documentary and archaeological records but also in the field-name evidence. The principal sources for the latter are the nineteenth-century tithe awards, although unfortunately no such award exists for Ashton parish. This evidence shows that there is a close match between the extent of medieval settlement as suggested by field-name evidence and as indicated by documentary, archaeological, and place-name evidence.

The distribution of field-names can be broken into two groups, those indicating waste and woodland clearance and those indicating arable agriculture (Fig 8.2). Clearance names, such as 'intake' or 'hey', can be found on the edges of woodland, mossland and waste areas such as Ashton Moss, Buckton Moor, Denton Moor, Hough Hill in Dukinfield, Hollingworth Moor and Werneth Low. This supports the distribution of 'leah' names discussed above, implying continued expansion in these areas after the Norman Conquest.

Field-names indicating arable agriculture, such as 'acre', 'dole' or 'butt', occur throughout the Borough (see Chapter 4), but are especially striking in such upland townships as Hollingworth, Stayley and Werneth. Indeed this evidence suggests that certain parts of Hough Hill in Dukinfield, Hollingworth Moor and Werneth Low were brought into production during the medieval period, presumably before the mid-fourteenth century. Thus both sets of field-name data suggest the continued expansion of settlement throughout the Borough during the medieval period.

The documentary and archaeological evidence intimates that this agricultural activity was based upon individual manors, the focus within each usually being the medieval hall. This was the case in Dukinfield, Godley, Hyde and Newton (Figs 3.13, 3.14, 3.21 & 3.24). However there were frequently subsidiary settlement foci within a manor, usually another hall, often for a junior branch of the family. This can be seen in Denton, Hollingworth and Matley (Figs 3.12, 3.18 & 3.22), although in Haughton it seems likely that the later village was the focus for settlement, and not the medieval hall, which lay further to the north (Fig 3.17). In the larger manors settlement appears to have been dispersed. Thus in Clayton manor the township of Droylsden had its own settlement focus, at the junction of Annett Lane, Lumb Lane and Ashton Hill Lane (Fig 3.11). In the fifteenth century there were also farmsteads along the western edge of Ashton/Droylsden Moss, and along Greenside Lane (Speake & Whitty 1953, 47-9). In Tintwistle township the manor was so large that it was divided into four divisions, each with its own core settlement. However, the Longdendale survey of 1360 implies the existence of two settlement cores within Micklehurst: 'Mukelhurst', which later gave its name to this northern division of the township, and 'Lytelhurst', which appears to be a lost place-name. The core of 'Mukelhurst' was probably Castle Farm (Booth *et al* 1976-8, no 121) (Fig 3.27). Although the eastern half of Hattersley manor was dominated by the medieval park around Botham's Hall, further settlement was recorded in the early fourteenth century at Higher and Lower Cliff, on the north-eastern edge of Werneth Low (Highet 1960, 64) (Fig 3.16). In Stayley manor the puture rolls for the mid-fourteenth century record settlement at two further locations within the township: at 'Arpurlegh', probably Herpley Farm in the southern part of the township (Highet 1960, 66-7), and at 'Haysteslegh', a lost place-name (Dodgson 1970, 319) (Fig 3.26). In Werneth manor settlement appears to have been dispersed around the flanks of Werneth Low, with Higham and Hydes farms and Beacon House occurring in the early fifteenth century (Highet 1960, 78) (Fig 3.28).

This evidence suggests that during this period settlement was expanding from the core of each manor, the medieval hall, usually resulting in further core settlements. However, there is very little to indicate that these core settlements formed the nuclei of later villages. In only two cases within the Borough can this be seen, at Ashton and Mottram. Nevertheless settlement across Tameside was sparse with fewer than forty sites recorded (Fig 8.3; Appendix 5).

The sixteenth- and seventeenth-century landscape

Our archaeological and historical evidence is considerably greater for this period, and undoubtedly in part accounts for the four-fold increase in sites recorded from this period (Fig 8.4; Appendix 5). However, since most of the 'new' sites appear to have been family farmsteads or hamlets, their occurrence may also have been in part due to the shifting economic circumstances of the later fourteenth and fifteenth centuries, which witnessed the break-up of demesne estates in favour of small tenant farmers. This process is illustrated by a number of surveys from the seventeenth century. The Longdendale survey of 1600, which only covered the demesne manors of Mottram and Tintwistle, indicates that there were seventeen tenant farmers in Mottram township and five in the Micklehurst division of Tintwistle farming an average of 33 acres each (Chester LRO DTW/2477/B/9). In 1609 a total of 61 tenant farmers were recorded in Denton and Haughton, holding on average 26 customary acres (Young 1982, Appendix A), while the Ashton parish survey of 1618 (Butterworth 1823, 155-66) recorded 300 tenants farming an average of 13 acres (see Chapter 5).

The expansion of settlement is particularly noticeable around lowland moss and waste lands, such as Denton Moor, enclosed in the 1580s, and Ashton Moss, the northern fringes of which were subject to piecemeal enclosure during the late sixteenth and early seventeenth centuries (see Chapter 7). However a number of upland waste areas were also exploited in this period. The case of Quick Edge has already been noted. Harrop Edge, in Matley, and Hough Hill, in

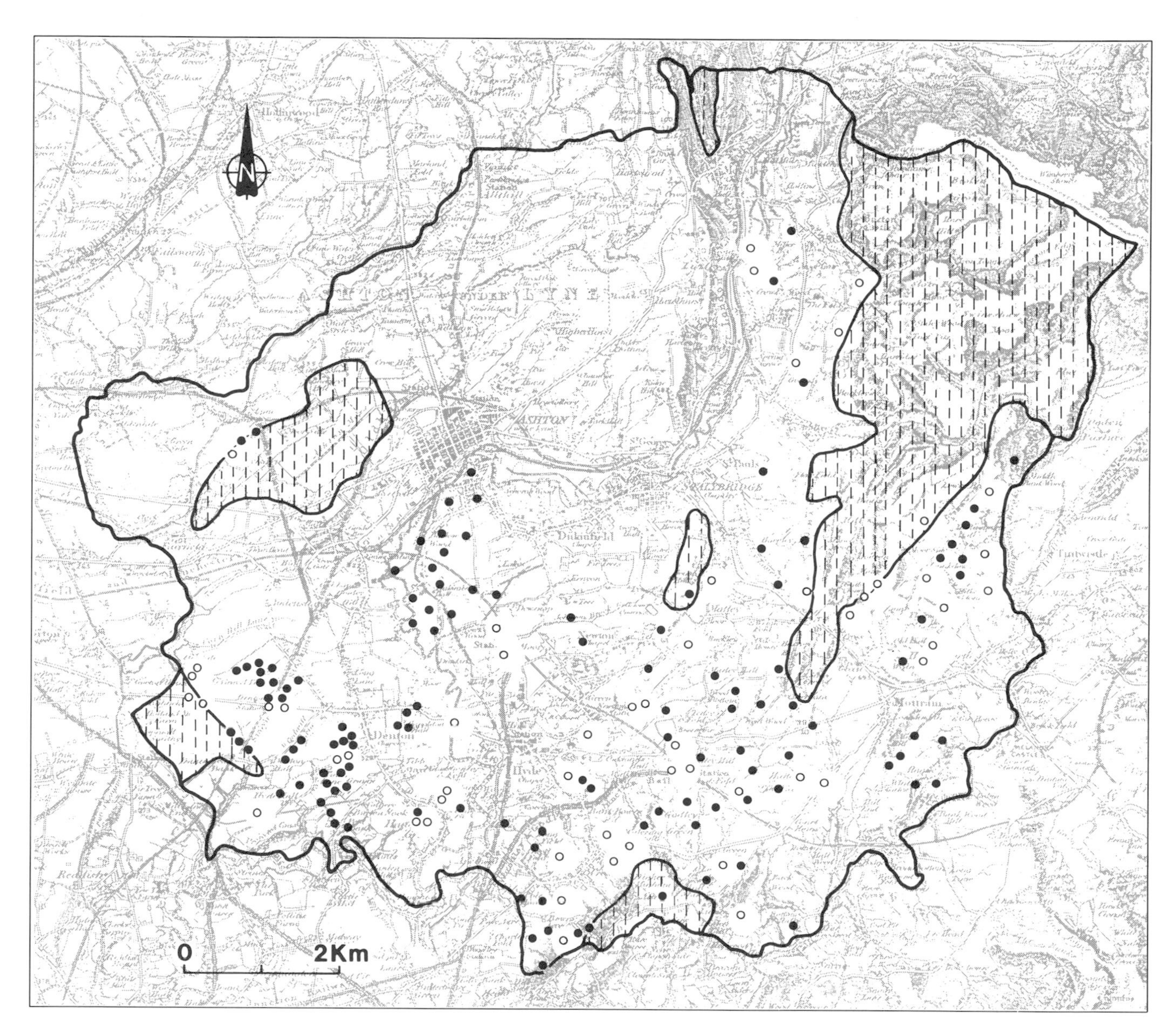

Fig 8.2 Distribution of field-names indicating arable agriculture and waste and woodland clearance.
Key: ● = arable agriculture; ○ = waste and woodland clearance; ¦¦¦ = moor.
These suggest that the main areas of medieval agricultural activity were the valleys, although a number of wastes were also exploited. The field-names are derived from the Dukinfield estate map of 1692 and the nineteenth-century tithe awards. No comparable evidence exists for Ashton-under-Lyne.

Dukinfield, also appear to have been partially enclosed during this period. Elsewhere new farmsteads appear to have completed the settlement and clearance of the lowland areas of the Borough.

One notable feature in the changing distribution of medieval and early modern settlements in Tameside was the impact of the villages of Ashton and Mottram. In the medieval period it is apparent that both formed the focus of local farming communities, with no indication of any subsidiary settlements within a 1km radius of Ashton, and only one such site, the Haigh, within the same radius of Mottram (Fig 8.3). However by the sixteenth and seventeenth centuries their roles within their respective parishes had changed. Ashton seems to have maintained its position as the central focus for settlement within the parish. Over 20% of the total number of households of the parish were resident in what is shown to be a small town in the sources for 1618 (Butterworth 1823, 155-66), 1643 (Bowman 1960, 243-5) and 1666 (Tait 1924, 114-15). Significantly no farmsteads were recorded within a 1km radius of the town throughout this period. However the case of Mottram village is somewhat different. The hearth tax returns for 1664 indicate that it accounted for only 10% of the total number of households in the parish (Chester LRO M13). Furthermore by the seventeenth century there were six farmsteads within a 1km radius of what was still a village, suggesting that the

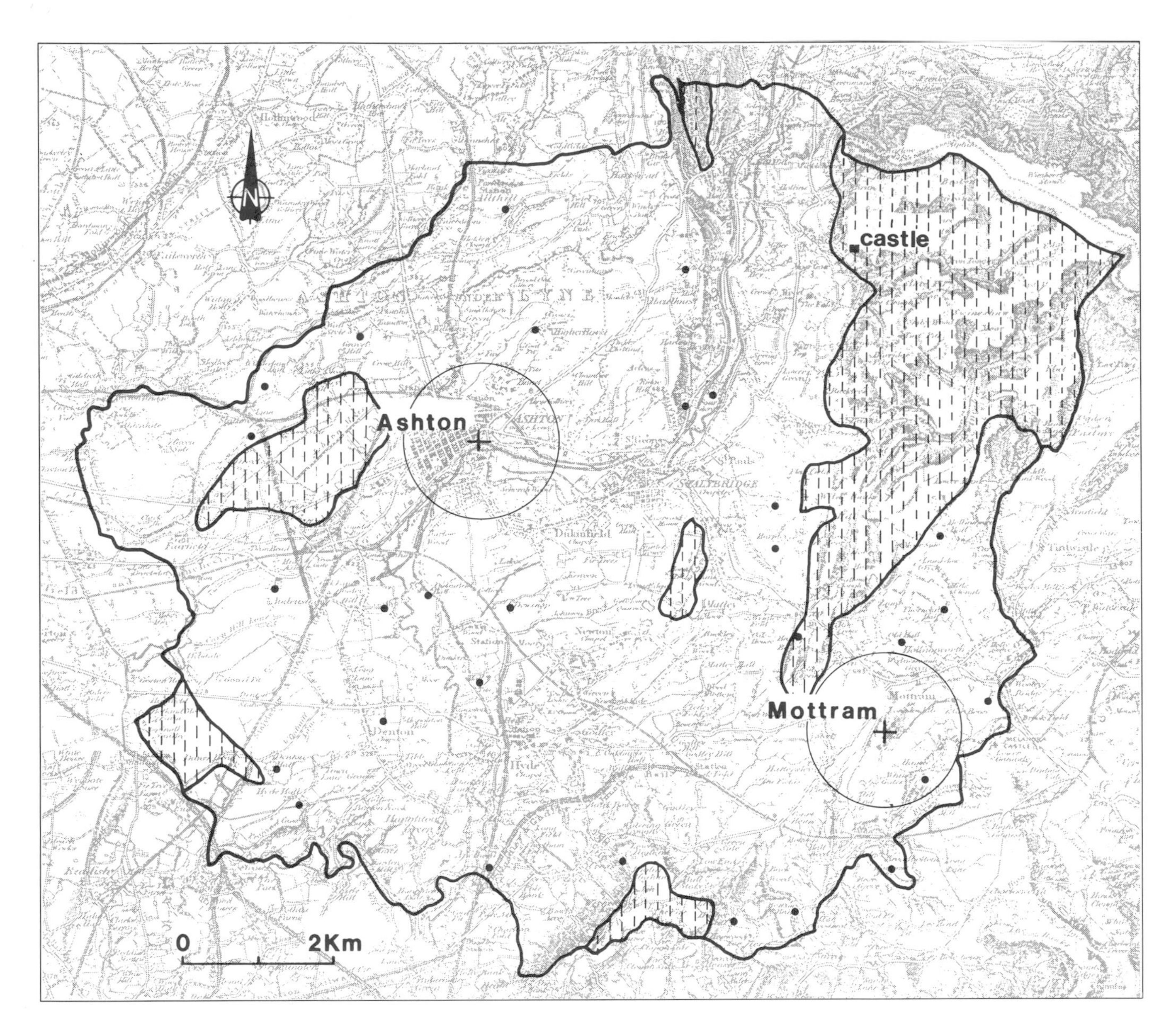

Fig 8.3 Medieval settlement in Tameside based on documentary evidence.
Key: ● = settlement site; ¦¦¦ = moor.
The distribution of sites suggests that Ashton and Mottram were each the centre of a local farming community, with no subsidiary sites within a 1km radius of Ashton, and only one within the same radius of Mottram. Elsewhere within the Borough the pattern is of dispersed settlement.

settlement was not as pre-eminent in its parish as Ashton had become (Fig 8.4). The reasons for this divergence in the development of these two settlements are best assessed by a brief analysis of their development.

The development of Ashton-under-Lyne

The ancient village and town of Ashton-under-Lyne lay on the northern bank of the River Tame. Sited on a small spur of boulder-clay covered high ground, on the first terrace, the settlement lay some 10m above the flood plain of the River Tame. The existence of a pre-Conquest settlement on this site is suggested not only by the Domesday reference to St Michael's church, but also by the place-name evidence. The 'lyne' element of the name would appear to have been derived from the British 'lemo', 'an elm', and according to Kenyon can be taken to mean 'the district of the elm', although in the North-West it appears to have been used also as a boundary term to refer to the limits of palatine jurisdiction (Kenyon 1991, 65). The 'tun' element of the place-name suggests an Anglo-Saxon origin for the settlement (Ekwall 1922, 29).

The descent of Ashton manor has been described in Chapter 3, and the medieval economy of the village and manor, which was a mixture of arable and pasture land held in common, in Chapter 4. However, apart

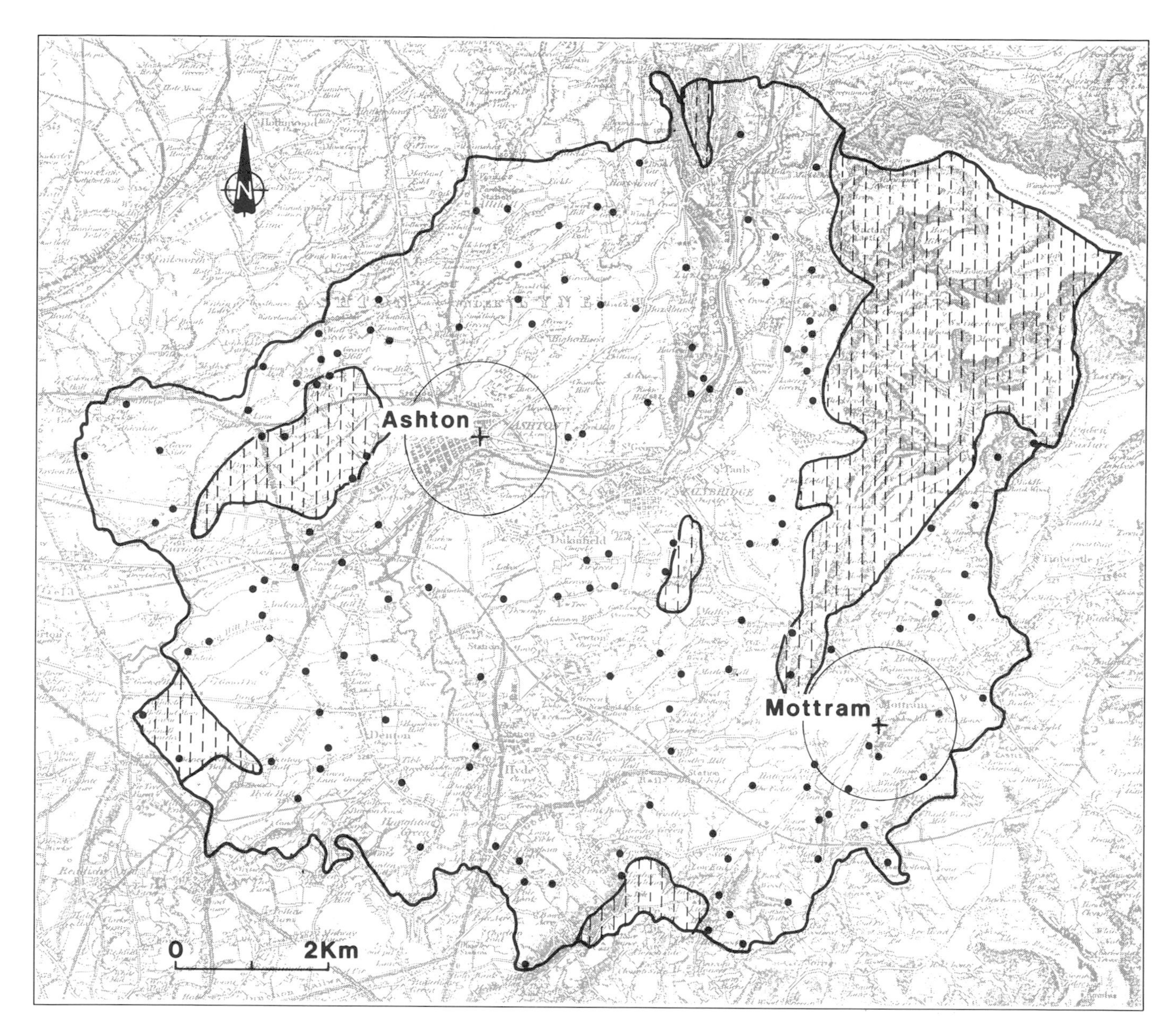

Fig 8.4 Farmsteads, hamlets and villages 1500-1700 based on documentary and archaeological evidence.
Key: ● = settlement site; ¦¦¦ = moor.
The primacy of Ashton town within its parish can be seen by the lack of farmsteads within a 1km radius. This contrasts with Mottram where six farmsteads lie within the same distance.

from Bowman's assessment of the post-1700 growth of the industrial town (Bowman 1960, 637-9), there has been no attempt to trace the early layout of Ashton-under-Lyne.

Fortunately a plan of Ashton has survived from 1765, which throws considerable light on the origins and development of the town (ESRCA/15; Fig 8.5). This indicates that the core of the old settlement lay along Scotland Street, or 'Towne' Street as it was called in 1422, between the church and the hall. In fact the settlement appears to have developed as a typical medieval village of irregular row plan (Roberts 1982, 11), with a village green acting as the market centre at its northern end. This is the situation suggested by the Ashton rental for 1422 which records twenty cottages within the village (Harland 1868, 96-8). If one includes the smithy of Roger Smyth, the bakehouse of Roger the Baxter, the kiln of Merget of Stayley, Jenkyn Cocker's 'croft at the town end', and six other tenants in this section of the rental, a possible total of 30 buildings in addition to the hall and church can be achieved for early fifteenth-century Ashton. In 1765 a total of 32 buildings lined Scotland Street from the hall in the south to the market cross in the north, and whilst this is not conclusive proof of the 1422 extent of the village it does imply that the general argument may be correct. A multiplier of 4.75 individuals per household, as suggested by Walton (1987, 25), gives a population for the town of approximately 152 in the early fifteenth century. The significance of this settlement, and its pre-eminent position both in the parish and in this area of south-eastern Lancashire, was confirmed by the granting of a market and fair here in 1414 (John Rylands Library EGR1/5/1/1).

By the mid-seventeenth century the village had expanded to the north, and was now concentrated on four roads, Town Street, Crickets Lane, Old Street and Cowhill Lane. The focus of the settlement was the area around the market place, where the court house was built in 1636 (Bowman 1960, 630). The market cross is attested in 1654 when the marriage banns for James Roades and 'Easter Smith' were published there (*ibid*, 292). In 1660 a Mr Newton held property at the junction of the southern end of Cowhill Lane (later Dungeon Street) and Old Street (*ibid*, 346). Old Street itself, running westwards from the cross, was referred to by the court leet records in 1683 as 'the highway between Newton Nook and Ashton Cross' (*ibid*). Cowhill Lane was described as the end of the town as late as 1713 (*ibid*, 353). Crickets Lane or 'Creekity lane' occurs in the court leet records of 1684 (*ibid*, 330). The 1765 town plan indicates that many buildings occupied long thin strips of land, possibly the remains of crofts, running back from either side of Old Street. These crofts are typical features of a fossilized medieval village layout, and may suggest that this part of the town saw expansion in the fifteenth century as well as in the sixteenth and seventeenth centuries (Roberts 1982, 8).

The population of the settlement in the seventeenth century can be estimated from a number of records, which indicate that the village had grown into a small town. The Ashton parish survey of 1618 records 49 households in the town, which when multiplied by 4.75 gives an approximate population of 233. However this figure may be too low, since only landholders were included in the tax list. In 1643 some 116 individuals signed the Solemn League and Covenant (Bowman 1960, 243), which, if every individual represented a household, would give a figure of 551. A similar figure can be achieved from the hearth tax returns of 1666 (Tait 1924, 114). This figure needs to be gauged against the other towns of the region. By the Restoration there were probably ten towns in Lancashire with a population of more than 1000, the largest of which was Manchester with more than 4000 inhabitants (Walton 1987, 25).

The economic importance of the settlement is emphasized by the survival of its market – 20% of the medieval markets of Lancashire had ceased by the sixteenth century (Morris 1983, 27) – and the jealousy with which its regulations were guarded (Bowman 1960, 40). It is also significant that in the 1660s the economy of the town was sufficiently developed to warrant the minting of trading tokens, in common with other larger towns in the region, such as Chester, Manchester and Lancaster (Heywood 1887, 73). Furthermore, there is evidence to suggest a growth in textile production in the parish during the late sixteenth and seventeenth centuries (see Chapter 7). Much of this may have centred on Ashton itself and contributed to its continuing economic success.

The development of Mottram

The evidence available for Mottram is considerably less than that for Ashton-under-Lyne, but is sufficient to indicate that by the end of the seventeenth century Mottram village was less than half the size of Ashton. As with Ashton, the place-name evidence suggests a pre-Conquest origin for the settlement, the most likely derivation being the Old English 'motere' meaning 'at the speakers' place' (Dodgson 1970, 202). The antiquity of the settlement is further implied by its probable reference in the Cheshire Domesday Book (see Chapter 2). The apparent absence of St Michael's church in the survey may be due to the omission of all church references in Hamestan (Macclesfield) hundred, rather than the absence of the building itself.

In the medieval period the village lay upon Warhill, probably in an irregular row plan between Parsonage Farm and St Michael's church (Fig 8.6). The present church is fifteenth-century, but there was probably a church on this site in the thirteenth century when Robert 'parson of Mottram' was a witness to two Godley charters of pre-1249 (PSA 1850, nos 3 & 6). The 'parsonage' farm and glebe lands are first mentioned in a document of 1547 and were in the occupancy of Robert Shawe in 1617 (Chester LRO P25/8/7 & 9). Buildings in the hamlet at the Mudd are also referred to in the seventeenth century (Chester LRO DTW Bundle J). Little has survived of the medieval core of the village between the Mudd and the church, although at least one house platform is still visible as an earthwork on the western edge of Littlemoor Road (Plate 11.1). The Longdendale survey of 1360 lists thirteen individuals as tenants in Mottram township, two of whom, 'Jordan and Wadkyn del Haghe', probably held land near the Haigh hamlet, whilst 'Stephen de Harap' may have held a farmstead on Harrop Edge (Booth *et al* 1976-8, no 104). The rest probably lived in Mottram itself, although only one, 'William de Wharell', can be firmly associated with the old medieval core of the settlement (*ibid*). This would suggest that by 1360 the village contained approximately 48 people, using a multiplier of 4.75.

By the seventeenth century the village had spread northwards beyond the church and along Church

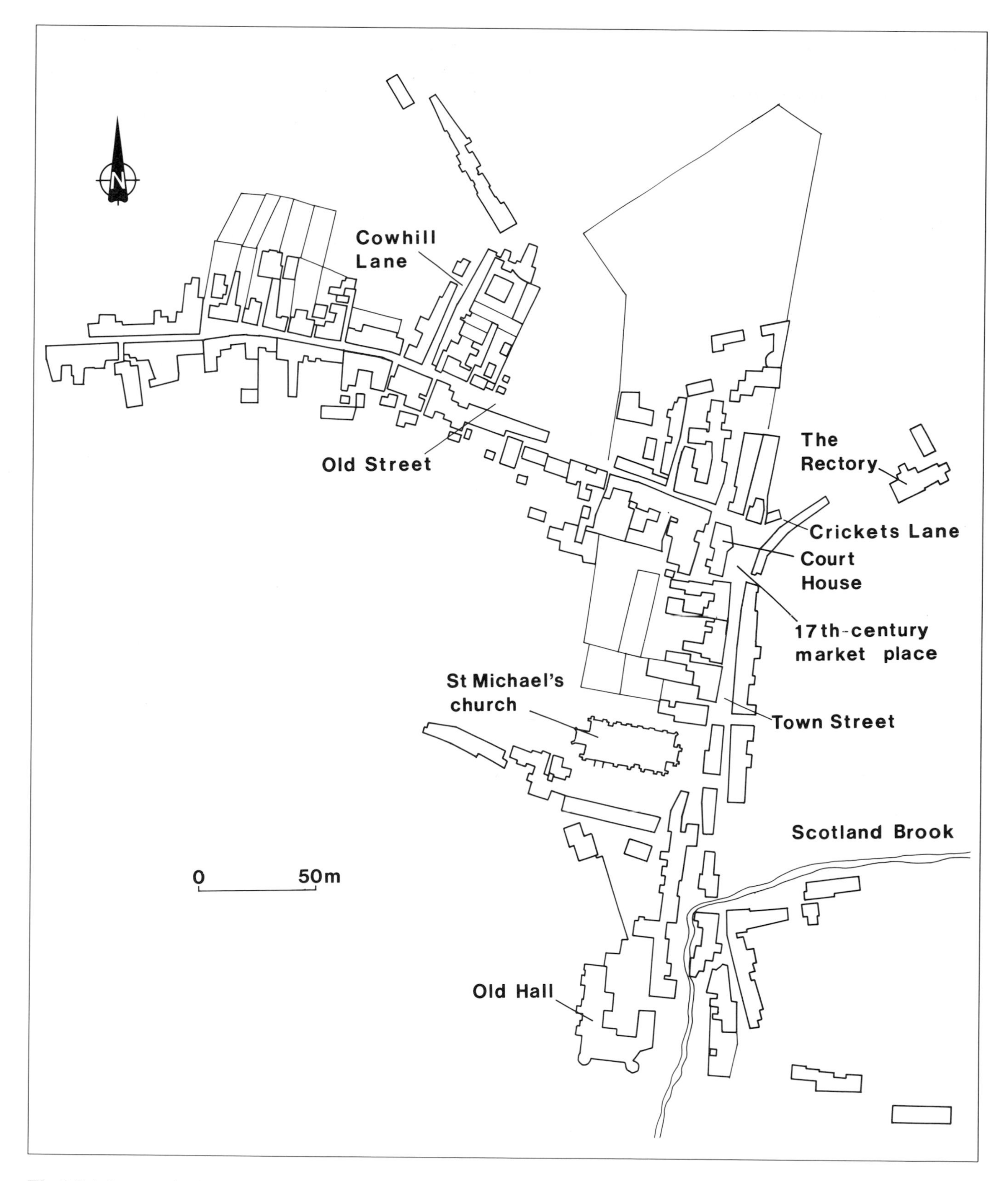

Fig 8.5 Ashton-under-Lyne in 1765, after the Stamford estate plan.
The medieval village lay between the Old Hall and the church. Documentary evidence suggests that the seventeenth-century town was largely coincident with that recorded in 1765.

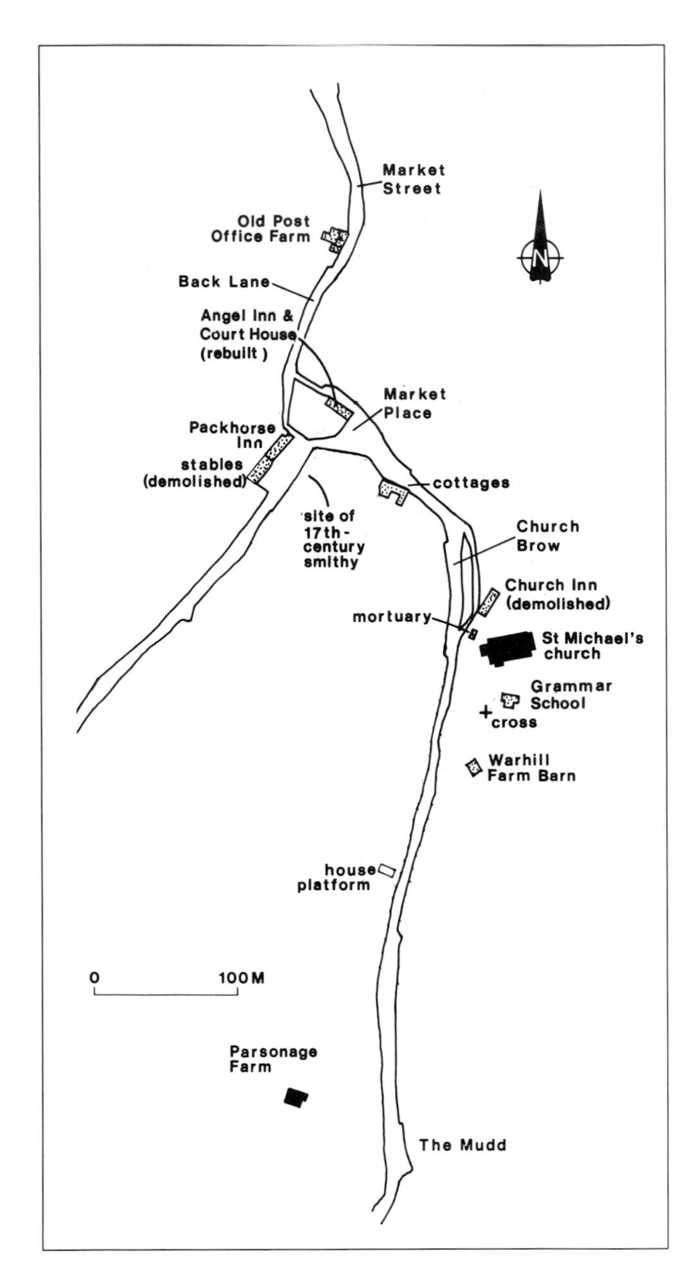

Fig 8.6 The development of Mottram to 1700.
Key: pre-seventeenth-century building or site.
seventeenth-century building.
The medieval village lay along the ridge between the church and Parsonage Farm. In the seventeenth century the settlement expanded onto the lower ground to the north, centred on the court house.

Brow. This is the area where the surviving seventeenth-century structures stand: the Market Place houses, the Packhorse Inn, the Old Post Office and No 4 Back Lane. However in the seventeenth century the main thoroughfare below the hill was not Market Street, but Back Lane. Market Street was built in the late eighteenth century as can be seen by comparing the Cheshire maps of Burdett from 1777 and Bryant from 1829-31 (Harley & Laxton 1974, plate X).

A survey of 1600 and a large collection of deeds survive from the seventeenth century which enable us to assess the size of the village and review its development at the end of our period. The survey of 1600 lists seventeen tenants in the township, of which three can be assigned to farmsteads at the Haigh and Hurstclough, and three to Mottram village (Chester LRO DTW/2477/B/9). Most of the remaining eleven tenants probably also lived in the village and, whilst we cannot be sure, these figures would imply a population for the village in excess of 66 individuals, and probably more.

A collection of deeds from 1684 mentions eight of the thirteen family names which appeared in 1600 – Ashworth, Bower, Dewsnape, Garside, Rowbotham, Tooterington, Walker and Winterbotham (Chester LRO DTW Bundle J) – suggesting a high degree of continuity in the population during this period. These deeds also record fourteen messuages, seven cottages and one smithy in the township, suggesting a population of about 104 in 1684. However this figure is almost certainly too low, since the hearth tax returns for 1664 recorded 50 households, giving a population of around 237 (Chester LRO MF13). Whilst it is not possible to assess the size of Mottram village from these figures alone, further evidence, from the parish registers and wills and inventories, indicates that there were in fact seven farmsteads in the township during this century, at Broadbottom, Brown Road, Carr House, the Haigh, Hillend, Hurstclough and Lower Roe Cross (Fig 3.23; Appendix 5). Even if one assumes that each contained on average two families, as certainly Broadbottom and the Haigh did, that would still leave approximately 36 households to account for. These presumably lived in Mottram itself, suggesting that by the latter half of the seventeenth century the village had a population of around 171.

Thus, although our evidence is diverse and imperfect, there is reason to believe that the village of Mottram was a fairly static community until the late sixteenth century. It was not until the seventeenth century that the village witnessed population growth, with perhaps the size of the settlement nearly doubling and accounting for its expansion into Market Place and along Back Lane.

The economic role of the settlement appears to have been limited for much of the period 1066-1700. The first clear indication of the village's economic role comes from the Longdendale survey of 1360. This indicates that the medieval borough of Tintwistle was the economic heart of the parish (Booth *et al* 1976-8, no 116), while Mottram was the administrative head of the lordship, the 'court of Mottrum' being mentioned in the same survey (*ibid*). Some industrial activity is suggested by the place-name 'wharell', meaning a quarry (Dodgson 1970, 315) and perhaps indicating the early exploitation of the millstone-grit bluff on which the settlement was located. However there are no other indications that the settlement was anything other than a small agriculturally based hamlet. There is no evidence of a medieval market, and the manorial corn-mill was probably situated on the Hollingworth/ Tintwistle township boundary at Woolley mill. Admittedly the presence of the place-name 'Oldemulneton' in 1313 suggests the possibility of a mill on the River Etherow at Broadbottom (*ibid*), but whatever its location this early mill appears to have been abandoned by 1360 (see Chapter 4).

It was not until the late sixteenth and early seventeenth centuries that the overwhelmingly rural economy of the village began to change. The initial impetus for this may have been the mining of coal where it outcropped on Littlemoor, immediately south of Parsonage Farm (see Chapter 7). By the second half of the century the settlement included a smithy, with possibly a kiln (Chester LRO DTW Bundle J/14) and was home to at least one linen weaver (*ibid*, J/4). It may also have held an informal market. In 1641 Ann Wood, a widow of Coatebank Greene, had debts owing to her which included 7s from a 'William Tomelinson' and 4s 8d from a 'James Wood', both 'due att Mottram wakes' (Chester LRO WS).

8.2 The Demography of Tameside 1570-1700

It is only with the advent of parish registers in the ecclesiastical reorganization of the mid-sixteenth century that it is possible to analyse in any detail the shifts and trends in the demography of Tameside. Prior to that date it is possible to draw only broad conclusions about the spread and density of population in the Borough. From the evidence discussed above it would seem that during the medieval period the population was dispersed thinly across the Borough, within a group of sixteen well defined townships. However the lay subsidy of 1334 indicates that half of Tameside lay in one of the poorest and most sparsely inhabited regions in the country, namely Lancashire (Kenyon 1991, 16). By the early sixteenth century the overall population of the county was between four and nine people per square mile. This compared to an average of between ten and fourteen in much of the South-East, which in places had more than twenty people per square mile. Similar figures for Cheshire are not available but it seems likely that east of the Dee and Gowy valleys the population was as sparse as that in Lancashire (Sheail 1972, 114-15).

Aggregative analysis of Ashton and Mottram parishes

In the early modern period it is possible both to assess the population of the parishes of Ashton and Mottram and to identify demographic trends within the two, albeit only approximately in each case. The hearth tax returns are the most commonly used, if not entirely reliable, source for overall population size in this period. For Ashton and Mottram parishes the 1666 and 1664 returns respectively would appear to be complete, since they list both those taxed and those discharged from payment (Tait 1924; Chester LRO MF13). These show Ashton parish to have had 413 households and Mottram parish 330 (85 of which were exempt), although Mottram parish only had six houses with more than three hearths, whereas Ashton had 24. Using Walton's multiplier of 4.75, these figures suggest a total population for Ashton of 1962, and 1568 for Mottram. These figures, which are for the parishes as a whole, may be compared with the totals of 551 and 171 or so which have been suggested above for Ashton town and Mottram village.

It is possible to analyse the demographic trends in these same parishes by aggregative analysis of the parish registers. However, although nationally each parish was required to register all baptisms, marriages and burials from 1538, few parishes have details from this early date (Riden 1987, 94). Ashton and Mottram are no exception, with the registers in Mottram surviving from 1570 onwards (Chester LRO MF41/1-9), but those for Ashton only from 1594 onwards (Brierley 1928). Furthermore in the case of Ashton records are missing for several periods in the seventeenth century. The worst of these was the period 1642-1655 when no records were kept, or if they were they have not survived. The record of marriages would appear to be mutilated for a number of other years, there being gaps for the periods 1624-30 and 1664-9. In the Mottram registers baptisms are missing for 1649, and marriages for 1648-50 and 1658-62. The annual totals of baptisms and burials for Mottram parish in the period 1570-1680 have been plotted by Powell (1976, 6). For the present work all baptisms, burials and marriages recorded between the years 1594 and 1700 for the Ashton parish have also been counted (Fig 8.7). To reduce the extremes created by haphazard elements in the series and to emphasize the underlying trends, ten year moving averages for Ashton parish were also calculated.

In both parishes comparison of the overall number of baptisms and burials suggests a modest rise in population over this period, with only 5.5%, or 373, excess baptisms over burials in Ashton in the period 1594-1700, and 10% to 12% in Mottram for the period 1570-1680 as noted by Powell (1976, 6). However, when the figures are broken down into smaller periods they show a far from uniform development. In Ashton the total number of baptisms for the period 1594-1641 was 4132 compared to 3090 burials, giving an excess of baptisms over burials of 34% and suggesting rapid population growth. However, for the period 1655-1700 there were only 2644 baptisms as opposed to 3313 deaths, giving an excess of deaths over baptisms of 25%, suggesting population decline. However, when the ten year averages are also taken into account, this picture may require some modification. Whilst the ten year averages for burials across the period 1594-1700 remain close to the hundred year average of 70 per year, the ten year averages for baptisms consistently fall below the hundred year average of 73 in the period after 1656. Indeed there is a decline in each of the ten year averages for the 1670s, the 1680s and the 1690s. Thus whilst the population of Ashton may have declined in the period 1670-1700, other factors, in particular the under-registration of baptisms associated with nonconformity, may have been more significant in producing these apparently grim figures. Attempts at family reconstruction, as undertaken by Wyatt for Nantwich (1989, 11-22), might indicate which was the major determining factor in this period.

While the picture from Ashton in the late seventeenth century is thus not entirely clear, the early period shows a population growth not inconsistent with Walton's argument that the population of Lancashire nearly doubled in the period 1563-1664 (Walton 1987, 24-5). However Young's survey of the Denton and Haughton entries in the parish registers of Ashton, Manchester and Stockport for the period 1594-1627 indicates that some areas of Tameside remained unaffected by these demographic changes. Both communities appear to have been static in terms of population growth during the early seventeenth century, with 139 baptisms and 139 burials recorded from Denton inhabitants, and 107 baptisms to 115 burials recorded by Haughton inhabitants (Young 1982, 36).

Furthermore even in the first half of the seventeenth century there were crisis years of excess mortality. The registers of both Mottram and Ashton show a high degree of coincidence in each of their crisis years. In the 1590s, the crisis year in Mottram was 1596 which produced 66 deaths, whilst in Ashton it was 1598 which produced 80 deaths. The 1620s were equally bad in both parishes, the worst years being 1621 which produced 75 burials in Mottram and 136 in Ashton, and 1623, which saw over 100 deaths in Mottram and 169 in Ashton. In Mottram 1642 and 1645 produced 75 and 46 burials respectively, and although there are no records from Ashton parish in this period there is a report in 1649 of plague striking Ashton town (Ormerod 1844, 278). Whilst the situation in the 1670s was not as bad, there were 59 burials in Mottram in 1671 and 115 in Ashton in 1675. The period 1680-1700 was particularly grim in Ashton, the number of burials exceeding the hundred year average of 70 in eleven of these twenty years. In the 1680s, 1684 and 1685 were bad years with 84 and 82 burials respectively, but these were overshadowed by the years 1698-1700 which saw burials reaching 117, 116 and 101 respectively.

When a national perspective is taken it is possible to see that the crisis years in the 1590s and 1620s coincided with periods of exceptionally bad harvests. 'In both periods in Cumberland and Westmorland people died of starvation; they may also have done so in Ashton-under-Lyne...in 1623-4, when burials reached a level three times above the normal, the number of births fell by half, and infant mortality greatly increased' (Coward 1980, 48). The period 1670-1700 was an era of agricultural stress; wool and grain prices were very sluggish in the 1670s and 1680s, whilst the 1690s were a period of bad harvests (*ibid*, 432). Since the economy of Ashton parish was still dependent upon mixed farming in the latter part of the seventeenth century these economic conditions may in part account for the coincident rises in burials and dips in baptisms visible for the years 1673, 1681, 1684, 1693 and 1699.

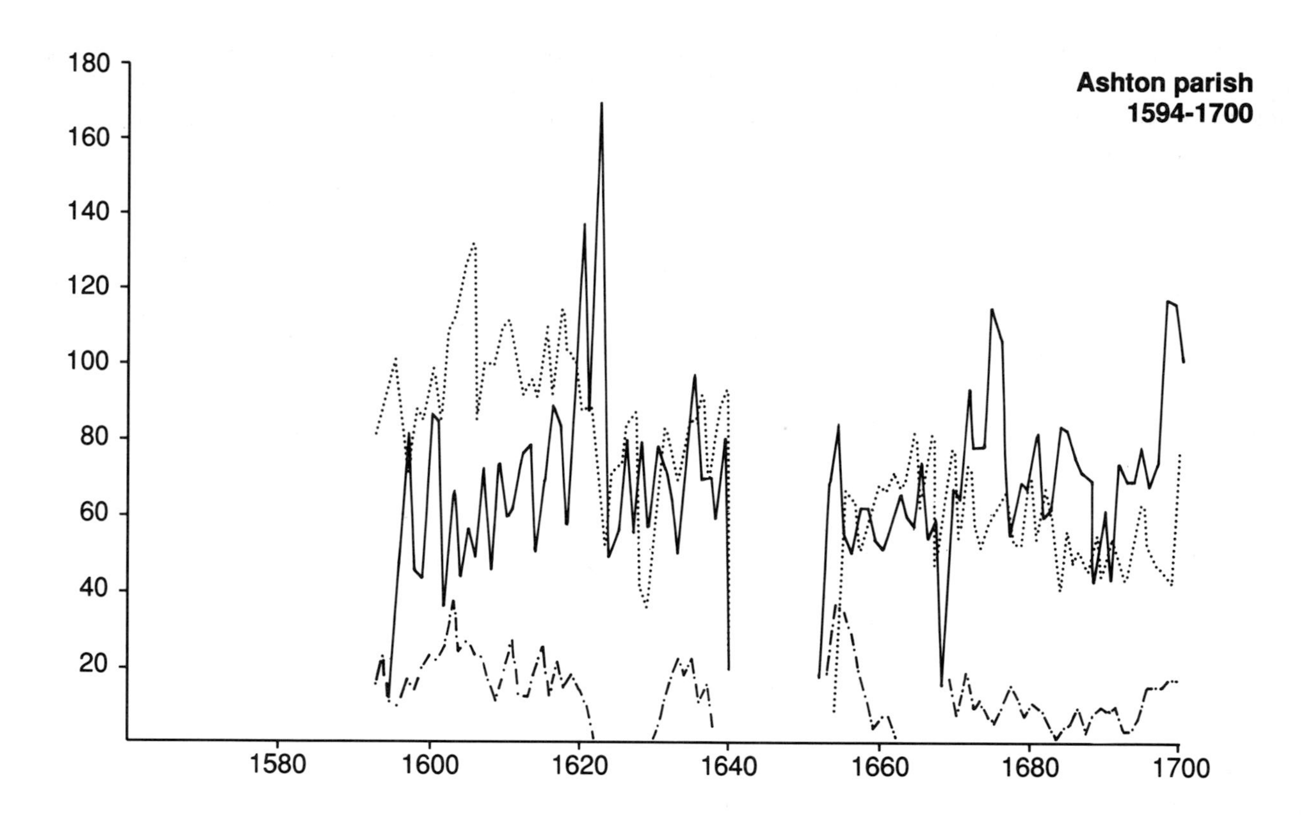

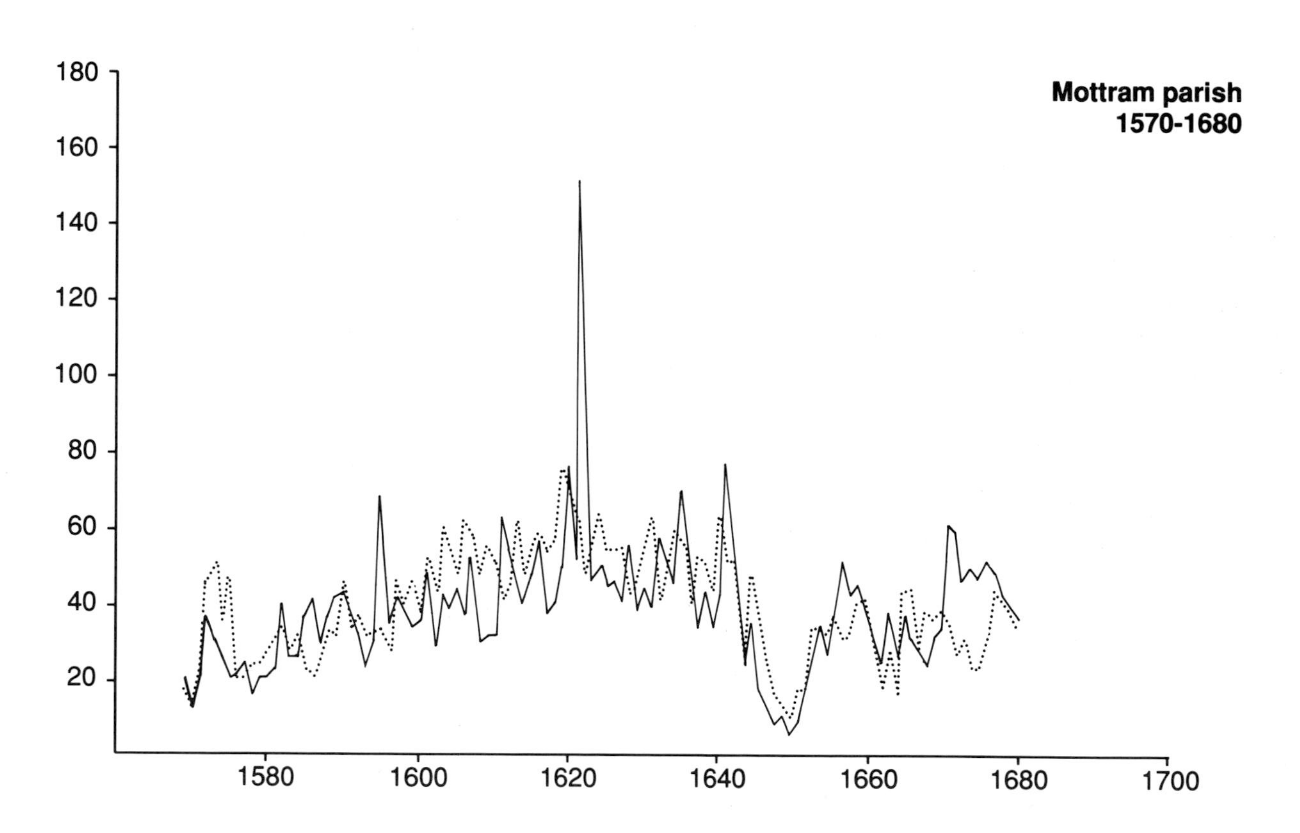

Fig 8.7 Aggregative analysis of Ashton and Mottram parish registers.
Key: —·—·— marriages ·················· births ———————— deaths.
Particularly noticeable are the crisis years of high mortality in the 1590s, 1620s and 1670-1700.

Chapter 9

House, Hall and Castle

'[The jury from Longdendale] say upon their oath that there is also one ruined castle called Buckeden [Buckton] and [it is] of no value'

(Booth *et al* 1976-8, no 83)

9.1 Medieval Vernacular Buildings in Tameside

Three main types of domestic building can be identified within Tameside during the medieval period: the cottage, the longhouse and the hall. Only documentary material survives for the first of these buildings, but there is notable physical evidence for the latter two categories, which when combined with documentary evidence highlights the relative social position of the inhabitants of these structures.

Cottages

The cottage was a small rectangular building of one or two rooms. With local variations this often constituted the main regional house type from the early medieval period onwards. The small and cheap nature of these structures implies that their occupants were at the lowest end of the social scale. In Cheshire examples of such buildings have been excavated at the medieval village in Tatton Park, where they have been dated to the thirteenth and fourteenth centuries (Higham 1985, 75). Although no physical evidence for structures of this type is known within Tameside, the Ashton rental of 1422 lists at least twenty cottages within the manor. Most were rented at 2s per annum, by far the lowest of all the rents listed, and all the residents were tenants-at-will (Harland 1868, 95-108).

Longhouses

The longhouse was a self-contained farming unit, rectangular in plan, and divided into three or four bays; one end provided accommodation for the household, while the other end was used for storage and the stalling of livestock. Such substantial structures were occupied by individuals of a higher social status than the peasants who occupied the cottages described above. In Tameside they were probably the dwellings of free tenants and perhaps also of tenants-at-will leasing a sizeable holding. This last group are most visible in the Ashton rental of 1422; here at least 46 such individuals are listed as holding as many tenements, with rents varying from 5s to 56s 11d per year, but averaging around 22s (Harland 1868, 96-101).

Apethorn Farmhouse, Werneth, dates from the fifteenth century and is a rare local survival of a medieval longhouse (Plate 4.3). Although now encased in seventeenth-century stone rubble and later brick, the building was originally cruck-framed, of four bays, and open to the roof. Cruck construction involved the use of pairs of substantial curving timbers, or blades, tied to make A-shaped frames, or trusses. These stood on foundations of timber and stone and were arranged in sequence to form the frame of the building. The walls, infilled with wattle and daub, were non-load bearing and were often replaced by a number of different building materials in later centuries, including brick and stone. At Apethorn four of the original five cruck trusses survive. They all had tie beams, collar ties and collar yokes supporting the original roof construction, although some of these elements have now been removed. No documentary material specifically concerning this site is known from the medieval period, but the relatively high status of the building can be seen in the decoration of one of the cruck blades which bears the unusual feature of a simply carved column and capital.

Halls

The third main type of medieval domestic building in Tameside was the hall. The halls were the homes of the manorial lords and, by the late medieval period, of the wealthiest free tenantry. In line with its higher status the hall lacked the integral agricultural storage and stallage of the longhouse and served primarily as accommodation for the owner and his household, and as the administrative centre of his estate. The common plan was of an open hall of one or two bays, heated by a central hearth. At one or both ends a further bay, divided into two storeys, provided private accommodation for the owner and also a separate service area. In Tameside the medieval hall is best represented by five sites: Taunton Hall and Newton Hall which still retain part of their original cruck-framed structures, Dukinfield Hall excavated in 1982, Denton Hall, partly excavated in 1980, and Ashton Old Hall, demolished in 1893 but known from early illustrations and descriptions.

Taunton Hall is one of the hidden gems of the Borough. The building is a cruck-framed structure within eighteenth-century brick walls and a stone slate roof. Originally the structure appears to have been a two-bay open hall, of which the central cruck truss and one other survive. In the post-medieval period a dividing wall was built across the central truss, an inglenook fireplace was built against this division and an upper floor inserted. A third cruck truss is at right angles to the others in a cross-wing which was added in the sixteenth century or earlier. The medieval Taunton estate was held by the Claydens of Clayden in Manchester as free tenants of the Asshetons. Richard de Clayden is attested as holding land in Ashton as early as 1315, while in 1422 Thomas de Clayden was a tenant of John de Assheton paying 3s 6d rent (Farrer & Brownbill 1911, 345 n 89; Harland 1868, 104).

Despite the fact that the manor of Newton was held by the Neuton family as early as 1211-25 (see Chapter 3), there do not seem to be any documentary references to the hall until the will of John Newton in 1557 (Chester LRO WS). The present building has been restored in recent years, but the original timbers have been radiocarbon-dated to *c* 1380, suggesting that this is one of the earliest timber-framed structures in Greater Manchester and northern Cheshire. What survives of the hall is a rectangular structure composed of three pairs of crucks, standing on a stone plinth (Plate 3.1). The two northern cruck trusses have double cruck spurs about 3m above the floor, connecting the oak wall-frame to the wide cruck blades. The southern cruck forms a gable end. The hall is open to the roof, and there are three windows with timber diamond-section mullions. The walls are formed by square-panel framing of oak, with wooden pegs securing the structure (Marsden 1971, 68-72). It would seem likely that the building had at least one, possibly two, further crucks, extending the hall northwards.

The site of Dukinfield Hall, which was demolished in 1950, was excavated by the Greater Manchester Archaeological Unit in 1982 (Walker & Tindall 1985, 39-42; GMAU archive M7). This excavation indicated that the hall buildings were composed of five main phases of which the earliest, phases 1a and 1b, were medieval in date (Fig 9.1). Phase 1a comprised a series of slots and post-holes, two with posts still in situ, forming a building *c* 12m by 6m, aligned east-west. Some of these post-holes showed signs of having been recut, indicating that there were at least two episodes in the development of this structure. To the east, on the same alignment, lay the evidence for phase 1b. Here sandstone footings formed a rectangular structure *c* 20m by 7.5m in size and may have supported a cruck-framed building. In the centre of the building lay a stone hearth 2m by 1m, set in a floor of compacted brown earth. This would suggest that the earlier timber-post structure was replaced by a building of hall-and-chamber plan, which originally may have been similar in appearance and perhaps also of similar date to Newton Hall.

Dukinfield Hall has sometimes been put forward as a moated site, but no evidence of a moat was found during the excavation in 1982. Only one site in Tameside is known to have been moated, namely Denton Hall. Moated sites are extremely common in England, with over 6000 known; more than 200 have been identified in Cheshire (Wilson 1987), and 70 in Greater Manchester (Walker & Tindall 1985, 63-5). Their floruit appears to have been between *c* 1200 and *c* 1325, although moats continued to be created in the later fourteenth and fifteenth centuries (*ibid*, 61). The role of the moated site in the medieval period is a vexed subject but, in the North-West at least, most were associated with the houses of manorial or sub-manorial lords and were probably constructed as an expression of the status of the local family (Wilson 1987, 143; Harrop 1983, 10-12). Their distribution is in part dependent on the suitability of the local geology. In the North-West most moated sites are to be found on the Keuper Marl/boulder clay soils of Cheshire and southern Lancashire (Wilson 1987, 145). The western foothills of the Pennines, which include the old parishes of Mottram and Ashton, are almost totally devoid of moats, since the soils overlie either millstone grit or shaley coal outcrops (Harrop 1983, 8).

At Denton Hall excavation in 1980 revealed a short length of the moat to the north of the hall. These investigations showed that the moat at this point was *c* 11.5m wide with a sandstone and timber revetment along at least its southern edge, but its full extent remains uncertain. It has been suggested that its line may be indicated by two ponds to the west and south of the hall, giving it an irregular, almost triangular shape (Bryant & Bryant 1985, 58-9). Although most of the moats in Greater Manchester and Cheshire are

Plate 9.1 Ashton Old Hall, *c* 1890.
This view of the hall shows (left) the stone-built south wing with one of its two round towers. This wing probably dates from the fifteenth century and suggests that the hall was a fortified manor house. The inner courtyard buildings (right) were substantially altered in the nineteenth century. The hall was demolished in 1893.

rectangular or subrectangular in plan, there are a number of irregular shaped examples which include a triangular moat at Heyes Lane, Timperley (Wilson 1987, 146). The date of the moat at Denton Hall is uncertain, but it pre-dates the sixteenth century when it was backfilled and a timber-framed building was constructed across its line (Bryant & Bryant 1985, 58-61). However, references to a manor house in Denton date to the fourteenth century, when in 1330 Thurstan de Holland granted to Alexander de Shoresworth 'all his messuages except the chamber in which his goods were contained in Denton' (Irvine 1902, 98).

The most important and impressive of Tameside's medieval vernacular buildings was Ashton Old Hall. The lords of Ashton manor are first referred to in the mid-twelfth century, and Bowman suggested that Ashton Old Hall was originally a motte and bailey castle of this period (Bowman 1960, 248). However, early views of the hall, on which the motte and bailey theory is largely based, emphasize that the hall was built on the edge of a natural river terrace spur, overlooking the River Tame flood plain, and not on an artificially raised mound. In view of the fact that the church was in existence in the eleventh century, and that the medieval village of Ashton probably developed between the hall and the church, it is tempting, nevertheless, to postulate an extremely early building on the site of the later Ashton Old Hall.

The earliest documented reference to this building occurs in 1379, in the Ashton custom roll and rental, in which the 'Hall-yards' are mentioned (Harland 1868, 112). The Old Hall is next documented in *c* 1422, again in the rental, where the occupants of the pews in St Michael's are given, the 'servant women of the hall' being allotted the first form on the south side of the church (*ibid*, 113). According to Aikin the hall, as it stood in his day, was 'supposed to have been built about the year 1483' (Aikin 1795, 226). In its final form, as recorded on the Ashton estate plan of 1765 (ESRCA/15), the building consisted of a U-shaped arrangement (Fig 8.5). The southern range was built of stone, with a round tower, reputedly serving as a garderobe, or latrine, at each corner of the south wall (Aikin 1795, 226) (Plate 9.1). The south elevation of this range was much altered in the nineteenth century, but an illustration published by Aikin suggests that it originally included a centrally placed narrow arched doorway, flanked on each side at the upper-floor level by a two-light trefoiled window in a square-headed surround (*ibid).* The pictorial view of the Old Hall on the 1765 plan shows this elevation capped with crenellations, or battlements (ESRCA/15; Bowman 1960, 637). The west wing was also built of stone. Its west elevation included at least three gables, possibly of seventeenth-century date, but these would appear to be additions to the original fabric. According to Aikin this elevation contained 'strong parts of immense thickness with numbers of loop holes' (Aikin 1795, 226). A description of the Old Hall given by Higson in 1862 (in Glover 1884) shows that this wing once contained an open hall, with a roof decorated with trefoil windbraces. The short east wing appears to have been built of timber. An enclosed courtyard was created by a separate range of buildings, covering the north-eastern angle of this inner courtyard, and a wall enclosing the north-western corner of the yard.

Aikin refers to a second 'outer' courtyard (1795, 226) and this appears on the 1765 plan as a triangular yard, with buildings on its northern and eastern sides. Both courtyards had 'strong walls', while over the 'outer gate' was a small timber-framed structure

> 'ascended to from the inside by a flight of stone steps and very ancient. It has always gone by the name of the Gaoler's Chapel...[but] was taken down in 1793' (*ibid*).

The basis of Aikin's date of 1483 for the hall is uncertain. However, similar roof decoration to that at Ashton survives in Cheshire at Tatton Old Hall and Sutton Weaver, both examples dating from the late fifteenth century, and at Bramall Hall, where a date in the late fifteenth or early sixteenth century has been put forward (Figueiredo & Treuherz 1988, 39, 166-7, 274-5). The principal features of the southern elevation, the trefoil-headed windows and the small corner towers, are also consistent with a fifteenth-century date.

This high status building is best categorized as a defended manor house. The closest parallel within Greater Manchester is Radcliffe Tower, Bury, where a stone tower flanked by a timber-framed hall was erected by James de Radcliffe in 1403 (Walker & Tindall 1985, 47-51, 102-3). The extent of the medieval hall at Ashton is uncertain, but the reference to the 'Hall-yards' in 1379 may indicate that the double courtyard arrangement recorded in the eighteenth century pre-dates the fifteenth-century rebuild.

9.2 The Vernacular Architecture of Tameside *c* 1500-1700

The 'Great Rebuilding'

From the mid-sixteenth century onwards the vernacular architecture of Tameside, as elsewhere in the North-West, was radically changed by three main, interrelated, innovations: an increase in the number of rooms within individual dwellings, the replacement of the open hearth by the chimney and, from the late sixteenth century, a movement away from the open hall to buildings which were of two storeys throughout. The 'Great Rebuilding' associated with these changes was a phenomenon which first affected the dwellings of the manorial lords and other wealthy gentry, who either incorporated these features into completely new buildings or altered and enlarged existing structures. However in the seventeenth century a no less significant revolution took place in the dwellings of the yeomanry. In this case new buildings were erected which, unlike the earlier longhouses, were essentially farmhouses, with the accommodation of livestock and storage of produce now removed to outbuildings.

The innovations in both the hall and farmhouse involved changes in methods of construction and choice of materials. The cruck frame, though suitable for a rectangular plan, open-hall building, was less so for the requirements of the more complex two-storey arrangements now being undertaken. In Tameside it may still have been employed in the seventeenth century in barns, and the example at Woodfield may date from this period. However, in domestic timber-framed buildings it would appear to have been replaced by the other main method of construction, in which vertical posts joined by horizontals formed the main components of the walls onto which were set the roof trusses. Timber was not the only material used. Stone, which in the medieval vernacular buildings of Tameside with the notable exception of Ashton Old Hall was used principally to provide a footing for timber-framing, was now used as a main material. Tameside is of particular interest in this respect, in that there is a division between the use of stone and timber, the first predominating in the western half of the Borough, the second in the eastern. This architectural division reflects the geographical position of Tameside. The Borough straddles the lowlands of south-east Lancashire and north-east Cheshire and the western foothills of the Pennines, and each of these two areas had its own predominant building tradition, depending largely on the local availability of materials. A third main material, brick, is found in the homes of the gentry of northern Cheshire from the

1570s onwards but it was not until after *c* 1660 that this material became common in the houses of the yeomanry and other classes (Groves 1990, 34-5). In Tameside the use of brick in the seventeenth century is found mainly in the western half of the Borough.

Halls

The development of the hall from the simple hall-and-chamber plan of the medieval period to the grander structures of the seventeenth century is best illustrated in Tameside by seven sites: Denton Hall, Dukinfield Hall, Hyde Hall, Hyde, Hyde Hall, Denton, Stayley Hall, Newton Hall and Hollingworth Hall.

Although the west wing of Denton Hall was demolished in 1895 and the remaining part of the building destroyed by fire in 1930 sufficient documentary and pictorial evidence survives to suggest the development of the building. The core of the structure was originally an open hall, probably dating from the late fifteenth or early sixteenth century. This was of a simple design, made up entirely of cross-pieces and uprights, with a cove under the eaves, but without any attempt at ornamentation, except in the mouldings of the beam under the cove (Farrer & Brownbill 1911, 314). However, probably in the sixteenth century this rectangular building was enlarged by the addition of a double-gabled western wing, separated from the open hall by a screens passage and housing the kitchen. This wing was also timber-framed but with more variety in the treatment of its parts. It had long windows on each storey, two overhanging gables and a line of quatrefoil panelling. Possibly contemporary with this wing was a square projecting bay at the eastern end of the hall. This sixteenth-century complex appears to have faced southwards (*ibid*; Smith 1971, 160).

In the late sixteenth or early seventeenth century the hall was again subject to alteration. At the east end of the great hall a smaller chamber, with a gable to the north and south, was added. The upper part of this wing was reached by an external brick and stone staircase. Further improvements included the insertion of impressively ornamented brick chimneys in the hall and the west wing.

Immediately north of the hall was a smaller, detached range, for which a sixteenth-century date has been put forward. This building, which was built across the line of the backfilled moat, was still standing in 1979, when it was dismantled and re-erected at Hough Lane, Wilmslow (Bryant & Bryant 1985, 55-7). It was a three-bay structure of two storeys, originally built in timber, but clad during the nineteenth century in brick. However one gable with its timber framework did survive in situ in 1979, although it appears to have been of a later date than the main timbers, possibly about 1600. The quatrefoil panelling which decorated this gable is similar to that found at Ordsall Hall, Salford. The roof timbers were possibly renewed sometime during the seventeenth century. Since no staircase was found inside the building access was presumably via an external stairway (Walker & Tindall 1985, 36). The surviving evidence in 1979 suggested that the north bay on the ground floor provided a separate service area with little or no decoration, while on the first floor the north and central bays formed the main room. The original function of this building is uncertain. Smith suggested that it may have been an autonomous dwelling (Smith 1971, 160). However, the absence of any essential domestic features, such as smoke-bays or chimneys, seems to tell against this and a more likely possibility is that it was a regular meeting place of high status, perhaps for the manorial court (Bryant & Bryant 1985, 57).

Dukinfield Hall was also rebuilt in the sixteenth and seventeenth centuries. Phase 2 of the excavated hall appears to have been constructed in the mid- to late sixteenth century, and involved the rebuilding of the medieval phase 1b open hall and the addition of an east wing to form an L-shaped structure (GMAU archive M7). The sandstone foundations of the phase 1b hall were reused, and now formed a plinth on which brick courses were laid. Documentary and photographic evidence shows that these sandstone and brick footings supported a timber-framed structure which faced north-eastwards. Associated with the brick and sandstone footings were the remains of a brick inglenook fireplace with a cobbled interior, situated at the eastern end of the hall. That a floor had been inserted into the open hall by the early seventeenth century is indicated by the will of Robert Duckenfield from 1621, which mentions his chamber 'over the hall' (Chester LRO WS). A further phase of building activity took place in the seventeenth century. Phase 3 saw the building of a second timber-framed wing, this time at the western end of the structure, and the refurbishment of many of the walls in brick, producing a building with two cross-wings at either end of a central hall (Plate 6.2). It was from this phase that the earliest floor levels survived. These produced seventeenth-century finds, including coins of the 1660s, which led the excavators to postulate a mid-seventeenth-century date for the beginning of this phase. However the will and inventory of Robert Duckenfield in 1630, which lists each of the rooms of the hall, mentions the hall, the parlour, several bedrooms, a buttery and a kitchen, which arguably could only be fitted into a building considerably larger than that of the sixteenth century (Chester LRO WS).

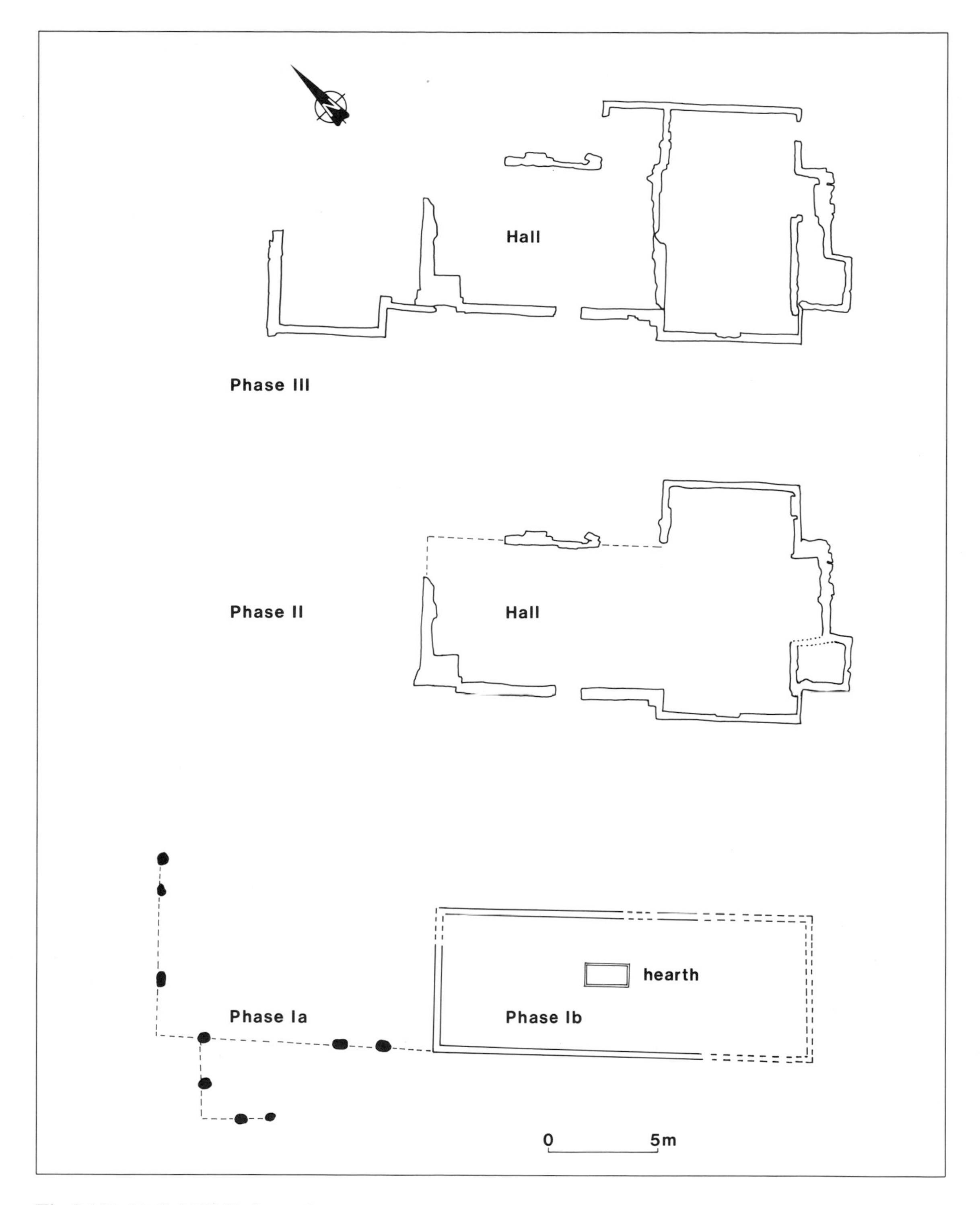

Fig 9.1 Dukinfield Hall phase plans.
Key: Phase 1a – medieval timber-post building; Phase 1b – medieval sandstone footings of possible cruck-framed hall; Phase 2 – sixteenth-century rebuild of the open hall and addition of the east wing; Phase 3 – seventeenth-century rebuild with the addition of the west wing.

The phase 3 hall is the building illustrated on the 1692 Dukinfield estate map (Stalybridge Local Studies Library DD 229/1). The hall was further enlarged in the nineteenth century, when a new chapel was added to the west wing and many of the external walls were replaced by machine-made brick (GMAU archive M7).

Hyde Hall, in Hyde, was demolished in 1857 (Lock 1981, 3) but there is a considerable body of documentary evidence which indicates that this was a timber, brick and stone structure. The tenure of a moiety of Hyde manor by the Hyde family from the late twelfth century (see Chapter 3) would imply the existence of a medieval hall on this site, but a manor house here is not recorded until Robert Hyde's will and inventory of 1639 (Chester LRO WS). There were then thirteen rooms in the hall including a 'chamber o'r the hall', a parlour, a 'wett larder', a lobby, and four 'chambers'. Ancillary structures included a brewhouse, a storehouse, a mill with its own chamber, a stable with its own chamber on a separate first floor, a malt garner and a hen-house. The whole complex was clearly substantial and was still being added to in the early seventeenth century, for the inventory mentions goods 'in the new buildinge'. Early map evidence indicates that in its final plan the hall complex had four wings entirely surrounding a courtyard, but the western wing appears to have been an eighteenth-century addition (Aikin 1795, 450), suggesting an H-planned hall, with cross-wings at either end of a central range. Ormerod, who saw the hall before it was demolished in 1857, suggested that it had been rebuilt in the mid-seventeenth century (Ormerod 1882, 809), but the above inventory implies that much of the 1639 hall was earlier, perhaps being sixteenth-century in origin.

Hyde Hall, Denton, formerly the home of a junior branch of the Hyde family, is built partly of timber-framing, partly of roughly dressed stone blocks and brick. In plan the present hall is T-shaped, of two storeys, with a two-storey porch, a one-bay brick addition, and a gabled cross-wing projecting to the front and the rear (Plate 6.1). However, at one time the building was H-shaped, one wing having been demolished. The porch has a plaque bearing the date 1625 below the Hyde coat of arms, but the principal feature is the two-storey bay to the upper end of the hall. This has coved jetties at first-floor and eaves levels, corner posts with carved capitals, and a ten-light window the full width of the first floor. All of the early windows have diamond-section timber mullions and leaded casements. The interior contains a large inglenook fireplace backing onto a cross-passage which contains the original studded oak doors at each end. The hall, as well as the chamber above, are entirely panelled, in some parts with Jacobean enrichment. The hall may originally have been open to the roof and the floor subsequently inserted to form two storeys.

Manorial residences east of the River Tame show a greater use of stone as the favoured building material perhaps from as early as the late sixteenth century onwards. Many local manor houses were totally rebuilt during the seventeenth century in this material, and it is this area that exhibits many of the features found in such high-class buildings in other parts of the North-West. The most unusual of these new buildings was Stayley Hall, which is a testament to the fusion of the lowland timber box-framed and upland stone building traditions then current in Tameside.

The present structure of Stayley Hall is usually ascribed to the sixteenth century (RCHME 1976), but there is reason to believe that it contains elements of a much older structure. The earliest documentary reference to the hall occurs in the Cheshire puture rolls for 1342-3, in which 'le Chaumbur' of Robert de Stavelegh of Stayley is mentioned (Highet 1960, 66-7). The hall is next referred to in a set of rentals and accounts of Sir Ralph Staveley from the period *c* 1399-1420. In these 'the new halle' is named, and Bowman suggests that this building may have been erected in consequence of the marriage of Sir Ralph to Elizabeth or Lucy, daughter of the second or third John de Assheton (Bowman 1960, 107 n 31). The next reference is in William Booth's will of 1579 (Chester LRO WS). The first illustration of the hall appears on Saxton's map of Lancashire of 1577 (Wilkins-Jones 1978, 49). The map of Stayley manor dated to *c* 1580, and perhaps compiled as a result of the death of William Booth, provides a detailed view of the southern elevation of the building. This indicates that the structure was timber-framed, with a five-gabled southern frontage (Bowman 1960, 113).

That ground-plan survives today although the building was clad in stone sometime in the seventeenth century (Plate 3.4). Halls of similar design are known from elsewhere in northern Cheshire and southern Lancashire and include the recently surveyed Bispham Hall which was probably built around 1600 (Nevell 1990, 13-18). On the west side of the main building is a second, smaller timber-framed building attached to the main hall by a timber-framed stair turret and chimney-stack. Both floors were divided into two rooms, although the ground floor was heated by a single fireplace.

Whether this partially detached wing is of contemporary construction to the main hall is debatable. It is aligned at a slight angle to the main hall and the linking door on the ground floor may have been inserted, although that at first-floor level is suggestive of contemporaneous construction. Also this wing is separately framed and lacks the moulding evident on the jetty of the main hall. Such evidence is indicative of two phases of construction and it is possible that the detached wing was rebuilt on the site of an earlier building about the same time as the hall was built (RCHME 1976). The Stayley manor plan of *c* 1580 is clear evidence that such a building arrangement existed by this time. The detached wing may have been built on the site of an earlier hall, possibly 'the new halle' mentioned in the Stayley rental of *c* 1399-1420 (Bowman 1960, 107).

By the seventeenth century Newton Hall had also been substantially expanded, the medieval hall forming but part of a larger complex of buildings set around three sides of a courtyard. These are described in Alexander Newton's will of 1617 (Chester LRO WS), which also suggests that the medieval hall had been given a first floor. A total of 21 rooms were mentioned, including a 'chamber over the hall', as well as two kitchens, a little parlour, a great parlour, both with rooms above, a wet larder, a buttery and a closet. Eight rooms contained beds but only three rooms, the parlour, hall and kitchen, had fireplaces. Ancillary buildings included a brewhouse, two shippons, two barns, a stable, an oxhouse and a mill.

Hollingworth Hall is first mentioned in connection with a petition of 15th February 1354, recorded in the Black Prince's register. In this John Hollingworth complained that 'his house at Holyngworth' had been broken into by William Hunt (Dawes 1932, 144). There must be some slight doubt as to which of the two halls in Hollingworth this refers to, but in all probability Hollingworth Hall is meant, rather than the Old Hall, the seat of the junior branch of the family. A cruck-framed structure of pre-seventeenth-century date, containing at least two crucks, survives in the northern range of the eighteenth-century Hollingworth Hall Farm. It is possible that this building was the medieval hall which was superseded by the seventeenth-century hall, immediately to the north. Little is known of this medieval building beyond this evidence. It is clear from John Hollingworth's will of 1661/2 that the new hall was an extensive building with sixteen rooms and a separate gatehouse (Chester LRO WS). The existence of a detached gatehouse occurs elsewhere in the region during the late sixteenth and seventeenth centuries, the earliest being at Lostock Hall, Bolton, which was built in 1590 (Smith 1971, 161, plate XXIV). Other elements of Hollingworth Hall in 1661/2 included a 'storehouse' and a 'weare house', the 'ould kitchen' and a dining room, while the presence of a gallery in the building might suggest that this structure itself included an open hall. Although the hall was demolished in 1944, surviving photographic evidence indicates that it was a stone structure of three storeys with mullioned windows and two gabled wings (Plate 3.2). There was an entrance offset towards the southern end of the building. The precise location of the detached gatehouse is unknown.

Yeoman and farm labourers dwellings

Although the halls are the best documented examples of vernacular architecture in early modern Tameside they formed only a small proportion of dwellings within the Borough. The divide between the homes of the manorial lords and wealthy freeholders and those of the majority of the local population may be gauged by the hearth tax returns of the 1660s. In Ashton parish in 1666 the highest assessments were those for Robert Assheton of Shepley Hall and William Bell of Cinderland Hall with ten and eight hearths respectively (Tait 1924, 114-15). However, out of a total of 413 households 368, or 89%, had two hearths or less (*ibid*), while in Mottram parish in 1664 out of 330 households a total of 318, or 96%, fell into this category (Chester LRO M13).

Although the 'Great Rebuilding' can be first detected in the houses of the gentry, by the beginning of the seventeenth century its influence was filtering down to the dwellings of the yeomanry. Among the earliest of the new buildings associated with this class is Hillend Farm in Mottram, which was probably built by Raphe Redditch following his marriage in the previous year (Powell 1976, 36). This stone-built house has a two-storey gabled porch, decorated with stone coping and kneelers (Plate 5.1), features which are also found at the end of the seventeenth century at the Old Post Office, Mottram, built in 1694. The ground floor arrangement at Hillend appears to have consisted of one large room, with one or two smaller rooms set to the rear and sharing a central chimney (Powell 1976, 36).

The major impact of the 'Great Rebuilding' on the houses of the yeomanry, however, appears to have taken place in the latter half of the seventeenth century. A rough guide to this development is provided by datestones, twelve of which survive from the seventeenth century. All bar one can be found on structures belonging to yeoman farmers, the exception being a row of cottages at Meadow Bank where the datestone reads '1698 IHAH'. This evidence is also concentrated on the Cheshire side of the Borough, where there are eight recorded datestones, compared with only four from the Lancashire side. After the 1604 datestone at Hillend, there are two examples from the 1640s, but it is not until after 1670 that the evidence begins to accumulate, with nine examples from the period 1671-1700.

Wills and inventories not only suggest that there was an increase in new buildings in the late seventeenth century but also provide evidence of a tendency towards larger dwellings. Of the 227 wills and inventories for Mottram parish during the period 1570-1680, 76, or 33%, list rooms, and of this total 53 had three or less. Of the remaining 23 references to four or more rooms, all bar four occur after 1660. They fall into six social categories, the largest being yeomen, with eight references, followed by three gentlemen, three tradesmen, two innkeepers, two yeomen/tradesmen and one husbandman (Powell 1976, 36). Of particular interest is the inventory of John Handforth of Newton in 1673, which shows that he had two dwellings, one with at least five rooms, and another, referred to as 'the old house' or 'little house'

Plate 9.2 Buckley Hill Farmhouse, Littlemoss.
This impressive brick-built farmhouse with its gabled facade was built in the late seventeenth century for the Buckley family, yeoman tenants of Ashton manor. The house displays a delicate use of brickwork around the windows and in its lozenged decoration and is an early example of the use of this material.

for which three rooms are listed, 'the lower part', 'the chamber' and 'the furthest room' (*ibid*). Further documentary evidence for new buildings is provided by the Werneth court book which records the erection of a number of dwellings and barns in the entries for 1657 and 1658 (Chester LRO DAR/I/16).

The developments of the late seventeenth century can also be traced in the stone-built dwellings of this period which still survive in some number in the upland areas of the Borough (see Appendix 4). Of particular note are Mossley Manor House and Broadbottom Hall, the latter of which was built in 1680 by the Wilde family, tenant farmers who also leased Broadbottom mill (Plate 5.2). A number of labourers cottages have also survived from the late seventeenth century. These include Lower Fold in Alt Hill, Clough End Farm in Mottram, Inglenook in Mossley and Moorgate Farm in Stayley (see Appendix 4). These were stone buildings of a single depth, the cottages usually being of one bay and two storeys, with three- or four-light mullion windows and low graduated stone roofs.

Within the lowlands of Tameside two high status houses were built not of timber, the more usual material in this area, but of brick, these being Buckley Hill Farm in Littlemoss and Red Hall in Audenshaw. Red Hall was demolished towards the end of the nineteenth century but is known to have been built in 1672 by Ralph Stopford, a wealthy local yeoman farmer (Butterworth 1823, 91). Buckley Hill Farm, the home of the Buckley family, is probably also of late seventeenth-century date. This is an imposing brick structure of three bays and two storeys. It is especially noteworthy for the finely detailed brickwork on the exterior. This includes raised lozenges and square panels on all elevations, as well as brick mullion windows (Plate 9.2).

9.3 Buckton Castle

Buckton Castle lies at 335m OD on a steep-sided sandstone spur overlooking the Carr Brook and River Tame valleys and commanding extensive views over the Mersey Basin to the south-west and north-west. The landscape around the site has been altered substantially over the years, mainly because of extensive sandstone quarrying which has left the earthwork on a peninsula of high ground (Booth & Cronin 1989, 61) (Plate 1.2; Fig 9.2).

Deceptively the site has the appearance of being an earthwork, consisting of a single bank and ditch enclosing a roughly oval interior, of 0.35 hectares, some 45m by 35m in size, with its long axis aligned north-west to south-east. The interior is raised to a height of *c* 1.5m above the exterior ground level, and is cratered extensively as the result of random excavations from the eighteenth to the twentieth centuries. It is surrounded by a rampart which survives in places up to 1.5m above the interior and has an overall width of 2.0-2.5m. However on closer examination it is apparent that this bank is the collapsed remains of a wall *c* 2m wide. This feature is most visible on the western side of the structure where a 15m length of the wall has been exposed by recent erosion. Here internal and external walls of mortared ashlar blocks retain a rubble mortared core.

The single ditch is continuous except to the south-west, where a natural slope of 1:2 renders it superfluous. Elsewhere it survives to a depth of *c* 6m, being up to 10m wide. Booth and Cronin suggest that the excavated ditch material may have supplied the sandstone for the wall (*ibid*), but there is no direct proof for this assertion. Two entrances are currently visible, to the south-east and the north-west. Both are shown on a mid-eighteenth-century plan and drawing of the site by Canon Raines, but only the north-west entrance appears on the plans by Thomas Percival (1756-1818) and Ormerod, the latter drawn in 1817 (*ibid*, 62). This entrance consists of a causeway *c* 5m wide, and Ormerod suggests that a paved road led from it north-westwards towards Saddleworth (*ibid*). Some authorities have noted the existence of a counterscarp bank to the south-east, although this is not obvious today, and indeed may have been destroyed by the recent expansion of the quarry into this area.

Two related external earthworks are visible to the north-west of the site, although these should not be confused with a mound at the north-western corner of the monument which probably represents a spoil-tip. A further large embankment some 75m down thc slope to the south-east also appears to be unconnected with the monument. The related earthworks run north-west-wards from the site, enclosing an oval area *c* 75m by *c* 80m, with a bank, visible only on the eastern side of this area, *c* 3-4m wide and up to 2m high, and an external ditch *c* 3m wide and up to 1.5m deep.

The date of the site has been the subject of much discussion since the eighteenth century, and the evidence has been recently reviewed by Booth and Cronin (*ibid*, 63-4). The site has sometimes been identified as an Iron Age hillfort, but Forde-Johnston, who studied all the Lancashire and Cheshire hillforts in 1962, asserted that 'a medieval rather than a prehistoric date might be more appropriate' (Forde-Johnston 1962, 11-12). The earliest documented reference to the site can be found in the Longdendale survey of 1360 which states that 'there is one ruined castle called Buckeden and of no value' (Booth *et al* 1976-8, no 83), suggesting that the site was a medieval castle which had fallen into disuse before that date. The next clear reference to the site occurs on a map of Stayley manor, drawn in *c* 1580. This shows Buckton Castle, which is specifically named, as a standing oval structure with an entrance to the north, defined by what appears to be a stone wall atop an embankment (Bowman 1960, 113).

Furthermore morphological and architectural parallels suggest that the site was a medieval ringwork castle. It is categorized as such by Cathcart King and Alcock in their survey of ringworks in England and Wales, although they overlooked the existence of a bailey to the north of the site (Cathcart King & Alcock 1969, 117 no 100). Of 204 ringworks listed by them, 53 had baileys, the most well known being Castle Acre and Castle Rising in Norfolk (*ibid*, 110-23). Further to this Cathcart King and Alcock note that 24 ringworks had artificially raised interiors, as has Buckton Castle.

The context of this medieval site is largely defined by the date of ringworks in general. The date range for these sites lies between the mid-eleventh and early thirteenth centuries (*ibid*, 96-8), although the possibility of an early site being reused in the medieval period was also noted. This occurred at Loddiswell, Devonshire, Dinas Powys, Glamorgan, Colwall, Herefordshire, and possibly at Rudbaxton Rath, Pembrokeshire, and Castle Combe, Wiltshire, (*ibid*, 113-22, nos 41, 60, 85, 149, 183). Thus it is not impossible that excavation may prove Buckton Castle to have been founded on an early, possibly Romano-British, domestic site.

During the early medieval period there are two contexts in particular when Buckton Castle may have been constructed: the years 1135-53 and 1165-73. During these periods and up until *c* 1200-3 the lordship of Longdendale was held directly by the earl of Chester. From 1135 until his death in 1153 Earl Ranulf II was the most important lord in the whole of

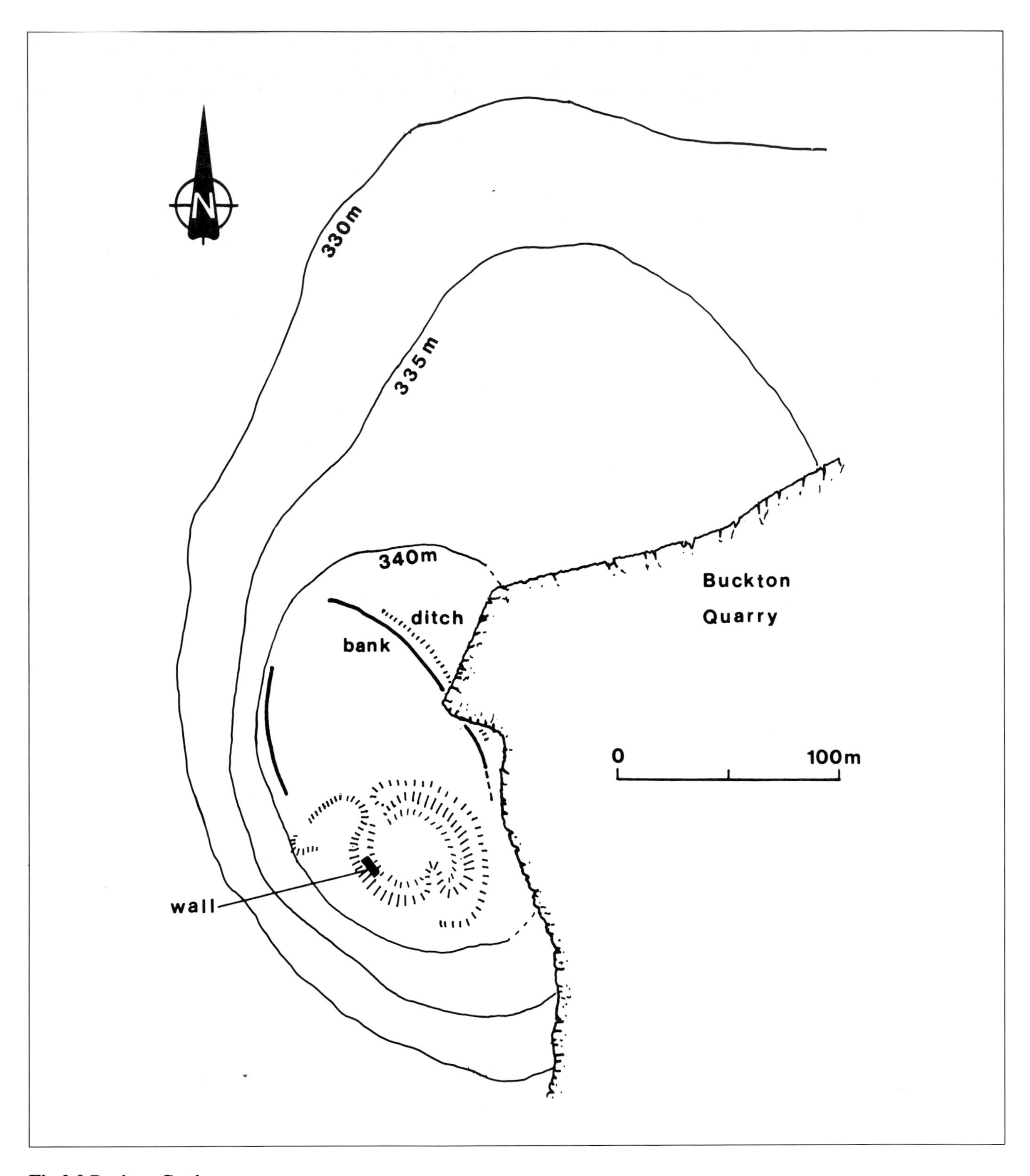

Fig 9.2 Buckton Castle.
Although the central 'earthwork', in reality an ashlar-faced wall with a rubble core, is the most prominent feature of the site, there is also evidence of an outer bank and ditch. This outer earthwork strengthens the identification of the site as a medieval castle, comprising a ringwork and bailey.

England, and during the civil wars between Stephen and Matilda amassed territory outside Cheshire, in eastern and central England, including the important fortresses of Lincoln and Coventry (Husain 1973, 110). However he favoured neither side in the civil wars, taking up a position of armed neutrality in 1141. The need to defend his territory from both parties may have been the cause for the construction of Buckton Castle, in order to guard the remote region of Longdendale and the Tame valley. It has been suggested that Mouselow Castle, in Glossop, on the southern banks of the Etherow, may also have been constructed in this period (Scott *et al* 1973, 18). Secondly in the 1160s Earl Hugh II was closely involved in Henry II's war against the northern Welsh. This ended in the catastrophic campaign of 1165, after which Henry abandoned North Wales, west of the River Dee, to Owain Gwynedd (Husain 1973, 110). Earl Hugh was left to defend the Welsh frontier of Cheshire on his own and eventually, along with a number of other earls, rose in rebellion in support of Henry II's three sons in 1173. It may be of significance that Stockport Castle was first mentioned in 1173, when it was held by the rebel Geoffrey de Costentin (Earwaker 1877, 330; Barraclough 1988, 192). Possibly both Buckton and Stockport castles were constructed as part of a scheme to secure Earl Hugh II's eastern flank, either while the earl was busy with the Welsh, or when he rebelled in 1173. However, such speculation can only be confirmed by the excavation of Buckton Castle itself.

Plate 10.1 St Michael's, Ashton-under-Lyne.
A church on this site is probably mentioned in the Domesday survey of 1086. St Michael's was rebuilt in the early fifteenth century, but the present church is largely a rebuild of the nineteenth century. The tower, 139ft 6in high, dates from 1886-8.

Chapter 10

Parish, Church and Chapel

'Let those present and to come know that I Matthew son of Edith...have given and granted and by this present charter confirmed to God and to the Cluniac order and house and monks of Kersal, a portion of my land in Audenshaw'

(Charter of 1190-1212, Farrer 1902, 328-9)

10.1 Parish Structure and Ecclesiastical Organization

During the period under study the three main types of small administrative unit in Tameside were the parish, township and manor, the parish being the territorial unit of ecclesiastical administration. In many parts of the English lowlands the parish was coterminous with the township, but in the sparsely populated North-West it more often consisted of a group of adjacent townships. Within Tameside Mottram-in-Longdendale parish fell into this pattern of a multiple township-parish unit. Denton and Haughton, and Dukinfield, Hyde and Werneth were also parts of multiple township-parish units, the first two being in Manchester parish, the others in Stockport. However Ashton-under-Lyne was a single parish-township, a much rarer phenomenon in Cheshire and Lancashire (Fig 10.1). The district of Quick lay in Saddleworth chapelry, which was itself part of the vast parish of Rochdale (Petford 1987, 79). Until the creation of a separate diocese of Chester in 1541, the Tameside parishes lay within the archdeaconary of Chester, a subdivision of the diocese of Lichfield (Lander & Thacker 1980, 12).

The early development of the Tameside parishes is obscure, but for most there is evidence of a pre-Conquest origin. This is almost certainly the case with Manchester parish, St Mary's church there being mentioned in the Domesday survey, and probably also with Ashton parish, given the likely identification of Ashton church with the St Michael's church recorded in the same Domesday entry (Morgan 1978a, R5.2; see Chapter 2). Domesday makes no mention of a church at Rochdale, but the holding of 2 plough-lands here by Gamel in 1066 may be an example of a pre-Conquest manorial estate which was coterminous with a parish also of pre-Conquest origin (Kenyon 1991, 144; Morgan 1978a, R5.2).

Although the Domesday survey lists no churches in Macclesfield hundred, the fact that the medieval Mottram parish included the Domesday manors of Tintwistle and Hollingworth suggests that Mottram church pre-dates the Conquest. The existence of a church at Stockport by the late twelfth century can be inferred from a Matthew, cleric of Stockport, attested *c* 1190 (Earwaker 1877, 354). However, Stockport itself is not mentioned in the Domesday survey and, although a pre-Conquest origin for the church has often been assumed, there is no clear indication that Stockport served as the head of an administrative unit, ecclesiastical or secular, prior to the twelfth century, when there is also the first evidence of the Stockport lordship. Of the three Tameside townships which formed part of Stockport parish in the medieval period, Werneth is listed in the Domesday survey as part of a group of multiple manors which also included Tintwistle and Hollingworth (Sawyer & Thacker 1987, no 66). It is possible that the township was itself originally part of Mottram parish and was given to Stockport parish as a result of the grant of Werneth manor to the lordship of Stockport in the early thirteenth century (see Chapter 3). The position of Dukinfield, as an outlying member of Stockport parish, also suggests that its parochial association once lay elsewhere. Unfortunately the early manorial links of the township are obscure (see Chapter 3), but on territorial grounds it is possible that this too may originally have been part of Mottram parish, the same being perhaps also applicable to Hyde.

Large medieval parishes, such as Manchester and Rochdale, were divided into parochial chapelries which were created to serve the more isolated members of the community. The Godley charters provide

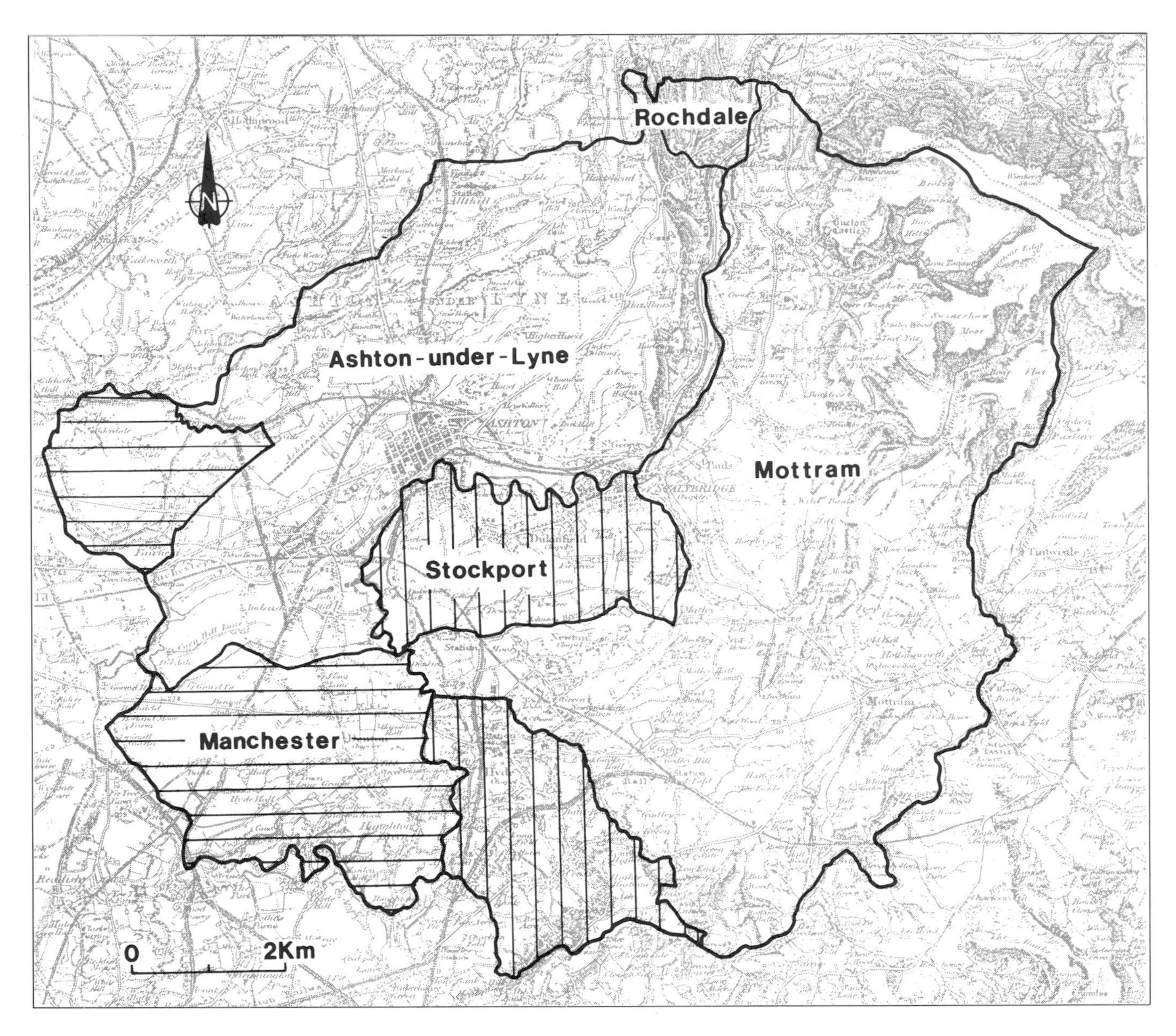

Fig 10.1 Tameside parishes pre-1700.
Manchester, Mottram and Rochdale parishes are all probably of pre-Conquest origin. It is possible that the three Tameside townships within Stockport parish, that is Dukinfield, Hyde and Werneth, were once part of Mottram parish and were transferred to Stockport parish during the medieval period.

evidence of a Robert, 'cleric of Dukinfield' as early as the mid-thirteenth century (PSA 1850, no 3; Middleton 1900, 39). It is possible that the provision of Dukinfield with its own cleric resulted from the transfer of the township from Mottram parish to Stockport parish suggested above. In 1445 Hamnet de Hyde obtained a licence for an oratory in Haughton manor (Ormerod 1882, 811). However, it was not until 1531 that the chapelry of Denton, which included neighbouring Haughton, was created with the construction of a church (Booker 1855, 41). On occasion such divisions were opposed by the diocesan authorities. The Ashton churchwardens tried several times to establish a chapel of ease in the parish during the seventeenth century, but only in the mid-eighteenth century did they meet with success. The best documented attempt took place during the Interregnum in 1650, when a detailed description of the boundaries of a new chapelry, based at Alt Edge, was proposed but never implemented (Bowman 1960, 193-4).

One feature of medieval religious life which was not represented in the Borough was the establishment of monastic houses. However through the gifts of local lords of the manor two monastic orders acquired land in Tameside. The Knights of St John held land in Ashton manor as early as 1292 (Farrer & Brownbill 1911, 345 n 94). According to the 1540 rental of their lands the widow of Richard Hunt paid 12d for Limehurst, and the heirs of Sir Thomas de Assheton 2d for 'Foulash'. A Richard Hunt died in 1587 holding a capital messuage and lands in Middlebrook formerly belonging to the priory of St John (*ibid*).

The earliest and best documented instance of monastic land refers to Audenshaw and the Cluniac monks of Kersal Cell. In a deed of the period 1190-1212 'Matthew son of Edith', probably Matthew de Reddish, lord of Denton, Haughton and Audenshaw (see Chapter 3), gave to the monks of Kersal a parcel of land in Audenshaw between 'the assart of William son of Gamel and Kettlescroft', being bounded by Nico Ditch on the east and Ashton Moss and Moss Brook on the north (Farrer 1902, 328-9) (Fig 3.7). In a deed of the period 1240-59 the northern half of this land, defined by Moss Brook, Ashton Moss, Nico Ditch and Gore Brook, was granted by the prior of Lenton (the mother house of Kersal) to Robert le Rous for 'half a mark due upon the feast of St Oswald the king' (*ibid*, 332-3). The monks of Kersal also held land in Alt, namely a moiety of 'Paldenlegh' granted to the cell *c* 1200 by Alban de Alt (*ibid*, 330). Following the dissolution of the cell, a three-fold division of its lands in 1548 between the Siddalls, Kenyons and Chethams gave each 4s 9d, or a third share of 14s 4d, as rent from lands 'in Ashton' (Arrowsmith & Hartwell 1989, 75, 78). The greater part of that income was evidently derived from the lands given to the cell by Matthew, son of Edith, for in 1588 and 1616 the Siddalls were described as in receipt of 3s 4d as rent from a messuage in Audenshaw (Booker 1859, 129, 137).

During the reign of Elizabeth I the parish acquired non-ecclesiastical functions. Alongside the churchwarden, whose responsibilities were confined to the upkeep of the church and its services, officers responsible for overseeing the new Poor Relief laws and the upkeep of the highways were appointed. The ecclesiastical and civil sides of the parish were not wholly separated, since wardens were also *ex officio* overseers and all the officers were either appointed or nominated by the parish in vestry assemblies, a general meeting of householders (Riden 1987, 91). Although in Ashton during the 1680s ex-churchwardens were usually elected as overseers, in 1696 the two offices were combined (Bowman 1950, 60-1). On the other hand, while the churchwardens were responsible for their actions to the archdeacon and through him to the bishop, the overseers and surveyor were accountable to the justices. In 1618, for example, the officers for Stayley and Mottram were ordered by the justices of Macclesfield hundred to repair their bridges over the rivers Tame (probably on the site of the later Stayley bridge) and Etherow (Chester LRO DAR/I/40, 77, 79) (Fig 3.7).

10.2 The Parish Churches

St Michael's, Ashton-under-Lyne

The present church of St Michael's, Ashton-under-Lyne, was virtually rebuilt in the nineteenth and early twentieth centuries and little survives of the early fifteenth-century church (Farrer & Brownbill 1911, 347) (Plate 10.1). However illustrations of the exterior of the church exist from 1765 (ESRCA/15) and 1827 (Butterworth 1827, frontispiece), which indicate that it was similar in style and plan to Mottram parish church. The illustration of 1765 is a view from the south-west and shows a church built in the Perpendicular style with a castellated six-bay aisle with a clerestory above, a porch in bay two, and a two-stage tower. The only surviving fragments of this late medieval church are some hoodmoulds with carved head stops on the southern exterior, and the late fifteenth- and early sixteenth-century stained glass, now in the aisles but originally in the east window. These windows are one of the treasures of the Borough and consist of eighteen scenes depicting the life of St Helena, members of the Assheton family and three saintly kings (Pugh 1902, 130-8).

As already noted, Ashton church is very likely the St Michael's church listed in the Salford hundred in the Domesday survey. Certainly the church was in existence by 1262, for Thomas Grelley, lord of Manchester, who died in that year, is recorded as holding the advowson (Farrer & Brownbill 1911, 348 n 124). The inquest of his successor Robert Grelley in 1282 lists the advowson as worth £20 per annum (Farrer 1903, 250). This same figure is mentioned in the survey of Manchester manor in 1320 or 1322 (Farrer 1907, 69), although in 1291 the ecclesiastical taxation of Pope Nicholas valued the church at not more than £10 (Farrer & Brownbill 1911, 348). In 1403 Thomas la Warre, lord of Manchester, agreed that after his death the advowson should pass to John de Assheton and his heirs (*ibid*). The rebuilding of the church followed, 1413 being given as the traditional date. A list of the pew arrangements survives from *c* 1422, and may stipulate the seating in the new church (Harland 1868, 112-15). In 1515 Thomas de Assheton left £40 in his will towards the rebuilding of the tower (ESRCA/13).

Although in 1538 all parishes were required by law to keep records of all births, marriages and deaths (Riden 1987, 94), the registers for Ashton parish do not survive from this early period. It is not until 1594 that records of baptisms and marriages begin, and 1596 for deaths, but barring the period 1642-55 there are records for most of the seventeenth century (Brierley 1928). The surviving churchwardens' accounts cover two periods in the seventeenth century, 1639-57 and 1684-1700 (Farrer & Brownbill 1911, 348). Although the parish records for the Interregnum are fragmentary, further material survives in the plundered ministers' accounts for the period 1650-60 (Shaw 1896, 95).

From the medieval period onwards one of the duties of the parish was to provide schooling for local children. However in Ashton the earliest reference to a school attached to the church dates from 1590 when Charles Davenporte, the parish clerk, was named in the will of John Cocke as 'schoolmaster' (Preston LRO WS). In 1613 the parish register states that 'about this tyme Thomas Jackson was admitted to be minister & schoolm'r' (Brierley 1928, 330). In 1623 a 'Richard Chambers, Schoolemaister' was buried at Ashton church (*ibid*, 354), whilst in the period 1696-1706 a Joshua Newton occurs as 'schoolemaster' in the parish registers (*ibid*, 186, 191, 207). According to Edwin Butterworth 'a school house was erected in the seventeenth century on land given by the manorial owners adjacent to the Church-yard, for the education of the children of the parishioners generally' (Butterworth 1842, 60-1). Bowman suggests that this building was on the site of the later eighteenth-century school in Ashton (Bowman 1960, 384).

St Michael's, Mottram-in-Longdendale

Although the interior of St Michael's was remodelled in 1854, with only the chancel piers and arch surviving from the previous structure, the exterior survives almost complete from the fifteenth and early sixteenth centuries (Plate 10.2). Built in the Perpendicular style the church has a nave and chancel flanked by aisles of six bays, with the porch in bay two of the south aisle. The aisles are topped by a castellated parapet. Each bay has a weathered buttress and a stepped three-light window with a cusped head and a hoodmould terminating in carved heads. The castellated porch has a four-centred arch opening and angled buttresses. The nave has a clerestory with windows of a similar design to the aisles, but dating from the nineteenth-century restoration. A view of the church published by Aikin shows a more haphazard arrangement of seven mullion windows above the south side of the nave (Aikin 1795, 458). At the western end of the building is a four-staged tower, built *c* 1486, which has angled weathered buttresses and a castellated parapet, below which, encircling the tower, is a row of carved stone heads. There is a three-light west window with Perpendicular tracery, and two-light belfry openings. The two-bay chancel has a five-light transomed Perpendicular-style east window and a vestry to the north. Flanking the chancel are two chapels. The chapel on the south side was attached to the manor of Stayley and that on the north side to the manor of Hollingworth, and both were probably erected by the owners of these manors as chantry chapels. In the Stayley chapel are two much defaced sandstone effigies representing a knight, traditionally identified as Sir Ralph Staveley who died *c* 1420, and his wife, Elizabeth (Ormerod 1882, 866). The Hollingworth chapel contains a monument to Reginald Bretland of Thorncliff Hall, who died in 1703.

Whilst Mottram parish church is not mentioned in the Domesday survey, there is good reason to believe that the parish and the church were late Anglo-Saxon foundations (see above). The first securely dated reference to the church is of no later than 1249, when Henry 'parson of Mottram' witnessed a grant to Roger Davenport by Robert Salemon (Highet 1960, 86-7). This is probably the same individual as the Henry, chaplain of Mottram, recorded alongside Sir Robert, parson of Mottram, in Godley charter no 3 and possibly also no 6 (PSA 1850, nos 3 & 6; Middleton 1900, 37-9). Ormerod dated Robert to the late thirteenth century (1882, 854). However in view of the early thirteenth-century date for these two Godley charters (see Appendix 1) it would seem much more likely that Robert was parson in the first quarter of the thirteenth century and was succeeded by Henry between *c* 1225 and 1249. The church is next referred to in the ecclesiastical taxation of 1291 when the advowson was valued at £10 per annum (Chester LRO P25/8/1). In 1300 Jordan de Macclesfeld was the parson, while the Black Prince's register records the presentation of William de Claydon in 1360 (Dawes 1932, 397). Both Ormerod (1882, 854-8) and Earwaker (1880, 118-38) provide much valuable information about the parsons, vicars and beneficiaries of the church during the medieval and early modern periods.

A number of documents provide evidence of the church's lands in the parish during the sixteenth and seventeenth centuries. In 1535 the parish income was £32 11s 6d, which included £2 10s from the glebe lands, £13 6s 8d from the 'tithes of grain', and £7 14s 8d 'in wool and lambs' (Chester LRO P25/8/2). In 1548 Nicholas Hyde was confirmed as vicar with lands which included a 'mansion with houses of office', glebe lands and tenements, meadows, leases, pastures, tithe corn, fruits and heriots (*ibid*, P25/8/7). In 1617 these lands included barns, stables, orchards, gardens and the glebe lands at Parsonage Farm (*ibid*, P25/8/9).

Like St Michael's at Ashton-under-Lyne, Mottram church was responsible for the education of the parish's children. There was a schoolmaster at Mottram as early as 1557 (Thacker 1980, 242). In 1612 Robert Garsett, an alderman of Norwich, left £100

Plate 10.2 St Michael's, Mottram-in-Longdendale.
Although the interior of the church was altered in the nineteenth century, the exterior retains much fifteenth-century work. Of particular note are the carved heads which terminate the hoodmoulds over the windows.

towards the maintenance of a free school at Mottram on condition that the lord of the manor or another gentleman did likewise. Richard Wilbraham, lord of Longdendale, raised £100 through voluntary contributions, and in 1619 he and Garsett's son each paid £100 to the school's trustees. The school benefitted from further gifts during the seventeenth century, including a covenant of £5 per annum made by Robert Hyde in 1684 (*ibid*). The school house was twice rebuilt at local expense. In 1623 William Hollingworth, a yeoman of Matley, left 13s 4d towards the cost of completing a new building (Earwaker 1880, 139), whilst in 1670 the structure was again renewed through contributions made by the parishioners (Chester LRO EDV/7/3/355). The school house was rebuilt for a second time in 1858, and is still standing (see Appendix 4).

10.3 Chapels

St James' (later St Lawrence's) Chapel, Denton

The chapel of ease at Denton was built on waste land in 1531-2 at the instigation of the Holland and Hyde families (Booker 1855, 41). This building still survives although it was heavily remodelled in 1872 when transepts were added to create a cruciform plan (Farrer & Brownbill 1911, 319). As originally built in the sixteenth century the chapel appears to have consisted of a nave of six bays, built of timber framing on a stone plinth with coved eaves and lit by mullion windows of three or more lights. Photographic evidence pre-dating the 1872 alterations shows a bellcote to the west and a chancel, also timber framed, to the east (Plate 6.3). Internally the six bays of the original timber-framed structure still remain. The shaped posts and curved braces support tie-beam roof

Plate 10.3 Dukinfield Old Hall Chapel.
The chapel was built in the mid to late-sixteenth century, close to Dukinfield Hall. It was here in 1641 that Samuel Eaton, chaplain to Robert Duckenfield, organized the first Congregational church in England.

trusses which have inclined struts, purlins with cusped bracing and a ceiling at collar level. The windows also incorporate fragments of early sixteenth-century stained glass from the former east window.

In 1534 it was agreed by the lord and freeholders of Denton and Haughton that for every acre of enclosed land 20d should be contributed to the upkeep of the chapel (Young 1982, 12). Further endowments were made to the chapel throughout the century. In 1571, for instance, Richard Holland and Robert Hyde of Denton wrote to Adam Hulton of Park Hall asking his consent to the enclosure by Raffe Collier of 3 acres of Denton Moor, the rent being £1 'employed for the maintenance of the chapel there' (*ibid*). During the seventeenth century the most notable incumbent was John Angier, a nonconformist whose election to the chapel was promoted by the Puritan Richard Holland in 1632 (Booker 1855, 71; Arrowsmith 1985, 6-13).

Dukinfield Old Hall Chapel

The remains of Dukinfield Old Hall Chapel now lie disused and disregarded but they form the elements of the oldest building in the township. The surviving structure probably dates from the mid- to late sixteenth century. It is built in ashlar stone with a later clay-tiled roof, the chapel consisting of a one-bay chancel and a two-bay nave, each bay having a stepped three-light round-headed, cavetto-moulded mullion window with segmental hoodmould. A door to the west of the nave has a chamfered surround, though the lintel is now missing. There is also a three-light east window in the same style as those described above, but double-chamfered with cusped heads and an elliptical hoodmould (Plate 10.3).

A licence for an oratory in Dukinfield was granted on 10th October 1398 to the lord of the manor, John de Dokenfeld. This may have been a regrant, given the existence in the first quarter of the thirteenth century of a Robert, cleric of Dukinfield (see above). It is possible that the sixteenth-century chapel lies on the site of a medieval predecessor.

In the seventeenth century the chapel acquired national importance as the home of the first Independent church to be set up in England (McGarvie 1980, 57). The man who organized this church at Dukinfield Hall was Samuel Eaton, chaplain to the hall's owner Colonel Robert Duckenfield. The son of the vicar of Great Budworth, Eaton was educated at Magdalen College, Cambridge, from where he graduated in 1624. Having taken Anglican orders he became rector of West Kirby, although in 1631 he was suspended for nonconformity. The following year Eaton went to Holland where he became a Congregationalist. He soon returned, ministering to a congregation in Southwark, and was consequently imprisoned in Newgate and fined £1550 (*ibid*). In 1637 Eaton travelled to New England but returned in 1640 and was soon involved in the tumultuous events of 1640-2. His preaching at St John's, Chester, on 3rd January 1641, and at Knutsford and Great Barrow near Chester, brought him to the attention of Robert Duckenfield who made him his chaplain, placing his own private chapel at Eaton's disposal. In 1647 the Old Hall Chapel was visited by George Fox, the founder of the Quaker movement, and it was here that he began his preaching career.

In 1653 the congregation split and Eaton with his adherents set up a new church in the grammar school at Stockport. The rump of the congregation continued to meet in Dukinfield until its suppression after the Restoration (*ibid*, 60). After 1660 the Old Hall Chapel does not seem to have been used for regular worship, even by the family, for Colonel Robert Duckenfield was buried at Denton Chapel in 1689 (Bulkeley 1889, 117). It was not until 1695 that the Old Hall Chapel was once more in regular use, when it was registered as a meeting-house (Stell 1987, 55-6). McGarvie has described the chapel as being 'of prime importance in the history of English Nonconformity, as the scene of the first Independent (Congregational) church, as the scene of George Fox's first sermon, and as the scene of the first provincial non-Trinitarian (Unitarian) church' (McGarvie 1980, 64).

Plate 11.1 Mottram, looking south from the church tower, *c* 1900.
The medieval village of Mottram lay between the church and Parsonage Farm (upper right, distance). Alongside Littlemoor Road an earthwork (immediately beyond the building in centre right) may be the remains of a house platform associated with the medieval settlement. The hamlet of the Mudd (upper left, distance) is attested from the late seventeenth century.

Chapter 11

Conclusion

'In so small a book on so large a matter...it would be absurd to pretend to have achieved proportion; but I will confess to some attempt to correct a disproportion'

(G K Chesterton, *A Short History of England*, 1917, 238)

To attempt to assess the history and archaeology of Tameside in the medieval and early modern periods is to admit not that there is too little information available but that there is too much. How to marshal the large array of deeds, inventories, wills, official documents and maps depends on the view-point of the writer. A work such as this is necessarily a synthesis of this database, the aim of which is to highlight some of the major themes of the period without being overwhelmed by the minute detail of much of the evidence. These themes are the development of the landscape, the growth of its people and the progress of society from feudalism towards industrial revolution.

When the Domesday survey was taken in 1086 Tameside was inhabited by a population which was both small in number and largely confined to isolated settlements along the major river valleys of the Tame and Etherow. Beyond these lay the wastes and woods not only of upland areas like Hollingworth Moor but also areas of lowland waste such as Denton Moor or Ashton Moss.

The next 600 years saw the steady exploitation of these resources so that by 1700 the predominantly woodland landscape of Domesday had been turned into the open pastures that can still be seen in surviving rural Tameside today. The impetus for this change was the growing population of the Borough, and the changing economic imperatives of the late medieval and early modern periods. Although in the early medieval period a growth in population had led to a phase of woodland clearance and colonization, the setbacks of the fourteenth century, characterized by plague and poor climate, did not necessarily lead to a halt in the exploitation of the landscape. Rather the areas that had been cleared for cultivation were now given over to sheep or cattle farming, pursuits which demanded more acres of land and so fuelled the continuing clearance of woodland and the enclosure of wastes.

How this society had altered from the Norman period is difficult to assess. The biggest change was the emergence of a large number of landholding free tenants, who by the seventeenth century were not confined to the gentry and the ruling county elites, but included a substantial body of what was known in the contemporary literature as yeoman farmers. By this stage most farmland was cultivated from family farmsteads whose inhabitants might number the size of a hamlet. These settlements were now spread across the landscape and were no longer concentrated around a few isolated clearings as they were in the Norman period.

Nevertheless whilst the population had increased dramatically during the sixteenth and seventeenth centuries, and the pattern of landholding and owning had shifted in favour of those groups outside the aristocracy, the society and industry of Tameside were still firmly established upon the rural economy. The emphasis may have changed – seventeenth-century families needed to support themselves from a number of different sources which included weaving, mining, husbandry, cultivation and farm labouring, rather than from just cultivation or stock-rearing – but nevertheless it was the agricultural cycle and the natural environment which dominated people's lives as it had done in the Norman period. Failure of harvests, combined with the deteriorating climate, still led to crises within the community. There is no surer sign of the dependency of such settlements as Ashton or Mottram on the countryside than the appalling mortality rates documented in the 1590s, 1620s or 1670s and 1680s, periods of natural disaster in the rural economy.

Appendix 1
The Godley Charters in the Society of Antiquaries Archives

The following catalogue deals with seventeen charters and deeds relating to the ancient Godelegh family of Godley manor in the thirteenth and fourteenth centuries. They formed part of a substantial donation by John Owen to the Society of Antiquaries in London in August 1849, and for convenience have been referred to in the text as the Godley charters (GC). A total of 51 documents, spanning the years *c* 1211 to 1645, were deposited. Whilst many are concerned with land and property in Godley, a number of other local manors and manorial families are mentioned. Amongst these are Ashton-under-Lyne (no 22, dated 1347), Matley (no 21, dated 1341), Mottram (no 9, dated 1313; nos 10 and 11, both early fourteenth-century) and Newton (no 24, undated but probably fifteenth-century; no 25, dated 1439; no 28, dated 1452; nos 31 and 32, dated 1482 and 1491; no 35, dated 1504; no 38, dated 1507; no 40, dated 1508; no 42, dated 1517). Although a summary list was published in the Society's proceedings in 1850, none of these documents was published in any detail until 1900, when Middleton (1900, 36-40) presented partial translations of charters nos 1, 2, 3, 6, 12, 14, 15, 18 and 19. A transcription of charter no 1 was added by Barraclough (1957, 42). Both Earwaker (1880, 156-7) and Helsby (in Ormerod 1882, 860) record the existence of a second group of documents, partially published in the *Manchester Guardian* newspaper by John Harland in 1849-50 and presented to the Manchester Free Library in 1874. The importance of the Godley charters now held by the Society of Antiquaries lies in the genealogical and manorial evidence which they contain relating to Mottram and Ashton parishes, particularly in the thirteenth and fourteenth centuries. The following catalogue is an attempt to summarize the existing published material relating to this group of documents.

GC1

A grant, undated, of the period 1211-25.
1) Thomas de Burgh.
2) Adam Fitz-Reginald.
A grant of lands in 'Mottram', probably the original grant of Godley manor. Adam was obliged to grind his corn at the manorial mill. For a transcription see Barraclough (1957, 42).
Witnesses: Nicholas de Tatton, Hugh parson of Tatton, Robert son of Adam, Robert de Stavelegh, Robert de Bredbury, Ralph de Hatterslegh, Ralph de Wolegh, Thomas de Hollinworth, Henry de Mattelegh.

GC2

A grant, undated, probably of the period 1225-49.
1) William de Godelegh son of Adam de Godelegh.
2) Robert his brother.
A grant of all the lands which William's uncle William held in Godley to Robert his brother except for 1 acre in 'Baldwinlie'. Of the witnesses Thomas de Godelegh occurs on GC3 making a date in the second quarter of the thirteenth century seem most likely (Middleton 1900, 38).
Witnesses: Robert de Stavelegh, William Rae, Radulf de Walegh [Woolley?], Henry de Mattelegh, Thomas de Godelegh, Hugh de Godelegh.

GC3

A grant, undated, probably pre-1249.
1) Thomas de Godelegh.
2) Thomas Faber.
A grant to Thomas Faber (Smith) of the lands and buildings in Godley which his brother Adam Faber held previously. Included licence to burn charcoal. Amongst the witnesses Henry, the chaplain of Mottram, is attested as parson there in 1249 (Highet 1960, 86-7), suggesting a date of no later than this year for the document (Middleton 1900, 38-9).
Witnesses: Sir Robert parson of Mottram, Henry chaplain, Thomas de Hollinworth, Ralph de Wolegh, Robert cleric of Dukinfield, Alexander de Mattelegh, Robert chaplain of Mottram.

GC4

A grant, undated, probably pre-1313/14.
1) Alexander de Mattelegh and his eldest son Richard.
2) Robert son of Hugh de Godelegh.
A grant by Alexander de Mattelegh and Richard his eldest son to Robert de Godelegh and his heirs of all their right in the lands of Robert son of Hugh de Godelegh. Richard de Mattelegh occurs in a document of 1313/14 (Ormerod 1882, 868), was a witness to GC15 and was dead by 1341, when his son William was described as his heir (GC21). Unpublished (PSA 1850, 40).

GC5

A grant, dated on the nativity of St John the Baptist, the ninth year of Edward II (1316).
1) William de Godelegh.
2) Robert de Godelegh.
A grant by William son of Henry de Godelegh to his brother Robert and his heirs of a place called the 'Breadherthe' in Godley. Unpublished (PSA 1850, 40).

GC6

A grant, undated, probably pre-1249.
1) Adam Faber.
2) Thomas Faber.
A grant by Adam Faber, of Simmundelegh, to his brother Thomas of the land held of Thomas de Godelegh and William de Godelegh, near Godley Brook. Thomas Faber also occurs in GC3, GC7 and GC8. All the witnesses to this

document occur on either GC2 and GC3 suggesting an early thirteenth-century date. Since they included Henry, the chaplain of Mottram, the document must be no later than 1249 (see GC3). A translation was published by Middleton (1900, 37).
Witnesses: Sir Robert parson of Mottram, Henry chaplain, Robert chaplain, Thomas de Hollinworth, Alexander de Mattelegh, Henry de Mattelegh.

GC7
A grant, undated, probably late thirteenth-century.
1) Ralph de Godelegh.
2) Thomas Faber.
A grant by Ralph son of Matthew de Godelegh to Thomas Faber of Godley and his heirs of all his right in the land in Godley, formerly belonging to his father and brother. This charter must therefore post-date GC6. However Ralph and Matthew de Godelegh only occur elsewhere in the undated charter GC8. Their relationship to the rest of the Godelegh family is unclear and a precise date is thus difficult to obtain. Henry Godelegh son of Thomas is attested in *c* 1270 (Earwaker 1880, 40), whilst Henry de Godelegh son of Robert is attested in 1294 and 1319 (GC12 & GC13). Barraclough notes two witnesses to this document, but there is no published translation (Barraclough 1957, 44; PSA 1850, 40).
Witnesses: Henry son of Thomas de Godelegh, Henry son of Robert de Godelegh.

GC8
A grant, undated, probably late thirteenth-century.
1) Thomas Faber.
2) Ralph de Godelegh.
A grant by Thomas Faber of Godley to Ralph son of Matthew de Godelegh of ½ acre of land in Godley. The date of this document is probably the same as GC7, late thirteenth-century. Barraclough notes two witnesses to this document, but there is no published translation (Barraclough 1957, 44; PSA 1850, 40).
Witnesses: Henry son of Thomas de Godelegh, Henry son of Robert de Godelegh.

GC12
A lease, dated 1294.
1) William de Godelegh and Agnes de Godelegh.
2) Henry de Godelegh.
A lease from William son of Henry and Agnes to Henry son of Robert de Godelegh of lands in Godley excepting 'Dewyscap'. A translation was published by Middleton (1900, 39).
Witnesses: Hamo de Dokinfield, Richard de Dewyscnap, Robert de Gattelegh, Rad de Woliegh, William de Tingetwysil.

GC13
A bill of sale, dated the Sunday next before the feast of All Saints 1319.
1) Henry de Godelegh.
2) William de Baggilegh.
A bill of sale by Henry de Godelegh of his goods and chattels to William de Baggilegh. Unpublished (PSA 1850, 40).

GC14
A release, dated 1308-9.
1) Robert de Godelegh.
2) Henry de Godelegh.
A release from Robert son of Henry de Godelegh to Henry son of Robert de Godelegh of all the homage, service and rents which Henry held of him for the sixth part of Godley. This document is almost certainly referred to by both Earwaker (1880, 156) and Ormerod (1880, 860), and dated by them to 1308-9. A partial translation was published by Middleton, but he omitted the witnesses (1900, 39).

GC15
A grant, undated, pre-1309.
1) Thomas Faber.
2) Henry de Godelegh.
A grant by Thomas Faber of Godley to Henry son of Robert de Godelegh and his heirs of land in Godley which Walter de Godelegh held from his brother Robert de Godelegh. Amongst the witnesses are Jordan de Bredbury who died in or before 1309 (Ormerod 1882, 820). A partial translation was published by Middleton (1900, 38).
Witnesses: Thomas bailiff of Macclesfield, Jordan de Bredbury, Roger de Maston, Richard de Dukinfield, Richard de Mattelegh, Robert de Mattelegh, John de Holynworth, Rodulph de Wolegh.

GC16
A grant, undated, possibly pre-1309.
1) Thomas Faber.
2) Henry de Godelegh.
A grant by Thomas Faber of Godley to Henry son of Robert de Godelegh and his heirs of land which Walter de Godelegh formerly held by grant from Robert Laysing his brother. Undated but in view of GC15 probably of the period before 1309, and certainly before 1319 when Henry sold his interests in Godley to William de Baggilegh. Unpublished (PSA 1850, 40).

GC17
A release, undated, pre-1319.
1) Margery Faber.
2) Henry de Godelegh.
A release by Margery daughter of Thomas Faber to Henry son of Robert de Godelegh and his heirs of her right and claim in a curtilage and house in Godley. Undated but before 1319 when Henry sold his interests in Godley to William de Baggilegh. Unpublished (PSA 1850, 40).

GC18
A grant, undated, late thirteenth-century.
1) Henry de Godelegh.
2) Henry de Godelegh.
A grant by Henry son of Thomas de Godelegh to Henry son of Robert de Godelegh and his heirs of lands in Godley which had been held of him by William, Thomas, William and Margery Faber. Undated but late thirteenth-century since Henry son of Thomas de Godelegh is last attested in *c* 1270 (Earwaker 1880, 40), whilst Henry son of Robert de Godelegh is not attested before 1294 (GC12). A translation

was published by Middleton (1900, 36).
Witnesses: Thomas bailiff of Macclesfield, Richard de Wrt [Worth?], John de Hatton, Robert de Balkares, Richard de Dewisnape.

GC19
A grant, undated, pre-1319.
1) Henry de Godelegh.
2) William de Godelegh.
A grant by Henry son of Robert de Godelegh to his brother William of land in Matley called 'assarta', and land in Godley. Undated but pre-1319 when Henry sold his interests in Godley to William de Baggilegh. A translation was published by Middleton (1900, 39).
Witnesses: William de Baggilegh, William the forester, Alexander de Mattelegh, Richard his son, William de Wae [Woolley?], Richard de Hatterslegh, Simon Bredbottom, Robert chaplain of Mottram.

GC20
A release, dated the Tuesday after the feast of St John the Baptist, 1325.
1) Helena de Godelegh.
2) William de Baggilegh.
A release by Helena the widow of Richard de Godelegh to William de Baggilegh of her right and claims in lands in Godley. Unpublished (PSA 1850, 40).

Appendix 2
The Earl of Stamford Records in the Cordingley Archives, Ashton-under-Lyne

Since 1819 the stewardship of the earl of Stamford's Cheshire and Lancashire estates has been held by the firm of estate agents and surveyors Cordingleys. On the death of the widow of the seventh earl in 1905 the Stamford estates were divided between Mrs Eileen Bissel and Lord Deramore. Cordingleys in Ashton-under-Lyne currently hold the documentary material for the Stamford estates in Lancashire, specifically for Ashton-under-Lyne, on behalf of Lord Deramore. Most of this material post-dates 1800, but a small group of manuscripts pre-dates 1700. Of these thirteen relate to property and persons in Tameside. These properties included the manors of Ashton and Stayley, the individuals concerned being members of the Assheton, Stavelegh and Booth families. Through the kind offices of Mr David Cordingley it was possible to catalogue and copy these documents. The catalogue is reproduced below. Translation of documents ESRCA (Earl of Stamford Records, Cordingley Archives) 4, 6, 7-9 and 12 was undertaken by Robert Dinn, and transcription of documents ESRCA 5, 10, 11 and 13 by Debra Stackwood and Michael Nevell. Copies of all of these documents, with the translations and transcriptions, are now held in the Tameside Local Studies Library, Stalybridge. All enquiries should be directed in the first instance to the Local Studies Librarian.

ESRCA 1
Indenture, sixth year of the reign of Edward I (1277/8).
1) Thomas de Macclesffeld.
2) Ralph [?] de Staveleg.
Property: grant of the manor of 'Staveleg' to Robert de Staveleg.
Witnesses: Thomas Assheton, Hamon de Dokinfeld, Robert de [?], Richard de Birch [?], Jordan de Tytheryngton, Henry Buran, John de Mottram [?], Richard de Dewysnape, Jacob de Brinnington, Henry rector of the church of 'Chedle', Roger de Prestbury, Adam de Both, John [?] de Brynnington.

ESRCA 2
Indenture, 13th May in the 33rd year of Edward I (1305).
1) Thomas de Assheton.
2) John de Assheton his son.
Property: tenements in the manor of Ashton-under-Lyne.
Witnesses: Adam de Walton, Henry de Stafforde, Richard rector of the church of 'Chedele', Thomas Le Waleye rector of the church of Ashton, Matthew de Haydocke, Richard de Moston, Richard de Assheton, Adam de Rossendale, Robert de Dokenfelde 'et aliis'.

ESRCA 3
Royal grant of free warren, 27th August in the ninth year of Edward III (1335).
1) Edward III.
2) John de Ashton and his heirs.
Transcription and photograph published by Bowman (1960, 49). Dated at Ashton.
Witnesses: John archbishop of Canterbury, John de Warenne earl of Surrey, Henry de Percy, William de Monte Alto, Ralph de Neville 'et aliis'.

ESRCA 4/1-3
Plea held at Mottram, 3rd March and 24th March 1377/8 [ESRCA4/1], and writ of right, 27th February 1377/8 [ESRCA 4/2-3].
1) Robert de Stavelegh and his son Ralph.
2) John de Oldum, chaplain, Richard de Morton, Thomas Gerberge (free tenants).
Trial by combat proceedings: dispute over 40 acres of land, 20 acres of meadow and 30 acres of woodland with appurtenances in the demesne lands of the manor of 'Stavelegh', which was claimed by the free tenants from Robert de Stavelegh. Other persons mentioned are John Lovell de Tichmersh, lord of Mottram-in-Longdendale, and his wife Matilda, Henry le Mareschal, clerk and steward of the manor of Mottram, Robert de Longedene, forester of Longedene, William de Leghs of Longedene, attorney. Partial translation published by Bowman (1960, 95-6, with photograph).
Witnesses: Thomas de Felton, justice of Cheshire [ESRCA 4/2-3].

ESRCA 5
Indenture, 1st September in the first year of Henry IV (1400).
1) John de Assheton.
2) John de Assheton his son.
Property: in the manor of Ashton-under-Lyne.
Witnesses: obscured by raised flap at the bottom of the document.

ESRCA 6
Deed of entail, the Monday after 3rd May in the third year of Henry IV (1402).
1) Simon Wagstav, vicar of Glossop, and John de Oldhum, clerk.
2) Robert de Staveley.
Property: the manor of Stayley and 'all our messuages, lands and tenements in the same township'. Others mentioned are Ralph de Staveley, brother of Robert, Oliver de Staveley, brother of Robert.
Witnesses: Robert de Legh, John de Assheton, knight, William de Hulme, John de Neuton.

ESRCA 7/1-3
Will, 29th September 1456, proved 29th April 1457 [ESRCA 7/1], and 23rd May 1457 [ESRCA 7/2-3].

1) Ralph Stayly.
Requests to be buried in the cemetery of St Martin's, Leicester. Wills that his daughter should marry Thomas Ashton. Relics including a silver cross left to Mottram church. Bequests to Edmund Vernon, Ralph Staveley, his servant Benedict. The will was proved before the prerogative court of Archbishop William of York, at his manor in Scroby, where administration of Staveley's goods was granted to Thomas Ashton, through his proxy Thomas de Holand, and before the prerogative court of Archbishop Thomas of Canterbury, held at Lambeth Palace, where probate was granted to Thomas Davenport. This shows that Staveley held land in the provinces of both York and Canterbury. Extracts are held in the Tameside Local Studies Library, Stalybridge.
Executors: Father [?] Thomas Ashton, Thomas Davenport, Thomas Holand acting as proxy for Thomas Ashton.

ESRCA 8
Illegitimacy case, heard at the archbishop of Canterbury's prerogative court, 27th July 1457.
Plaintiff: Elizabeth Ashton, wife of Thomas Ashton and daughter and heiress of the late Ralph Staveley.
Defendant: James Staveley.
The case concerns the 'legitimacy or illegitimacy of James Staveley of Coventry and Lichfield diocese, which before us [is] pending and undecided'. The first part of the document comprises transcripts of documents from the archdeacon's court in Chester, empowering Robert Kent, Roger Maden and various other people to represent them in court, dated 10th June 1457 and 6th July 1457. The core of the case is contained in the latter part of the document, which states that the case went against James Staveley.
Other persons mentioned: Edward Stanley, archdeacon of Chester, Master Nicholas Parker, custodian of the register, John Dey, proctor of the court of Canterbury in London, Henry Trevonwall, clerk of Exeter diocese, Thomas Kengey, John Lord, John Naseby, Thomas Holond, William Bryan, William Doraunt, Geoffrey Langbroke and William Chaunt.

ESRCA 9
Indented charter, 1st March in the 36th year of Henry VI (1458).
1) Ralph Staveley esquire.
2) Thomas Robotham, priest, Thomas Davenport esquire.
Ralph 'by means of a certain charter' gave lands in Cheshire, Lancashire and Yorkshire to the above named. These lands by charter of Thomas Assheton and his son Thomas are to be granted to Elizabeth 'daughter and heiress of the same Ralph'. Otherwise they are to revert to (2).
Witnesses: John Docunfeld, John Arden, John Huyde 'and others'.

ESRCA 10
Marriage indenture, 26th September in the 22nd year of Edward IV (1483).
1) Raufe Lord of Graystok, William Layton of Sproxton, Thomas Pole of Kykham, Harry Gray of Barton in Rydale.
2) John Assheton, knight, Rauf Assheton of Ffrytton, Sir William Mirfeld of Honley, Thomas Wentlvorth of Elmesall, Piers Rowme of Beston, and 'Thomas son and heir apparante to the forsaid Sir John Laurence Assheton parson of the Churche of Assheton'.
Thomas was to marry Anne, daughter of Lord Graystok, on 13th October 1483, with a dowry of £1000 4s. Inaccurate and incomplete transcription by Bowman (1960, 109-10).
Witnesses: (1) and (2).

ESRCA 11
Marriage indenture, 22nd January, third year of Henry VII (1487/8).
1) Sir Thomas Assheton of Ashton-under-Lyne manor.
2) James Haryngton.
Agnes Haryngton to marry Thomas Assheton. Bowman inaccurately dates this document to 1496 not 1487/8 (Bowman 1960, 110).
Witnesses: (1) and (2).

ESRCA 12
Inquisition post mortem, 7th October in the 19th year of Henry VII (1503).
Subject: 'Mathilda Staveley'.
Held: 'Altryngham', Cheshire.
Mathilda held four messuages, one toft, 40 acres of land, 10 acres of meadow, 20 acres of pasture and 16 acres of woodland in Stayley, 'in her demesne land, freely held as dowry'. To revert to Elizabeth, wife of Ralph Assheton, 'one of the daughters and heiresses of Elizabeth wife of Thomas Assheton and daughter and heiress of Ralph Staveley. Also to revert to George Bothe son and heir of Margaret, once wife of William Bothe and the other daughter and heiress of Elizabeth, wife of Thomas. Matilda died on 4th August 1503.
Witnesses: Hamon Masty, George Bonden.

ESRCA 13
Inquisition post mortem, 11th September in the 8th year of Henry VIII (1517).
Subject: Sir Thomas Assheton.
The inquisition starts in Latin, quotes Sir Thomas' will in English, and then finishes in Latin. His heirs were George Bothe, son of Margaret Bothe daughter of Thomas Assheton, Elizabeth Assheton, his wife, and Alicia Hoghton, also a daughter of Thomas. By a deed of 22nd July 1513 his executors were Sir Alexander Radclyffe, Richard Assheton of Middleton, Robert Longley, Thurstan Tyldysley, Gervase Assheton, parson of Ashton-under-Lyne', and Thomas Longley parson of 'Prestwyche'. Sir Thomas' will is dated 20th July 1515, and he died on 21st July 1515. A complete transcription of the will is held at Tameside Local Studies Library, Stalybridge. Bowman has published an incomplete and inaccurate transcription of this inquisition. In particular she incorrectly dates the will and the deed to 20th July 1514 and 27th July 1513 (Bowman 1960, 111-13).
Witnesses: Sir Richard Assheton, John Gibson, Sir Robert Longton, Peter Assheton, Thomas Wrightyngton, Thomas Tyldysley, Thomas Penketh [?], William Issherwoode, William Chorley, Arthur Tempest, Thomas Standysshe, William Asston.

Appendix 3
Colonel Duckenfield and the Jolly Letter

The following is a transcript of a document now held in the Tameside Local Studies Library, Stalybridge Library (DD 229/2). For the context of this letter see Chapter 6, p 75.

> 'I have noted ye contents of your's with reference to Justice / Dukenfield's grand father, but having examined Mr James / Jolly's, my great grand father's, memoirs, find no notice taken / of Col. Duckenfield except up[on?] an occassion once offered / Mr Jolly to be a Captain under ye said Col. for the Irish / Service, but after he had raised a Company of foot he / desisted perceiving ye design to fail, & had 2 Comissions / one to be Quarter Master of ye forces in Chester, ye other / to be Provost Marshal of ye said City & of ye Regiment / in garrison, there, at Shrewsbury, Ludlow, Lancaster, & / Liverpool, to hold under Colonell Duckenfield. This is all ye Account I find in those papers.
>
> By Commission dated 15th of September Ano. 1647 under / ye Hand of ye Lord General Fairfax Mr. James Jolly was nominated & appointed to be a Captain of a foot Company against ye Rebels in ye Ki[n]gdom of Ireland under ye Re= / giment of Collonell Robert [D]uckenfield of Duckinfield in / ye County of Chester Esq. & r[a]ised ye said Company on his / own people, Cost & Charges.
>
> Also by a Commission dated ye 3d. of February Anno 1647 [ie 1648] under / ye hand & Seal of Arms of ye said Sr. Thos. Fairfax Kt.[?] / Commander in Chief of all ye land forces under ye pay of ye / Parliament in ye Kingdom of England, Dominion of Wales, / & ye Islands of Gernsey & Jersy ye said James was Constituted / Provost Marshal to ye Garrison of Chester & of ye Regi= / ment of foot under ye Command of Col. Robert Dukenfie[ld] / above said, who hath ye Comand of ye Garrisons of Shrewsbur[y] / Lancaster, Liverpool, & Ludlow. And by like Commission fro. / ye said Sr. Thos. Fairfax Kt.[?] also under his hand & Seal of / Arms dated 13th of February Anno 1647 [ie 1648] he was appointed / & Constituted Quarter Master to ye Regiment of foot of ye / said Col. Duckenfield raised or to be raised for ye defence / of ye City of Chester.'

Appendix 4
Gazetteer of Standing Sites, Excavated Sites and Earthworks, 1066-1700

Ashton-under-Lyne

1 Alt Hill Farmhouse
SD 9444 0196

A T-shaped timber-framed farmhouse with two storeys and three units. There is a great hall, a small solar and servants' quarters, as well as a cross-wing to the north. The building was rebuilt in the early eighteenth century, and the date 1713 can be seen on one of the drop spouts.

2 Barn to the west of Audenshaw Lodge
SJ 9076 9637 Listed Building Grade 2

A late seventeenth-century brick barn, with a graduated stone slate roof, stone plinth and nineteenth-century alterations. There are opposed cart and winnowing doors with animal accommodation at the east end of the building. The tall elliptical-arched wagon entrance, now blocked, has a gauged brick arch and a brick dripmould. There is a similar arch to the smaller eastern doorway. A dripmould runs continuously over two two-light double-chamfered stone mullion windows. There is a raised lozenge and heart decoration built into the brickwork.

3 Buckley Hill Farmhouse, Littlemoss
SJ 9181 9968 Listed Building Grade 2*

A seventeenth-century farmhouse built of brick on a three-unit plan with two storeys and an attic. The first bay was rebuilt in the nineteenth century. There is some finely detailed brickwork on the exterior of the building, which includes raised lozenges and square panels on all elevations. There are two ground-floor and three first-floor windows, all with stone sills and continuous hoodmoulds using shaped bricks. The front of the building has three gables, as does the rear. Each gable has a blocked two-light mullion window under an elliptical brick arch and hoodmould. The interior of the structure includes an inglenook fireplace with a cambered bressumer beam and heck post, an oak dogleg staircase and original oak six-panel doors. In the roof are tie-beam roof trusses with curved struts. This farm complex also includes a seventeenth-century brick barn.

4 Cinderland Hall, Littlemoss
SJ 9135 9976 Listed Building Grade 2

A timber-framed hall of the sixteenth and seventeenth centuries, now partly rendered and encased in brickwork of the eighteenth and nineteenth centuries. In plan the structure has three units and a cross-passage, the service end, to the east of the cross-passage, having been substantially rebuilt. The main body of the hall is formed by four bays of two storeys, although the hall appears to have originally been open to the roof. There is a two-storey cross-wing to the west. The building has two brick chimney-stacks. The interior contains a cruck truss, immediately left of the cross-passage, incorporating three Tudor-arched doors, now blocked, below the tie-beam. There is also a large inglenook fireplace.

5 Debdale Farmhouse
SJ 9032 9620

The existing farmhouse is an L-shaped two-storey brick structure of the nineteenth century. However during conversion work in the 1980s the remains of a single cruck frame were uncovered within the building suggesting the existence of a pre-1700 building on this site.

6 Fairbottom Farmhouse, Alt Hill
SD 9406 0187 Listed Building Grade 2

A four-bay, two-storey house of probable seventeenth-century origin. Built of squared rubble with quoins, it has a continuous dripmould and eaves cornice, and a graduated stone slate roof. The ridge and gable chimney-stacks are built of brick. Reputed to contain datestones of 1653 and 1673.

7 Hartshead Green Farmhouse
SD 9570 0203 Listed Building Grade 2

A late seventeenth-century farmhouse of irregular plan with three bays and two storeys, with many eighteenth-century additions. Built of hammer-dressed stone, the earliest portion is the ground floor of bay three which has a two-light fire window and four-light double-chamfered mullion windows.

8 Jeremy Cottage, Hartshead Green
SD 9580 0190 Listed Building Grade 2

A three-unit plan farmhouse of two storeys, with an additional bay of a slightly later date. Built of squared rubble with a graduated stone slate roof with three ridge chimney-stacks, two built of brick. There is a datestone '1642 AH' on one of the ground-floor windows.

9 Lower Fold Farmhouse and Cottage, Alt Hill
SD 9440 0175 Listed Building Grade 2

The farmhouse is a timber-framed structure probably of the seventeenth century, which has been encased in eighteenth- and nineteenth-century brick. It has three gables and a tie-beam roof truss. The most significant feature of the interior is a fine carved oak staircase. In plan it is a three-unit, two-storey building, with later lean-to additions against the rear. The cottage, which is built of hammer-dressed stone and projects as a two-unit cross-wing, would appear to be early eighteenth-century, since there is a datestone 'TAI 1710' on the lintel.

10 **No 169 Old Hall Fold, Taunton**
SD 9267 0040 Listed Building Grade 2*

Medieval cruck-framed structure within eighteenth-century brick walls and stone slate roof. This building was originally part of the medieval Taunton Hall. In plan the building is of three bays and two storeys. The principal feature of the building is the survival of three cruck trusses. The two oldest are at each end of the principal room, being particularly large in both overall size and cross-section of the blades. The truss to the right of the principal room has an arch-braced collar and probably identifies the centre of the original open hall which has now been floored over. An inglenook fireplace backs onto it, with a large bressumer beam supported on a carved heck post. The third cruck truss is at right-angles to the others in the cross-wing, with blades which are not markedly curved, a tie-beam at floor level, a collar and wattle and daub panelling of the sixteenth century or earlier.

11 **Ridge and furrow earthworks, Littlemoss**
SD 9180 0015

Ridge and furrow earthworks covering two adjacent fields. The ridges are *c* 3-5m apart and up to 50m in length with curves at both ends, lying at *c* 110m OD. Aligned north-south.

12 **St Michael and All Angels' Church, Ashton-under-Lyne**
SJ 9415 9900 Listed Building Grade 1

The present church of St Michael's, Ashton-under-Lyne, was virtually rebuilt in the nineteenth century, the northern side dating from 1821, the nave and southern side from 1840-4, the east wall of the chancel from 1883, the tower from 1886-8 and the north porch from *c* 1920. Little survives of the early fifteenth-century church, or the later rebuild under the bequest of Sir Thomas de Assheton in 1515 which saw the replacement of at least the church tower (ESRCA/13). However illustrations of the exterior of the church exist from 1765 (ESRCA/15) and 1827 (Butterworth 1827, frontispiece), which indicate that it was similar in style and plan to Mottram parish church. The illustration of 1765 is a view from the south-west which shows a church built in the Perpendicular style with a six-bay aisle, topped by a castellated parapet. There was a porch in bay two. Each bay had a buttress and a stepped four-light window with cusped head and dripmould. The porch had a four-centred arch opening, angled buttresses and castellations. There was a six-bay clerestory with windows of similar design, and a two-staged tower. The only surviving fragments of the late medieval church are some hoodmoulds with carved head stops on the southern exterior and the late fifteenth- and early sixteenth-century stained glass, now in the aisles, but originally in the east window. A total of eighteen scenes depict the life of St Helena, members of the Assheton family and three saintly kings.

13 **Woodfield Barn**
SJ 9692 9947 Listed Building Grade 2

Although much altered a four-bay single-aisled barn survived on this site until 1990 when the building was dismantled with a view to re-erection. Whether the structure dates from the seventeenth century or earlier is unclear. The walls and roof were of squared rubble and slate, and bay four was incomplete having had the side-walls and roof removed. Three closed cruck trusses, supporting the original purlins, were relatively complete, having collar yokes. Unused windbrace notches and other structural anomalies suggest that the building may have undergone a change in use, or a restructuring.

14 **Woodfield Farmhouse**
SJ 9690 9945 Listed Building Grade 2

A two-unit, two-storey, seventeenth-century farmhouse with a single-storey porch, built of hammer-dressed stone and squared rubble. The farmhouse was dismantled in 1990 with a view to re-erection. To the right of the porch was a two-light double-chamfered mullion window with a hood-mould, to the left blocked windows. The first floor had a three-light double-chamfered window. To the rear were two two-light mullion windows.

Clayton (Droylsden)

15 **Greenside Farm**
SJ 8988 9885

A late seventeenth-century stone-built L-shaped building with a graduated stone slate roof, and ridge and gable chimneys. There is a two-storey porch with a round headed two-light window set in a stone surround on the first floor. Originally there were two sets of three-light mullion windows and one two-light mullion window on the south-eastern facade, but these have now been removed. The building has been restored and is now 'The Pig on the Wall' public house.

Denton

16 **Denton Hall**
SJ 9139 9468

Documentary and pictorial evidence for the now demolished hall indicate that it was a timber-framed structure standing on stone footings and of a three-unit plan. The original hall was open to the roof, with the western and eastern wings being added later. The building faced south where there were three bays and three gables, the western wing being a double jettied gable. Excavations in 1979, along with documentary evidence, suggest a three-phase development of this hall spanning the fourteenth to seventeenth centuries. In a deed of 1330 Thurstan de Holland granted to Alexander de Shoresworth 'all his messuages except the chamber in which his goods were contained in Denton' (Irvine 1902, 98).

The core of the building comprised a rectangular central hall, 10.7m by 7.6m, probably originally heated by a central hearth. The date of this hall is uncertain, but a late fifteenth- or early sixteenth-century date has been suggested. This portion was burnt down in 1930. It was of a simple design, made up entirely of crosspieces and uprights, with a cove under the eaves, but without any attempt at ornamentation, except in the mouldings of the beam under the cove. However, probably in the sixteenth century, this rectangular building was expanded by the addition of a double-gabled western wing, projecting slightly in front of the hall, from which it was divided by a cross-passage from east to west. The elevation of this wing continued the timber construction of the hall, but with more variety in the treatment of its parts. It had long windows on each storey, two overhanging gables and a line of quatrefoil panelling. This wing was demolished in 1895. A single projecting bay to the eastern end of the hall, again in timber-framing, may also have been part of this sixteenth-century remodelling.

In the late sixteenth or early seventeenth century the hall was again subject to alteration. At the east end of the great hall a smaller chamber, entirely faced in brick, with a gable to the north and south, was added. The upper floor was approached by an external brick and stone staircase. Further improvements included the insertion of impressively ornamented brick chimneys in the hall and the west wing.

To the north of the hall was a further, detached, wing, for which a sixteenth-century date has been put forward. This building, which was dismantled in 1979, was a three-bay structure of two storeys, originally built of timber. The northern gable with its timber framework survived in situ in 1979, although it appears to have been of a later date than the main timbers, possibly about 1600. The quatrefoil panelling which decorated this gable was similar to that found at Ordsall Hall, Salford. The roof timbers were possibly renewed sometime during the seventeenth century. Since no staircase was found inside the building, access was presumably from an exterior stairway. The north bay on the ground floor provided a separate service area with little or no decoration, while on the first floor the north and central bays formed the main room.

17 **Hyde Hall, Denton**
SJ 9180 9427 Listed Building Grade 2*

The surviving structure is probably sixteenth- and seventeenth-century in origin. The building is built partially of timber-framing, partially of roughly dressed stone blocks and brick. In plan the hall is T-shaped, of two storeys, with a two-storey porch and a one-bay brick addition. The gabled cross-wing projects to the front and the rear. The porch has a plaque bearing the date 1625 below the Hyde coat of arms, and a five-light mullion and transom first-floor window. The hall has two weathered buttresses and two cross-windows with segmental heads. There is also a six-light mullion and transom first-floor window. Similar six- and seven-light windows are found in the cross-wing. The left gable has exposed square-panel timber framing and a small two-storey gabled wing. The rear of the hall has a buttress and a four-light mullion window, but the principal feature is the two-storey bay at the upper end of the hall. This has coved jetties at first-floor and eaves levels, corner posts with carved capitals, a three-light mullion ground-floor window and a ten-light window the full width of the first floor. All of the early windows have diamond-section timber mullions and leaded casements. The principal features of the interior are a large inglenook fireplace with a chamfered bressumer beam, which backs onto the cross-passage which retains studded oak doors at each end. The hall, as well as the chamber above, is entirely panelled, in some parts with Jacobean enrichment.

18 **St James' (later St Lawrence's) Chapel**
SJ 9263 9506 Listed Building Grade 2*

The church, first built in 1531-2, originally consisted of a timber-framed nave and chancel, but was remodelled by J Medland and Henry Taylor in 1872 to create a cruciform building with transepts. Internally the six bays of the original timber-framed structure remain. The shaped posts and curved braces support tie-beam roof trusses which have inclined struts, purlins with cusped bracing and a ceiling at collar level. The windows incorporate fragments of early sixteenth-century glass from the former east window.

Dukinfield

19 **Dukinfield Hall**
SJ 9348 9702

Dukinfield Hall, described by Aikin in 1795 as 'an ancient building of venerable appearance' (Aikin 1795, 452), was demolished in 1950, and the site excavated by the Greater Manchester Archaeological Unit in 1982. Photographic evidence indicates an irregularly planned timber-framed building of two storeys facing east. The eastern facade was composed of three bays with three gables projecting at either end, the northern wing being a double gable. These gables formed cross-wings which also projected westwards. The back, or western, facade had a number of lean-to additions. Excavations indicated that the hall building had five main phases, of which Phases 1a and 1b dated from the medieval period. Phase 1a consisted of a series of slots and post-holes, two with posts still in situ, forming a building *c*12m by 6m, aligned east-west. Some of these post-holes showed signs of having been recut, indicating that there were at least two episodes to this phase of the 'hall' structure.

To the east of this structure, on the same alignment, lay the evidence for Phase 1b. Here were found sandstone footings forming a rectangular structure *c* 20m by 7.5m in size, that may have supported a timber structure similar to that at Newton Hall, that is one based on cruck frames. In the centre of the building lay a stone hearth 2m by 1m, set in a floor of compacted brown earth.

Phase 2 of the building appears to have been constructed in the mid- to late sixteenth century, and took the form of a new eastern wing to the hall, making an L-shaped structure.

The sandstone foundations of the hall were reused, and now formed a plinth on which brick courses were laid. Documentary and photographic evidence indicates that these sandstone and brick footings supported a timber-framed structure which faced north-eastwards. Associated with the brick and sandstone footings were the remains of two brick inglenook fireplaces, typical of those which became popular from the mid-sixteenth century onwards. These were located at the eastern end of the hall, and in the western wing, and had sandstone footings and cobbled interiors.

A further phase of building activity took place in the seventeenth century. Phase 3 saw the building of a second timber-framed wing, this time at the western end of the structure, and the refurbishment of many of the walls in brick, producing a building with two cross-wings at either end of a central hall. It was also from this period of activity that the earliest floor levels survived. These produced late seventeenth-century finds, such as coins of the 1660s, which initially led the excavators to postulate a mid-seventeenth-century date for the beginning of this phase. However the will and inventory of Robert Duckenfield in 1630 lists the hall, the parlour, several bedrooms, a buttery and a kitchen, which arguably could only be fitted into a building that was considerably larger than that of the sixteenth century (Chester LRO WS). This is the building illustrated on the 1692 Dukinfield estate map (Stalybridge Local Studies Library DD 229/1), although the hall was further enlarged in the nineteenth century, when a new, larger, chapel was added to the west wing, and many of the external walls were replaced by machine-made brick.

20 **Dukinfield Old Hall Chapel**
SJ 9436 9797 Listed Building Grade 2

The remains of Dukinfield Old Hall Chapel form the elements of the oldest surviving building in the township. The present structure probably dates from the mid- to late-sixteenth century. It is built of ashlar stone with a later clay-tiled roof, the chapel consisting of a one-bay chancel and a two-bay nave, each bay having a stepped three-light round-headed, cavetto-moulded mullion window with a segmental hoodmould. A door to the west of the nave has a chamfered surround, though the lintel is now missing. There is also a three-light east window in the same style as those described above, but double-chamfered, with cusped heads and an elliptical hoodmould.

Godley

21 **Godley Hall**
SJ 9667 9492

A substantial stone house built of squared rubble with a graduated stone slate roof, and modern brick chimney-stacks on the ridge. The house is of three storeys and three bays. The original doorway can be found on the eastern elevation. The lintel, with the inscription 'ICE 1718,' would appear to be a later addition. Attached to the west elevation is a two-storey stair wing, now used as the main entrance. This structure has two round-headed stone surround windows, a projecting plinth, an off-centre door, and a coped gable with kneelers and a ball finial, now removed. Either side of this wing are two double-chamfered three-light mullion windows, with the mullions now removed. This building is now used as a public house.

22 **Tetlowfold**
SJ 9673 9546

A two-storey, two-unit stone-built farmhouse from the mid-seventeenth century. Two datestones read 'RT 1645' and 'TWS 1726', indicating that the structure was rebuilt in the early eighteenth century. Only three walls of the original building remain, the rear wall, front bay and main entrance being rebuilds of *c* 1726. Among the early features to survive are three-, four- and five-light mullion windows.

Hattersley

23 **Botham's Hall**
SJ 9831 9298 Listed Building Grade 2

A T-shaped building of two storeys with a graduated stone slate roof. The seventeenth-century part of the house, the stem of the T, has a projecting plinth, quoins, first- and second-floor continuous dripmoulds and two-, three- and four-light double-chamfered mullion windows, and a five-light window. The door is in bay two and has an ovolo-moulded surround and a three-light gable mullion window.

24 **Clough End Farmhouse and Cottage**
SJ 9866 9403 Listed Building Grade 2

A stone and timber seventeenth-century farmhouse with attached cottage forming a two-storey, two-bay structure. There is a rear outshut and a two-storey extension. Built of coursed rubble and hammer-dressed stone with a graduated stone slate roof. The doors of each dwelling are placed centrally and have square-cut surrounds. Two-, three-, and four-light flat-faced stone mullion windows can be found on each house. The interiors have deep ceiling beams and box-framed dividing walls.

25 **Higher Cliff Farm**
SJ 9731 9269

A substantial L-shaped building, built of watershot stone, with a graduated stone slate roof and three gables. Now used as a barn. The greater part of the structure would appear to be a later eighteenth- or early nineteenth-century barn, but the short western wing contains much of an original seventeenth-century domestic dwelling. The western elevation survives intact and includes a blocked ground-floor two-light wooden mullion window, and a badly damaged first-floor wooden mullion window. The southern elevation has the remnants of a two-light wooden mullion window. Within the western wing survives some timber-framing now infilled with stone.

Haughton

26 **Haughton Green Glasshouse**
SJ 9400 9480

The first coal-fired glasshouse to be located and excavated in England was found during the laying of a new sewer line along the valley of the River Tame. Four years of excavation, directed by Ruth Hurst Vose for the Pilkington Glass Museum, revealed three well preserved subsidiary furnaces, used for annealing, and the main glassworking furnace, approximately 6m away. The furnace was a unique design with a deep wind tunnel running beneath the sieges to cope with the new coal fuel. A soda-lime glass was produced, with a high alumina content. Fine vessels in green, blue, black, and possibly amber were made.

Hollingworth

27 **Hollingworth Hall Farm**
SK 0021 9770 Listed Building Grade 2

Although the seventeenth-century Hollingworth Hall has been demolished the attached farm buildings still survive. Most of these are eighteenth-century in origin but elements of a much earlier timber-framed building, that may well have been part of the medieval Hollingworth Hall, survive in the farmhouse. Here in the northern range of the eighteenth-century stone building can be found at least two cruck frames, now largely concealed by a later ceiling. This suggests a building similar to Newton Hall, although it is not clear whether the remains of an open hall survive in the Hollingworth structure.

28 **Nos 3-5 Meadow Bank**
SK 0073 9675 Listed Building Grade 2

Two cottages built of coursed rubble with ashlar dressings and a graduated stone roof. No 3 is double-depth, of two storeys and two bays, with a gabled porch in bay two with an arched window and a lintel inscribed '1698 IH AH'. A three-light double-chamfered stone mullion window can be found on the ground floor and a similar two-light window on the first. There is a wing to the rear. No 5 has a lower roof-line, a three-light window on the ground floor and two two-light windows on the first.

29 **Mottram Old Hall**
SJ 9935 9637

An ashlar Greek Revival facade of *c* 1825 fronts the earlier sixteenth/seventeenth-century hall. The new facade is symmetrical with five bays, a central pediment, a single-storey porch and a cast-iron balcony with railings. The earlier hall survives as a wing to the rear of the nineteenth-century structure. It is a stone building with flat-faced mullions on the ground floor and square-cut surrounds on the first, with a surviving seventeenth-century doorway. Also from the seventeenth century are parts of the stables, which lie to the rear of the hall and include a cruck truss. The junior branch of the Hollingworth family were resident here from the fourteenth century to the eighteenth.

30 **Ridge and furrow earthworks, Hollingworth Moor**
SJ 9944 9780 & SJ 9926 9766

Two areas of ridge and furrow earthworks near Moorside Farm, Hollingworth Moor. SJ 9926 9766 lie at 350m OD and cover an area 40m by 60m. Ridges are aligned north-west to south-east and are *c* 5m apart. SJ 9944 9780 also lie at 350m OD but cover an area 70m by 80m. Ridges are aligned north-west to south-east and are *c* 5m apart.

31 **Thorncliffe Farm**
SK 0021 9682

Seventeenth-century stone-built farmhouse of three units, with an attached stable block to the east, and a later nineteenth-century two-bay stone-built house to the west. The ground floor includes two three-light mullion windows and one four-light mullion window. The first floor includes two three-light and one two-light mullion windows. It has a pitched stone slate roof and stone quoins.

32 **Thorncliff Hall Barn**
SK 0023 9680 Listed Building Grade 2

The only surviving element of the pre-1700 hall complex is a stone barn of the late seventeenth century. Built of squared rubble with hammer-dressed stone it has five bays and central opposed cart entries. There are two rows of vents and three buttresses. A fourth buttress was removed from bay one during nineteenth-century rebuilding. The interior contains four king-post fish-bone pegged oak trusses, with slightly cambered tie-beams.

33 **Woolley Mill**
SK 0090 9700

Earthworks probably relating to the medieval Woolley mill survive immediately north of Woolley Mill Lane where it crosses Hollingworth Brook. Remains of the earthen dam and the associated mill-pond can still be seen at this point.

Hyde

34 **Higher Higham Farm**
SJ 9608 9325

The current domestic dwelling is an eighteenth- or early nineteenth-century farmhouse. However attached to the western end of this structure is an earlier, probably late seventeenth-century structure, which appears to have been used as a dwelling. This is built of irregularly coursed and dressed stone. The southern wall has been removed, so that the structure forms an open garage. On the western elevation is a blocked doorway with a wooden lintel, and on the first floor a blocked square stone-framed window. A further blocked doorway and square window, both partially framed in stone, also survive in the northern elevation. Some of the roof timbers appear to be original.

Matley

35 **Higher Matley Hall**
SJ 9753 9597 Listed Building Grade 2

A T-shaped, two-storey building with a two-storey porch dated to 1733. Bay one, at the head of the 'T', has three-light double-chamfered stone mullion windows with hoodmoulds on each floor and two segmental-headed stone-dressed windows. The other mullion windows appear to have been heavily restored in this century, along with the coped gables. Although ostensibly a seventeenth-century stone building this facade hides the remains of an earlier timber-framed structure. The interior reveals elements of the original timber building in the head of the 'T', where the main posts are diagonally braced. A cambered tie-beam truss with a carved roundel panel on the underside supports a roof structure with curved windbraces.

36 **Paddock Farm**
SJ 9832 9600

A three-storey house of squared coursed rubble with a graduated stone slate roof and a gable chimney, probably late seventeenth-century. There is a two-storey extension to the south. Modern windows set in recessed stone frames which may originally have held stone mullions. The second-floor windows retain a single flat-faced stone mullion each. There is also a small light to the second floor of the south gable.

Mottram-in-Longdendale

37 **Broadbottom Hall**
SJ 9947 9363 Listed Building Grade 2

An L-shaped two-storey building with a two-storey porch, built in hammer-dressed stone with a graduated stone slate roof. A datestone on the door lintel reads 'JW 1680'. The former front has a projecting plinth and stone quoins. Bay one has two two-light and one three-light double-chamfered mullion windows with hoodmoulds. Bay three, which is gabled, has two three-light windows. The central porch has a cyma-moulded door surround with dated lintel, a continuous dripmould, and a two-light double-chamfered first-floor window. There has been some nineteenth-century restoration to the chimney-stacks and rear windows. The interior boasts wattle and daub panelling, chamfered and ovolo-moulded beams with stepped stops, the original staircase and doors.

38 **Coal pits, Littlemoor**
SJ 9931 9473 & SJ 9933 9477

Two ponds on Littlemoor now mark the probable position of the remains of early seventeenth-century bell pits in this area. Lying at *c* 230m OD the ponds are directly above the Warhill coal seam which outcrops here. Early map evidence suggests that until the late nineteenth century there were two further ponds, or pits, in this area, one to the north and one to the south of the surviving examples.

39 **Hodgefold**
SJ 9870 9345 Listed Building Grade 2

An L-shaped two-storey building built of irregularly coursed squared rubble. There are five bays with stone quoins and four square-cut stone door surrounds. The ground floor has a five-light double chamfered stone mullion window, a three-light mullion window and a three-light flat-faced stone mullion window. The first floor has two casement windows and three three-light mullion windows. A datestone on the building reads 'RW MW GW 1676'. The structure has been converted into five cottages.

40 **Mottram Grammar School**
SJ 9945 9524 Listed Building Grade 2

The existing structure is the school as rebuilt in 1858. This is a T-shaped Jacobean style building of one storey and a basement. The basement contains remains of the seventeenth-century structure, the door here, probably of this date, having a chamfered surround and a Tudor-arched head stone.

41 **Old Hill End Farmhouse**
SJ 9906 9445 Listed Building Grade 2

Built of coursed rubble, watershot stone and brick with a graduated slate and stone roof. The building is of two storeys with a central two-storey porch with a one-bay cottage added as a wing in the eighteenth century. The central porch has a chamfered door surround with a lintel with the date 1604. Above is a two-light double-chamfered stone mullion first-floor window and a coped gable with kneelers incorporating a dovecote. To the left of the porch are two three-light chamfered stone mullion ground-floor windows, and two flat-faced three-light first-floor windows. To the right are two five-light double-chamfered mullion windows. The internal walls and floors have all been removed and the building is now used as a barn and stable.

42 **Old Parsonage, Mottram**
SJ 9932 9499 Listed Building Grade 2

A building of squared rubble with a graduated stone slate roof and later brick chimney-stacks. It has a double-depth central staircase plan with two storeys. Three-light double-chamfered mullion windows can be found either side of the central door, each with a hoodmould. The interior is much altered but retains some original beams. Probably late seventeenth-century with later alterations.

43 **Old Post Office Farm, No 2 Back Lane Mottram**
SJ 9930 9558 Listed Building Grade 2

A two-bay, two-storey, baffle-entry building, with a two-storey porch. There is a slightly later wing added to the rear. A datestone on the door lintel reads 'NWM 1694'. The eastern frontal facade is symmetrical with a five-light house-part window and three three-light windows, all with double-chamfered stone mullions. The central porch has an off-centre chamfered door surround. Above is a round-headed first-floor light, owl and dove holes and coped gables with kneelers and ball finials. The rear facade has two windows with the mullions removed and a round-headed attic gable light. The interior contains wattle and daub partitions on two floors.

44 **Packhorse Inn**
SJ 9927 9543

The present east-facing facade was rebuilt in 1927 in mock-Tudor style. However the core of the building would appear to be early seventeenth-century. Plans from 1927 and pre-1927 photographs indicate that the structure was built of coursed rubble, as a double-depth, four-bay farmhouse on two storeys. A large stone barn lay immediately to the south, divided from the farmhouse by a cross-passage.

45 **Ridge and furrow earthworks, Mottram**
SJ 9910 9510

Ridge and furrow earthworks, aligned north to south, covering one field to the west of Little Moor Road, between Parsonage Farm and Mottram village. The ridges are *c* 5-8m in width, up to 100m or more in length and curved, lying at 210-30m OD.

46 **Ridge and furrow earthworks near Mottram Old Mill**
SJ 9890 9590

Aligned east-west these earthworks lie at *c* 200m OD. These ridges appear to be quite narrow, and a medieval date is not certain.

47 **St Michael's Church, Mottram**
SJ 9941 9530 Listed Building Grade 2*

Although the interior of St Michael's was remodelled by Shellard in 1854, with only the chancel piers and arch surviving from the previous structure, the exterior survives almost complete from the fifteenth and early sixteenth centuries. Built in the Perpendicular style the church has a nave with a six-bay aisle, with the porch in bay two. This is topped by a weathered plinth and a castellated parapet. Each bay has a weathered buttress and a stepped three-light window with cusped head and dripmould which is terminated in carved heads. The porch has a four-centred arch opening, angled buttresses and castellation. A six-bay clerestory with windows of a similar design can be seen above the main aisle. At the western end of the building is a four-staged tower, built around 1486, which has angled weathered buttresses, stone bands, and a castellated parapet. There is a three-light west window with Perpendicular tracery, a clock-face above and two-light belfry openings. The two-bay chancel has a five-light transomed Perpendicular-style east window and a vestry to the north. There are two chapels. The chapel on the south side seems to have been attached to the manor of Stayley and that on the north side to the manor of Hollingworth. They were probably erected by the owners of these manors as chantry chapels. In the Stayley chapel are two much defaced sandstone effigies representing a knight, probably Sir Ralph Staveley *c* 1400, and his lady. The Hollingworth chapel contains a monument to Reginald Bretland of Thorncliff Hall, who died in 1703.

48 **Warhill Farm Barn**
SJ 9941 9521

Stone-built late seventeenth-century barn, with stone quoins, graduated stone slate roof, and two blocked three-light flat-faced mullion windows to the upper floor on the south elevation.

Newton

49 **Newton Hall**
SJ 9420 9580 Listed Building Grade 2

The existing building is one of the earliest timber-framed structures in Greater Manchester or northern Cheshire, and has been radiocarbon-dated to *c* 1380. What survives of the hall is a rectangular structure composed of three pairs of crucks, standing on a stone plinth. The two northern cruck trusses have double cruck spurs about 3m above the floor, and these connect the oak wall frame to the wide cruck blades. The southern cruck forms a gable end. The hall is open to the roof, and there are three windows with timber diamond mullions. The walls are formed by square-panel framing, of oak, with wooden pegs securing the structure (Marsden 1971, 68-72). This structure is merely a part of a larger building visible on the Newton tithe map. It would seem likely that the building had at least one, possibly two, further crucks, extending the hall northwards.

'Quick Manor', Saddleworth

50 **Mossley Manor House**
SD 9759 0297

A three-storey stone house built sometime during the seventeenth century. The south facing facade of the building is very imposing being symmetrical with three storeys, three bays and two gables, with a central entrance with a rusticated and pedimented surround. There are two four-light ground-floor windows, two two- and four-light windows on the first floor, and two three-light windows on the second floor. Now converted into four cottages, Nos 3-6 Quickwood off Roughtown Road, Mossley. Extended in the nineteenth century to create Nos 4 and 6.

Stayley

51 **Hilltop Farm**
SD 9832 0013

A two-storey stone building, with a graduated stone slate roof and two- and three-light mullion windows. The exterior is rendered and the building has been heavily restored. A later eighteenth-century farmhouse forms an additional wing.

52 **Inglenook, Mossley**
SD 9765 0188 Listed Building Grade 2

Two houses, formerly three cottages of the late seventeenth, early and mid-eighteenth centuries. The seventeenth-century cottage (No 28 Audley St) is built of hammer-dressed stone and has a door obscured by a lean-to beneath a two-light double-chamfered mullion window. The right elevation has quoins, a four-light recessed chamfered ground-floor mullion window and two- and four-light double-chamfered stone mullion windows on the first floor.

53 **Little Bank Farm**
SD 9841 0051

A stone built two-storey farmhouse with a barn at its southern end. The farmhouse has a graduated stone slate roof, and ridge chimneys. There are two three-light chamfered mullion windows and one five-light chamfered mullion window on the northern elevation. The eastern elevation has two three-light mullion windows either side of a central doorway.

54 **Lukes Fold Farmhouse**
SJ 9790 9760 Listed Building Grade 2

A two-storey, six-bay building with a two-storey porch. Built in the late seventeenth century of squared rubble and hammer-dressed stone but much altered in the eighteenth century. A datestone on the door lintel reads 'HIE 1699'. The original porch wing has quoins and two two-light double-chamfered stone mullion windows with hoodmoulds, below a coped gable with kneelers.

55 **Moorgate Farmhouse Cottage**
SD 9831 0123 Listed Building Grade 2

Most of this complex would appear to date from the early eighteenth century. No 3 School Lane is a seventeenth-century cottage. Built of squared rubble and watershot stone with a graduated stone slate roof, the building is now, due to later additions, a long single-depth range with two storeys, including a shippon and a barn at the right end. No 3 has two four-light ground-floor windows and three- and four-light first-floor windows, all with chamfered stone mullions. The rear elevation has three blocked window openings.

56 **Ridge and furrow earthworks, Stayley**
SJ 9805 9915

A small area of ridge and furrow earthworks lying at *c* 160m OD, due east of Stayley Hall. The ridges are approximately 7-8m apart and up to 70m long. Two orientations are visible, north to south and south-west to north-east.

57 **Stayley Hall**
SJ 9757 9969 Listed Building Grade 2*

The first illustration of the hall appears on Christopher Saxton's map of Lancashire from 1577, while a map of Stayley manor dated to *c* 1580, and perhaps compiled as a result of the death of William Booth, provides a detailed view of the southern elevation of the building. This indicates that the structure was timber-framed, with a five-gabled southern frontage. This is the ground plan of the main hall as it exists today, although the building was clad in local stone after *c* 1580. To the west of the main house, beyond a chimney-stack, lies a second flush-walled timber-framed building of three bays and of two storeys, aligned at an angle of *c* 10 degrees from the principal structure, and latterly known as the kitchen building. The space in between the two is filled partially by a brick chimney and a further timber-framed structure containing a stair. The ground floor was heated by a large fireplace, possibly contemporary with the later main hall, and both floors appear to be divided into two rooms, a large one in the two northern bays, and a small one in the southern bay.

Tintwistle (Micklehurst district)

58 **Buckton Castle**
SD 9892 0161 Scheduled Ancient Monument

A ringwork defined by a stone wall, probably on top of an embankment, and a deep rock-cut ditch. One entrance to the north-west. The interior is raised. There is an outer earthwork to the north-west which is defined by an inner bank and outer ditch. The earliest documented reference to the castle is 1360 when it was described as disused, but its typology suggests that it was built in the twelfth or early thirteenth century. There is no indication that it was an Iron Age hillfort as has been suggested.

59 **Howard's Farmhouse and Cottages**
SK 9854 0249 Listed Building Grade 2

Little of the pre-1700 farmstead survives, most of the stone buildings on this site being three early to mid-eighteenth-century cottages and a farmhouse. However the right-hand cottage contains a four-light cavetto-moulded window and a hoodmould from the seventeenth century, although the rest of the structure would appear to be of eighteenth-century date.

Werneth

60 **Apethorn Farmhouse**
SJ 9432 9359 Listed Building Grade 2*

A fifteenth-century cruck-framed farmhouse now encased in external brick and squared rubble walls of the seventeenth to nineteenth centuries. This was originally a four-bay cruck-framed open-hall long-house, but in the seventeenth century a floor was inserted into the hall after its conversion into cottages. The western elevation consists of a small gabled stone wing in bay one, and a second stone bay. The other three bays are in brick and have three doors relating to their use as a shippon. The eastern elevation is similar except there are three dormer windows rising from the eaves, one of them gabled. The internal cruck frames and roof construction are especially noteworthy since four out of the original five cruck trusses survive. They all had tie-beams, although some have now been removed, collar ties and collar yokes, and support the original roof construction. The second frame was re-erected in the shippon and bears the unusual feature of a simply carved capital, with a rudimentary column beneath, on the east blade.

61 **Lower Higham Farm**
SJ 9604 9358

The current visitor centre of the Werneth Low country park is an eighteenth-century farmhouse. However a small wing, on the east side of this later structure, is probably late seventeenth-century in date. This wing is stone-built, of two storeys with a modern graduated slate roof, but with an original stone-surrounded window on the northern gable. A doorway on the western elevation has been blocked and is now a window.

Appendix 5
Sources for Pre-1700 Farmsteads and Buildings in Tameside

This appendix summarizes the evidence for medieval and sixteenth- and seventeenth-century settlement sites in the Borough of Tameside, and should be used in conjunction with the manor and township maps in Chapter 3 (Figs 3.6-8, 3.11-14, 3.16-18 & 3.21-8), and with the site distribution maps in Chapter 8 (Figs 8.3 & 8.4). The dates given for the medieval period represent the earliest reference that can be associated with a specific site, rather than a general area.

Ashton, Ashton town division (Fig 3.6)

1. Hayes Farm (later Slade Edge Farm) - 1599 (Brierley 1928, 308).
2. Clay Hill - 1681 (*ibid*, 165).
3. Knowl Farm - 1600 (*ibid*, 15).
4. Moss Side - 1636 (*ibid*, 103).
5. St Michael's Church - see Appendix 4.
6. Ashton Old Hall - 1379 (Harland 1868, 112).
7. Parks Hall Farm - 1630 (Brierley 1928, 89).

Ashton, Audenshaw division (Fig 3.7)

1. Lower Lumm - 1597 (Brierley 1928, 9).
2. Cinderland (Sunderland) Hall - 1422 & 1618 (Harland 1868, 104-5; Butterworth 1823, 158); see Appendix 4.
3. Buckley Hill - 1618 (Butterworth 1823, 158); see Appendix 4.
4. Jaum Fields - 1685 (Brierley 1928, 452).
5. Blake Rake - 1689 (Bowman 1960, 355).
6. Well Style - 1605, will of John Bardsley (Preston LRO WS).
7. Gravel Hill - 1682 (Brierley 1928, 447).
8. Hope Fold - 1603 (*ibid*, 250).
9. Saxon Farm - 1611/12 (*ibid*, 45).
10. Shepley Hall - 1422 & 1618 (Harland 1868, 103; Butterworth 1823, 157).
11. High Ashes - 1475 & 1664 (Butterworth 1823, 90-1; Brierley 1928, 135).
12. Red Hall - 1672, datestone (Butterworth 1823, 91).
13. Carrington Barn - 1573 (Farrer & Brownbill 1911, 344).
14. Hiltons Farm - 1598/9 (Brierley 1928, 11).
15. Audenshaw Lodge Barn - see Appendix 4.
16. Debdale Farm - see Appendix 4.

Ashton, Hartshead division and parts of Knott Lanes division (Fig 3.8)

1. Taunton Hall - 1337 (Farrer & Brownbill 1911, 341 nn 34 & 37); see Appendix 4.
2. Taunton Farm - 1621 (Brierley 1928, 70).
3. Tree House Bank - 1620 (*ibid*, 68).
4. Smallshaw - 1669, will of Katherine Hudson (Preston LRO WS).
5. Hurst Cross - 1637, court leet records (Bowman 1960, 203).
6. Broadoak Farm - 1596/7 & 1673, will of Martha Lees (Brierley 1928, 7; Preston LRO WS).
7. Fairbottom House - see Appendix 4.
8. Althill Farmhouse - 1422 (Harland 1868, 106); see Appendix 4.
9. Cock Bank Farm - 1590, will of John Cocke (Preston LRO WS).
10. Greenhurst - 1597 (Brierley 1928, 9).
11. Lilly Lanes - 1631 (*ibid*, 91).
12. Hartshead Green Farm - see Appendix 4.
13. Jeremy Cottage - see Appendix 4.
14. Broad Carr Farm - 1615 & 1672, will of Jervas Winterbothom (Brierley 1928, 55; Preston LRO WS).
15. Luzley - 1602 (Brierley 1928, 19).
16. Hazelhurst - 1337 & 1599/1600 (Farrer & Brownbill 1911, 341 nn 34 & 37; Brierley 1928, 13).
17. Moss de Lee - 1663, will of Ralph Hall (Preston LRO WS).
18. Heyrod Old Hall - 1318 & 1603, will of John Ashton (Ormerod 1882, 866; Preston LRO WS).
19. Heyrod Farm - 1663 (Brierley 1928, 133).
20. Woodfield Barn - see Appendix 4.
21. Woodfield Farm House - 1597/8 (Brierley 1928, 9); see Appendix 4.
22. Ridge Hill - 1627, will of Jane Ashton (Preston LRO WS).
23. Luzley End - 1690 (Brierley 1928, 178).

Clayton, Droylsden township (Fig 3.11)

1. Edge Lane - 1617 (Higson 1859, 46).
2. Old Clock House - 1666 (Speake & Whitty 1953, 46).
3. Greenside Farm - see Appendix 4.
4. Upper Lumm - *c* 1425 (Speake & Whitty 1953, 47).
5. Moorside Farm - 1688 (*ibid*, 46).
6. Birch Fold - 1613 (Higson 1859, 46).
7. Clock House - 1613 (*ibid*).

Denton (Fig 3.12)

1. Holland Moor Farm - 1645 (Booker 1855, 6).
2. Thornley Lane Farm - *ibid.*
3. Denton Hall - 1325-6 & 1619, will of Richard Holland (Farrer & Brownbill 1911, 311 n 10; Preston LRO WS); see Appendix 4.
4. Hyde Hall - 1320-2 & 1639, will of William Hyde (Farrer 1907, 56; Preston LRO WS); see Appendix 4.
5. Town Lane Farm - 1645 (Booker 1855, 7).
6. Lees House -1645 (*ibid*).
7. St James' (Lawrence's) Church - see Appendix 4.
8. Bridge House Fold - 1674 (Manchester LRO L695).
9. Taylor Lane Farm - 1645 (Booker 1855, 6).

Dukinfield (Fig 3.13)

1. Dukinfield Hall and Chapel - 1398 & 1546, will of Robert Dokenfeld (McGarvie 1980, 57; Chester LRO WS); see Appendix 4.
2. Dewsnip Farm - 1290, 1692 (Dodgson 1970, 277; Dukinfield estate map, Tameside Local Studies Library DD 229/1).
3. Unnamed farm - 1692 (Dukinfield estate map, Tameside Local Studies Library DD 229/1).
4. Yewtree Farm - *ibid.*
5. Bazier Farm - *ibid.*
6. Firtree Farm - *ibid.*
7. Knights House Farm - *ibid.*
8. Linehedge Farm - *ibid.*
9. Broadbentfold - *ibid.*
10. Hough Hill - *ibid.*
11. Gorse Old Hall - *ibid.*

Godley (Fig 3.14)

1. Tetlowfold - 1676, will of John Tetlaw (Chester LRO WS); see Appendix 4.
2. Godley Hall - 1608 (Chester LRO MF41/1); see Appendix 4.
3. Oliverfield Farm (later Godley Lane) - 1660, will of John Chadwick (Chester LRO WS).

Hattersley (Fig 3.16)

1. Fields - 1564 (Nicholas Platt Chester LRO WS).
2. Millhill - 1681 (Chester LRO MF41/2).
3. Pinfold - 1634 (Manchester LRO M95 Chapman Papers Box 13).
4. Clough - see Appendix 4.
5. Butterworths (later Greenside) - 1592 (Chester LRO MF41/1).
6. Lane End - 1604 (Chester LRO MF41/1).
7. Rhodesfold - 1638, will of John Rodes (Chester LRO WS).
8. Bothams Hall - early 14th century (Highet 1960, 64); see Appendix 4.
9. Lower Cliff - 1608 (Chester LRO MF41/1).
10. Higher Cliff - early 14th century (Highet 1960, 64); see Appendix 4.

Haughton (Fig 3.17)

1. Thorp Fold - 1661, will of Robert Thorpe (Preston LRO WS).
2. Haughton Hall - 1455 & 1581, will of Alexander de Hoghton (Ormerod 1882, 811; Preston LRO WS).
3. Glass House Fold - 1677 (Young 1982, 32).
4. Lowe's Farm - 1583, will of John Lowe (Preston LRO WS).
5. Haughton Green - 1645 (Booker 1855, 134).

Hollingworth (Fig 3.18)

1. Higher Bank - 1672-84 (DDX 87/1a).
2. Middle Bank - *ibid.*
3. Lower Bank - *ibid.*
4. Hollingworth Hall - 1354 (Dawes 1932, 144); see Appendix 4.
5. Moorside Farm - 1672-84 (DDX 87/1a).
6. Widowscroft Farm - *ibid.*
7. Thorncliffe Farm - see Appendix 4.
8. Thorncliff Hall - 1360 (Booth *et al* 1976-8, nos 83 & 116); see Appendix 4.
9. Meadowbank Cottages - see Appendix 4.
10. Hollingworth Old Hall (later Mottram Old Hall) - see Appendix 4.
11. Woolley Farm - 1286 & 1600 (Dodgson 1970, 310; Chester LRO DTW/2477/B/9).

Hyde (Fig 3.21)

1. Hyde Hall - 1639, will of Robert Hyde (Chester LRO WS).
2. Foxholes - *ibid.*
3. Smithyfold - 1645 (Booker 1855, 133 n 1).
4. Higher Higham Farm - 1685 (Chester LRO DDX/67/5); see Appendix 4.

Matley (Fig 3.22)

1. Lower Matley Hall - *c* 1620 (King 1656, 92).
2. Wrigleyfold - 1610 (Chester LRO MF41/1).
3. Higher Matley Hall - *c* 1620 (King 1656, 92); see Appendix 4.
4. Harrop Edge - 1360 & 1613 (Booth *et al* 1976-8, nos 104 & 116; Earwaker 1880, 135).
5. Paddock Farm - see Appendix 4.
6. Taylor Fold - 1607 (Chester LRO MF41/1).
7. Bardsley Gate - 1602 (*ibid*).

Mottram (Fig 3.23)

1. Lower Roe Cross - 1626, will of Reynold Hollingworth (Chester LRO WS).
2. Old Post Office - 1694, datestone; see Appendix 4.
3. Packhorse Inn - 1623/4 (Chester LRO DTW Bundle J/1); see Appendix 4.
4. Warhill Farm - 1360 (Booth *et al* 1976-8, no 104); see Appendix 4.
5. Carr House Farm - 1615 (Chester LRO MF41/1).
6. Parsonage Farm - 1547 (Chester LRO P25/8); see Appendix 4.
7. The Haigh (later Hague) - 1360, 1600 & 1684 (Booth *et al* 1976-8, no 98; Chester LRO DTW/2477/B/9; DTW Bundle J/8).
8. Hillend - 1599, will of John Redditch (Chester LRO WS); see Appendix 4.
9. Brown Road - 1613 (Chester LRO MF41/1).
10. Hurstclough - 1600 & 1684 (Chester LRO DTW/2477/B/9; DTW Bundle J/19).
11. Hodgefold - see Appendix 4.
12. Broadbottom Hall - 1286 (Dodgson 1970, 314); see Appendix 4.
13. Mottram Grammar School - 1619 (Thacker 1980, 242); see Appendix 4.
14. St Michael's Church - see Appendix 4.

Newton (Fig 3.24)

1. Newton Hall - *c* 1380 & 1580, will of George Newton (Marsden 1971, 68; Chester LRO WS); see Appendix 4.
2. Goodiers Farm - 1692 (Chester LRO MF41/2).

Quickmere (Fig 3.25)

1. Mossley Manor House - see Appendix 4.

Stayley (Fig 3.26)

1. Inglenook Cottages - see Appendix 4.
2. Spring Bank Farm - *c* 1580 (Preston LRO DDX 350).
3. Moorgate Farm - see Appendix 4.
4. Oakfield - *c* 1580 (Preston LRO DDX 350).
5. Unnamed farm - *ibid.*
6. Little Bank - see Appendix 4.
7. Unnamed farm - *c* 1580 (Preston DDX 350).
8. Wood Farm - *ibid.*
9. Hilltop Farm - see Appendix 4.
10. Sungreen - *c* 1580 (Preston LRO DDX 350).
11. Buckley Hill - *ibid.*
12. Stayley Hall - 1356-7 & 1579, will of George Booth (Highet 1960, 71; Preston LRO WS); see Appendix 4.
13. Sidebottom Fold - *c* 1580 (Preston LRO DDX 350).
14. Cockers Farm (formerly Harpelegh Farm) - early 14th century & *c* 1580 (Highet 1960, 63, 67, 71; Dodgson 1970, 318; Preston LRO DDX 350).
15. Herpley Farm (later Lukes Fold) - 1342-3 & 1388 (Highet 1960, 63, 67; Dodgson 1970, 319; Ormerod 1882, 866); see Appendix 4.
16. Heaps Farm - 1623/4, will of Thomas Heape (Chester LRO WS).

Tintwistle, Micklehurst division (Fig 3.27)

1. Howard's Farm - see Appendix 4.
2. Castle Farm - 1659 (Brierley 1928, 125).

Werneth (Fig 3.28)

1. Apethorn Farm - see Appendix 4.
2. Gerrards Wood Farm - 1658 (Chester LRO DAR/I/16).
3. Gerrards Fold - 1691 (Chester LRO DDX/67/10).
4. Geecross Fold - 1494 & 1682 (Earwaker 1880, 110; Chester LRO DDX 67/3).
5. Lower Higham Farm - 1406-7 & 1657 (Highet 1960, 78; Chester LRO DAR/I/16; DDX/67/8); see Appendix 4.
6. Hillside (later Hillend) - 1682 (Chester LRO DDX 67/3).

Glossary

Advowson - the right to appoint the incumbent of a parish church.

Assarting - the clearing of woodland for agriculture.

Bailey - a defended outer area of a castle, usually associated with a motte.

Barons - in Lancashire and Cheshire a privileged group of lords holding several manors usually directly from the holder of the honour.

Bay - the distance between roof trusses or load-bearing walls.

Borough (medieval) - a chartered town with its own court.

Burgage - tenement plots in a medieval town; usually long and narrow, with the narrow end fronting the street.

Castellation - ornamental battlements.

Collar - a short horizontal timber linking and tying together two main beams, such as two principal rafters or two crucks, a short distance below their apex.

Court leet - the judicial court of a manor.

Croft - a piece of land adjoining a house, used for agriculture.

Cruck spur - a horizontal timber projecting outwards from the cruck to enable the walls to be fixed to the structure.

Cruck truss - a pair of curved timbers, or blades, rising from the floor and meeting at an apex to support a roof.

Demesne - the land reserved and exploited by the manorial lord.

Four-centred arch - a pointed arch of four arcs, all centred on different points and creating a flattening effect.

Hide - originally the land necessary to sustain a household. The size varied according to locality and date, although most figures centre on 120 acres.

Honour - a large landholding held directly from the king.

Hoodmould - a moulding above a window or door to protect the opening from rainwater.

Hundred - an administrative subdivision of the county.

Inquisition post mortem - inquest taken by the authorities of a hundred before a jury to establish the heir and inheritance of the deceased.

Kneeler - a decorative stone projecting from the corner of the gable.

League - a unit of distance, often taken to be between 1 and 1½ miles. However this varied according to local usage.

Manor - a territorial and administrative unit held by a lord.

Moiety - a half.

Motte - part of a Norman castle, comprising a flat-topped conical mound of earth, usually erected with material from a surrounding ditch and surmounted by a wooden tower.

Mullion - the vertical structural member subdividing a window into lights.

Open field - a large unhedged field, divided into many strips, all individually held but farmed in common.

Oxgang - an eighth of a hide.

Plough-land - the area of land which a plough-team could keep in cultivation during a year, varying according to local conditions.

Plough-team - often assessed as 8 oxen, but depending on local agricultural potential this figure could be as low as a single ox.

Puture - a tax paid by lords of the manor and chief tenants for the upkeep of the serjeants.

Quarter sessions - the law court of a hundred, meeting four times a year.

Quatrefoil - a decorative architectural feature or aperture in the form of four lobes.

Ringwork - an early, simple form of castle comprising a circular or subcircular bank and ditch.

Serjeants - officers responsible for enforcing court judgments within a hundred.

Tie-beam - the horizontal timber of a truss linking the main rafters at eaves level.

Township - an ancient division of a parish.

Trefoil - a decorative feature or aperture in the form of three lobes.

Virgate - a quarter of a hide, often 20-30 acres.

Windbrace - supporting timbers set between the verticals and horizontals of a roof.

Sources

Primary Sources

Chester Local Records Office (LRO)

D/73/1 & 2 Deeds for Duckenfield property in Mobberley, 1662, 1753.
DAR/I/16 Werneth manor court book 1588-1658.
DAR/I/40 A book of notes from the Utkinton library 1753, revised 1754.
DDX 16/1-5 Leases of Hyde and Duckenfield property in Brinnington, Romiley & Hyde, 1605-57.
DDX 67 Ashton of Hyde collection.
DDX 87/1 The particulars of Hollingworth manor, 1672-84.
DDX 87/2 Hollingworth moor, access to, 1638.
DDX 464/3 Lease of lands in Godley, Sale, Matley and Newton, 1665/6.
DTW/2477/B/9 A survey of the land and tenements of Thomas Wilbraham, esquire, 1600.
DTW Bundles B, C, H-L Tollemache records.
EDT 143/1 & 2 Tithe map and apportionment for Dukinfield, 1849.
EDT 166/1 & 2 Tithe map and apportionment for Godley, 1845.
EDT 192/1 & 2 Tithe map and apportionment for Hattersley, 1839.
EDT 204/1 & 2 Tithe map and apportionment for Hollingworth, 1845.
EDT 217/1 & 2 Tithe map and apportionment for Hyde, 1839.
EDT 268/1 & 2 Tithe map and apportionment for Matley, 1840.
EDT 281/1 & 2 Tithe map and apportionment for Mottram, 1845.
EDT 292/1 & 2 Tithe map and apportionment for Newton, 1845.
EDT 366/1 & 2 Tithe map and apportionment for Stayley, 1840.
EDT 397/1 & 2 Tithe map and apportionment for Tintwistle, 1845.
EDT 417/1 & 2 Tithe map and apportionment for Werneth, 1839.
EDV/7/3/355 Parish Bundle, Mottram.
MF13 Hearth tax returns, Macclesfield Hundred 1664.
MF41/1-9 Mottram parish registers 1559-1939.
P25/8 Mottram parish records.
WS Wills and inventories.

Handlist of the Dunham Massey Archives in the John Rylands University Library of Manchester

EGR1/5/1 Deeds relating to the manor of Ashton-under-Lyne, 1413/14-1709.
EGR1/5/2 Property in Littlemoss, part of Ashton-under-Lyne, and Droylsden, part of Manchester, 1614-1700.

Manchester Local Records Office (LRO)

L695 Miscellaneous deeds
M95 Chapman Papers Box 13 Hattersley court book and suite rolls.

Preston Local Records Office (LRO)

DDEg 4d/13 Grain accounts for Denton and Haughton, 1693.
DDHu 12/2 & 3 Hulton family papers.
DDX 350 Mrs Bowman collection.
DRM 1/37 Tithe map and apportionment for Denton, 1849.
DRM 1/50 Tithe map and apportionment for Haughton, 1845.
DRM 1/39 Tithe map and apportionment for Droylsden, 1847.
QSP Quarter sessions papers.
Slater Heelis Collection Box D Bundle 57 Suit concerning Denton Moor, 1595-7.
WS Wills and inventories.

Tameside Local Studies Library, Stalybridge

DD 229/1 Dukinfield estate map, 1692.
DD 229/2 The Jolly letter, undated
E 179/250/11 PT6 Hearth tax returns for Macclesfield and Salford hundreds, on microfilm.

The Earl of Stamford Records in the Cordingley Archives, Ashton-under-Lyne

ESRCA 3 Grant of free warren in Ashton, 1335.
ESRCA 4 Property in Stayley manor – 'trial by combat', 1377/8.
ESRCA 6 Property in Stayley manor, 1402.
ESRCA 7 Will of Ralph Staveley, 1456.
ESRCA 8 Illegitimacy case re Stayley manor, 1457.
ESRCA 13 Inquisition post mortem of Sir Thomas Assheton 1517.
ESRCA 15 Ashton estate plan, 1765.

Greater Manchester Archaeological Unit

M7 Dukinfield Hall excavation archive, level 3, 1982.

Secondary Sources

Aikin J, 1795, *A Description of the Country Thirty to Forty Miles round Manchester*. London.

Arrowsmith A, 1985, 'John Angier: the 'Angel on Horse-Back'', *in* Lock (ed), 6-13.

Arrowsmith P & Hartwell C, 1989, 'Kersal Cell: A House of the Lesser Gentry in Salford, *Greater Manchester Archaeol J* 3 (for 1987-8), 71-93.

Ashmore O, 1958, 'Household Inventories of the Lancashire Gentry, 1550-1700', *Trans Lancashire Cheshire Antiq Soc* 110, 59-105.

Aston M, 1985, *Interpreting the Landscape: Landscape Archaeology in Local Studies*. London, Batsford.

Atkinson Rev J A (ed), 1909, *Tracts Relating to the Civil War in Cheshire 1641-1659*. Chetham Soc, new series, vol 65.

Axon E (ed), 1901, *The Manchester Quarter Sessions Records 1616-1623*. Rec Soc Lancashire Cheshire, vol 22.

Bagley J J, 1956, *A History of Lancashire*. London, Darwin Finlayson.

Barnes B, Buckley P M, Hunt J M & Petford A J, 1983, *Saddleworth Surveyed. Selected Maps of the Township 1625-1821*. Saddleworth Historical Society.

Barraclough G, 1957, *Facsimiles of Early Cheshire Charters*. Oxford, Blackwell.

Barraclough G (ed), 1988, *The Charters of the Anglo-Norman Earls of Chester, c. 1071-1237*. Rec Soc Lancashire Cheshire, vol 126.

Beck J, 1969, *Tudor Cheshire*. A History of Cheshire vol 7. Cheshire Community Council.

Bennett J H E & Dewhurst J C, 1940, *Quarter Sessions Records, with other Records of the Justices of the Peace for the County Palatine of Chester 1559-1760*. Rec Soc Lancashire Cheshire, vol 94.

Blackwood B G, 1967, 'The Cavalier and Roundhead Gentry of Lancashire', *Trans Lancashire Cheshire Antiq Soc* 77, 77-96.

Blackwood B G, 1976, 'The Economic State of the Lancashire Gentry on the eve of Civil War', *Northern History* 12, 53-83.

Blackwood B G, 1978, *The Lancashire Gentry and the Great Rebellion 1640-60*. Chetham Soc, 3rd series, vol 25.

Booker Rev J, 1855, 'A History of the Ancient Chapel of Denton in Manchester Parish', *in* W Langton (ed), *Cheshire Miscellanies*. Chetham Soc, vol 37.

Booker Rev J, 1859, *A History of the Ancient Chapel of Birch in Manchester Parish*. Chetham Soc, vol 47.

Booth K & Cronin J, 1989, 'Buckton Castle: A survey of the evidence', *Greater Manchester Archaeol J* 3 (for 1987-8), 61-8.

Booth P H W, 1981, *The Financial Administration of the Lordship and County of Chester 1272-1377*. Chetham Soc, 3rd series, vol 28.

Booth P H W, 1991, 'Calendar of Cheshire Inquisitions Post Mortem: Part 2', *Cheshire History* 27, 3-5.

Booth P H W, Harrop J M & Harrop S A, 1976-8, 'The Extent of Longdendale, 1360', *Cheshire Sheaf*, 5th series, nos 57, 68, 83, 98, 104, 116, 121, 126 and 131.

Bott O, 1983, 'Cornmill Sites in Cheshire 1066-1850: Part 1. *Cheshire History* 10, 53-72.

Bott O, 1984a, 'Cornmill Sites in Cheshire 1066-1850: Part 3. Medieval Mills and Agriculture', *Cheshire History* 13, 33-8.

Bott O, 1984b, 'Cornmill Sites in Cheshire 1066-1850: Part 4. Sites Recorded to 1486-1700', *Cheshire History* 14, 29-36.

Bowman W M, 1950, *Five Thousand Acres of Old Ashton: The History of the Limehurst Rural District*. (Republished 1990; Leeds, MTD Rigg Publications.)

Bowman W M, 1960, *England in Ashton-under-Lyne*. Ashton-under-Lyne Corporation.

Brierley H (ed), 1928, *The Parish Registers of Ashton-under-Lyne, 1594-1720*. Lancashire Parish Record Society, vol 65.

Bryant V A & Bryant S R, 1985, 'Excavations at Denton Hall', *Greater Manchester Archaeol J* 1, 55-67.

Bulkeley E W (ed), 1889, *The Parish Registers of Saint Mary, Stockport, containing the baptisms, marriages and burials from 1584-1620*. Stockport.

Butterworth E, 1842, *An Historical Account of the Towns of Ashton-under-Lyne, Stalybridge and Dukinfield*. Ashton.

Butterworth J, 1823, *History and Description of the town and Parish of Ashton-under-Lyne in the county of Lancaster and the village of Dukinfield in the county of Chester*. Ashton.

Butterworth J, 1827, *History and description of the towns and parishes of Stockport, Ashton-under-Lyne, Mottram-long-den-dale and Glossop*. Oldham.

Cathcart King D J & Alcock L, 1969, 'Ringworks of England and Wales', *Chateau Gaillard* 3, 90-127.

Chadwick W, not dated (*c* 1870), *Reminiscences of Mottram*. (Republished 1972; Longdendale Amenity Society.)

Clarke H, 1984, *The Archaeology of Medieval England*. Oxford, Blackwell.

Clayton D J, 1990, *The Administration of the County Palatinate of Chester 1442-1485*. Chetham Soc, 3rd series, vol 35.

Coward B, 1980, *The Stuart Age*. Longman.

Crofton H T, 1889, 'Lancashire and Cheshire Coalmining Records', *Trans Lancashire Cheshire Antiq Soc* 7, 26-73.

Crowe P R, 1962, 'Climate', *in* C F Carter (ed), *Manchester and its Region*, 17-46. Manchester University Press.

CRR 1875, *Calendar of the Recognizance Rolls to Henry IV: Extracted from the 36th Report of the Deputy Keeper of the Public Records. Appendix II, 1-548.* HMSO.

Cunliffe-Shaw R, 1958, 'Two Fifteenth-century Kinsmen: John Shaw of Dukinfield, Mercer, and William Shaw of Heath Charnock, Surgeon', *Trans Lancashire Cheshire Hist Soc* 110, 15-30.

Davies S, 1960, *The Agricultural History of Cheshire 1750-1850*. Chetham Soc, 3rd series, vol 10.

Davis R H C, 1966, 'The Norman Conquest', *History* 51, 279-86.

Dawes M C B, 1932, *Register of Edward the Black Prince, preserved in the Public Record Office. Part III (Palatinate of Chester), AD 1351-1365*. HMSO.

Dodd J P, 1986, 'Domesday Cheshire', *Cheshire History* 18, 10-20.

Dodgson J McN, 1970, *The Place-Names of Cheshire. Part I*. English Place-Name Society, vol 44 (for 1966-7). Cambridge University Press.

Dore R N, 1966, *The Civil Wars in Cheshire*. A History of Cheshire vol 8. Cheshire Community Council.

Dore R N (ed), 1984, *The Letter Books of Sir William Brereton, vol 1, January 1st - May 29th 1645*. Rec Soc Lancashire Cheshire, vol 123.

Dore R N (ed), 1990, *The Letter Books of Sir William Brereton, vol 2, June 18th 1645 - February 1st 1645/6*. Rec Soc Lancashire Cheshire, vol 128.

Driver J T, 1953, 'A Subsidy Roll for the Hundred of Macclesfield, A.D. 1610', *Trans Lancashire Cheshire Antiq Soc* 62 (for 1950-1), 54-67.

Earwaker J P, 1877, *East Cheshire Past and Present*, vol 1. London.

Earwaker J P (ed), 1879, *An Index to the Wills and Inventories now preserved in the Court of Probate at Chester. From AD 1545 to 1620*. Rec Soc Lancashire Cheshire, vol 2.

Earwaker J P, 1880, *East Cheshire Past and Present*, vol 2. London.

Earwaker J P (ed), 1881, *An Index to the Wills and Inventories now preserved in the Court of Probate at Chester. From AD 1621 to 1650*. Rec Soc Lancashire Cheshire, vol 4.

Earwaker J P (ed), 1884, *Lancashire and Cheshire Wills and Inventories at Chester*. Chetham Soc, new series, vol 3.

Earwaker J P (ed), 1887a, *An Index to the Wills and Inventories now preserved in the Court of Probate at Chester. From AD 1660 to 1680*. Rec Soc Lancashire Cheshire, vol 15.

Earwaker J P (ed), 1887b, *The Court Leet Records of the Manor of Manchester*, vol 4. Manchester.

Ekwall E, 1922, *The Place Names of Lancashire*. Chetham Soc, new series, vol 81.

Ffarington S M (ed), 1856, *The Ffarington Papers*. Chetham Soc, vol 39.

Farrer W, 1899, *Final Concords of the County of Lancaster. Part I, 7 Richard I to 35 Edward I: A.D. 1196 to A.D. 1307*. Rec Soc Lancashire Cheshire, vol 39.

Farrer W, 1902, *Lancashire Pipe Rolls and Early Cheshire Charters*. Liverpool.

Farrer W (ed), 1903, *Lancashire Inquests, Extents and Feudal Aids. Part I A.D. 1205-A.D. 1307*. Rec Soc Lancashire Cheshire, vol 48.

Farrer W, 1907, *Lancashire Inquests, Extents and Feudal Aids. Part II A.D. 1310-A.D. 1333*. Rec Soc Lancashire Cheshire, vol 54.

Farrer W & Brownbill J (eds), 1906, *The Victoria History of the County of Lancaster*, vol 1. Constable & Co.

Farrer W & Brownbill J (eds), 1911, *The Victoria History of the County of Lancaster*, vol 4. Constable & Co.

Figueiredo P de & Treuherz J, 1988, *Cheshire Country Houses*. Chichester, Phillimore.

Forde-Johnston J, 1962, 'The Iron Age Hillforts of Lancashire and Cheshire', *Trans Lancashire Cheshire Antiq Soc* 72, 9-46.

Gelling M, 1984, *Place Names in the Landscape*. Dent.

Glover W, 1884, *History of Ashton-under-Lyne and the surrounding district*. Ashton-under-Lyne.

Groves J, 1990, 'Houses in North East Cheshire in the Age of the Great Rebuilding 1600-1700', *Cheshire History* 25, 30-9.

Hall J (ed), 1889, *Memorials of the Civil War in Cheshire and the Adjacent Counties by Thomas Malbon, of Nantwich, Gent.* Rec Soc Lancashire Cheshire, vol 19.

Harland J (ed), 1868, *Three Lancashire Documents of the fourteenth and Fifteenth Centuries*, Chetham Soc, vol 74, 93-133.

Harley J B & Laxton P (eds), 1974, *A Survey of the County Palatine of Chester by P P Burdett 1777*. Historical Society of Lancashire and Cheshire, Occasional Series, vol 1.

Harris B E (ed), 1979, *The Victoria History of the County of Chester*, vol 2. University of London Institute of Historical Research.

Harris B E (ed), 1980, *The Victoria History of the County of Chester,* vol 3. University of London Institute of Historical Research.

Harris B E (ed), 1987, *The Victoria History of the County of Chester*, vol 1. University of London Institute of Historical Research.

Harrop S A, 1983, 'Moated Sites in North-East Cheshire and their links with the Legh Family in the Fourteenth Century', *Cheshire History* 11, 8-15.

Hewitt H J, 1967, *Cheshire under the Three Edwards*. A History of Cheshire vol 5. Cheshire Community Council.

Heywood N, 1887, 'Lancashire and Cheshire Tokens of the Seventeenth Century', *Trans Lancashire Cheshire Antiq Soc* 5, 64-105.

Higham N J, 1985, 'Tatton Park: Interim report on the 7th season of excavation of the deserted village', *Cheshire Archaeological Bulletin* 10 (for 1984-5), 75-82.

Highet T P, 1960, *The Early History of the Davenports of Davenport*. Chetham Soc, 3rd series, vol 9.

Higson C E, 1917, 'The Mesne Field in Lees', *Trans Lancashire Cheshire Antiq Soc* 35, 40-9.

Higson J, 1859, *Historical and Descriptive Notices of Droylsden Past and Present*. Manchester.

Hodson J H, 1978, *Cheshire 1660-1780: Restoration to Industrial Revolution*. A History of Cheshire vol 9. Cheshire Community Council.

Hughes A, 1980, *Seventeenth-century England: A Changing Culture. Vol 1: Primary Sources*. Ward Lock Educational/The Open University.

Hurst Vose R, 1989, 'Haughton Green Denton: A Seventeenth-Century Coal-Fired Glass Furnace', *Greater Manchester Archaeol J* 3 (for 1987-8), 115-16.

Husain B M C, 1973, *Cheshire under the Norman Earls*. A History of Cheshire vol 4. Cheshire Community Council.

Irvine W F, 1902, *A History of the Family of Holland of Mobberley and Knutsford*. Privately printed.

Ives E W (ed), 1976, *Letters and Accounts of William Brereton of Malpas*. Rec Soc Lancashire Cheshire, vol 116.

Kenyon D, 1991, *The Origins of Lancashire*. Manchester University Press.

King D, 1656, *The Vale-Royall of England or the County Palatine of Chester*. London.

Lamb H H, 1982, *Climate, History and the Modern World*. Methuen.

Lander S J & Thacker A T, 1980, 'The Diocese of Chester', *in* Harris (ed), 12-87.

Lock A, 1981, *Hyde in Old Photographs*. Tameside Metropolitan Borough.

Lock A (ed), 1985, *Looking Back at Denton*. Tameside Metropolitan Borough.

Lowe N, 1972, *The Lancashire Textile Industry in the Sixteenth Century*. Chetham Soc, 3rd series, vol 20.

Lumby J H, 1939, *A Calendar of the Norris Deeds (Lancashire) 12th to 15th century*. Rec Soc Lancashire Cheshire, vol 93.

McGarvie M (ed), 1980, 'Dukinfield Old Hall Chapel Manchester', *Transactions of the Ancient Monuments Society* (new series) 24, 57-64.

Mackey C H M, 1983, *Public Opinion and the Interregnum 1649-1660*. Unpublished BA dissertation, University of Manchester History Dept.

Marsden T L, 1971, 'Newton Hall, Hyde, Cheshire: A Cruck Frame, c. AD 1380', *Transactions of the Ancient Monuments Society* (new series) 18, 65-76.

Middleton T, 1900, *Old Godley: Historical, Descriptive, Biographical, Legendary*. Hyde.

Middleton T, 1932, *The History of Hyde and its Neighbourhood*. Hyde.

Middleton T, 1936, *The History of Denton and Haughton*. Hyde.

Miller E, 1975, 'Farming in Northern England during the twelfth and thirteenth centuries', *Northern History* 11, 1-16.

Morgan P (ed), 1978a, *Domesday Book: Cheshire*. Chichester, Phillimore.

Morgan P (ed), 1978b, *Domesday Book: Derbyshire*. Chichester, Phillimore.

Morrill J S, 1974, *Cheshire 1630-1660: County Government and Society during the English Revolution*. Oxford University Press.

Morrill J S, 1975, 'William Davenport and the 'silent majority' of early Stuart England', *Journal of the Chester Archaeological Society* 58, 115-29.

Morrill J S, 1979, 'The Northern Gentry and the Great Rebellion', *Northern History* 15, 66-87.

Morrill J S & Dore R N, 1967, 'The Allegiance of the Cheshire Gentry in the Great Civil War', *Trans Lancashire Cheshire Antiq Soc* 77, 47-76.

Morris M (ed), 1983, *Medieval Manchester: A Regional Study*. The Archaeology of Greater Manchester vol 1. Greater Manchester Archaeological Unit.

Nevell M D, 1990, 'A Survey of Bispham Hall', *Council for British Archaeology Regional Group 5 Newsletter* 60, 13-18.

Ormerod G, 1819, *The History of the County Palatine and City of Chester*. London.

Ormerod G, 1844, *Tracts relating to Military Proceedings in Lancashire during the Civil War*. Chetham Soc, vol 2.

Ormerod G, 1882, *The History of the County Palatine and City of Chester* (revised and enlarged by T Helsby), vol 3. London.

Page W (ed), 1912, *The Victoria History of the County of Yorkshire*, vol 2. London.

Parker Col J, 1904, *A Calendar of the Lancashire Assize Roll preserved in the Public Record Office, London. Part II*. Rec Soc Lancashire Cheshire, vol 49.

Petford A J, 1987, 'The Process of Enclosure in Saddleworth, 1625-1834', *Trans Lancashire Cheshire Antiq Soc* 84, 78-117.

Platt C, 1978, *Medieval England: A social history and archaeology from the Conquest to 1600 AD*. London, Routledge & Kegan Paul Ltd.

Powell J, 1976, *The Parish of Mottram-in-Longdendale, 1570-1680*. Unpublished Local History Certificate dissertation, University of Manchester Dept of Extra-mural Studies.

PSA, 1850, *Proceedings of the Society of Antiquaries* 2, 40-2.

Pugh Rev G A, 1902, ' The Old Glass Windows of Ashton-under-Lyne Parish Church', *Trans Lancashire Cheshire Antiq Soc* 20, 130-8.

Quintrell B W (ed), 1981, *Proceedings of the Lancashire Justices of the Peace at the Sheriff's Table during Assizes Week, 1578-1694*. Rec Soc Lancashire Cheshire, vol 121.

RCHME, 1976, *Stayley Hall, Stalybridge, Greater Manchester*. Unpublished report.

Riden P, 1987, *Record Sources for Local History*. London, Batsford.

Roberts B K, 1982, *Village Plans*. Shire Archaeology 27. Aylesbury, Shire Publications.

Savage A, 1982, *The Anglo-Saxon Chronicles*. Phoebe Phillips/ Heinemann.

Sawyer P H & Thacker A T, 1987, 'The Cheshire Domesday', *in* Harris (ed), 293-371.

Scott J, Smith J H & Winterbottom D, 1973, *Glossop, Dale, Manor and Borough*. Glossop & District Historical Society.

Shaw W A, 1896, *Minutes of the Committee for the relief of Plundered Ministers and of the Trustees for the Maintenance of Lancashire and Cheshire 1643-60. Part 2 1650-60*. Rec Soc Lancashire Cheshire, vol 34.

Sheail J, 1972, 'The distribution of taxable population and wealth in England during the early sixteenth century', *Transactions of the Institute of British Geographers* 55, 111-26.

Smith J T, 1971, 'Lancashire and Cheshire Houses: Some problems of architectural and social history', *Archaeol J* 127,155-181.

Smith W J, 1987, *Saddleworth Buildings*. Saddleworth Historical Society.

Speake R & Whitty F R, 1953, *A History of Droylsden*. Stockport, Cloister Press.

Stanning J (ed), 1891, *The Royalist Composition Papers, being the Proceedings of the Committee for Compounding AD 1643-1660, so far as they relate to the County of Lancaster, Vol I, A-B*. Rec Soc Lancashire Cheshire, vol 24.

Stell C, 1987, 'Dukinfield Old Chapel', *The Archaeology of Greater Manchester. Proceedings of the 133rd Summer Meeting of the Royal Archaeological Institute at Salford in 1987*, 55-6.

Stewart-Brown R (ed), 1934, *Cheshire Inquisitions Post Mortem, Stuart Period, 1603-60. Vol 1, A-D*. Rec Soc Lancashire Cheshire, vol 84.

Stewart-Brown R (ed), 1935, *Cheshire Inquisitions Post Mortem, Stuart Period, 1603-60. Vol 1, E-O*. Rec Soc Lancashire Cheshire, vol 86.

Studd J R, 1985, 'A Calendar of the Acts of the Lord Edward relating to Cheshire', *Cheshire History* 15, 7-12.

Sylvester D, 1956, 'The Open Fields of Cheshire', *Trans Lancashire Cheshire Hist Soc* 108, 1-33.

Tait J, 1904, *Medieval Manchester and the Beginnings of Lancashire*. Manchester University Press.

Tait J, 1924, *Taxation in Salford Hundred, 1524-1802*. Chetham Soc, new series, vol 83.

Taylor C, 1975, *Fields in the English Landscape*. (Republished 1987, Gloucester, Alan Sutton.)

Taylor F, 1951, *Hand-list of the Crutchley Manuscripts in the John Rylands Library*. The John Rylands University Library of Manchester.

Taylor F, 1975, *Hand-list of Charters, Deeds and similar Documents in the Possession of the John Rylands University Library of Manchester: IV*. The John Rylands University Library of Manchester.

Thacker A T, 1980, ' Schools', *in* Harris (ed), 223-54.

Thirsk J (ed), 1967, *The Agrarian History of England and Wales, vol IV: 1500-1640*. Oxford.

Walker J S F & Tindall A (eds), 1985, *Country Houses of Greater Manchester*. The Archaeology of Greater Manchester vol 2. Greater Manchester Archaeological Unit.

Walton J K, 1987, *Lancashire: A Social History 1558-1939*. Manchester University Press.

Watson J B, 1966, 'The Lancashire Gentry and Public Service, 1529-1558', *Trans Lancashire Cheshire Antiq Soc* 73-4 (for 1963-4), 11-59.

Wilkins-Jones C, 1978, *Tameside: An Outline History*. Tameside Metropolitan Borough.

Willan T S, 1980, *Elizabethan Manchester*. Chetham Soc, 3rd series, vol 27.

Wilson D, 1987, 'The Medieval Moated Sites of Cheshire', *Trans Lancashire Cheshire Antiq Soc* 84, 143-54.

Wood M, 1986, *Domesday: A Search for the Roots of England.* BBC Publications.

Wyatt G M, 1989, 'Nantwich and Wybunburg 1680-1819: a demographic study of two Cheshire Parishes', *Trans Lancashire Cheshire Hist Soc* 139, 1-30.

Youd G, 1961, 'The Common Fields of Lancashire', *Trans Lancashire Cheshire Hist Soc* 113, 1-41.

Young J, 1982, *Some Aspects of the History of Denton and Haughton, Lancashire, prior to the Eighteenth Century.* Unpublished Local History Certificate dissertation, University of Manchester Dept of Extra-mural Studies.

Young J, 1985, 'Denton and Haughton in Tudor and Stuart Times, *in* Lock (ed), 14-26.

Index